MANGA
IWA

Iwashiro, Toshiaki, 1977-
Psyren.

Toshiaki Iwashiro

When I have a manga in serialization, there's just never time to watch movies or read novels. I can put movies on in the background while I work, but reading novels is impossible. All I can do is gaze longingly at the new release displays in the bookstores and satisfy myself with my imaginings...

Toshiaki Iwashiro was born December 11, 1977, in Tokyo and has the blood type of A. His debut manga was the popular *Mieru Hito*, which ran from 2005 to 2007 in Japan in *Weekly Shonen Jump*, where *Psyren* was also serialized.

PSYREN VOL. 8
SHONEN JUMP Manga Edition

STORY AND ART BY TOSHIAKI IWASHIRO

Translation/Camellia Nieh
Lettering/Annaliese Christman
Design/Matt Hinrichs
Editor/Joel Enos

PSYREN © 2007 by Toshiaki Iwashiro
All rights reserved.
First published in Japan in 2007 by SHUEISHA Inc., Tokyo.
English translation rights arranged by SHUEISHA Inc.

The rights of the author(s) of the work(s) in this publication to be so
identified have been asserted in accordance with the Copyright, Designs
and Patents Act 1988. A CIP catalogue record for this book is available
from the British Library.

Printed in the U.S.A.

Published by VIZ Media, LLC
P.O. Box 77010
San Francisco, CA 94107

10 9 8 7 6 5 4 3 2 1
First printing, January 2013

www.viz.com

PARENTAL ADVISORY
PSYREN is rated T for Teen and is
recommended for ages 13 and up.
This volume contains fantasy violence.
ratings.viz.com

THE WORLD'S
MOST POPULAR MANGA

www.shonenjump.com

SHONEN JUMP MANGA EDITION

PSYREN

8

LIGHT

Story and Art by
Toshiaki Iwashiro

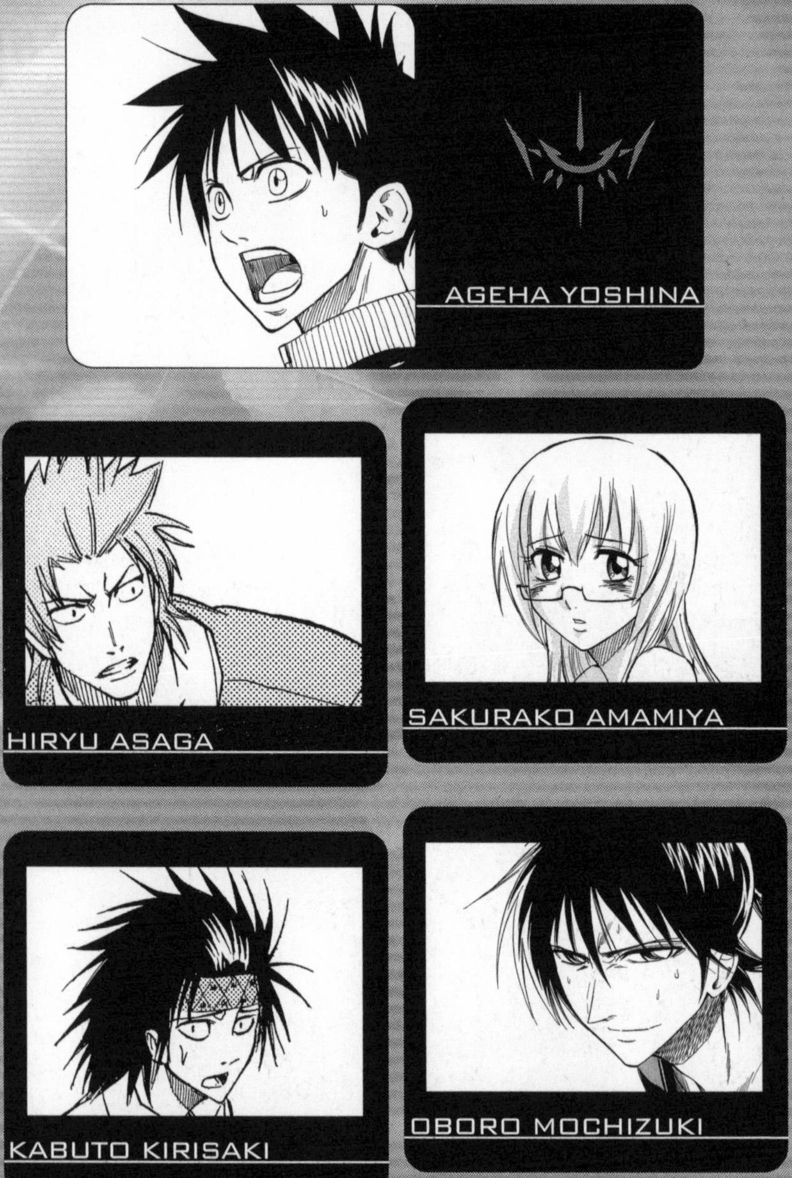
AGEHA YOSHINA
SAKURAKO AMAMIYA
HIRYU ASAGA
OBORO MOCHIZUKI
KABUTO KIRISAKI

Characters

DOLKEY

THE ELMORE WOOD GANG

SHINER

ELMORE TENJUIN

Story

HIGH-SCHOOLER AGEHA YOSHINA HAPPENS UPON A RED
TELEPHONE CARD EMBLAZONED WITH THE WORD PSYREN
WHILE SEARCHING FOR HIS MISSING FRIEND SAKURAKO
AMAMIYA. USING THE CARD TRANSPORTS HIM INTO A
LIFE-OR-DEATH GAME IN A BIZARRE WORLD.

AGEHA AND FRIENDS ENCOUNTER MIROKU AT THE MOUNTAIN
CABIN AND ARE OVERWHELMED BY HIS HORRIFIC POWERS.
BUT THE ENCOUNTER LEADS TO CHANGES IN THE CONTENT
OF THE VIDEO THEY'VE BEEN WATCHING THAT SHOWS THE
FUTURE. AGEHA AND THE OTHERS VOW TO SAVE ELMORE
AND THE CHILDREN FROM THE DEATHS THE RECORDING
FORETELLS, BUT IN THE ATTEMPT THEY ARE CRUELLY
WHISKED BACK TO PSYREN FOR THE FOURTH TIME!

PSYREN

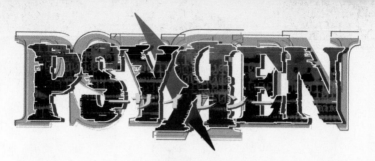

VOL. 8
LIGHT
CONTENTS

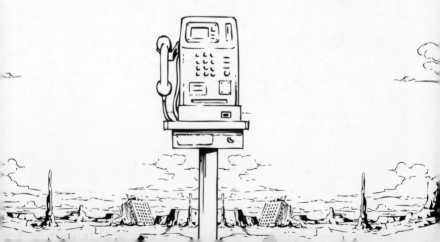

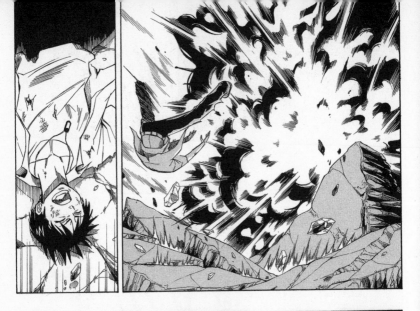

WHASSA MATTER? I THOUGHT YOU'D BE MORE FUN THAN THIS!

CALL. 63: DESPAIR

GHAK!

YOU'RE NOT GOOD FOR MUCH WITHOUT YOUR BLACK BLAST, ARE YOU?

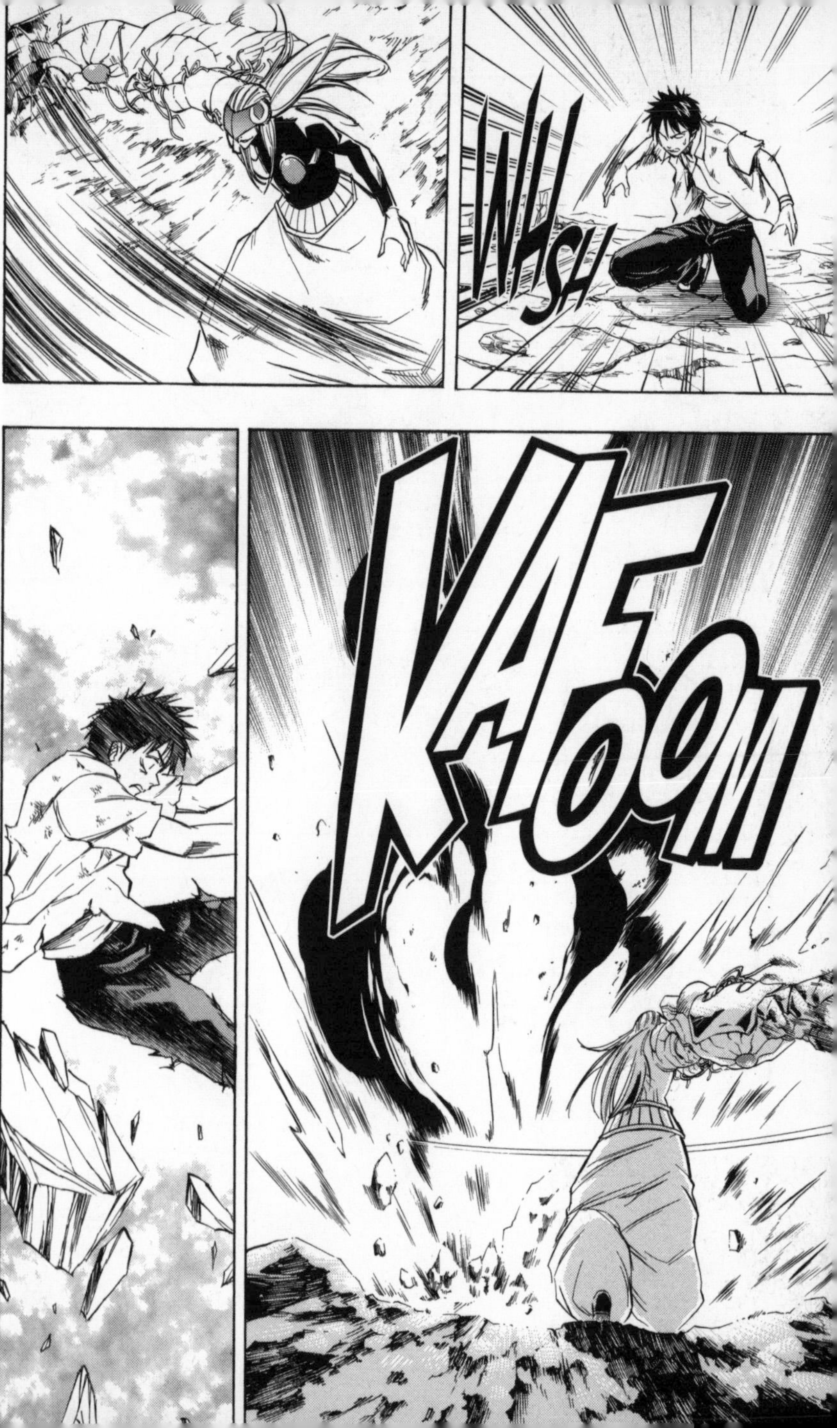
WHSH
KABOOM

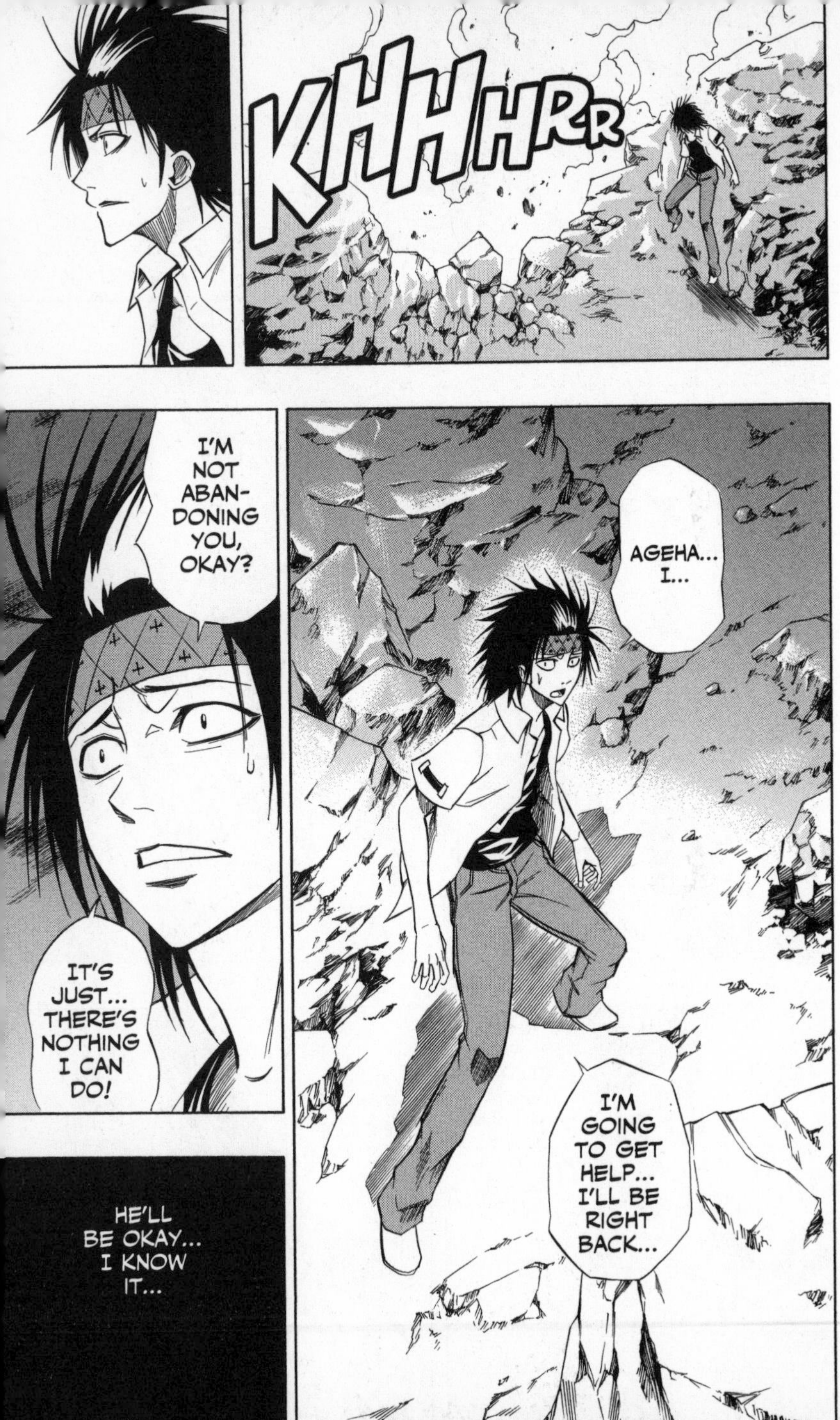
KHHHRR
AGEHA... I...
I'M GOING TO GET HELP... I'LL BE RIGHT BACK...
I'M NOT ABAN-DONING YOU, OKAY?
IT'S JUST... THERE'S NOTHING I CAN DO!
HE'LL BE OKAY... I KNOW IT...

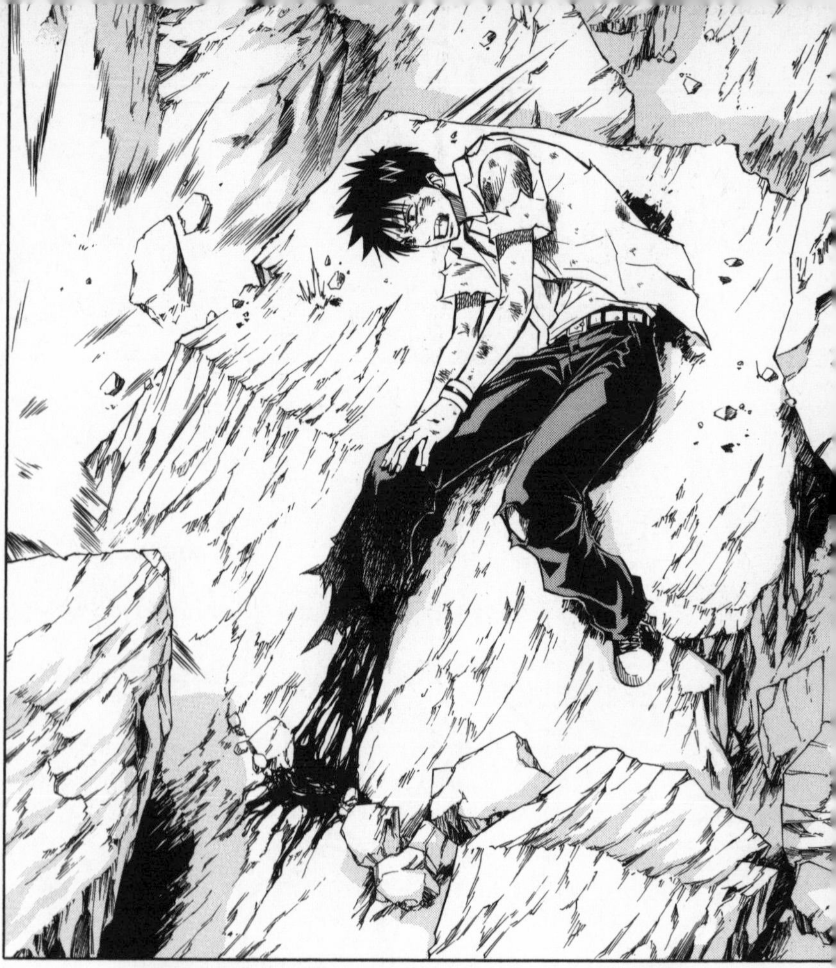

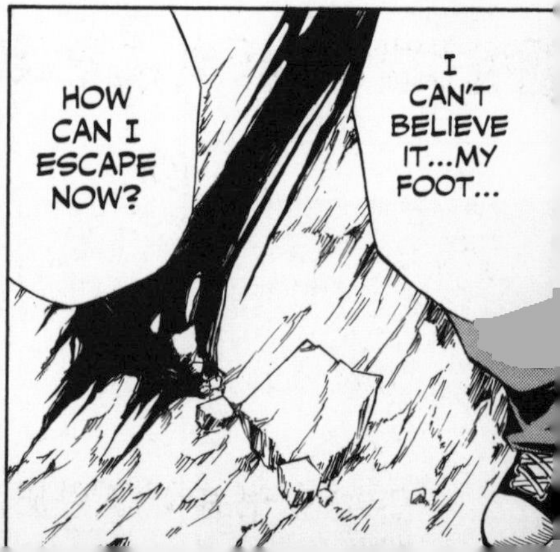
I CAN'T BELIEVE IT...MY FOOT...
HOW CAN I ESCAPE NOW?

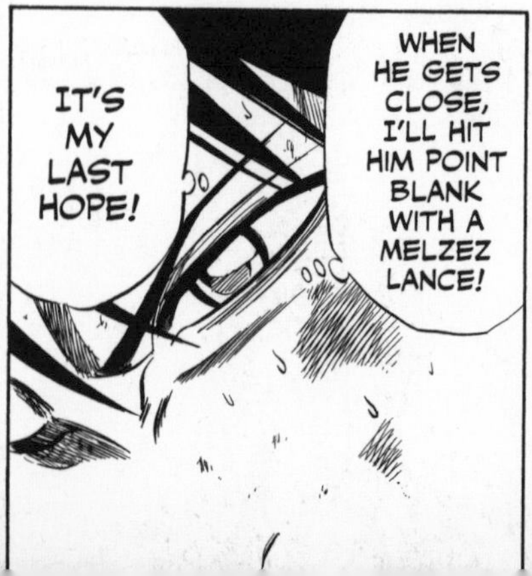
WHEN HE GETS CLOSE, I'LL HIT HIM POINT BLANK WITH A MELZEZ LANCE!
IT'S MY LAST HOPE!

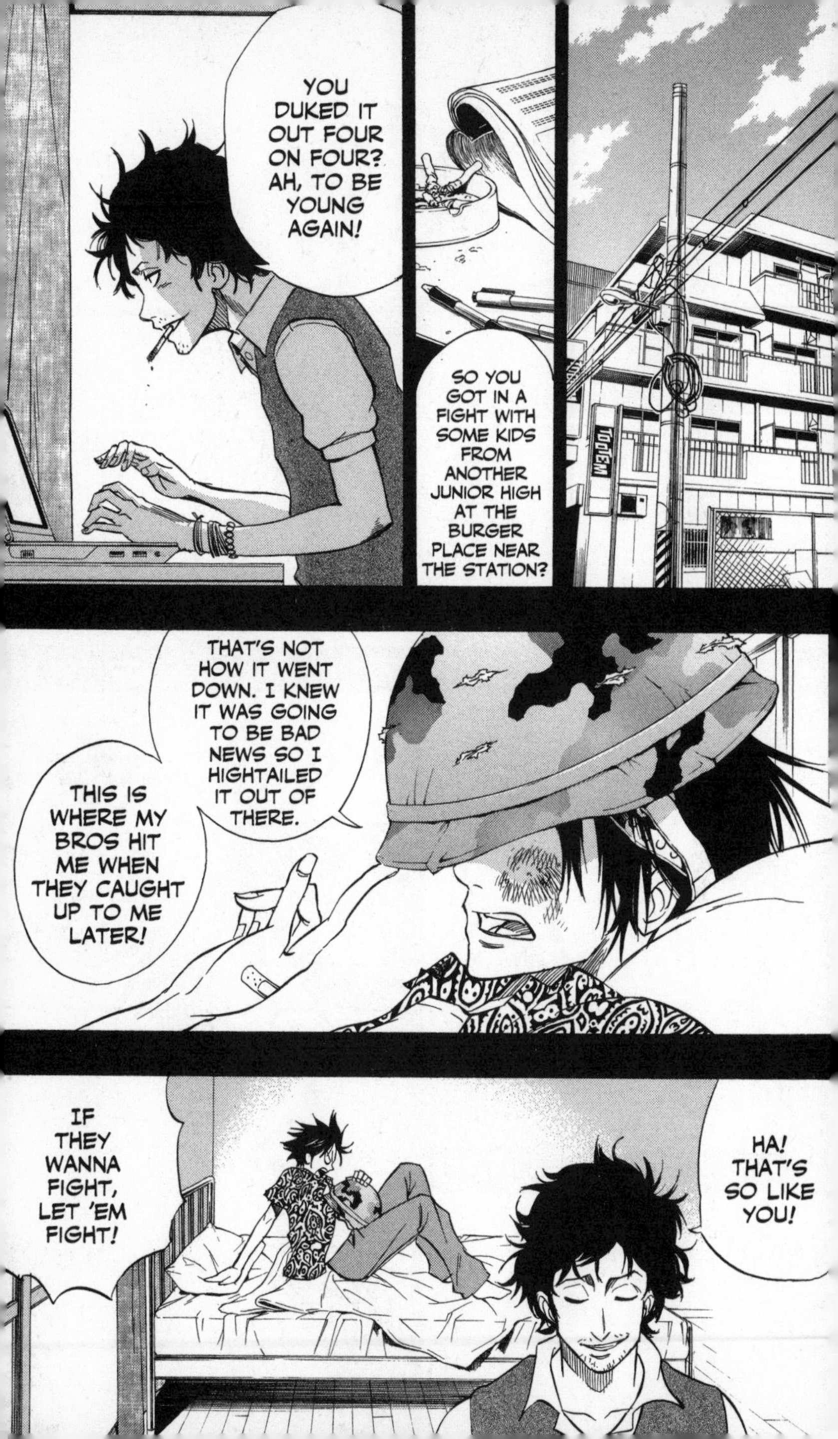
SO YOU GOT IN A FIGHT WITH SOME KIDS FROM ANOTHER JUNIOR HIGH AT THE BURGER PLACE NEAR THE STATION?
YOU DUKED IT OUT FOUR ON FOUR? AH, TO BE YOUNG AGAIN!
THAT'S NOT HOW IT WENT DOWN. I KNEW IT WAS GOING TO BE BAD NEWS SO I HIGHTAILED IT OUT OF THERE.
THIS IS WHERE MY BROS HIT ME WHEN THEY CAUGHT UP TO ME LATER!
HA! THAT'S SO LIKE YOU!
IF THEY WANNA FIGHT, LET 'EM FIGHT!

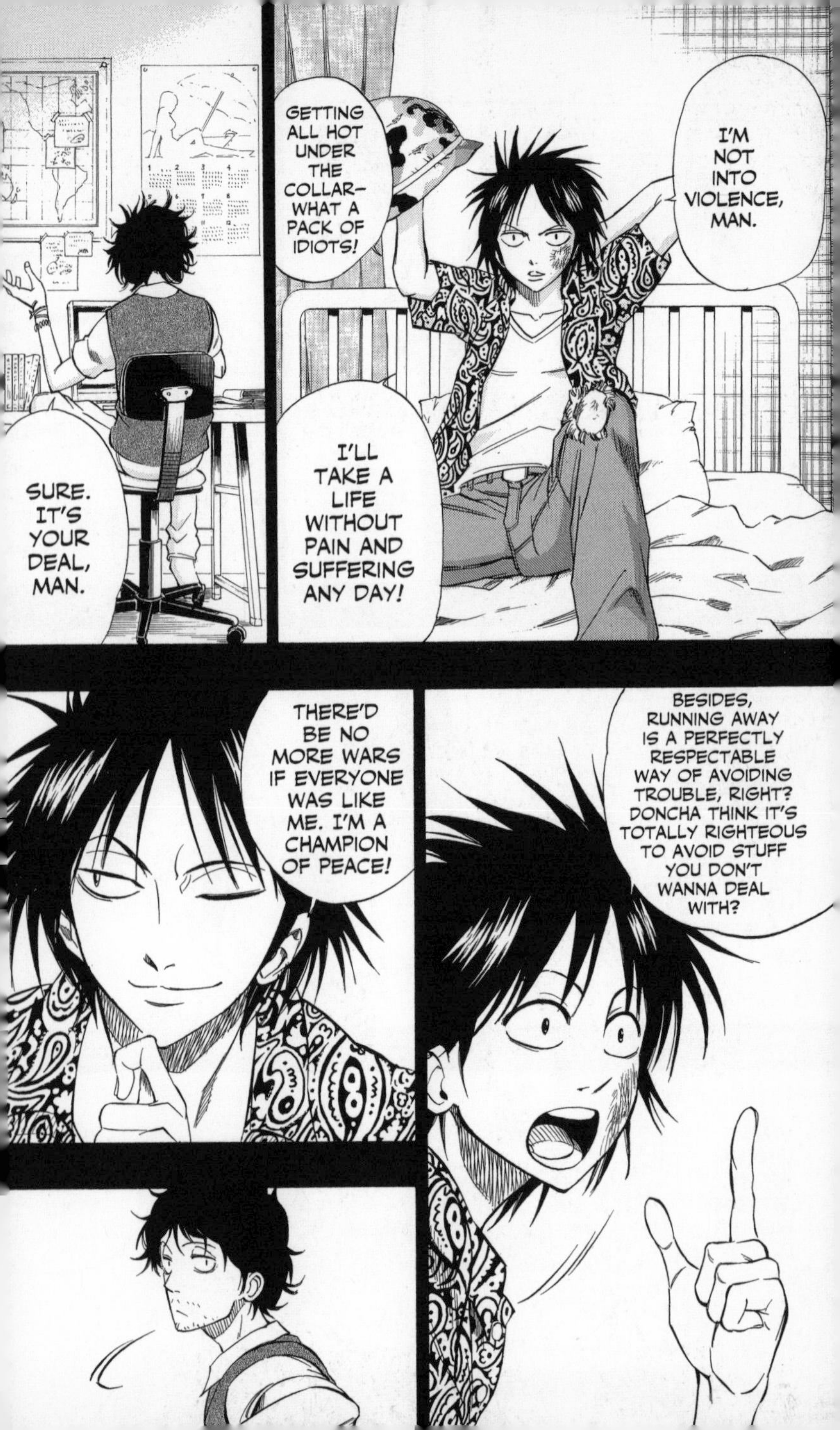
I'M NOT INTO VIOLENCE, MAN.
GETTING ALL HOT UNDER THE COLLAR— WHAT A PACK OF IDIOTS!
I'LL TAKE A LIFE WITHOUT PAIN AND SUFFERING ANY DAY!
SURE. IT'S YOUR DEAL, MAN.
BESIDES, RUNNING AWAY IS A PERFECTLY RESPECTABLE WAY OF AVOIDING TROUBLE, RIGHT? DONCHA THINK IT'S TOTALLY RIGHTEOUS TO AVOID STUFF YOU DON'T WANNA DEAL WITH?
THERE'D BE NO MORE WARS IF EVERYONE WAS LIKE ME. I'M A CHAMPION OF PEACE!

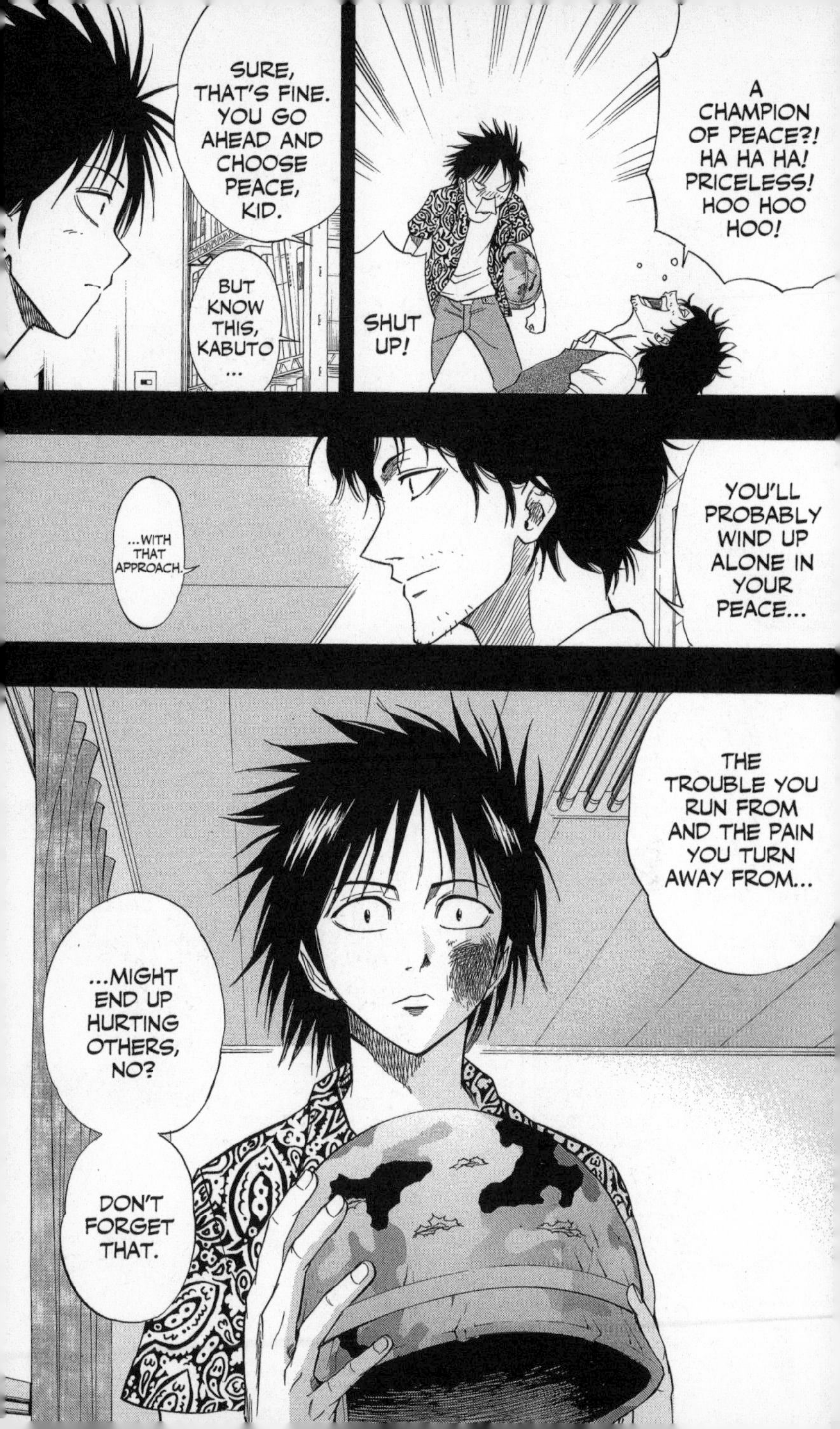
A CHAMPION OF PEACE?! HA HA HA! PRICELESS! HOO HOO HOO!
SHUT UP!
SURE, THAT'S FINE. YOU GO AHEAD AND CHOOSE PEACE, KID.
BUT KNOW THIS, KABUTO...
YOU'LL PROBABLY WIND UP ALONE IN YOUR PEACE...
...WITH THAT APPROACH.
THE TROUBLE YOU RUN FROM AND THE PAIN YOU TURN AWAY FROM...
...MIGHT END UP HURTING OTHERS, NO?
DON'T FORGET THAT.

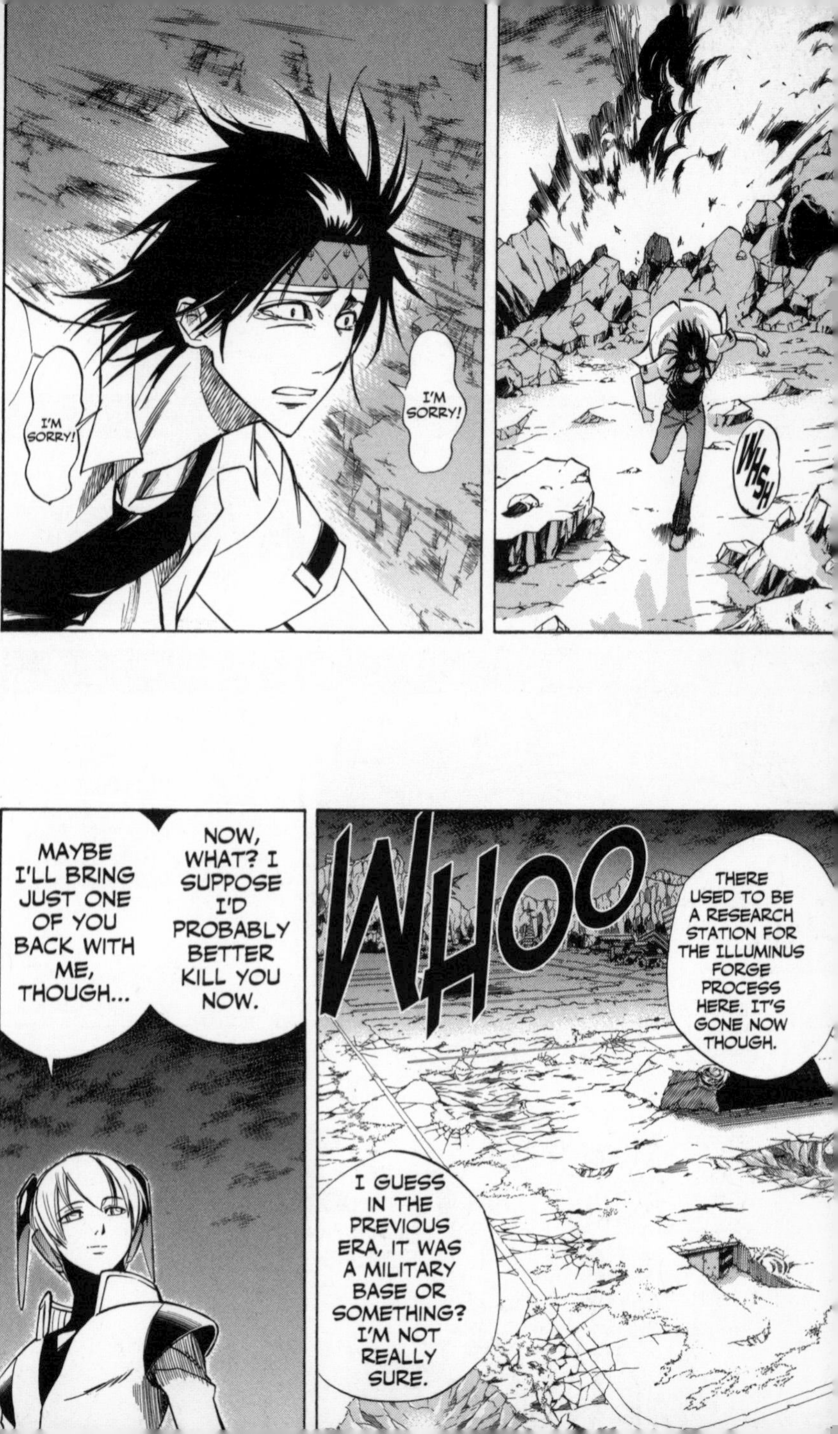
WHSH
I'M SORRY!
I'M SORRY!
WHOO
THERE USED TO BE A RESEARCH STATION FOR THE ILLUMINUS FORGE PROCESS HERE. IT'S GONE NOW THOUGH.
I GUESS IN THE PREVIOUS ERA, IT WAS A MILITARY BASE OR SOMETHING? I'M NOT REALLY SURE.
NOW, WHAT? I SUPPOSE I'D PROBABLY BETTER KILL YOU NOW.
MAYBE I'LL BRING JUST ONE OF YOU BACK WITH ME, THOUGH...

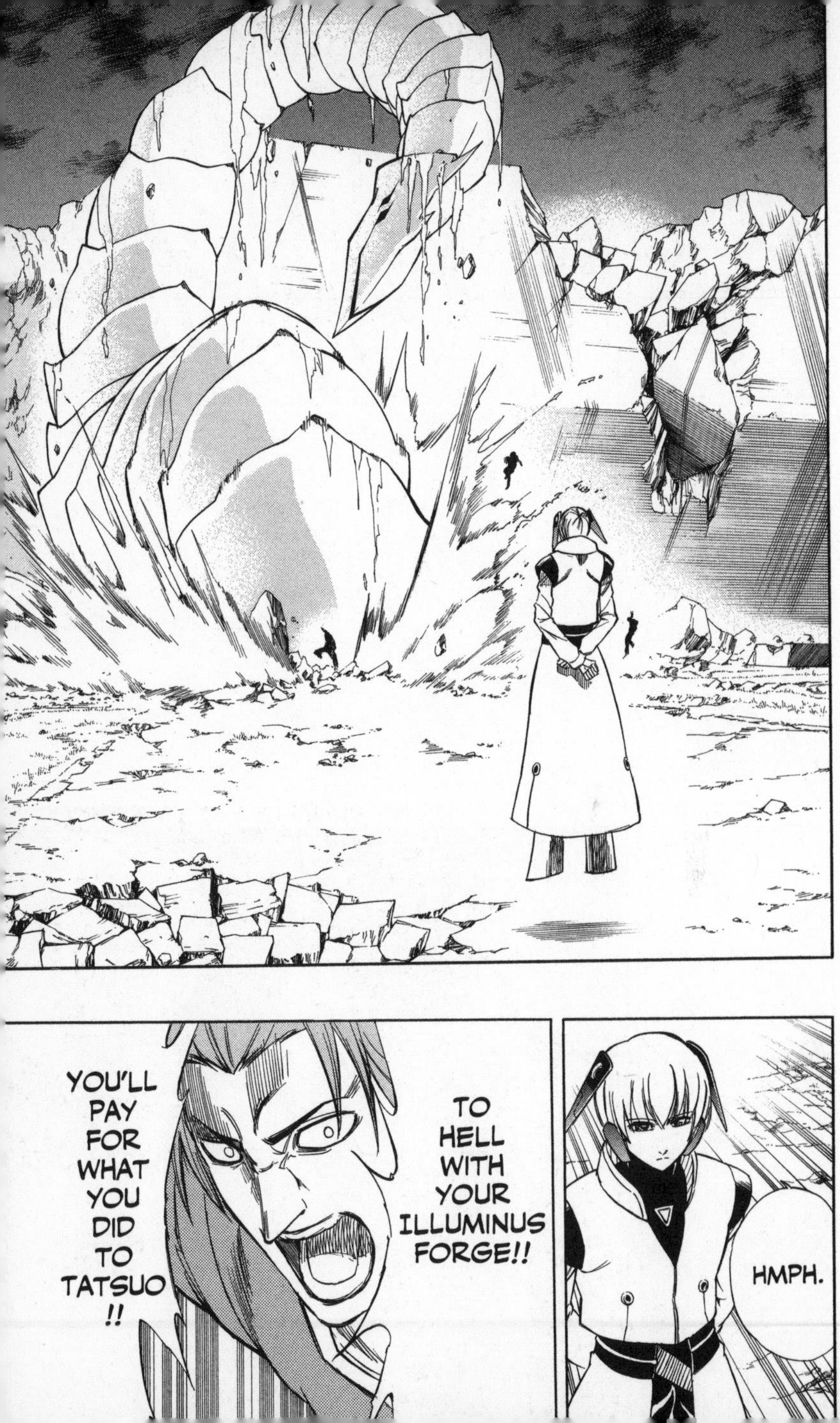
HMPH.
TO HELL WITH YOUR ILLUMINUS FORGE!!
YOU'LL PAY FOR WHAT YOU DID TO TATSUO!!

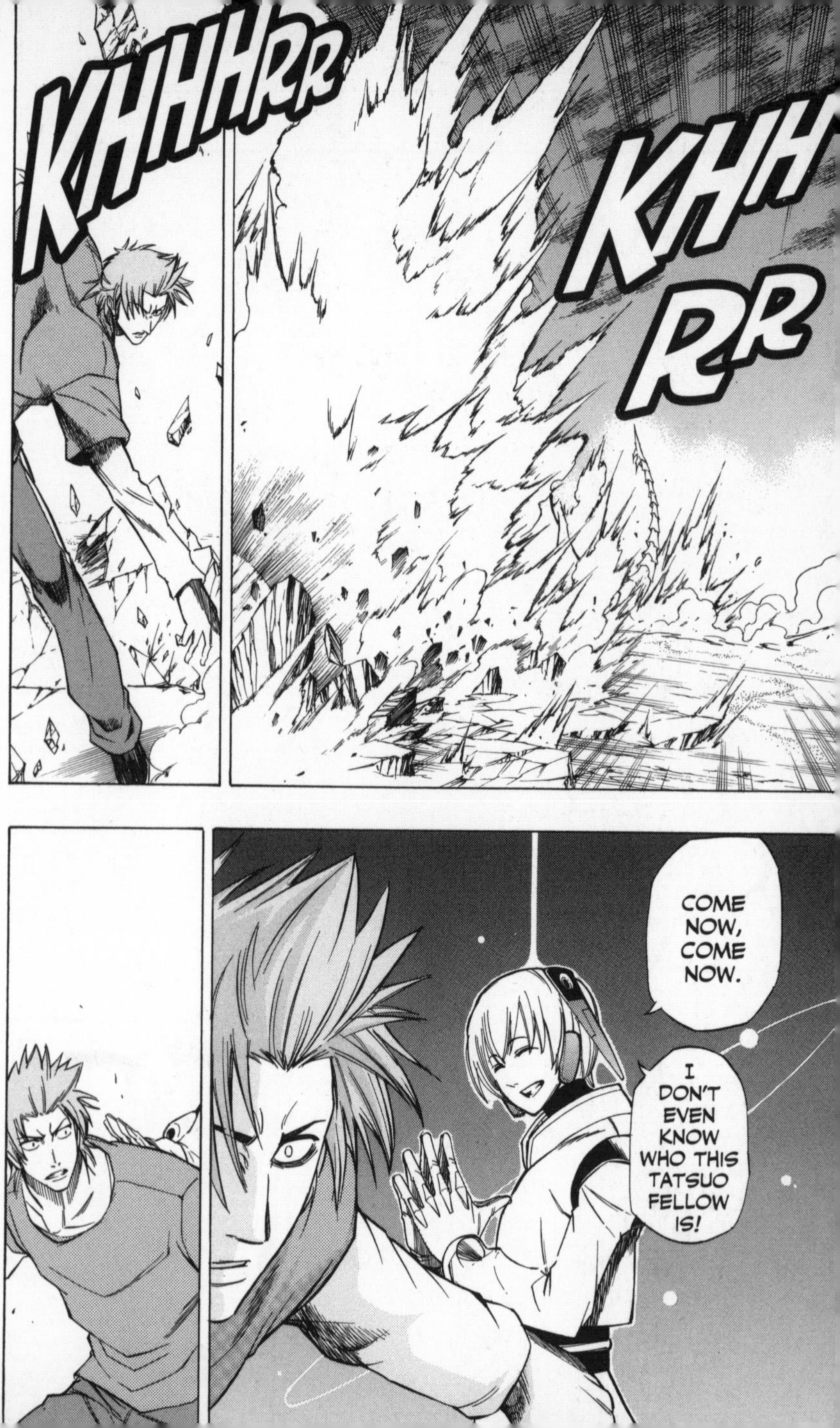
KHH RR
KHHHRR
COME NOW, COME NOW.
I DON'T EVEN KNOW WHO THIS TATSUO FELLOW IS!

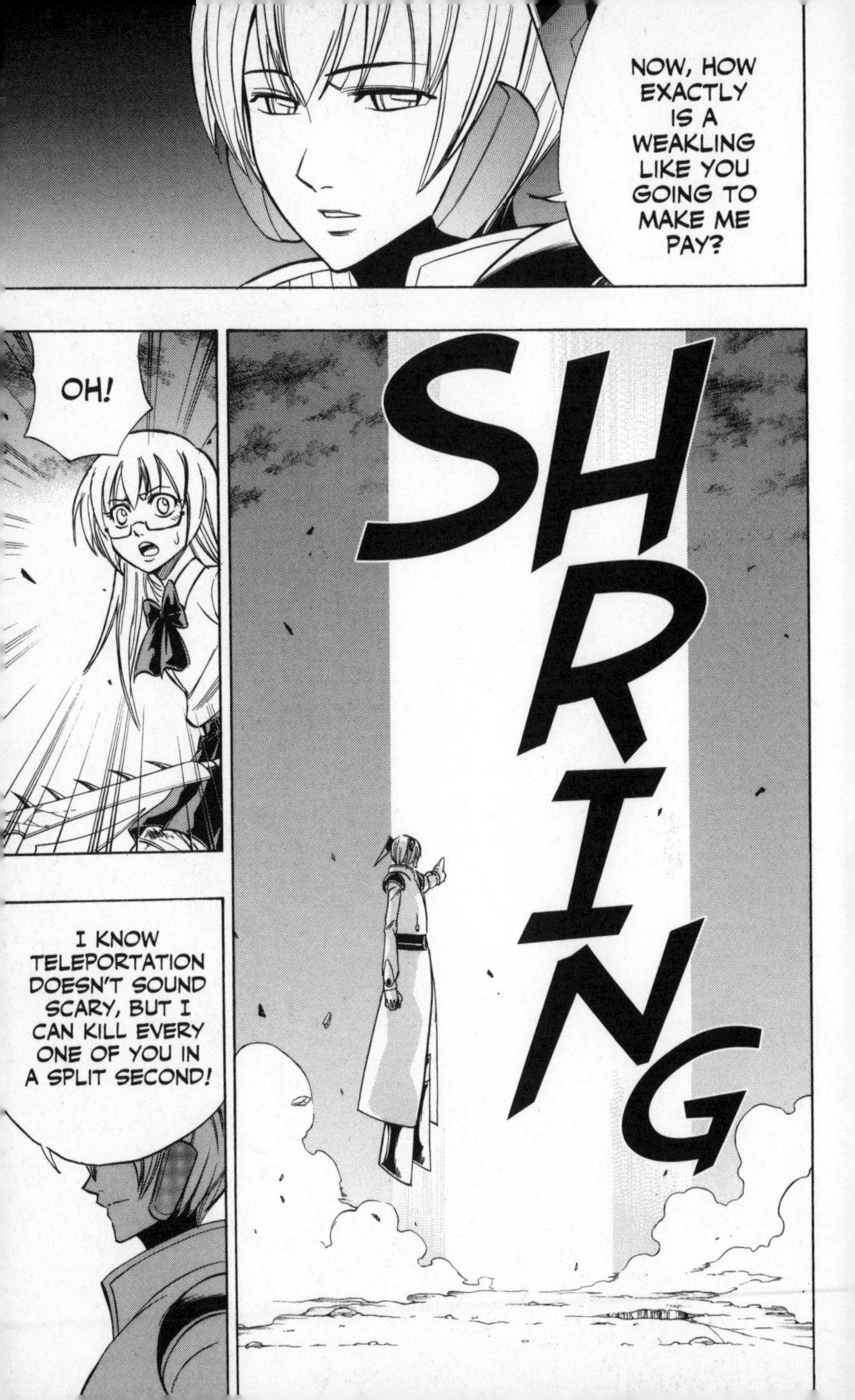
NOW, HOW EXACTLY IS A WEAKLING LIKE YOU GOING TO MAKE ME PAY?
SHRING
OH!
I KNOW TELEPORTATION DOESN'T SOUND SCARY, BUT I CAN KILL EVERY ONE OF YOU IN A SPLIT SECOND!

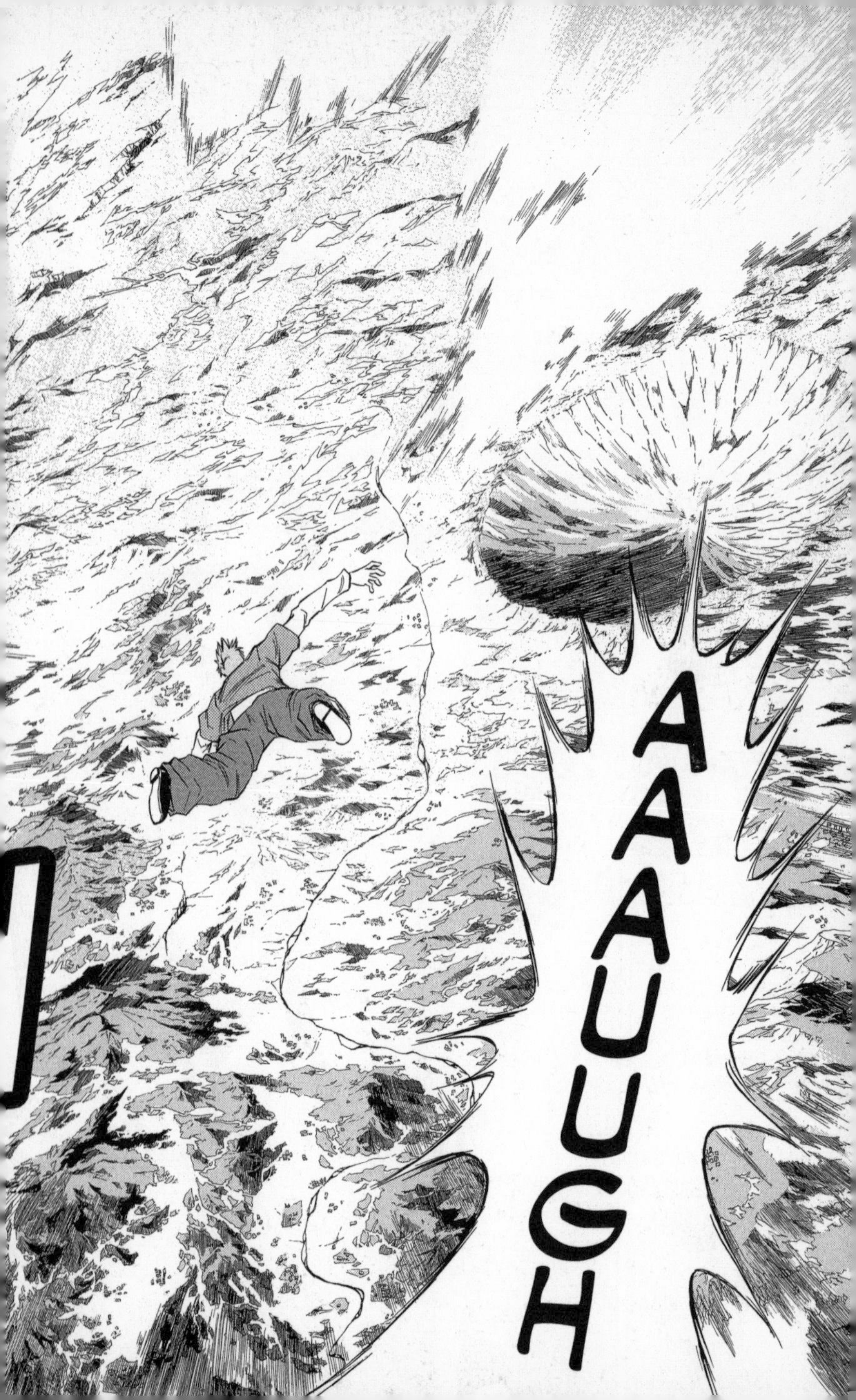
AAAAUGH

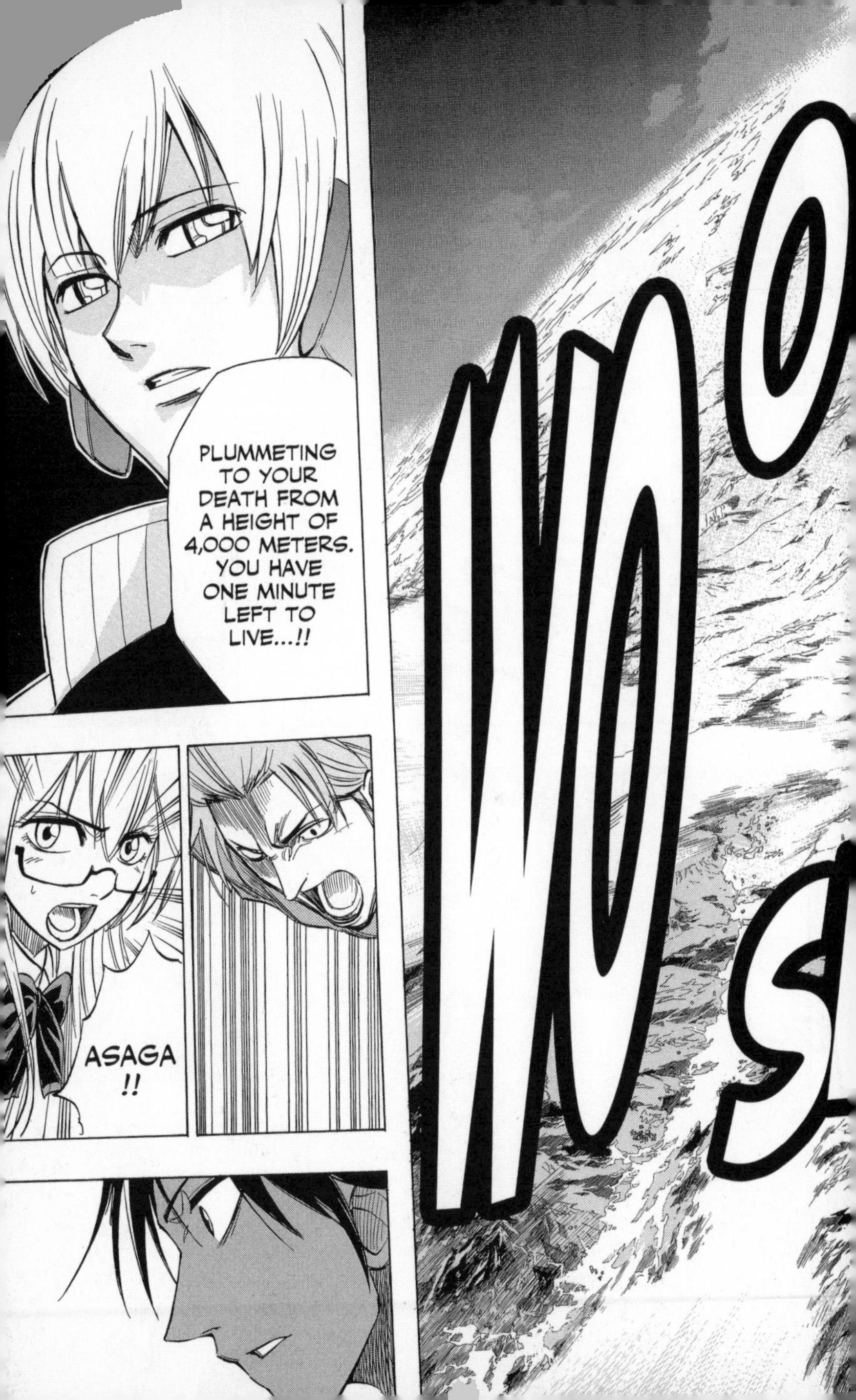
WOOS
PLUMMETING TO YOUR DEATH FROM A HEIGHT OF 4,000 METERS. YOU HAVE ONE MINUTE LEFT TO LIVE...!!
ASAGA !!

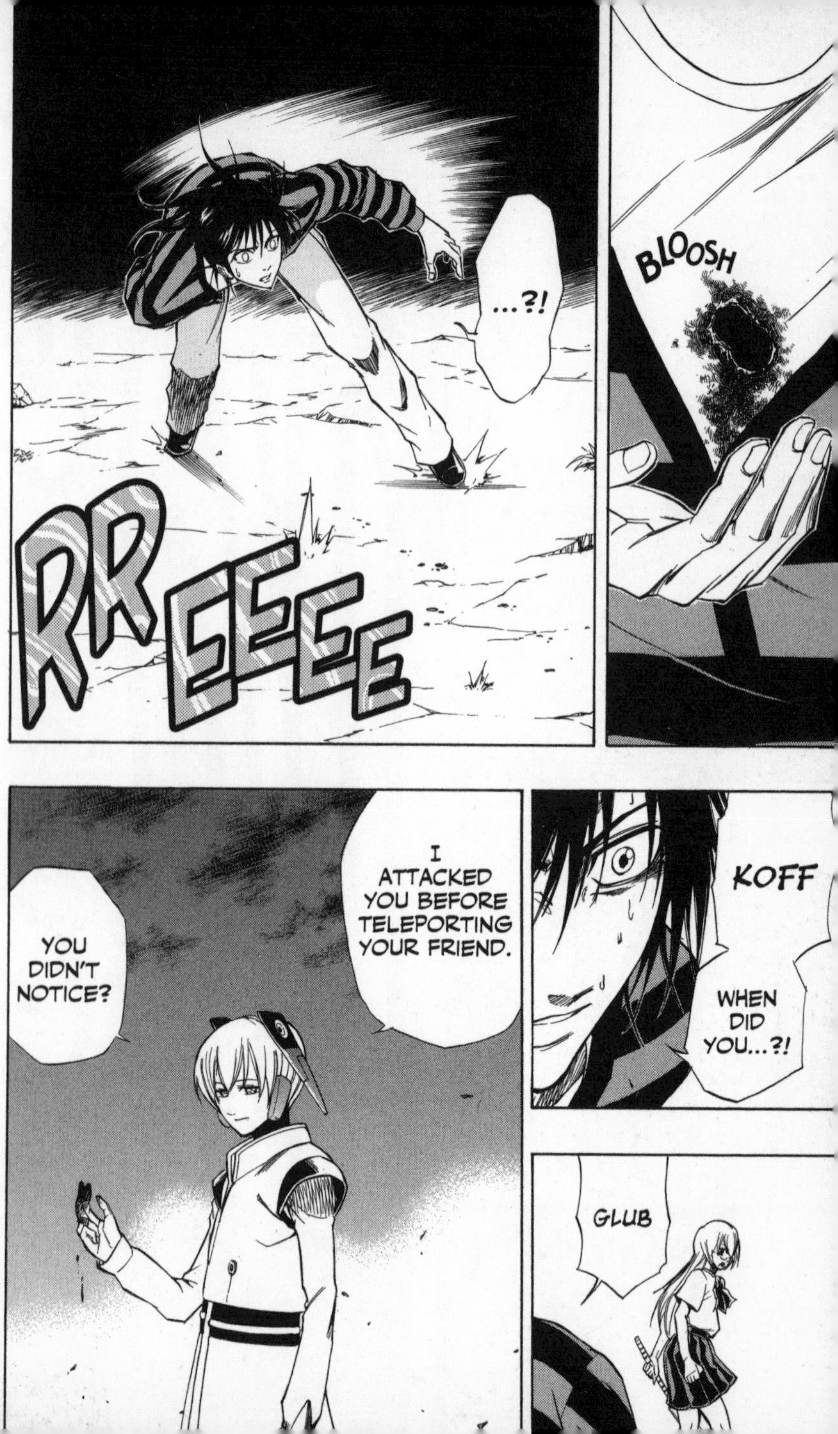
BLOOSH
...?!
RREEEE
KOFF
WHEN DID YOU...?!
GLUB
I ATTACKED YOU BEFORE TELEPORTING YOUR FRIEND.
YOU DIDN'T NOTICE?

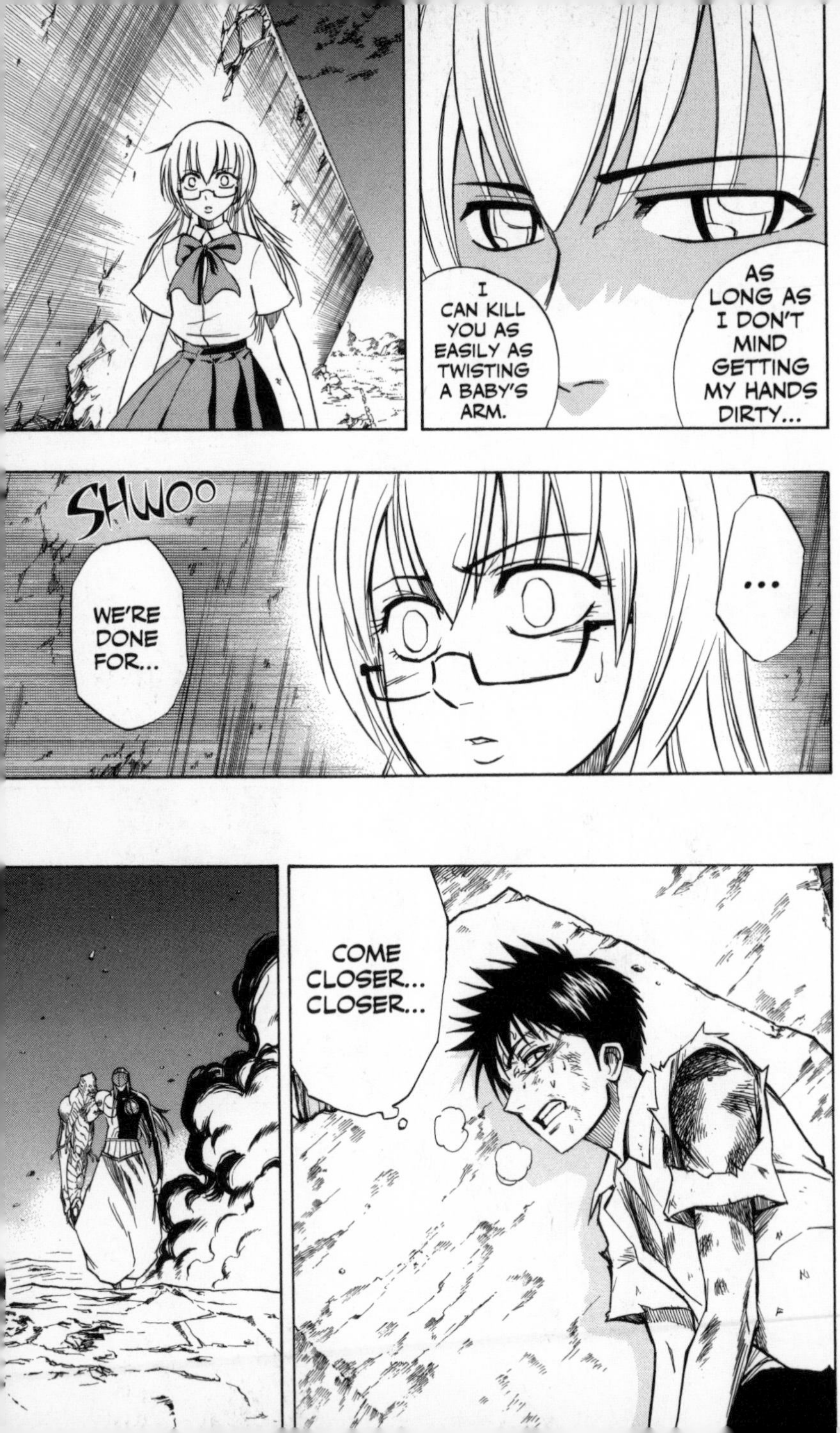
AS LONG AS I DON'T MIND GETTING MY HANDS DIRTY...
I CAN KILL YOU AS EASILY AS TWISTING A BABY'S ARM.
...
SHWOO
WE'RE DONE FOR...
COME CLOSER... CLOSER...

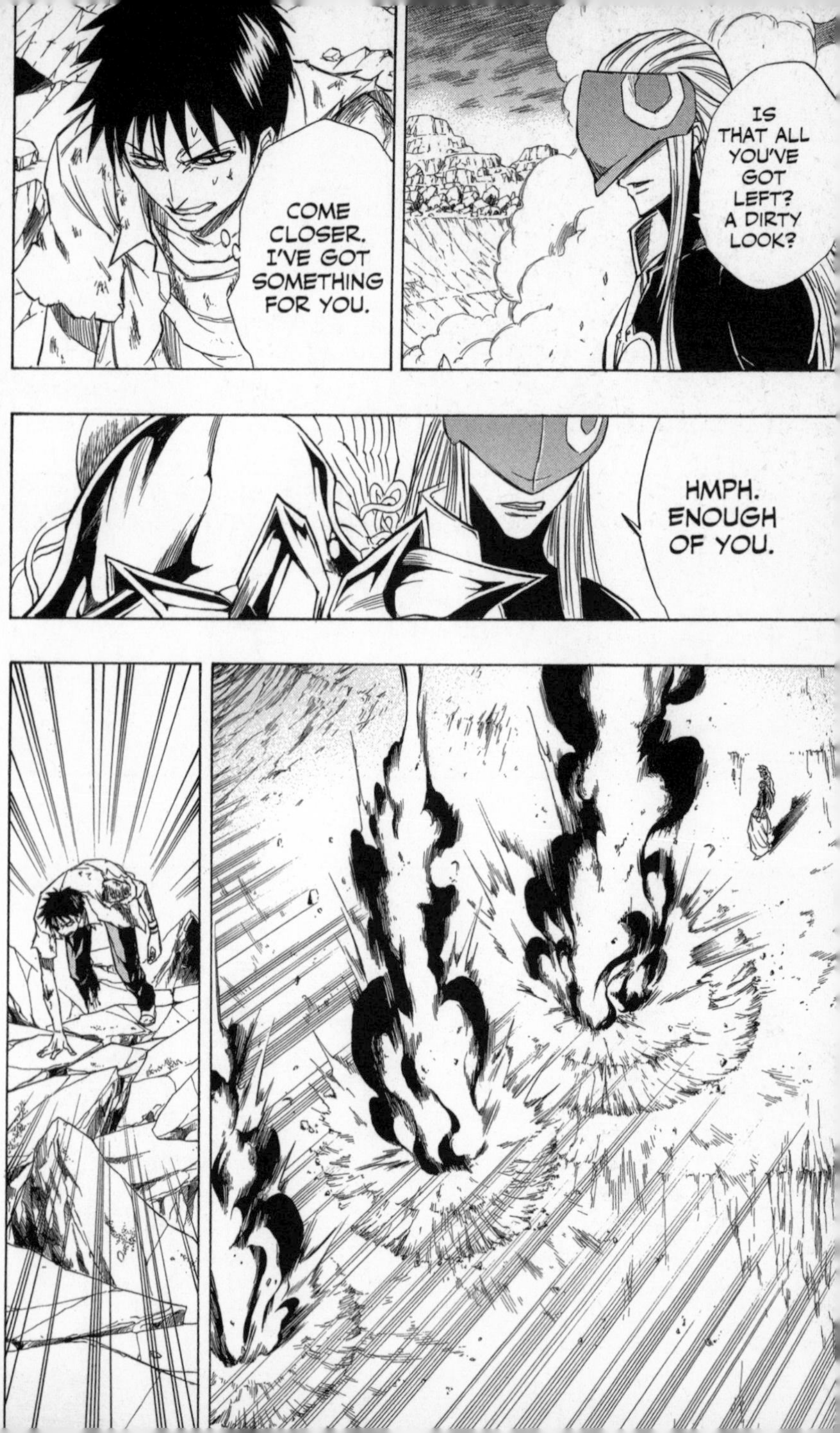
IS THAT ALL YOU'VE GOT LEFT? A DIRTY LOOK?
COME CLOSER. I'VE GOT SOMETHING FOR YOU.
HMPH. ENOUGH OF YOU.

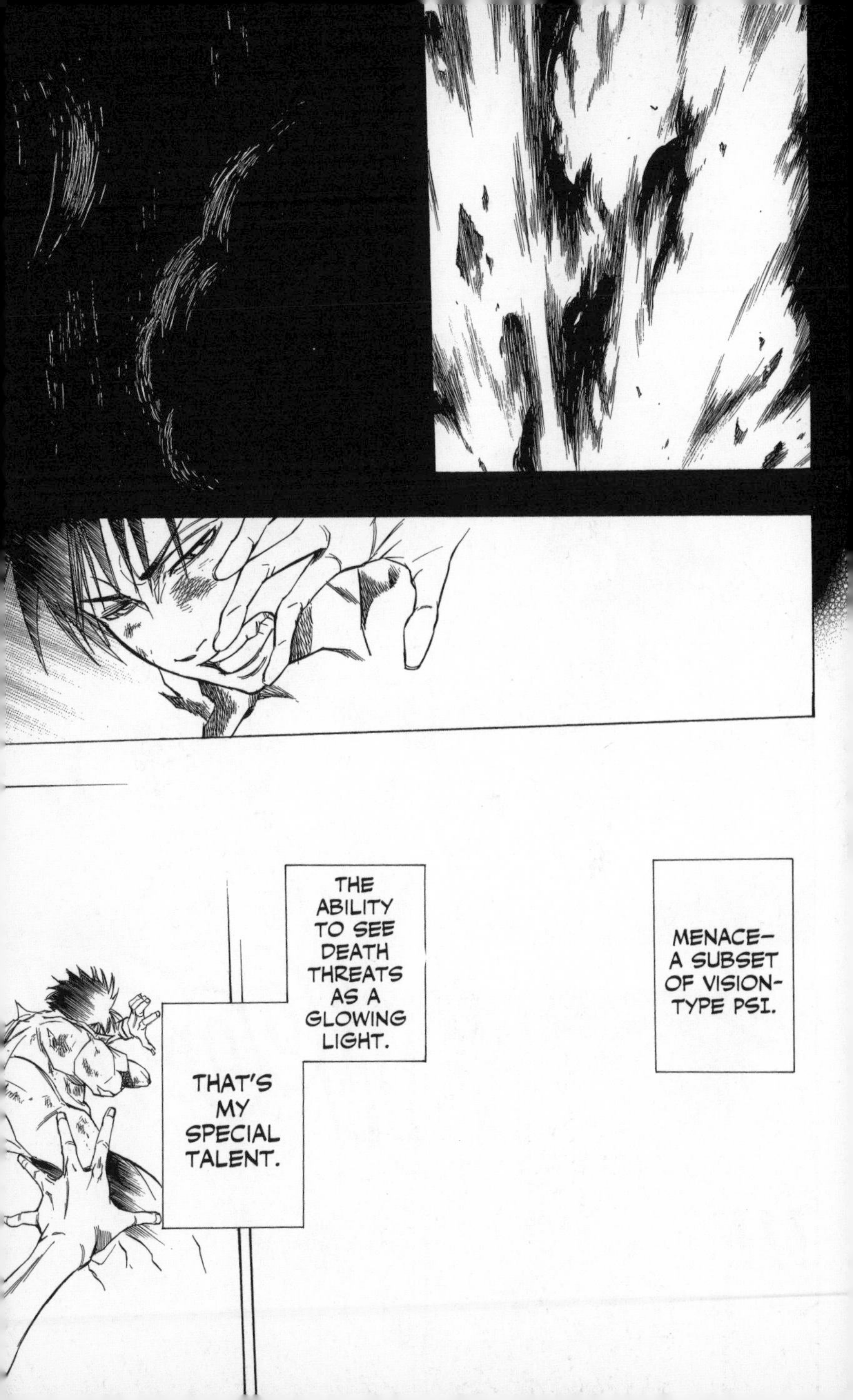
MENACE—A SUBSET OF VISION-TYPE PSI.
THE ABILITY TO SEE DEATH THREATS AS A GLOWING LIGHT.
THAT'S MY SPECIAL TALENT.

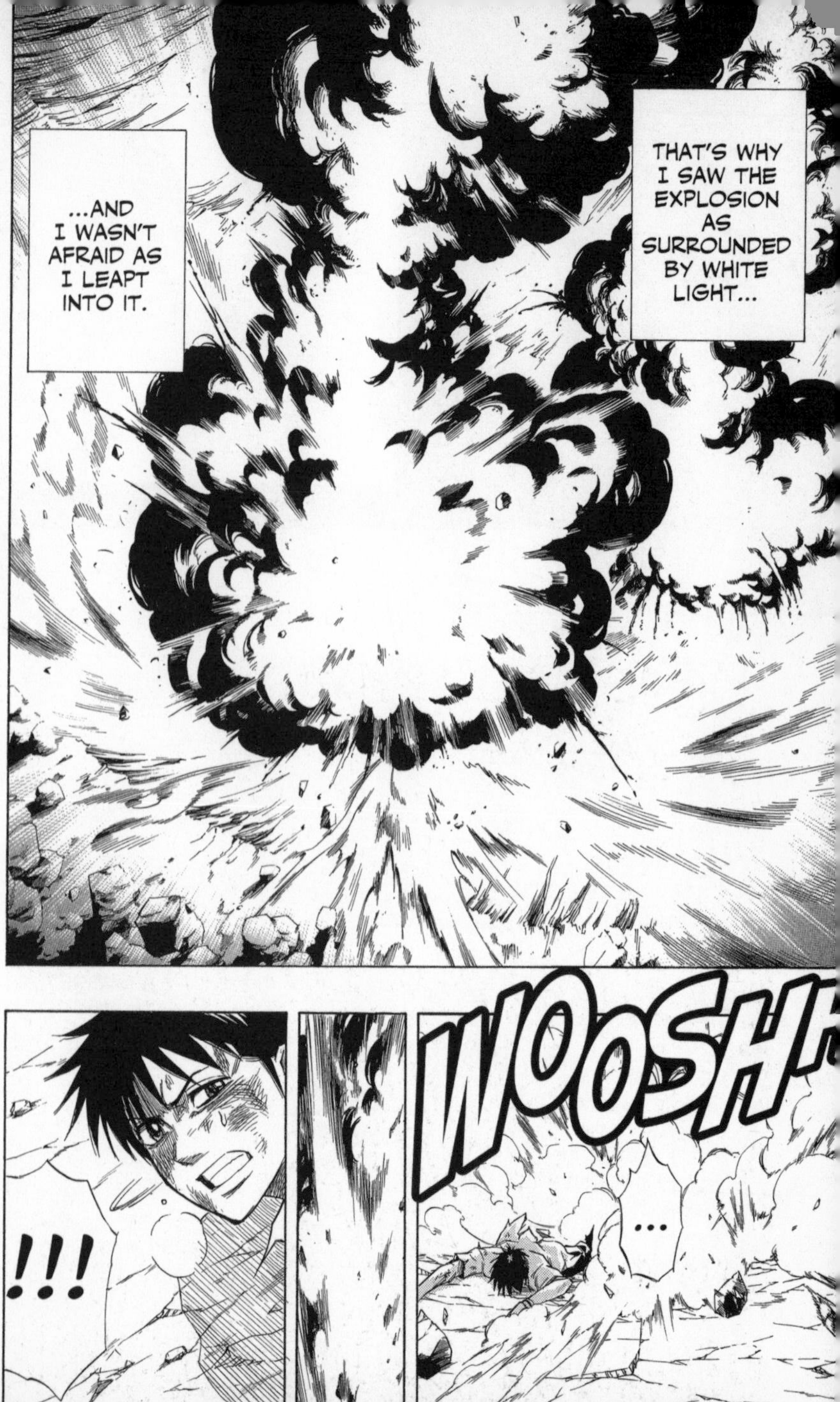
THAT'S WHY I SAW THE EXPLOSION AS SURROUNDED BY WHITE LIGHT...
...AND I WASN'T AFRAID AS I LEAPT INTO IT.
WOOSH
...
!!!

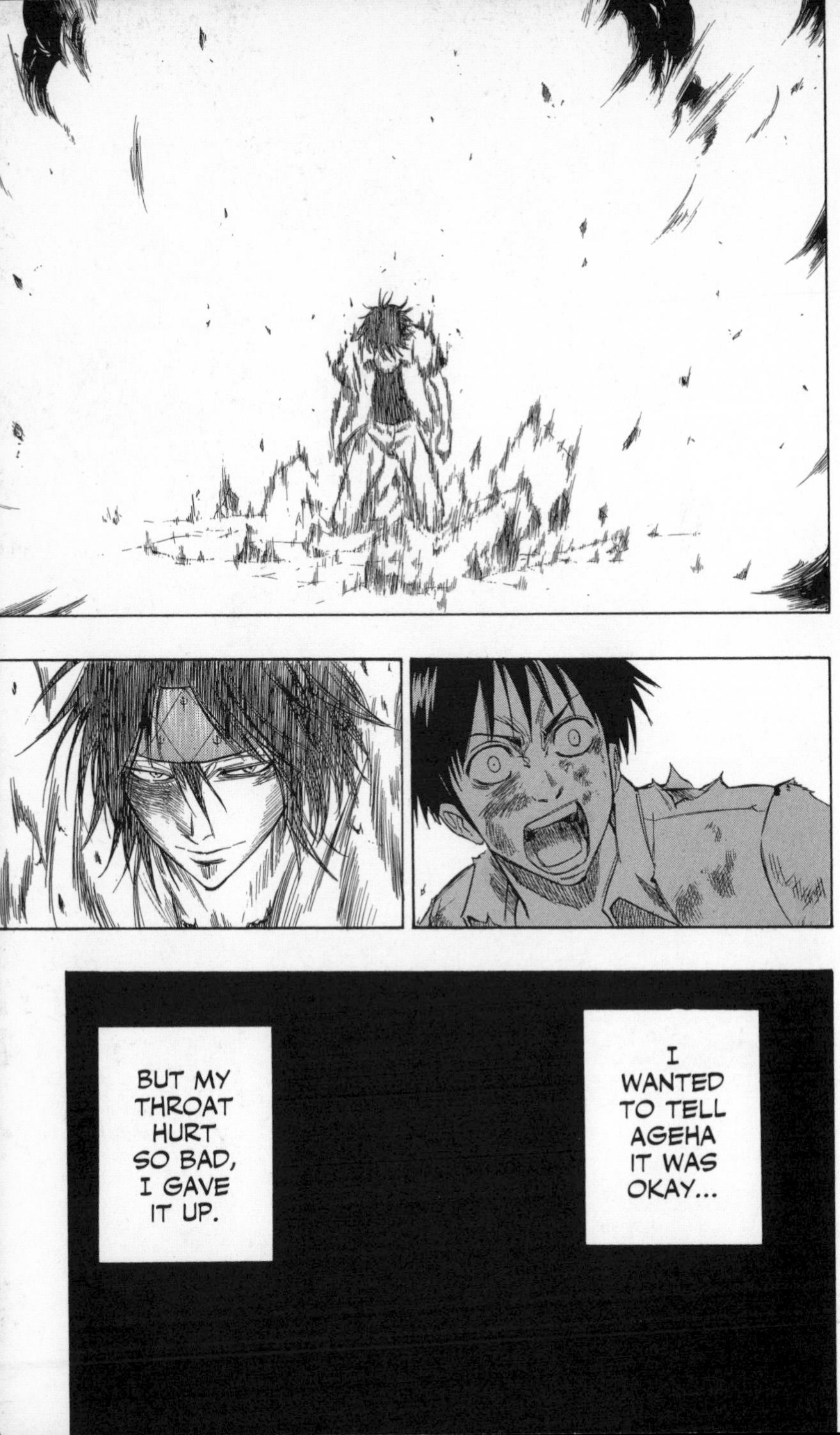
I WANTED TO TELL AGEHA IT WAS OKAY...
BUT MY THROAT HURT SO BAD, I GAVE IT UP.

Mutters and mumblings

STUFF THAT'S ON MY MIND THESE DAYS:
CHOOSING A NEW CELL PHONE
THE FINAL SEASON OF *PRISON BREAK*
SEASON 7 OF *24*
A NEW LCD TV
THE BROKEN OLD LIGHT BOX I'VE BEEN USING FOREVER
THE RELEASE DATE FOR *EVANGELION 2.0*
THE COVER ART FOR *PSYREN* VOLUME 9
MY DECEMBER SCHEDULE
CLEANING UP MY ROOM

STUFF THAT'S ALWAYS ON MY MIND: THESE SURVEYS

Call.64: Light

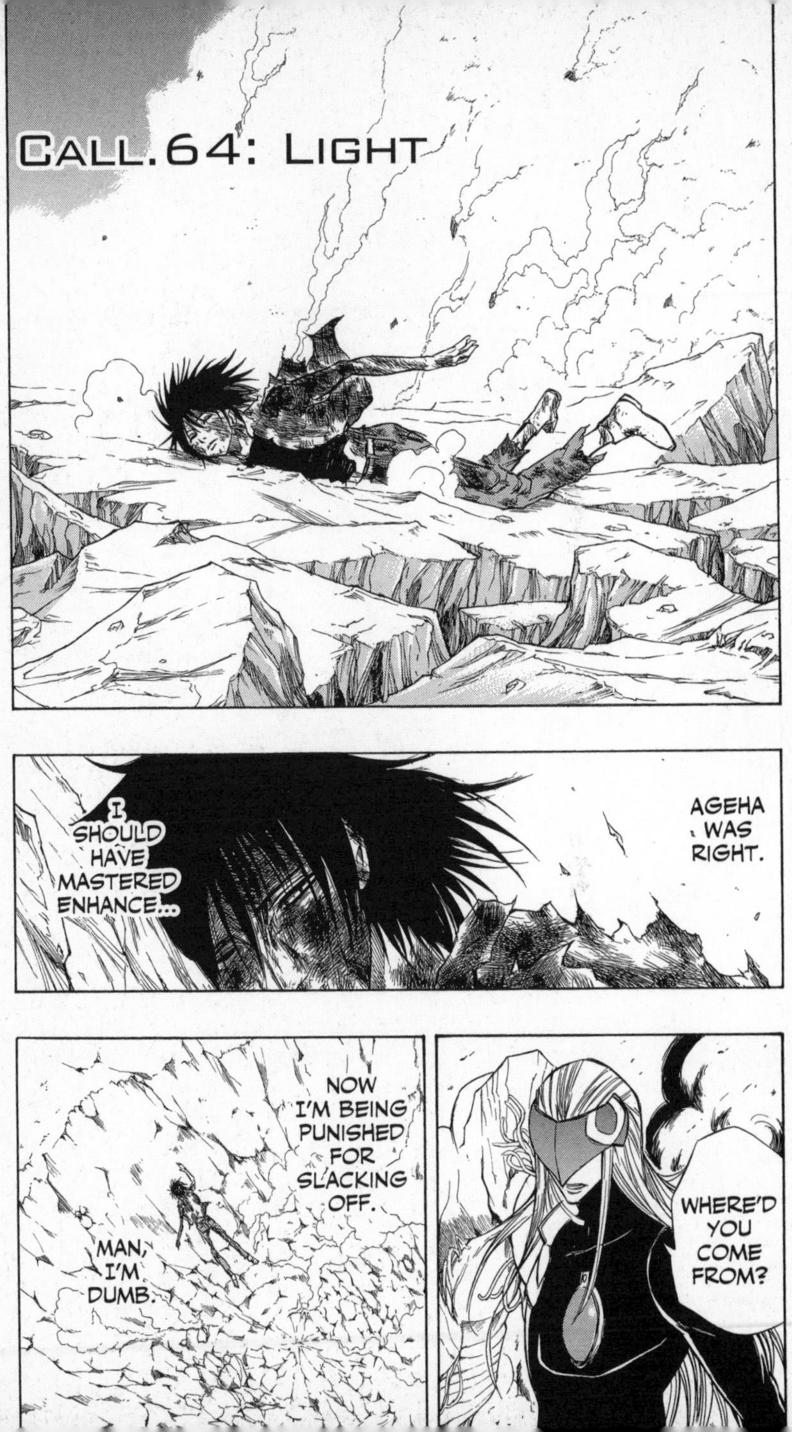

AGEHA WAS RIGHT.
I SHOULD HAVE MASTERED ENHANCE...
WHERE'D YOU COME FROM?
NOW I'M BEING PUNISHED FOR SLACKING OFF.
MAN, I'M DUMB.

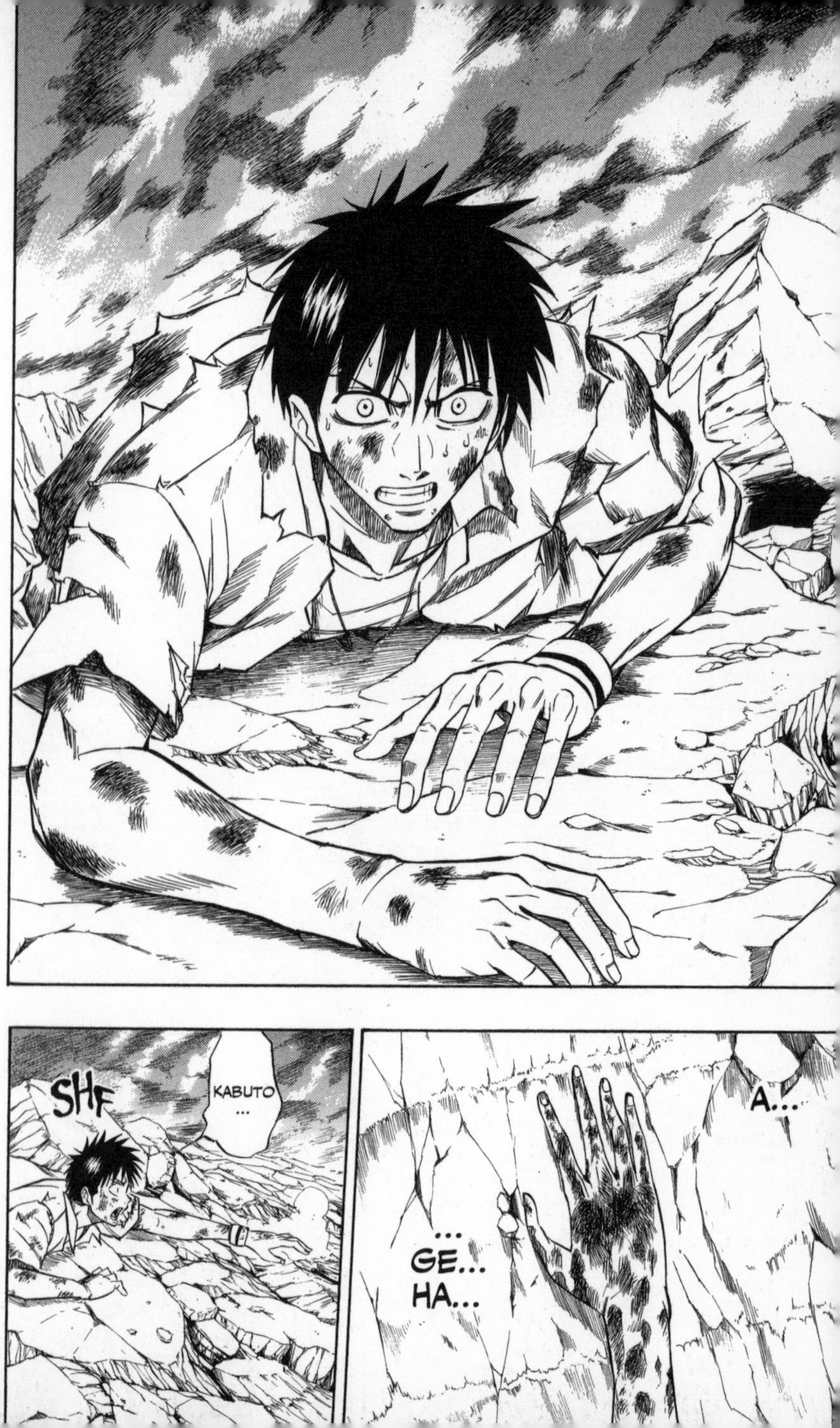
A...
... GE... HA...
SHF
KABUTO ...

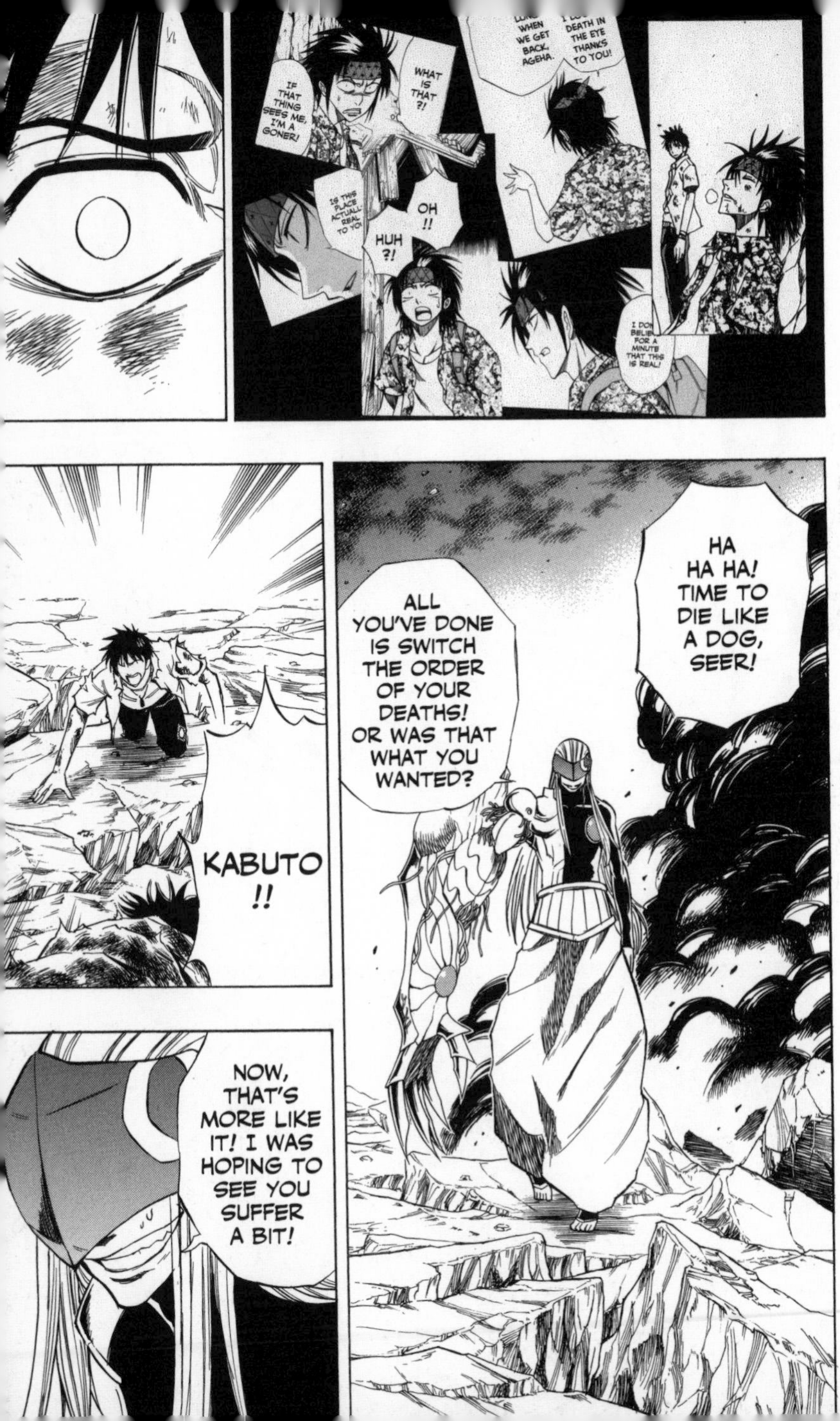
FOR A MINUTE THAT THIS IS REAL!
DEATH IN THE EYE THANKS TO YOU!
WHEN WE GET BACK, AGEHA.
WHAT IS THAT ?!
IF THAT THING SEES ME, I'M A GONER!
OH !!
HUH ?!
IS THIS PLACE
HA HA HA! TIME TO DIE LIKE A DOG, SEER!
ALL YOU'VE DONE IS SWITCH THE ORDER OF YOUR DEATHS! OR WAS THAT WHAT YOU WANTED?
KABUTO !!
NOW, THAT'S MORE LIKE IT! I WAS HOPING TO SEE YOU SUFFER A BIT!

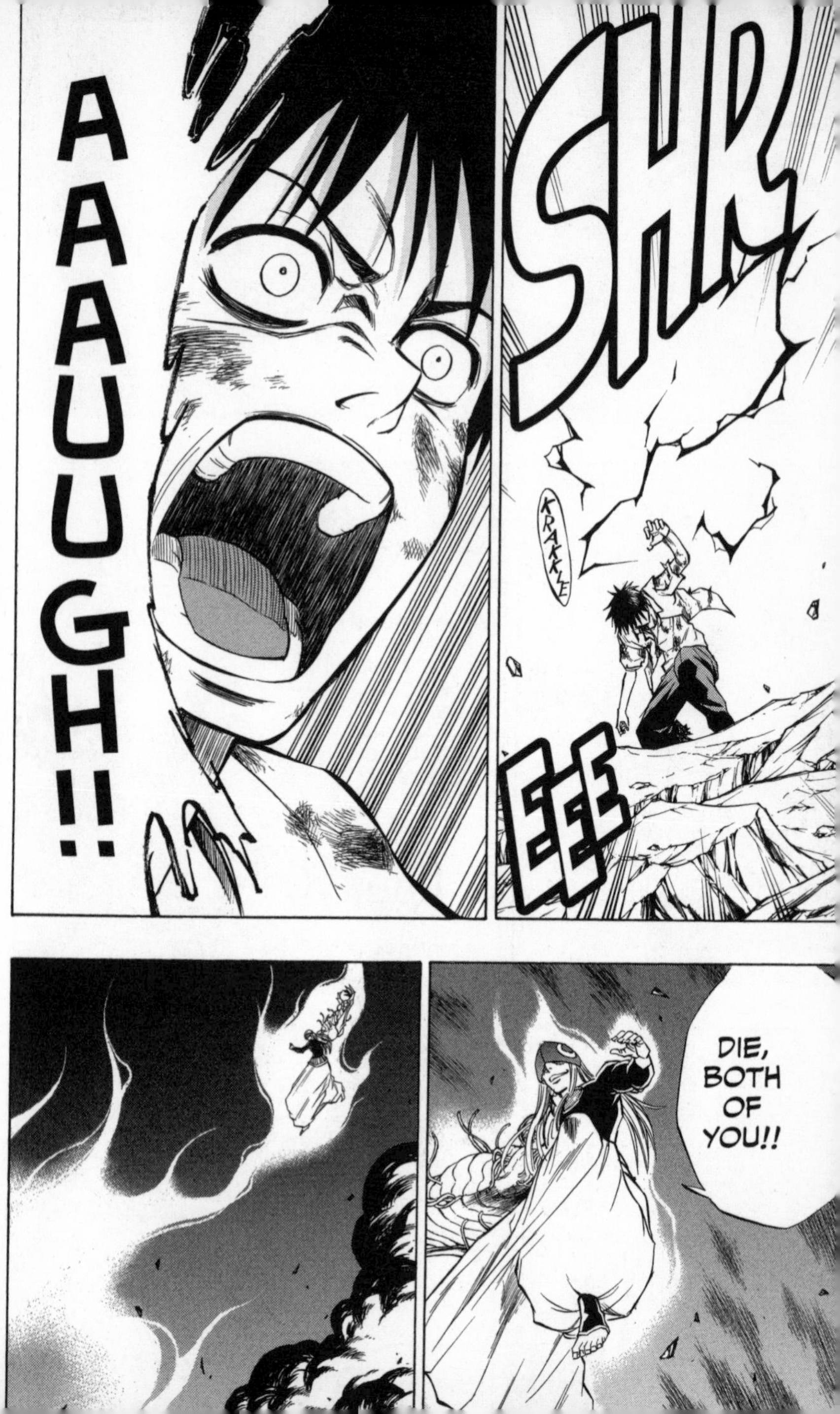
SHR
KRAKKLE
EEE
AAAUUGH!!
DIE, BOTH OF YOU!!

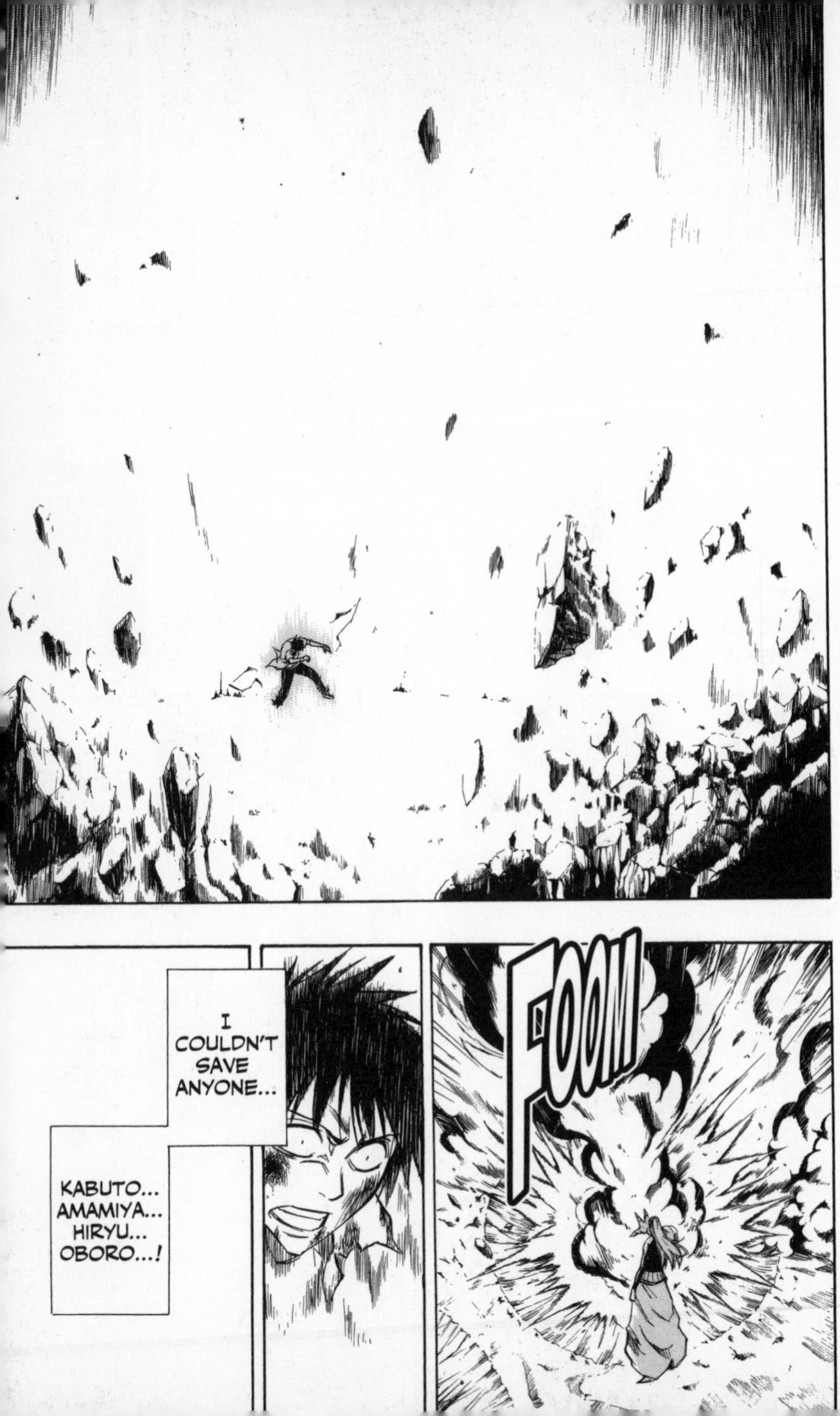
FOOM
I COULDN'T SAVE ANYONE...
KABUTO... AMAMIYA... HIRYU... OBORO...!

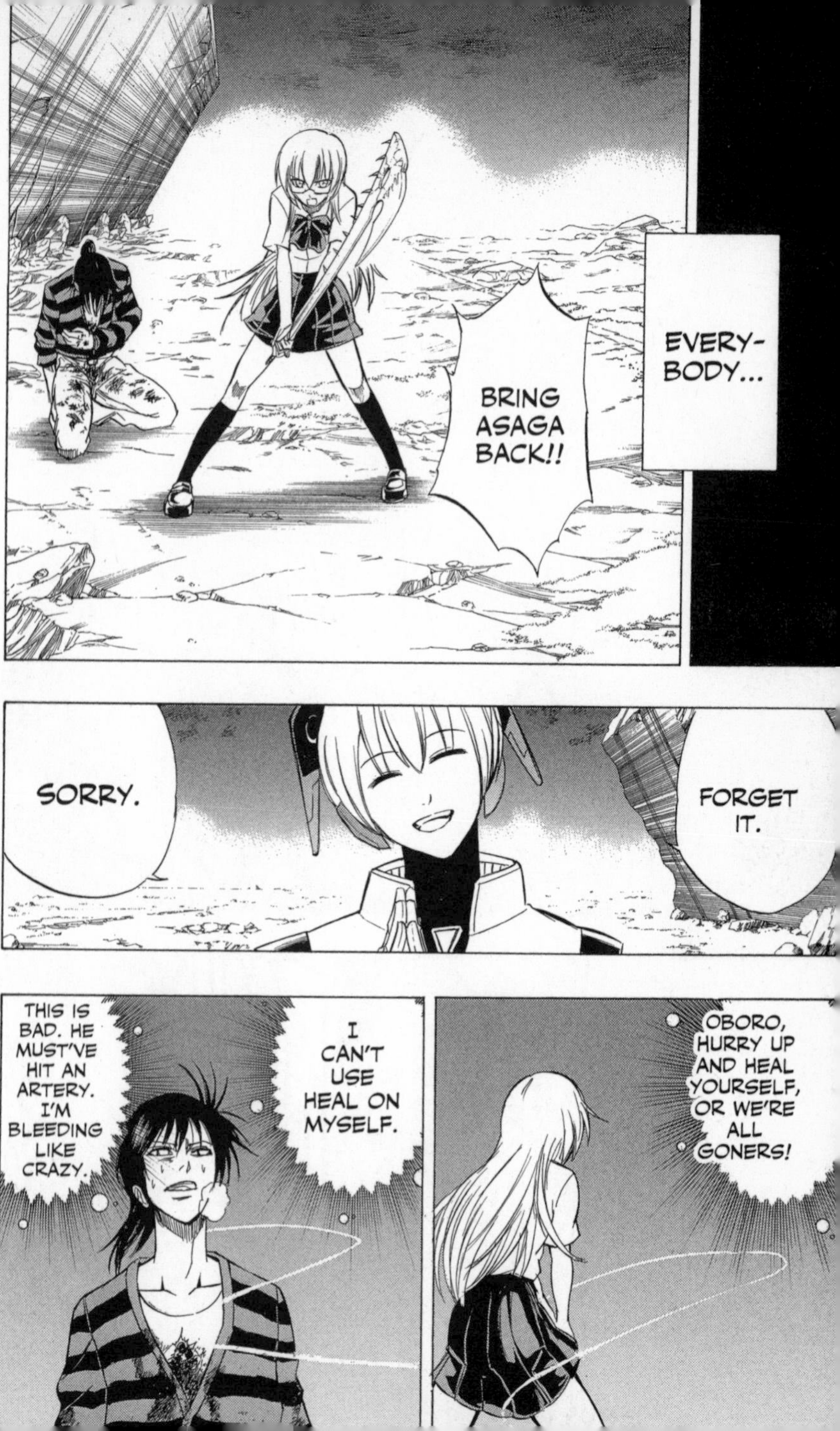
EVERY-BODY...
BRING ASAGA BACK!!
FORGET IT.
SORRY.
OBORO, HURRY UP AND HEAL YOURSELF, OR WE'RE ALL GONERS!
I CAN'T USE HEAL ON MYSELF.
THIS IS BAD. HE MUST'VE HIT AN ARTERY. I'M BLEEDING LIKE CRAZY.

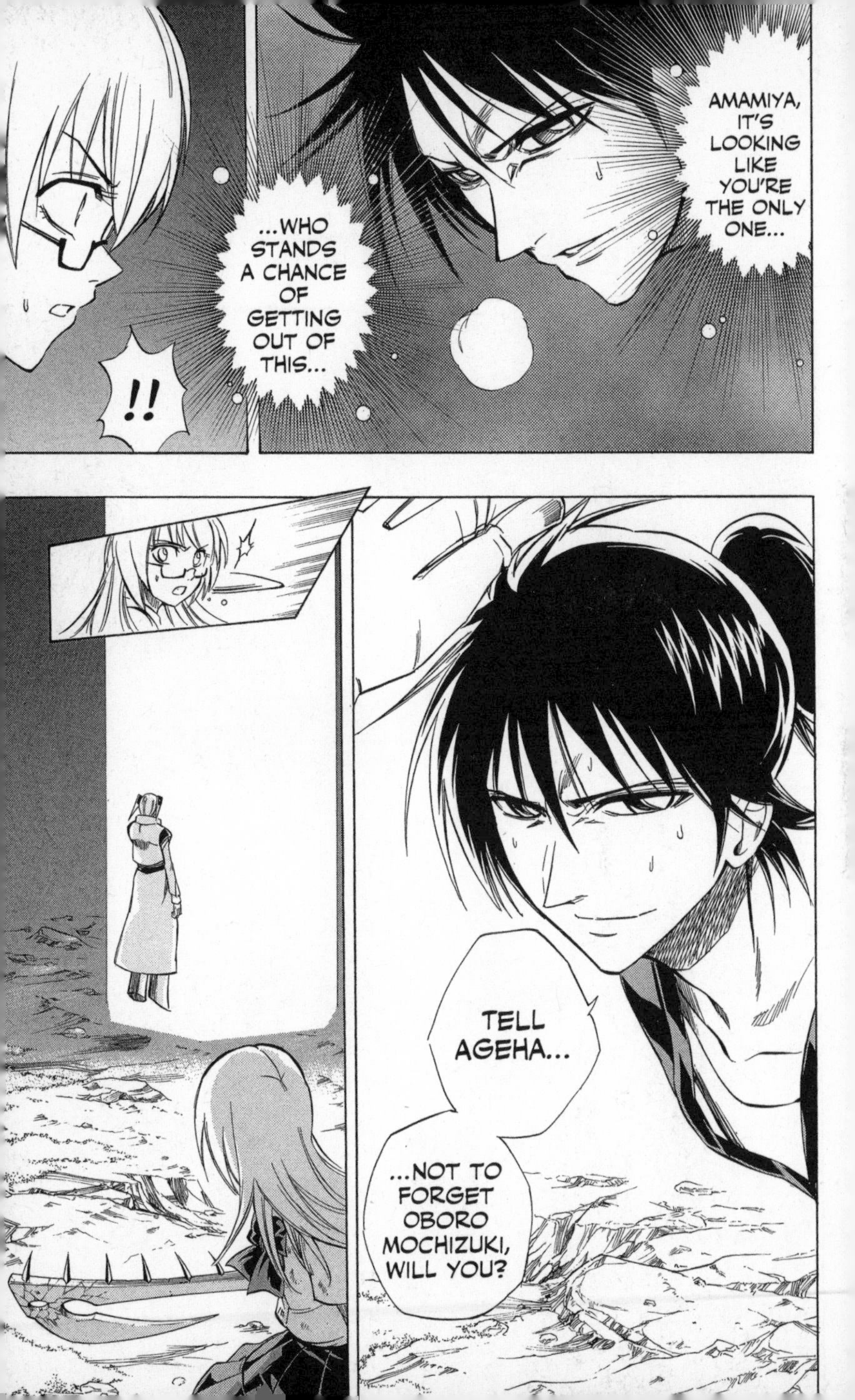
AMAMIYA, IT'S LOOKING LIKE YOU'RE THE ONLY ONE...
...WHO STANDS A CHANCE OF GETTING OUT OF THIS...
!!
TELL AGEHA...
...NOT TO FORGET OBORO MOCHIZUKI, WILL YOU?

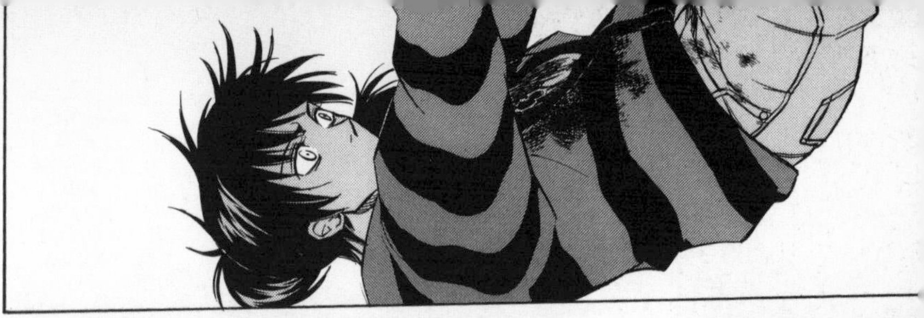

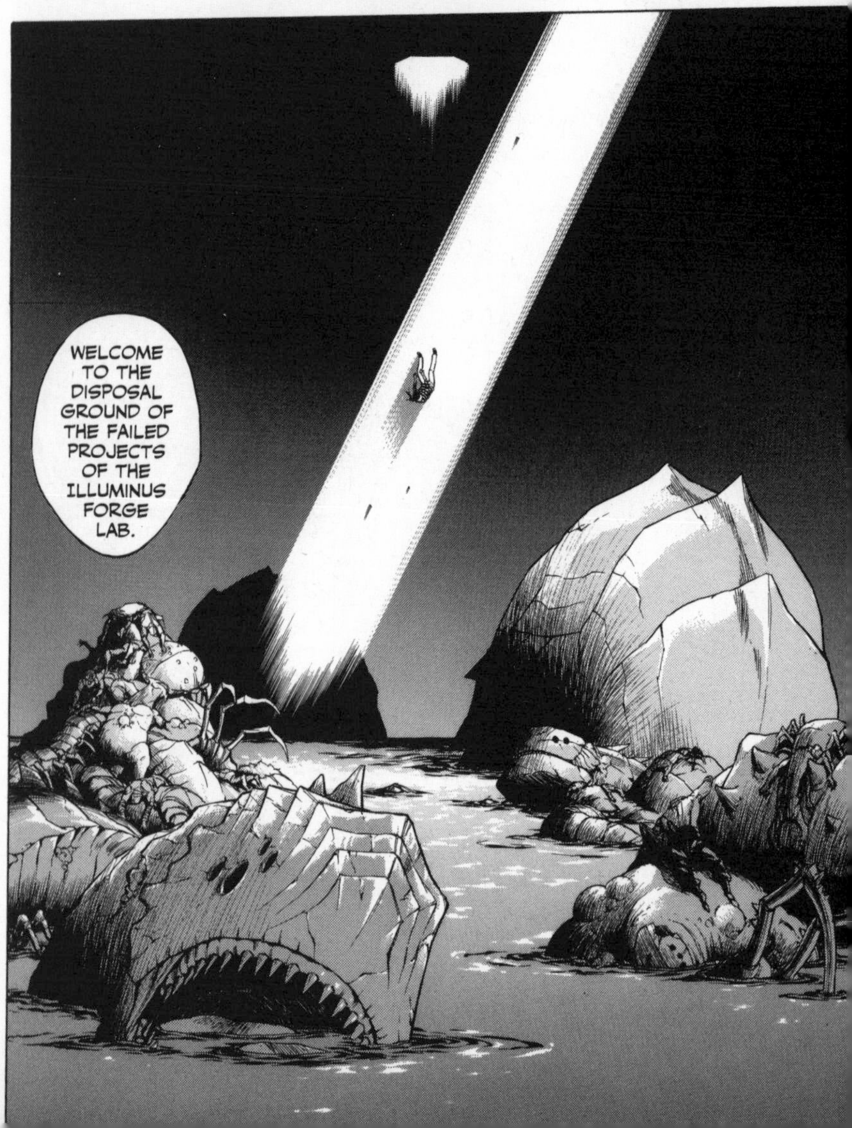
WELCOME TO THE DISPOSAL GROUND OF THE FAILED PROJECTS OF THE ILLUMINUS FORGE LAB.

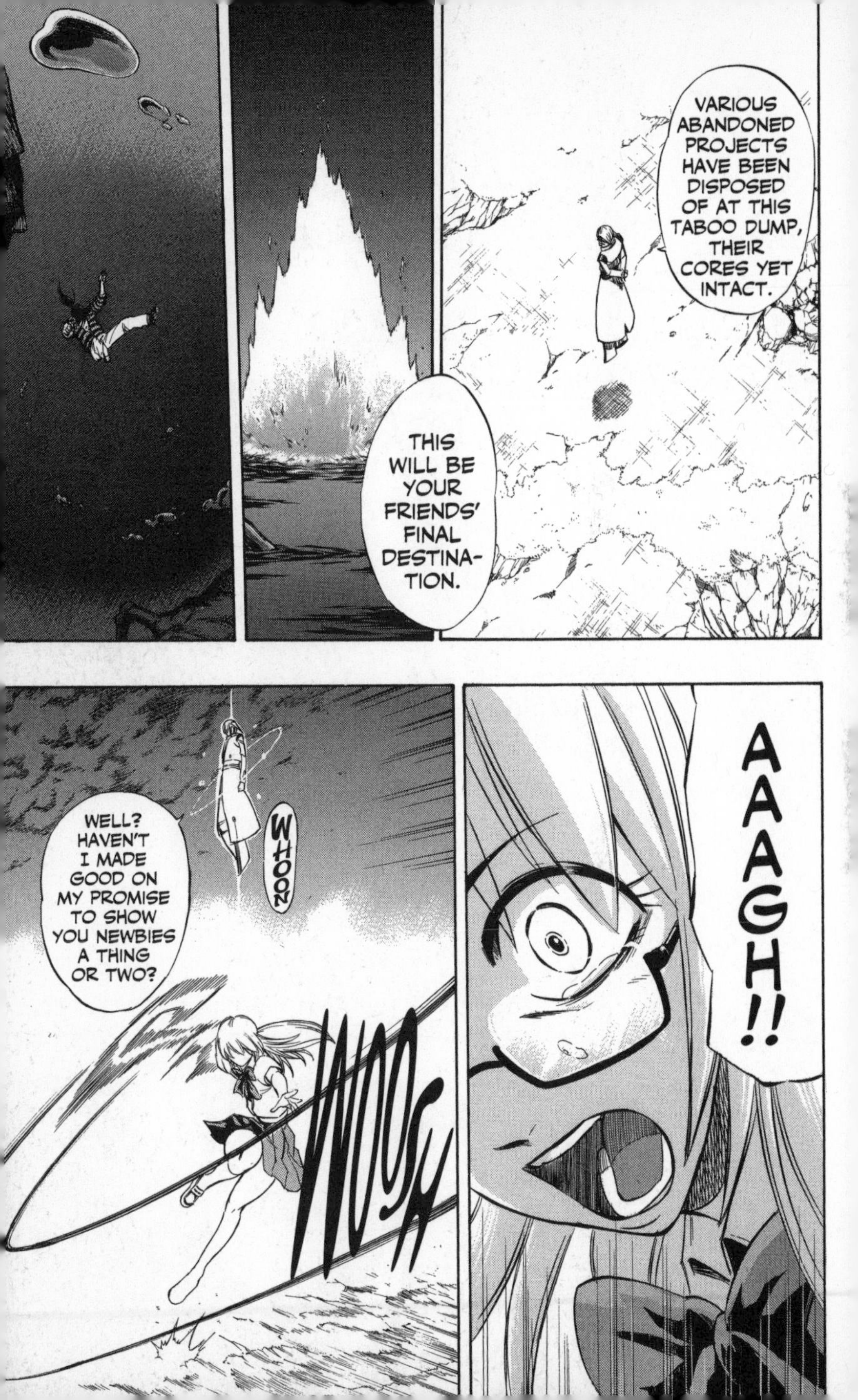
VARIOUS ABANDONED PROJECTS HAVE BEEN DISPOSED OF AT THIS TABOO DUMP, THEIR CORES YET INTACT.
THIS WILL BE YOUR FRIENDS' FINAL DESTINA-TION.
AAAGH!!
WHOON
WELL? HAVEN'T I MADE GOOD ON MY PROMISE TO SHOW YOU NEWBIES A THING OR TWO?

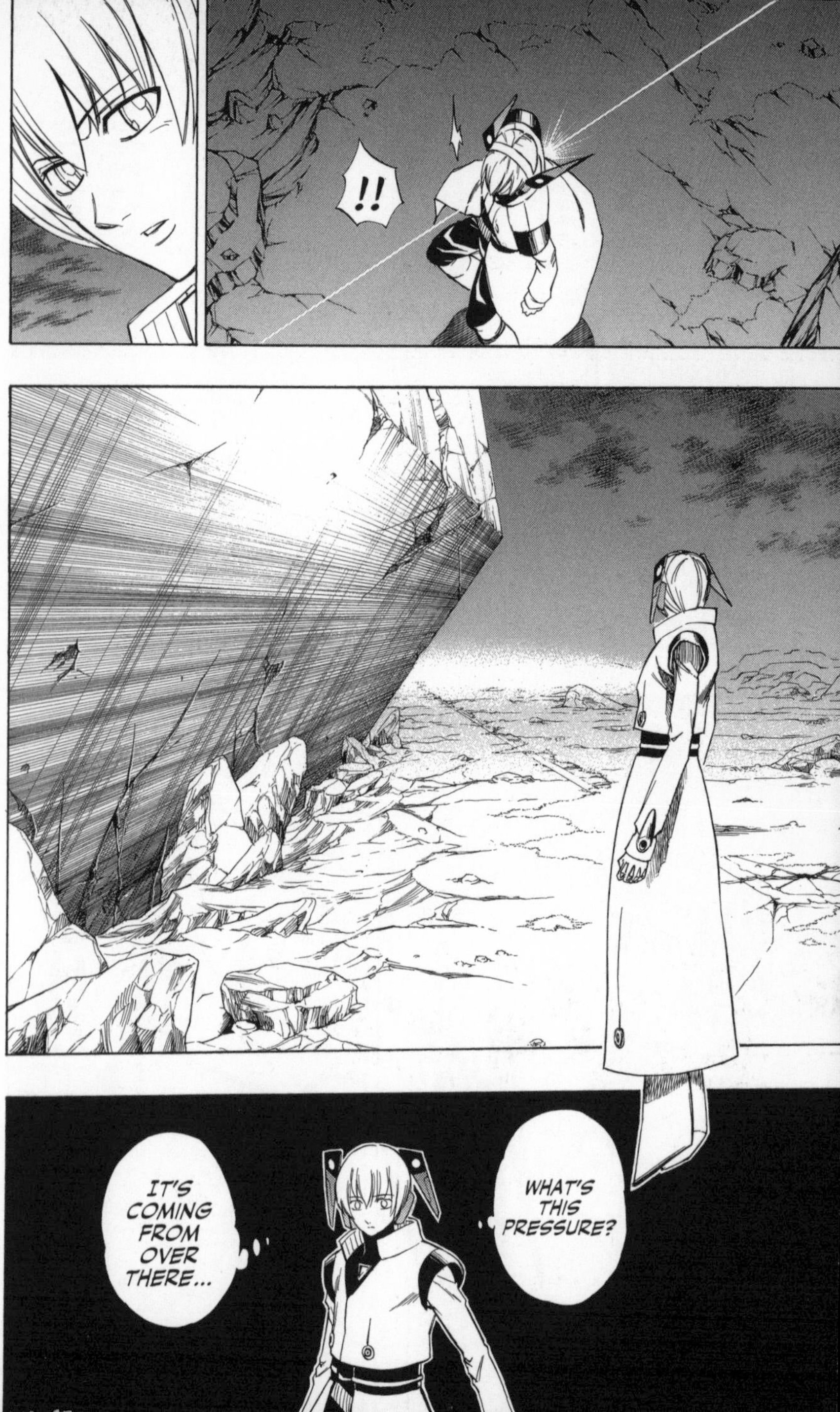
!!
WHAT'S THIS PRESSURE?
IT'S COMING FROM OVER THERE...

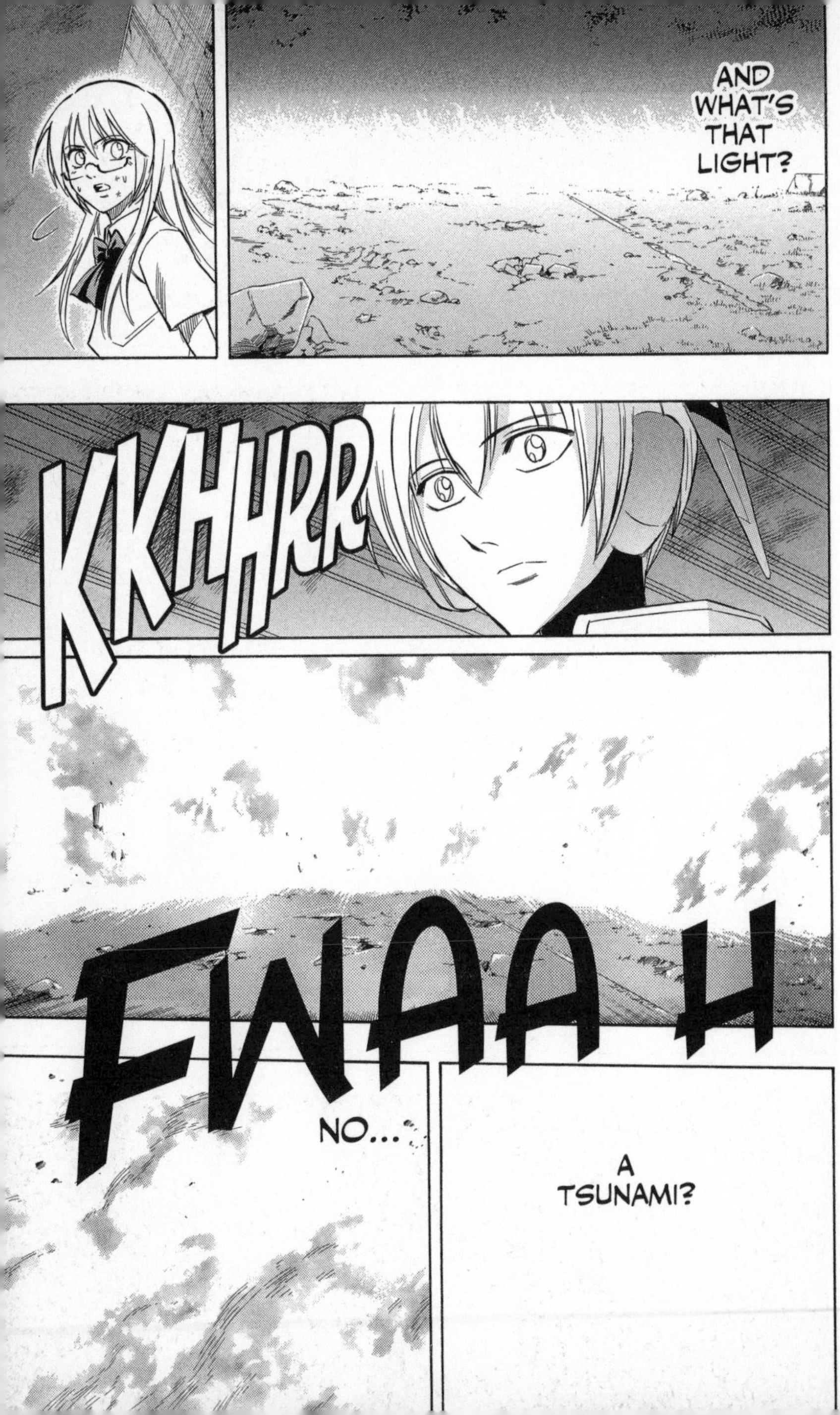
AND WHAT'S THAT LIGHT?
KKHHRR
FWAA H
A TSUNAMI?
NO...

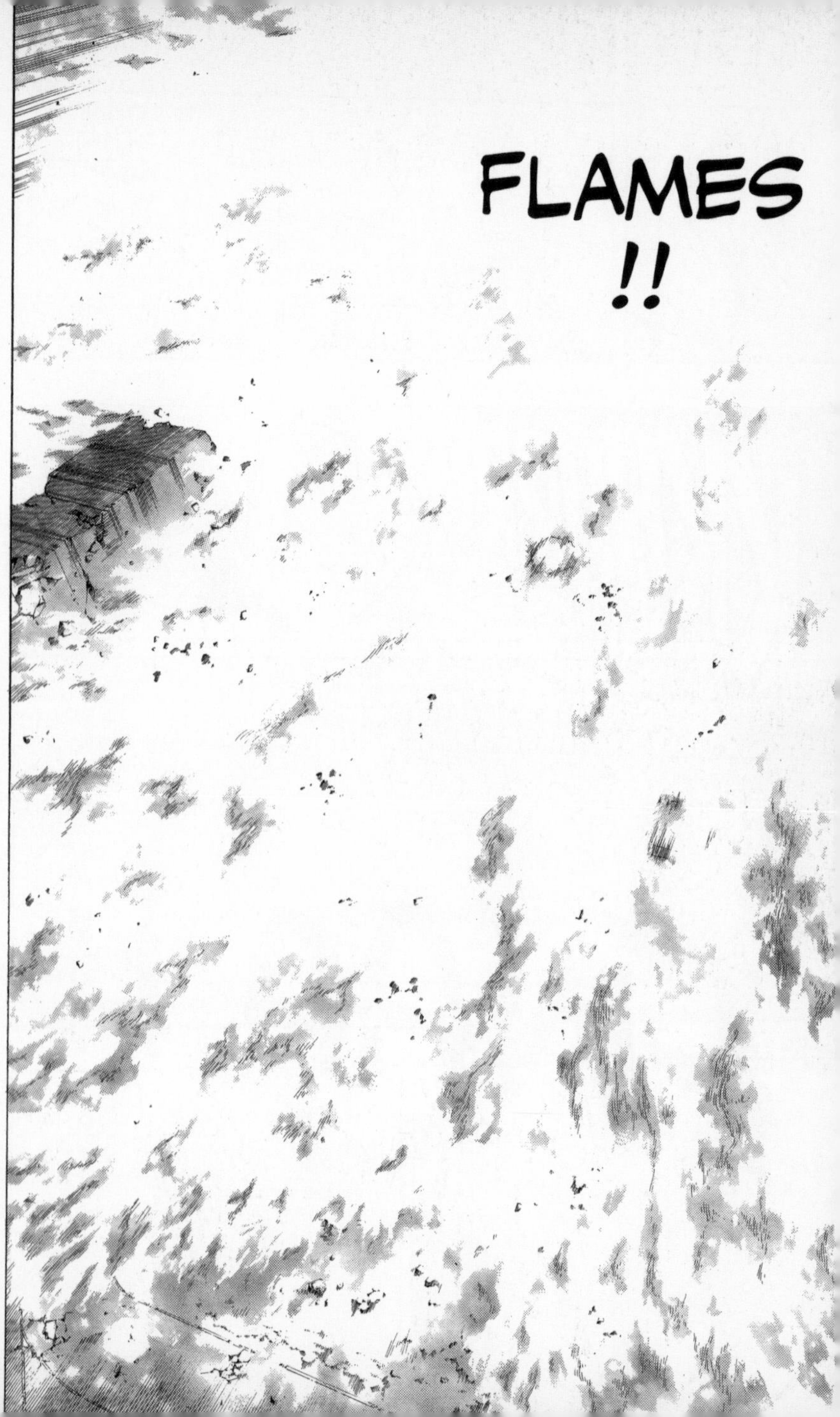
FLAMES !!

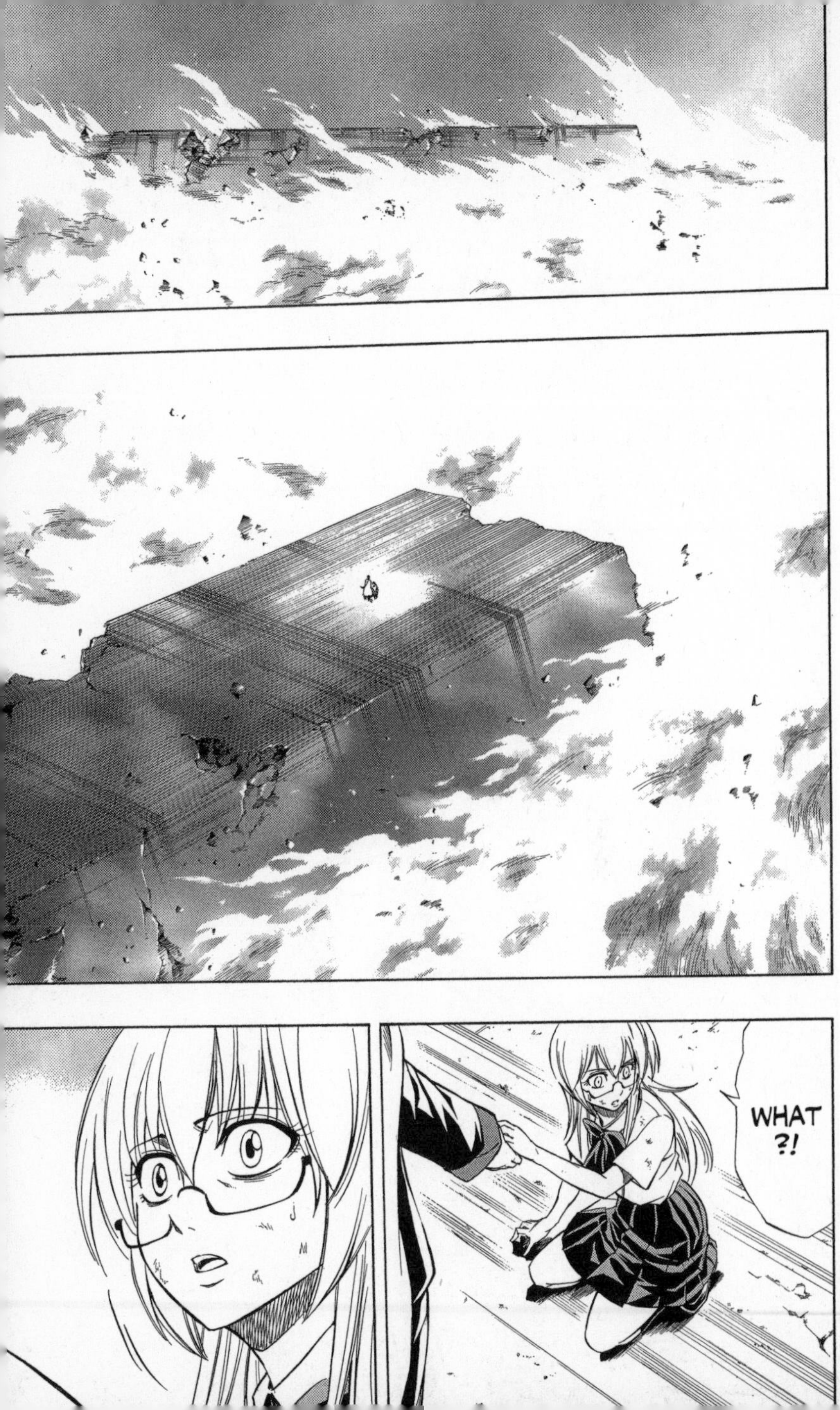
WHAT ?!

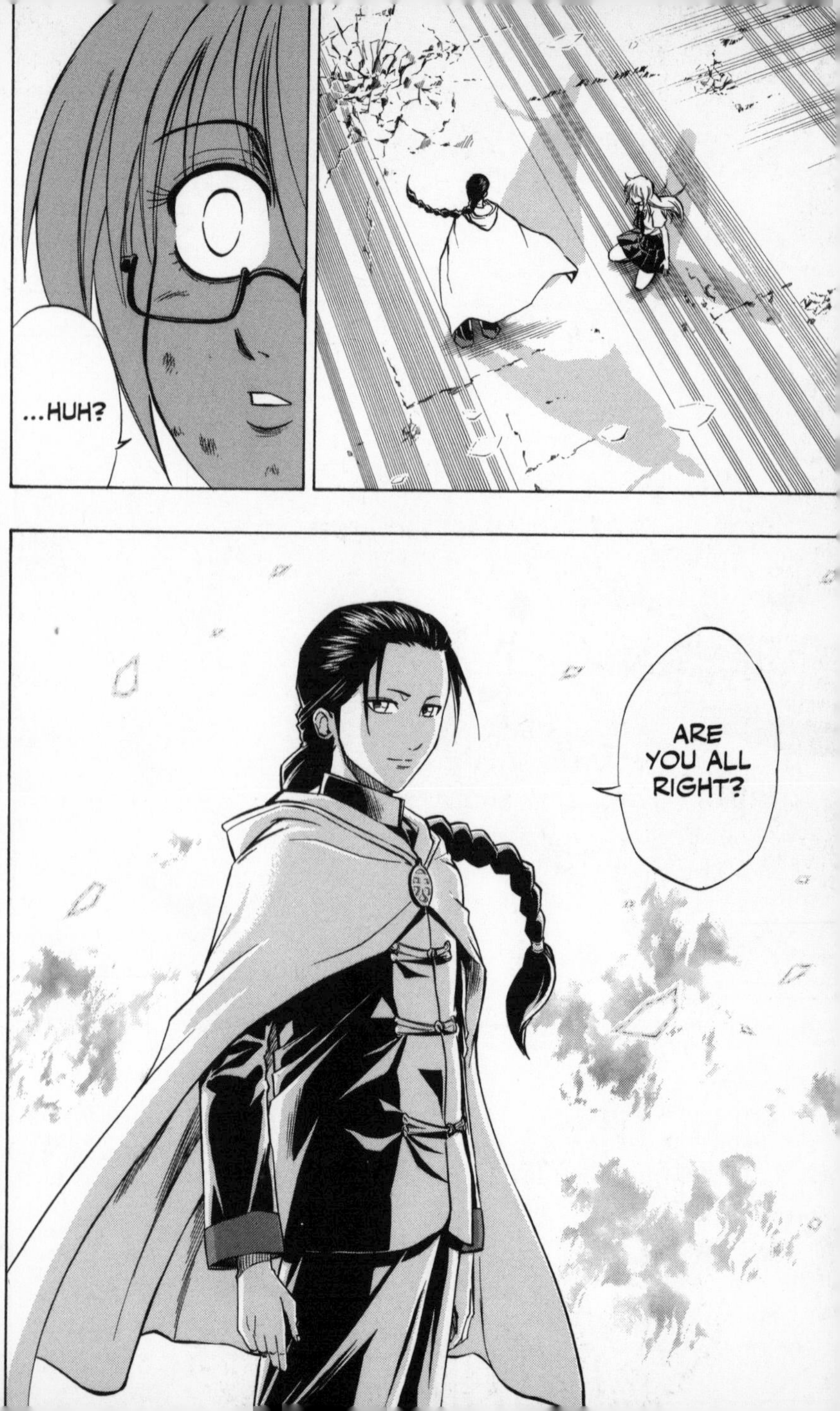
...HUH?
ARE YOU ALL RIGHT?

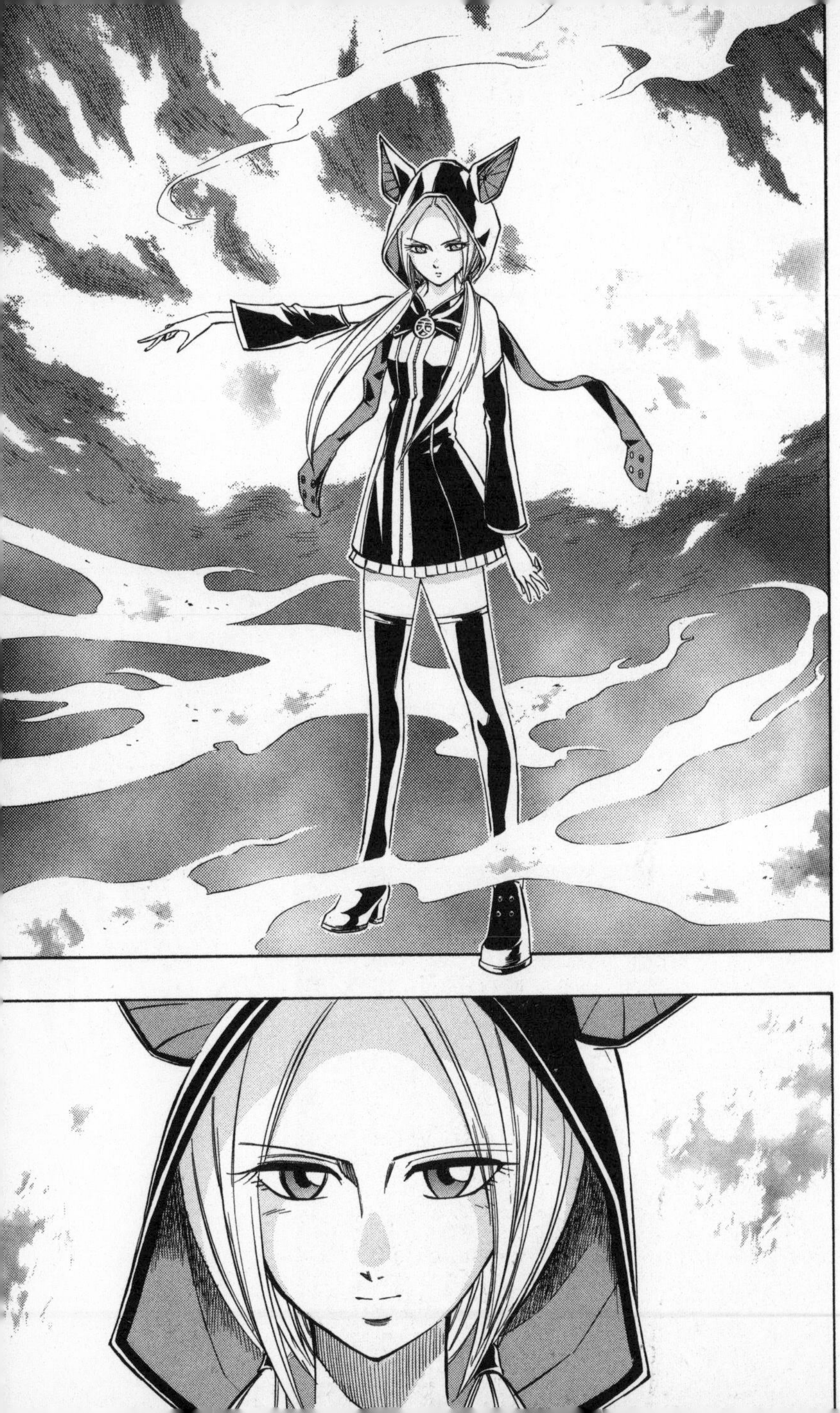

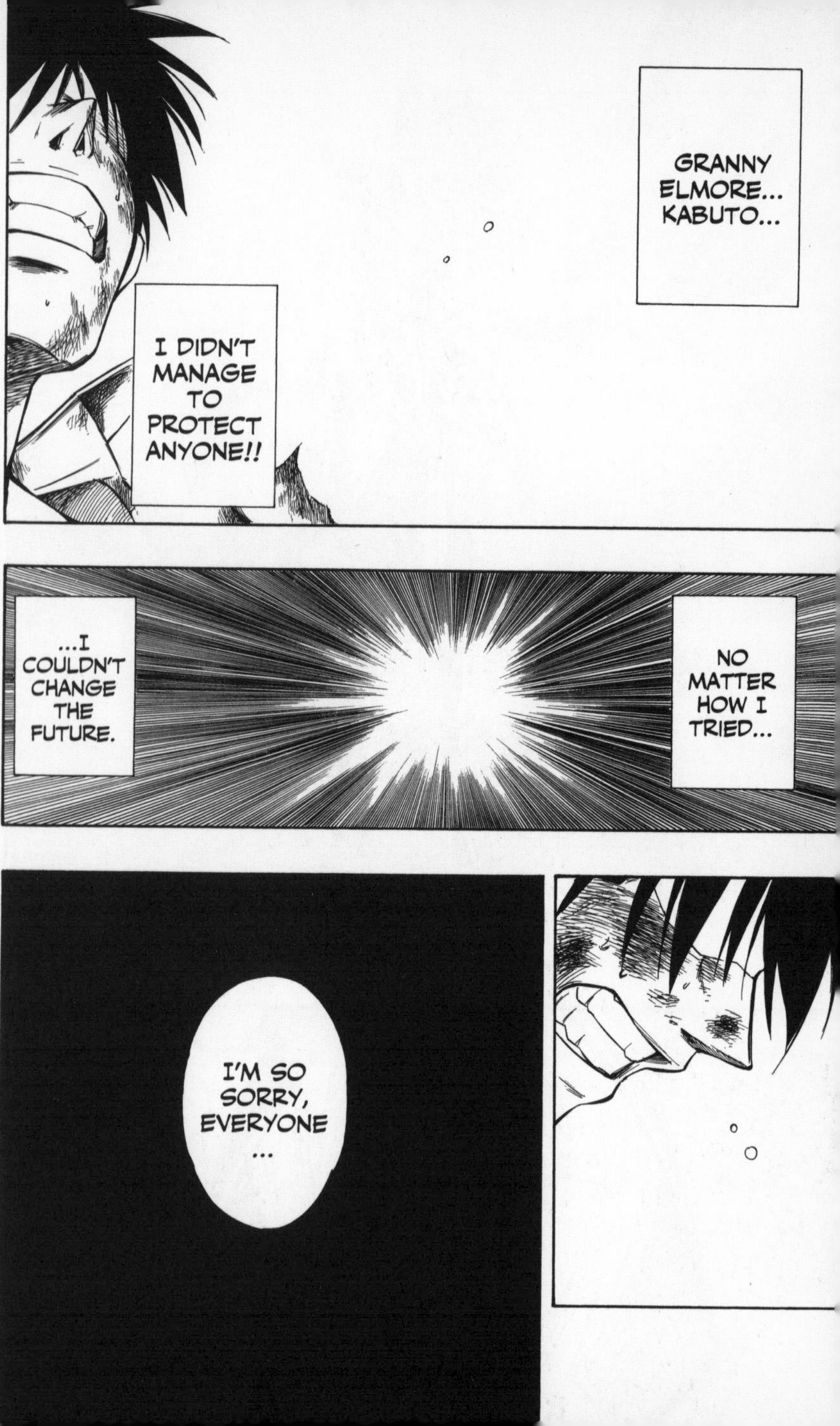
GRANNY ELMORE... KABUTO...
I DIDN'T MANAGE TO PROTECT ANYONE!!
NO MATTER HOW I TRIED...
...I COULDN'T CHANGE THE FUTURE.
I'M SO SORRY, EVERYONE...

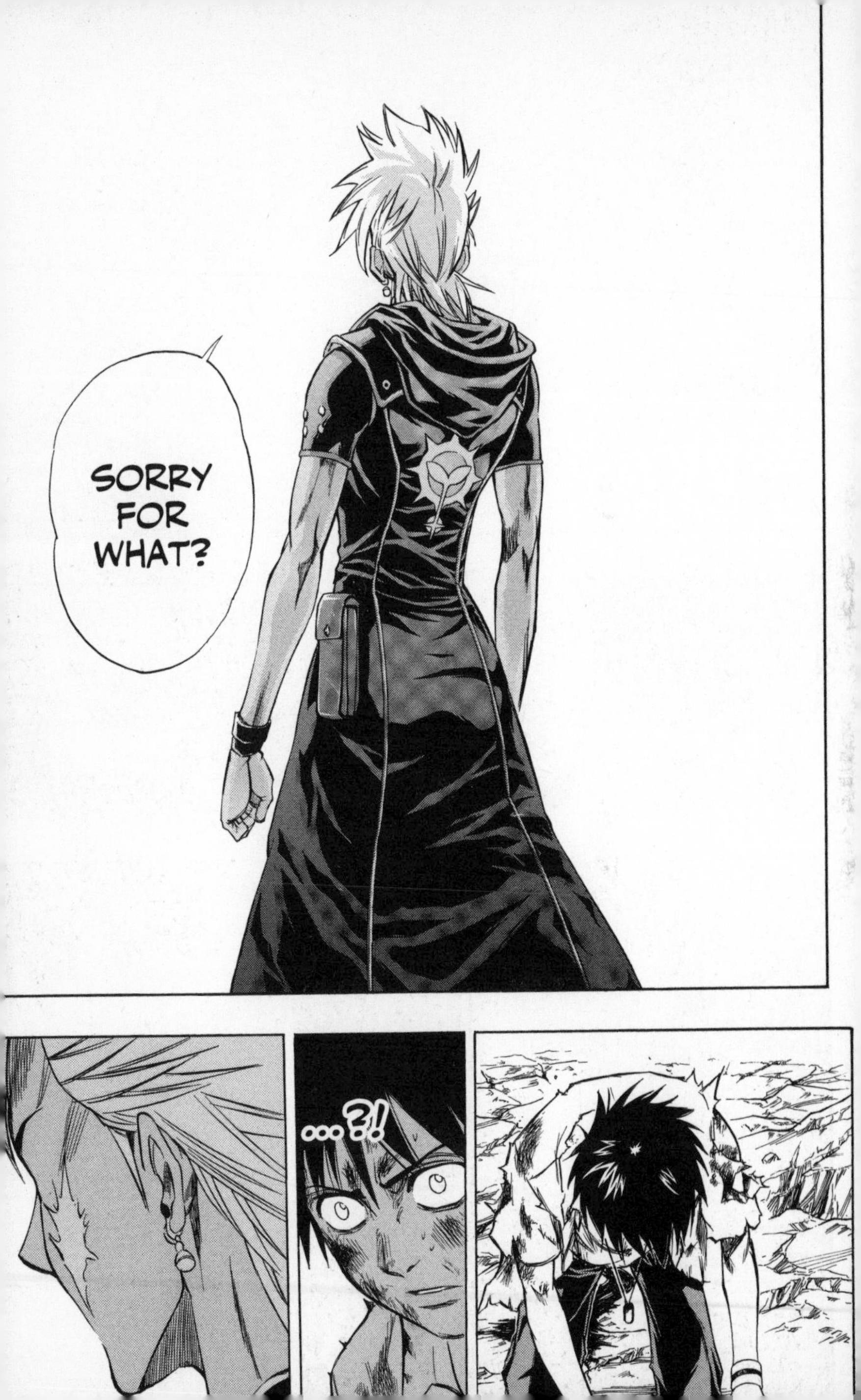
SORRY FOR WHAT?
...?!

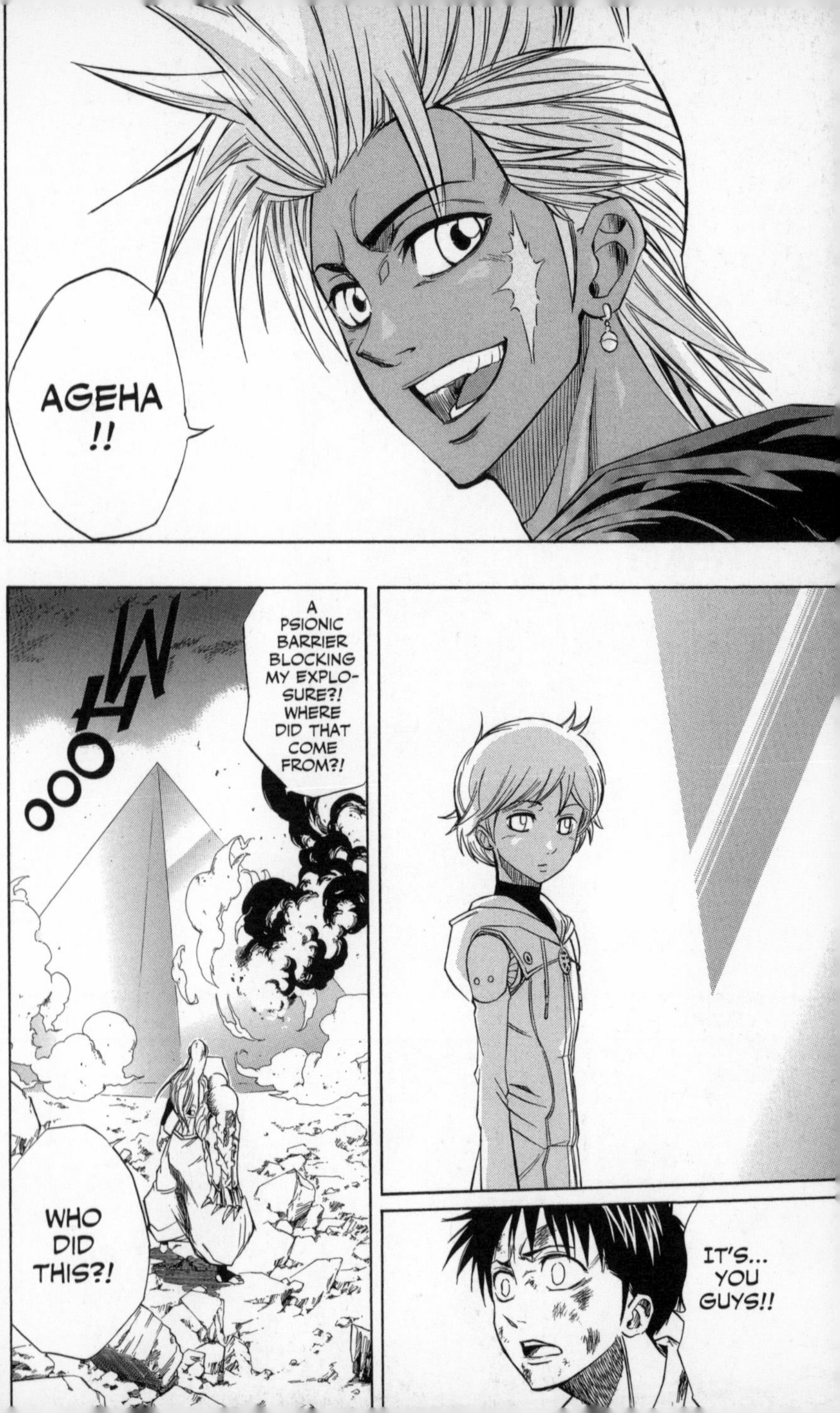
AGEHA !!
IT'S... YOU GUYS!!
WHOOO
A PSIONIC BARRIER BLOCKING MY EXPLO-SURE?! WHERE DID THAT COME FROM?!
WHO DID THIS?!

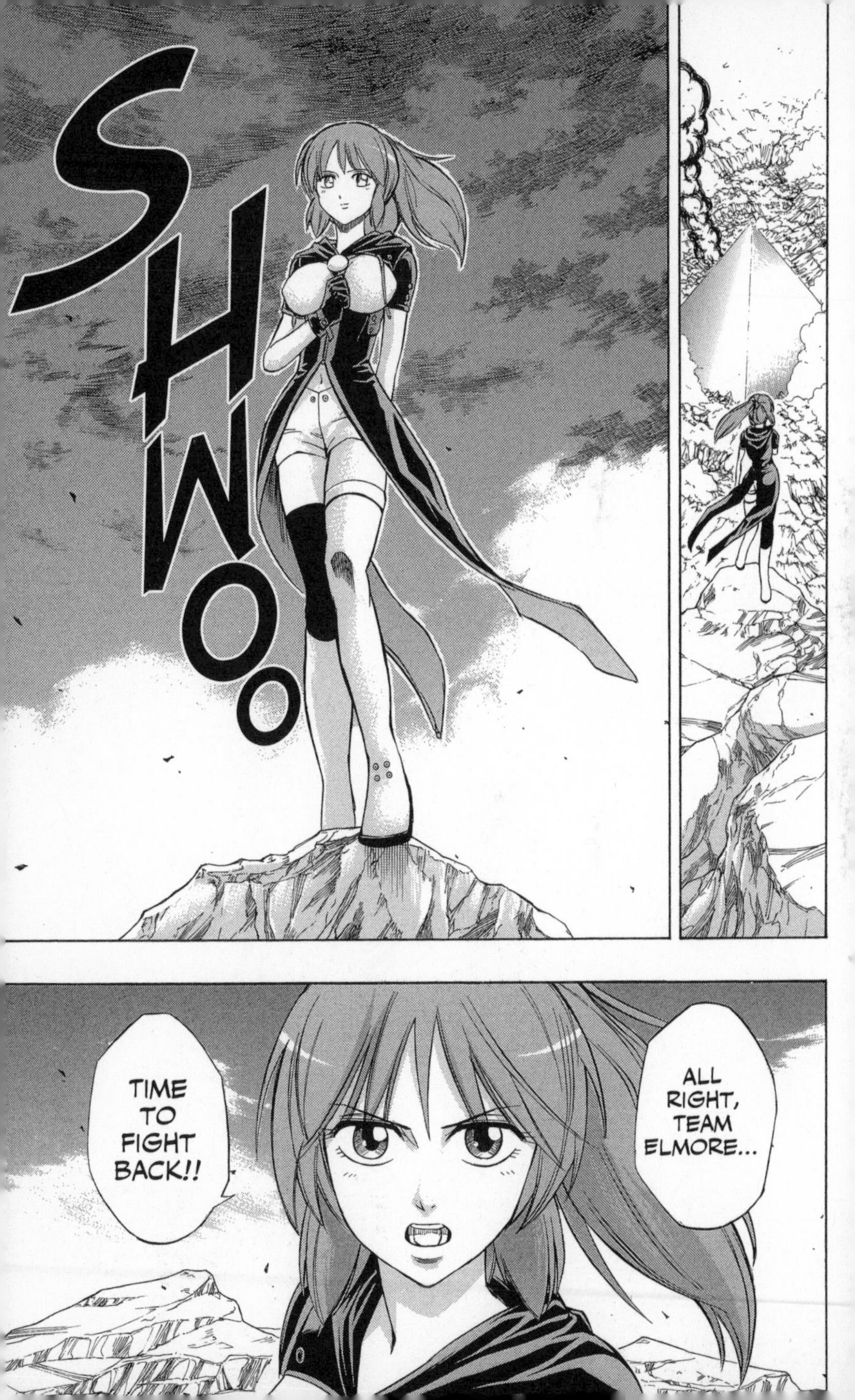
SHWOO
ALL RIGHT, TEAM ELMORE...
TIME TO FIGHT BACK!!

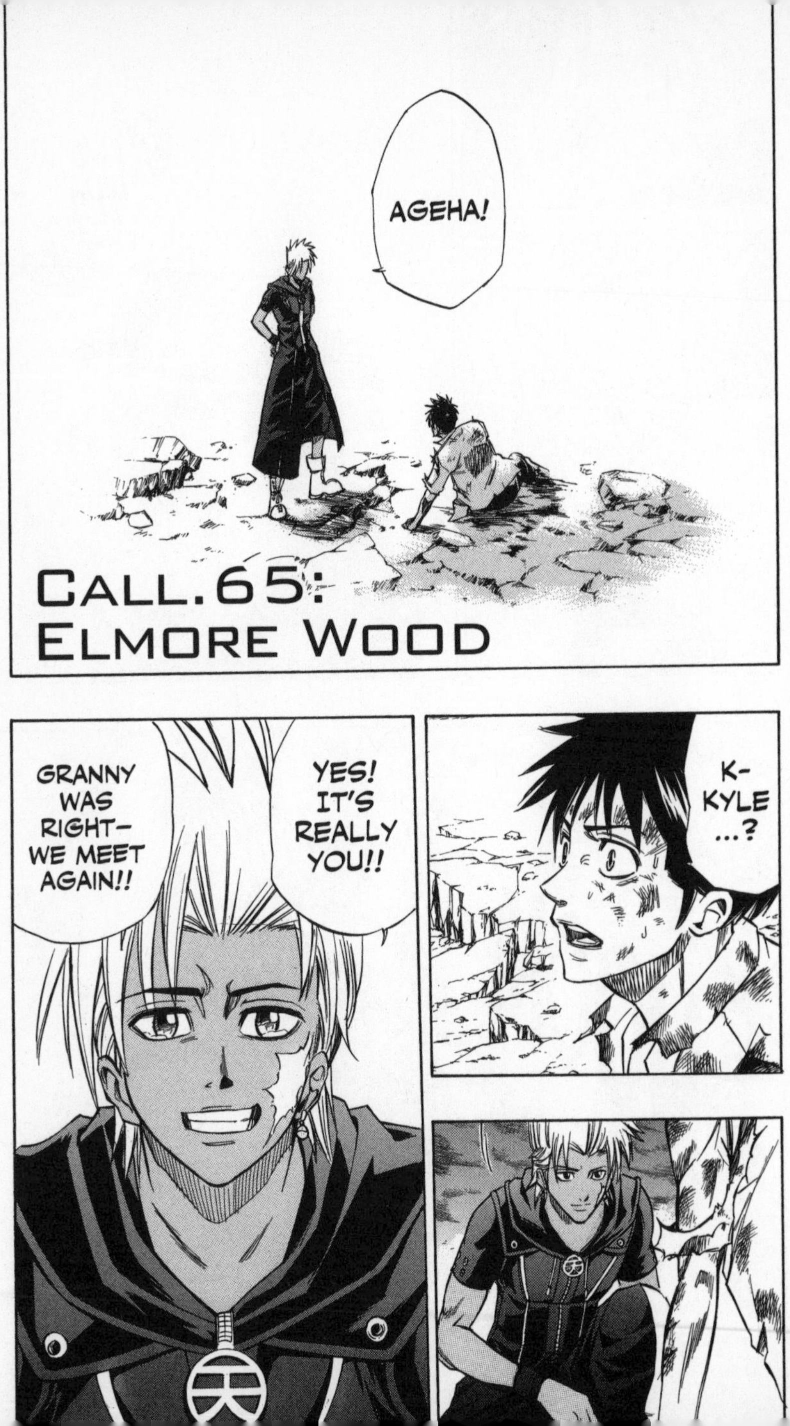
AGEHA!
CALL.65: ELMORE WOOD
K-KYLE ...?
YES! IT'S REALLY YOU!!
GRANNY WAS RIGHT— WE MEET AGAIN!!

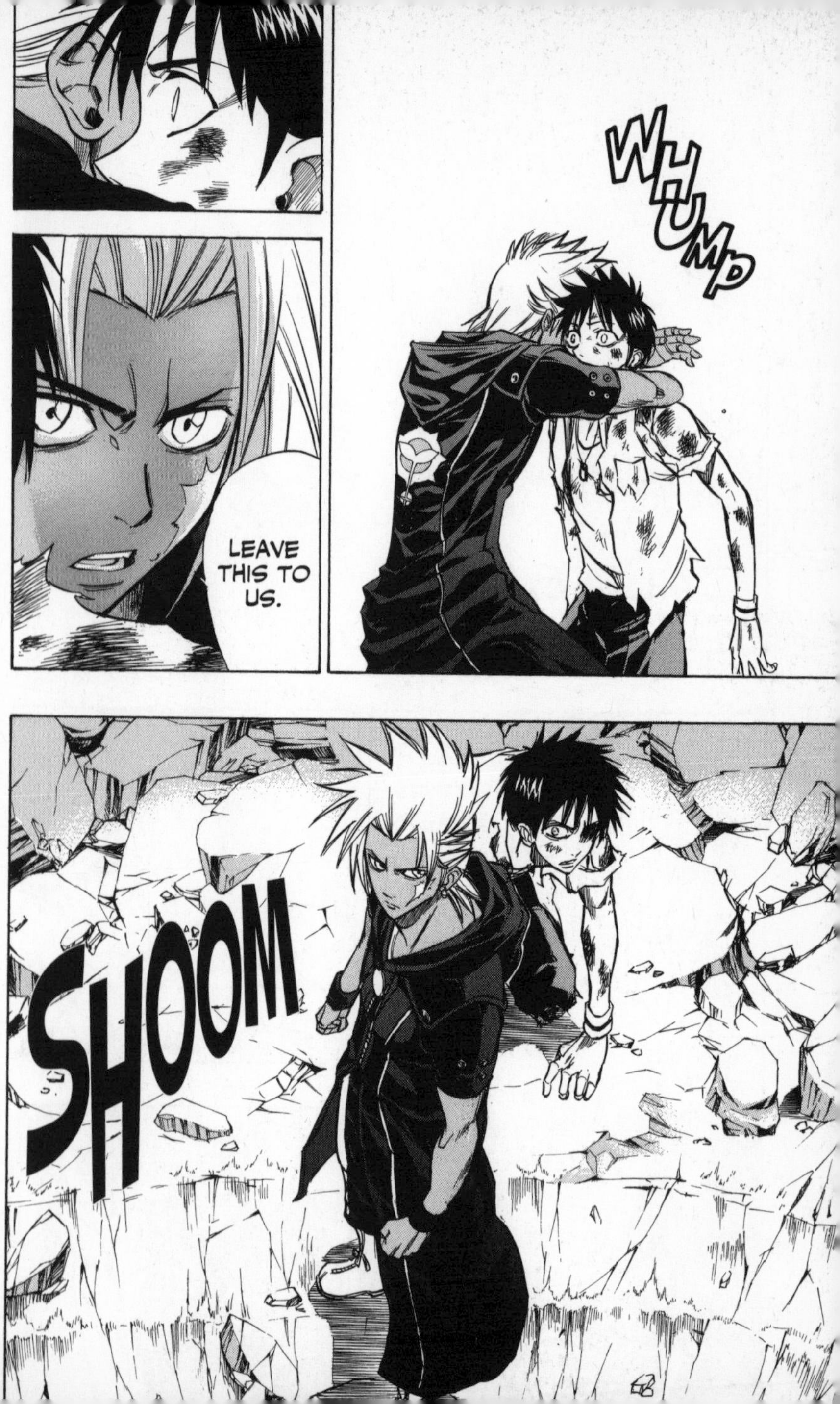
WHUMP
LEAVE THIS TO US.
SHOOM

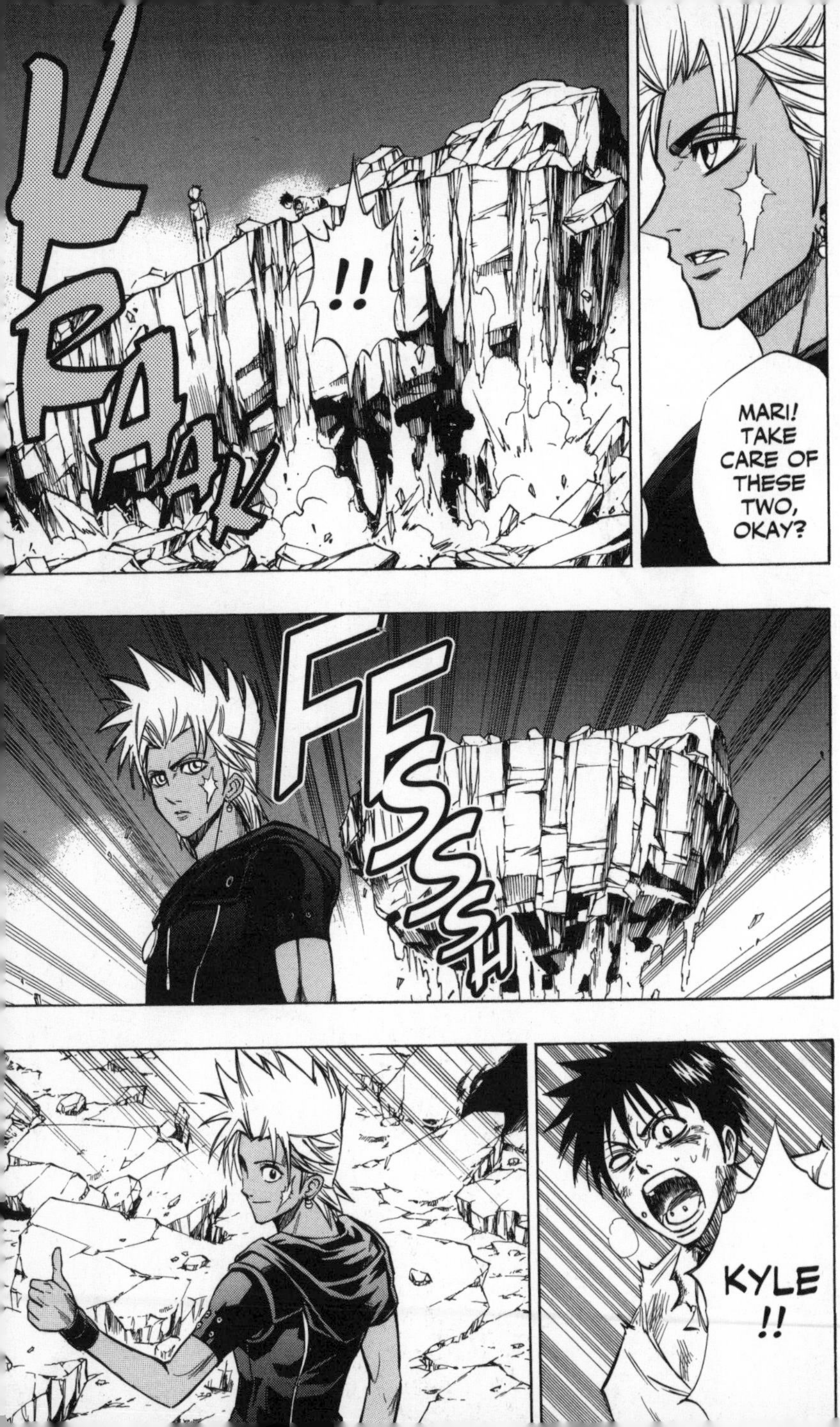
MARI! TAKE CARE OF THESE TWO, OKAY?
KRAAK
!!
FFESSSH
KYLE !!

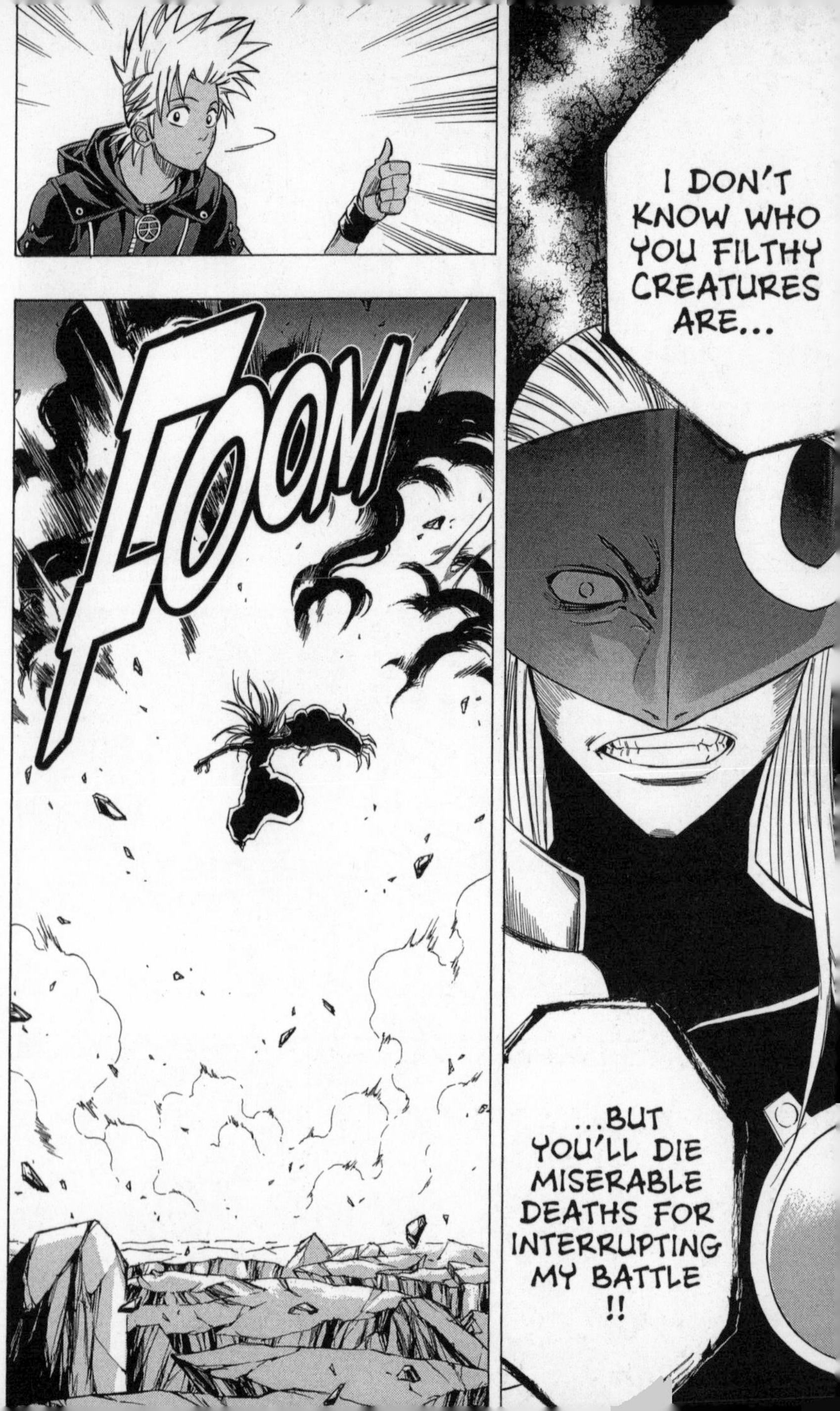
I DON'T KNOW WHO YOU FILTHY CREATURES ARE...
...BUT YOU'LL DIE MISERABLE DEATHS FOR INTERRUPTING MY BATTLE !!
FOOM

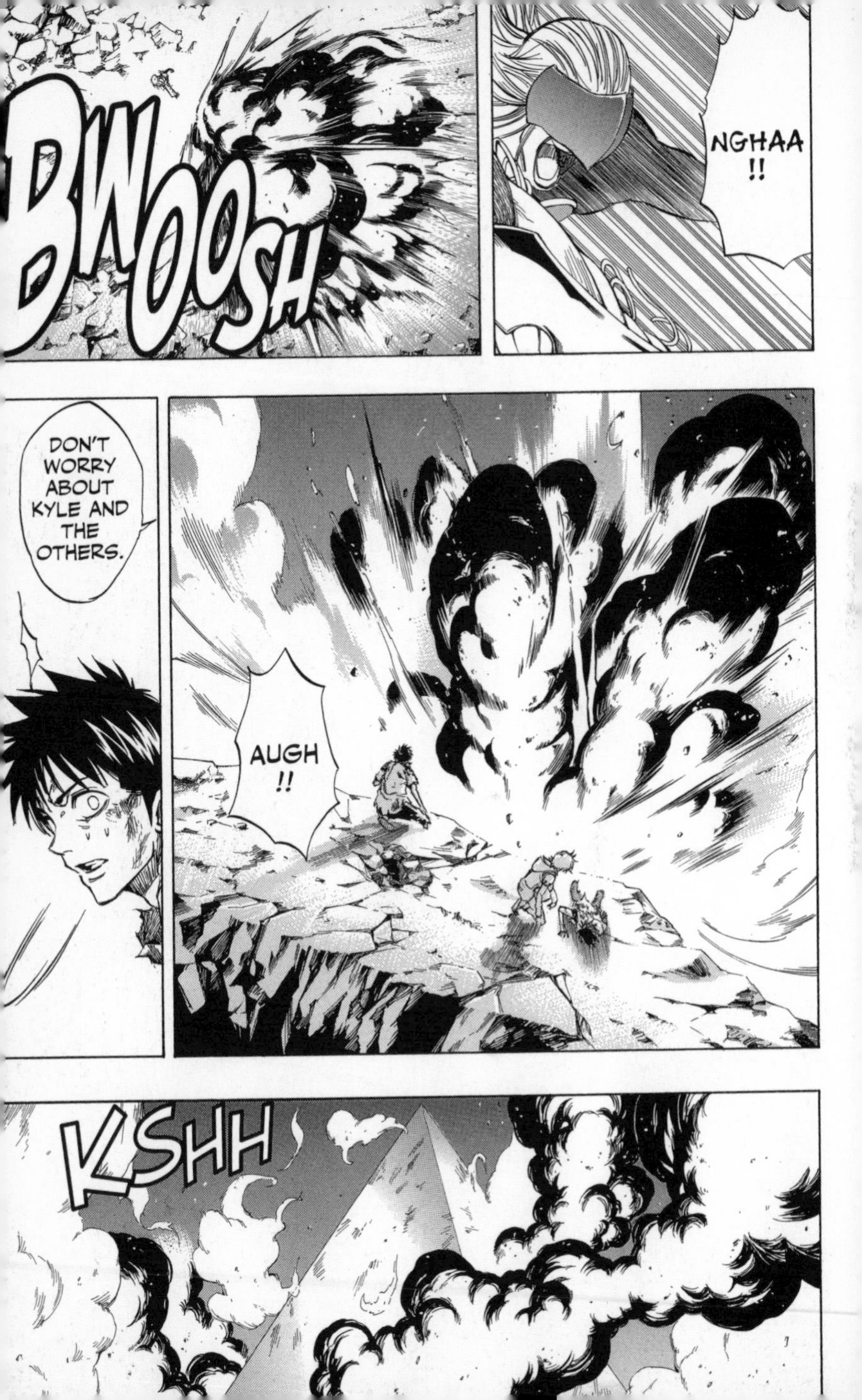
NGHAA !!
BWOOSH
AUGH !!
DON'T WORRY ABOUT KYLE AND THE OTHERS.
KSHH

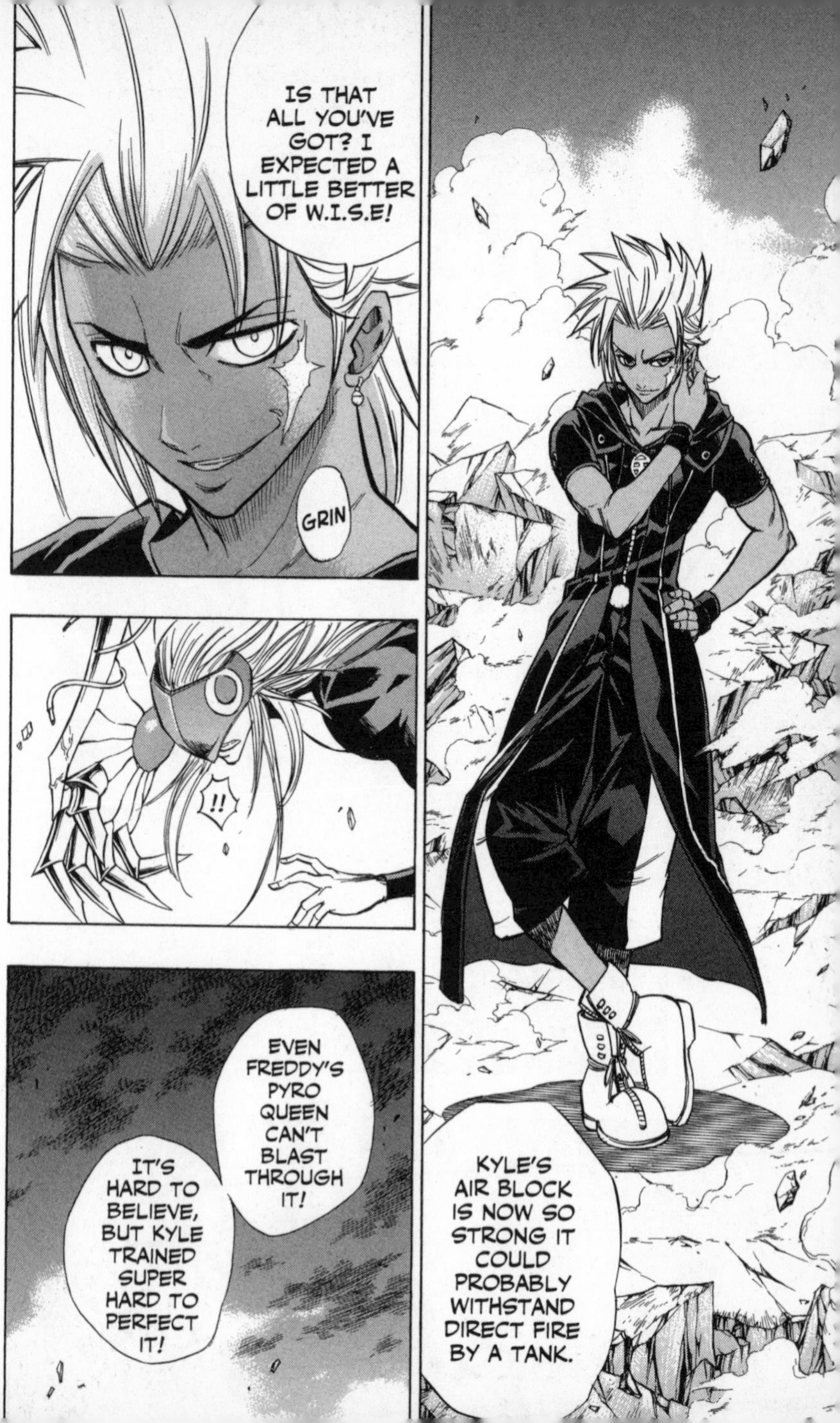
KYLE'S AIR BLOCK IS NOW SO STRONG IT COULD PROBABLY WITHSTAND DIRECT FIRE BY A TANK.
IS THAT ALL YOU'VE GOT? I EXPECTED A LITTLE BETTER OF W.I.S.E!
GRIN
!!
EVEN FREDDY'S PYRO QUEEN CAN'T BLAST THROUGH IT!
IT'S HARD TO BELIEVE, BUT KYLE TRAINED SUPER HARD TO PERFECT IT!

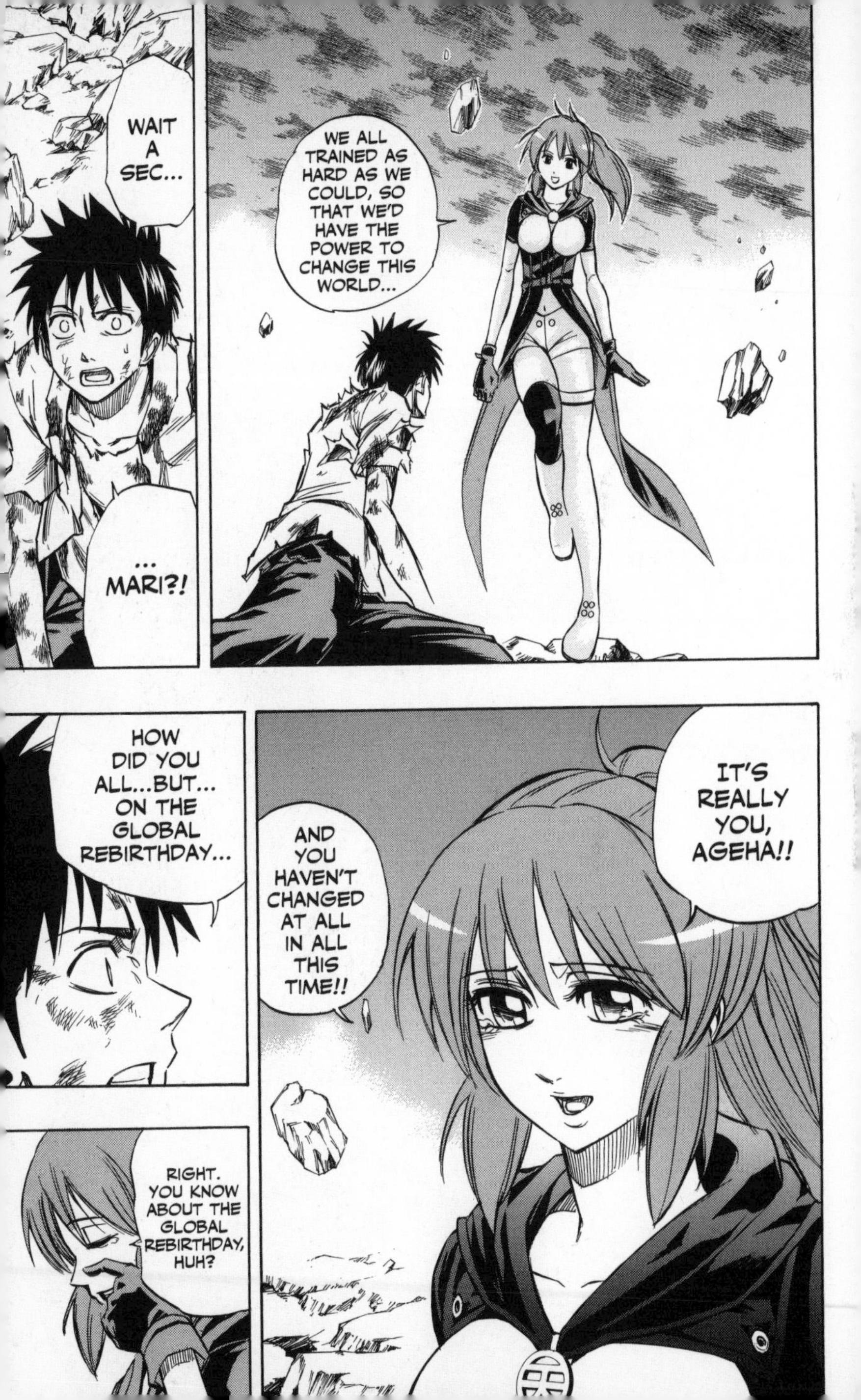
WE ALL TRAINED AS HARD AS WE COULD, SO THAT WE'D HAVE THE POWER TO CHANGE THIS WORLD...
WAIT A SEC...
...MARI?!
IT'S REALLY YOU, AGEHA!!
AND YOU HAVEN'T CHANGED AT ALL IN ALL THIS TIME!!
HOW DID YOU ALL...BUT... ON THE GLOBAL REBIRTHDAY...
RIGHT. YOU KNOW ABOUT THE GLOBAL REBIRTHDAY, HUH?

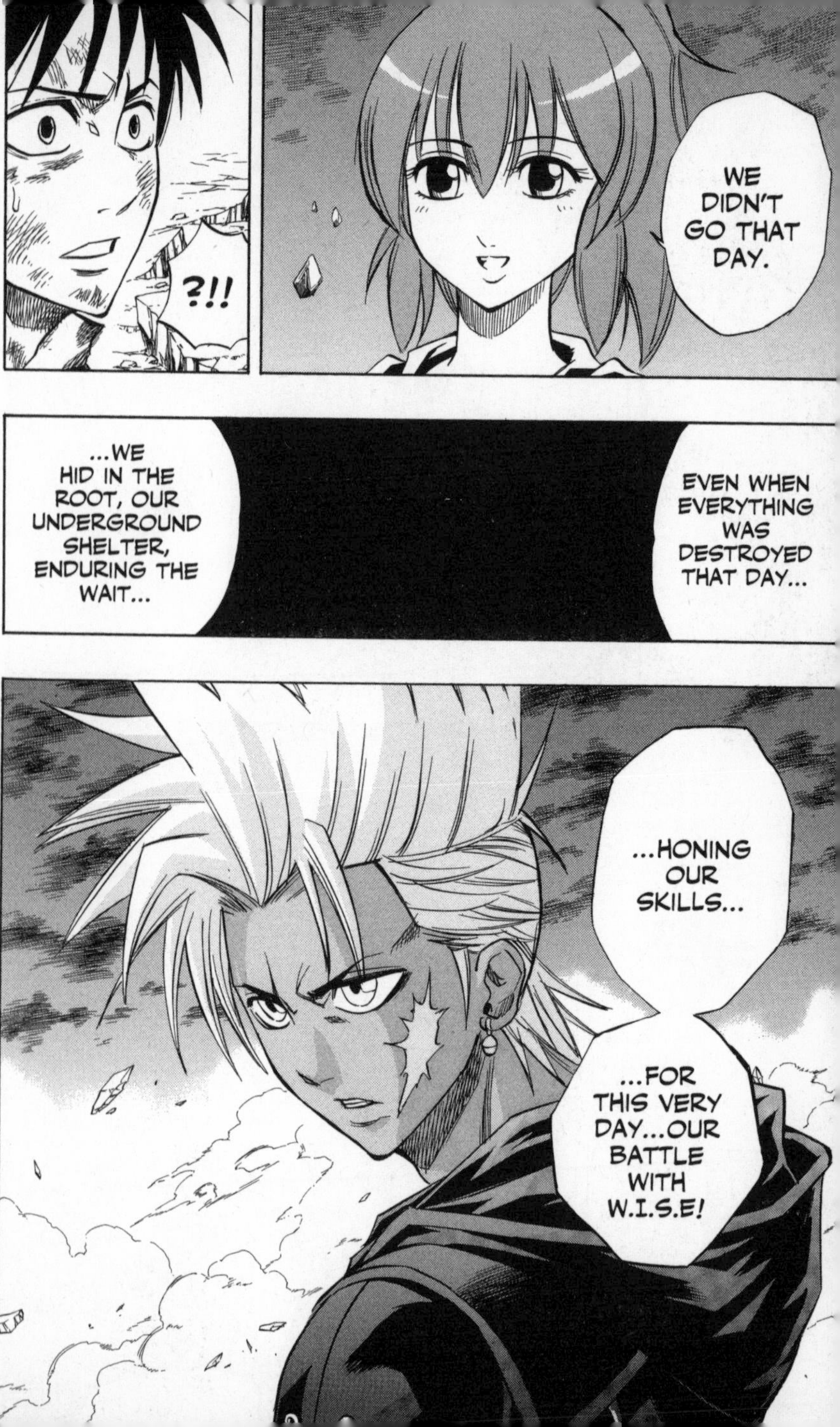
WE DIDN'T GO THAT DAY.
?!!
EVEN WHEN EVERYTHING WAS DESTROYED THAT DAY...
...WE HID IN THE ROOT, OUR UNDERGROUND SHELTER, ENDURING THE WAIT...
...HONING OUR SKILLS...
...FOR THIS VERY DAY...OUR BATTLE WITH W.I.S.E!

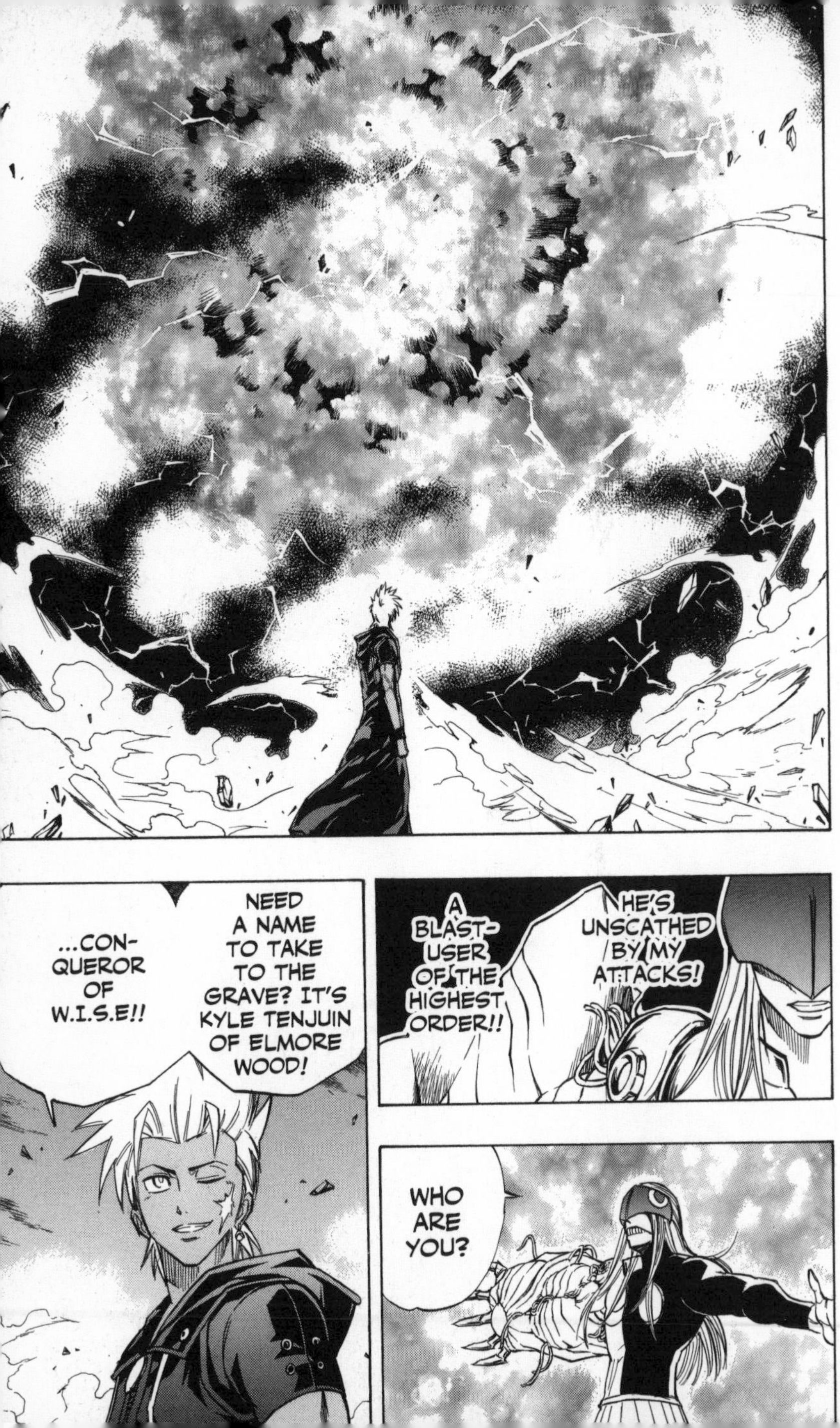
HE'S UNSCATHED BY MY ATTACKS!
A BLAST-USER OF THE HIGHEST ORDER!!
WHO ARE YOU?
NEED A NAME TO TAKE TO THE GRAVE? IT'S KYLE TENJUIN OF ELMORE WOOD!
...CON-QUEROR OF W.I.S.E!!

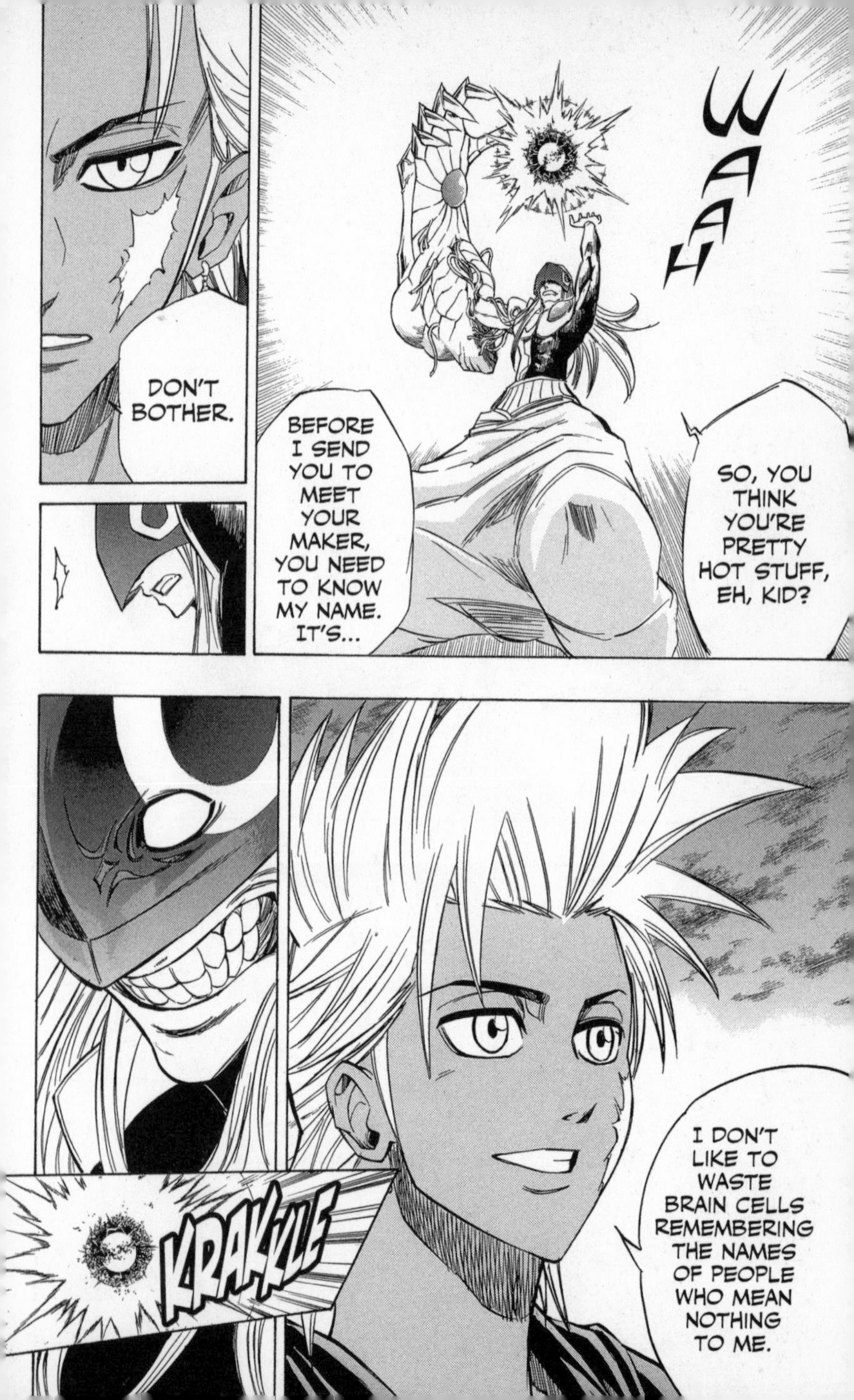
WAAAH
SO, YOU THINK YOU'RE PRETTY HOT STUFF, EH, KID?
BEFORE I SEND YOU TO MEET YOUR MAKER, YOU NEED TO KNOW MY NAME. IT'S...
DON'T BOTHER.
I DON'T LIKE TO WASTE BRAIN CELLS REMEMBERING THE NAMES OF PEOPLE WHO MEAN NOTHING TO ME.
KRAKKLE

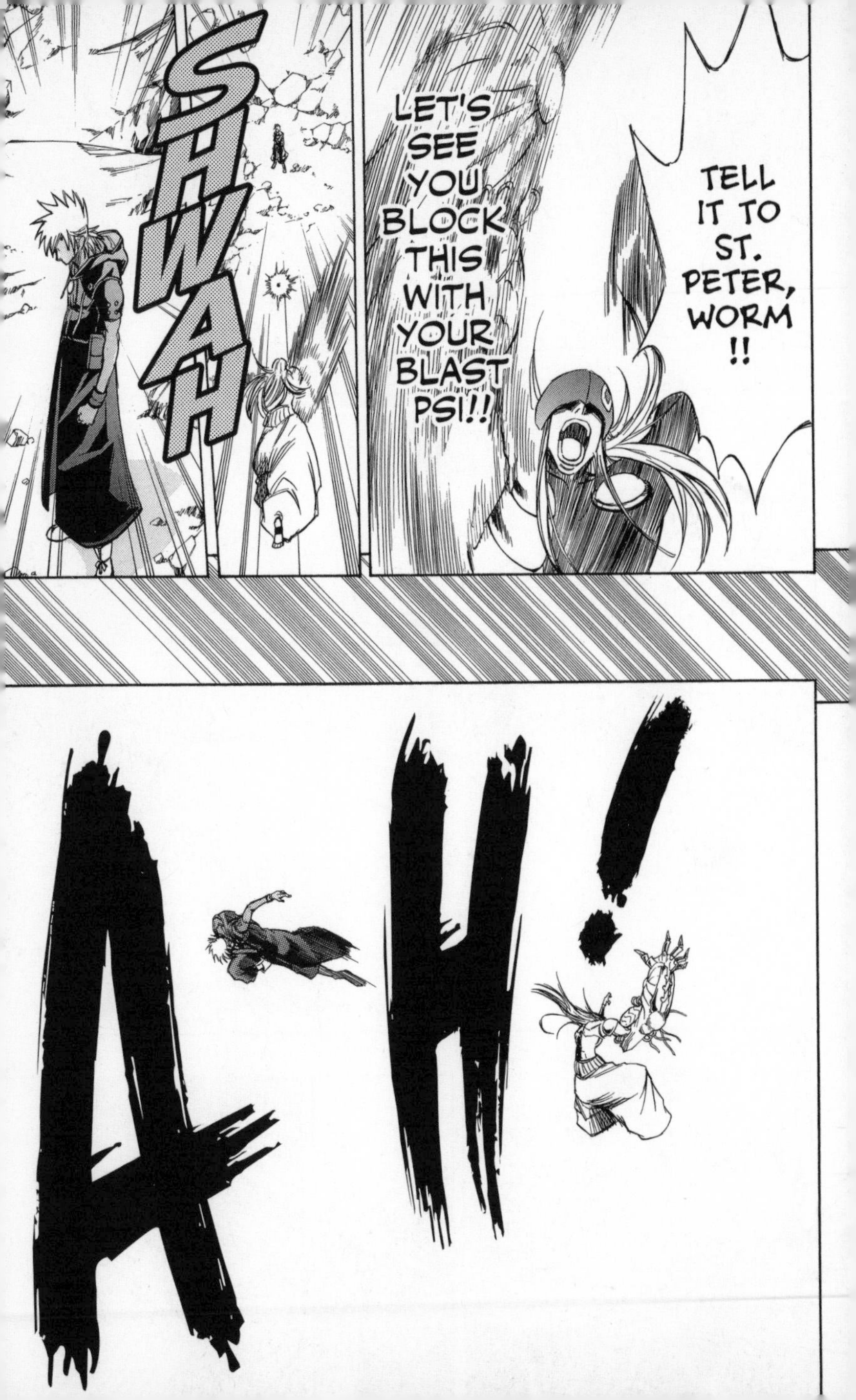
TELL IT TO ST. PETER, WORM!!
LET'S SEE YOU BLOCK THIS WITH YOUR BLAST PSI!!
SHWAH
AH!

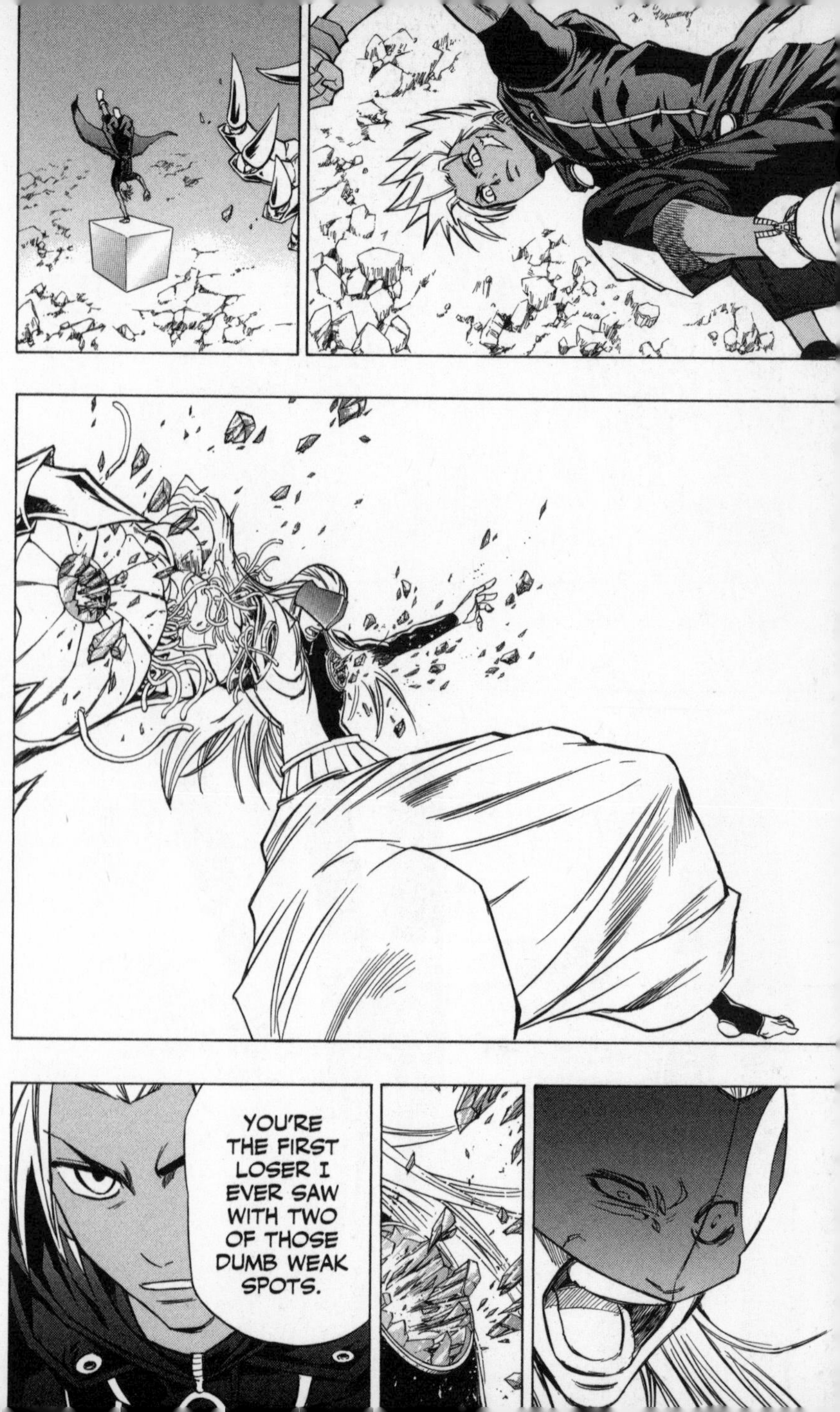
YOU'RE THE FIRST LOSER I EVER SAW WITH TWO OF THOSE DUMB WEAK SPOTS.

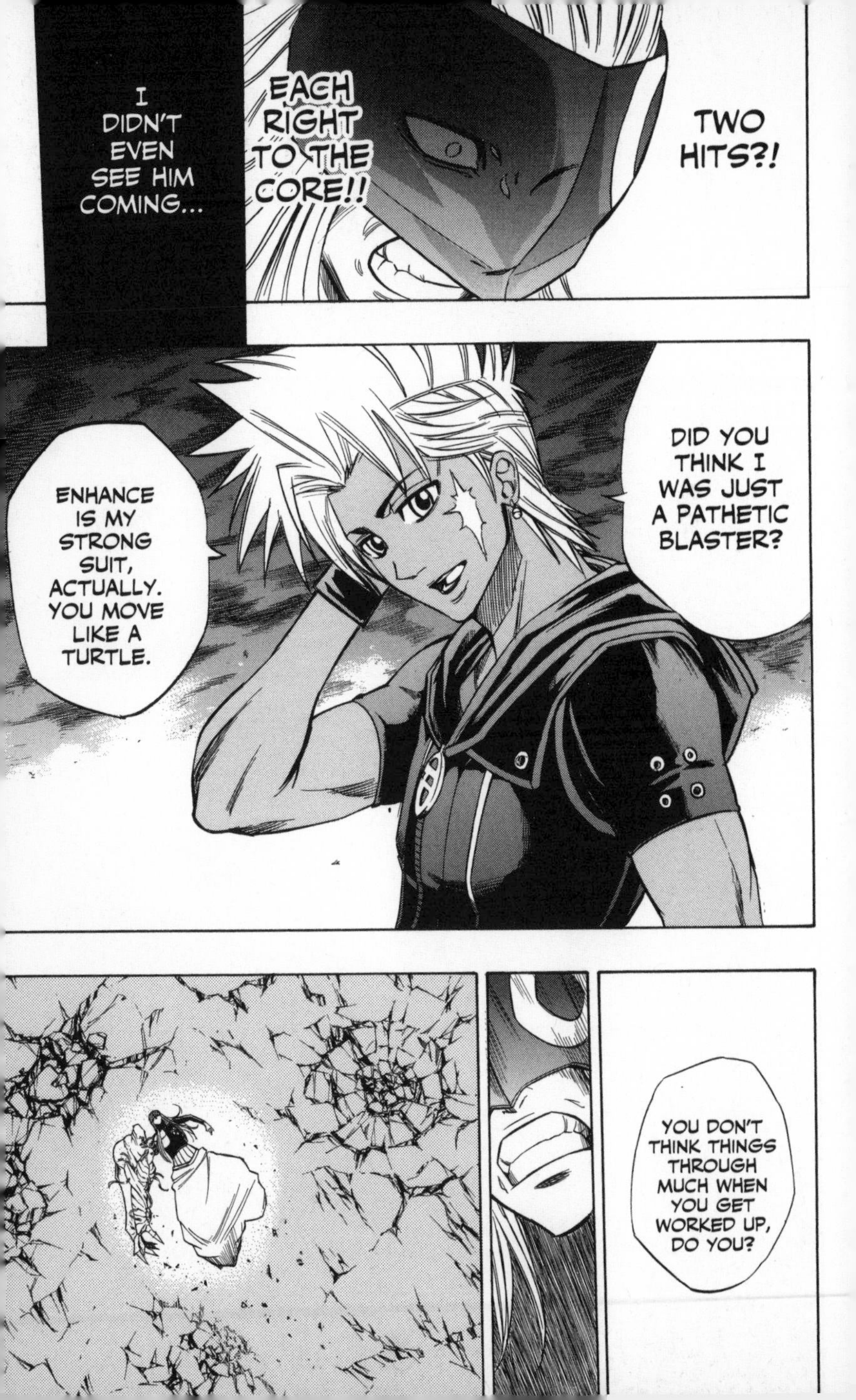
TWO HITS?!
EACH RIGHT TO THE CORE!!
I DIDN'T EVEN SEE HIM COMING...
DID YOU THINK I WAS JUST A PATHETIC BLASTER?
ENHANCE IS MY STRONG SUIT, ACTUALLY. YOU MOVE LIKE A TURTLE.
YOU DON'T THINK THINGS THROUGH MUCH WHEN YOU GET WORKED UP, DO YOU?

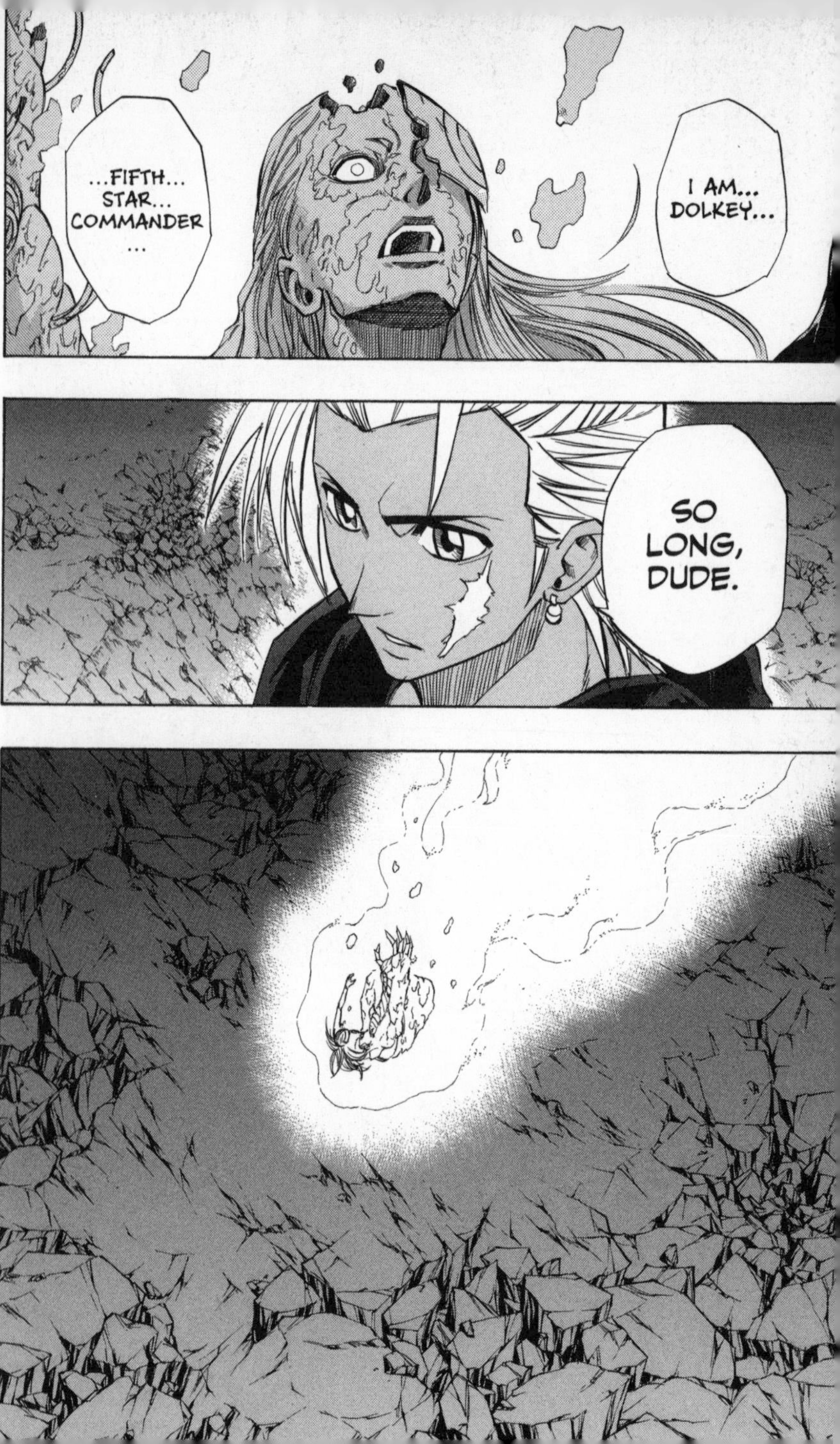
I AM... DOLKEY...
...FIFTH... STAR... COMMANDER ...
SO LONG, DUDE.

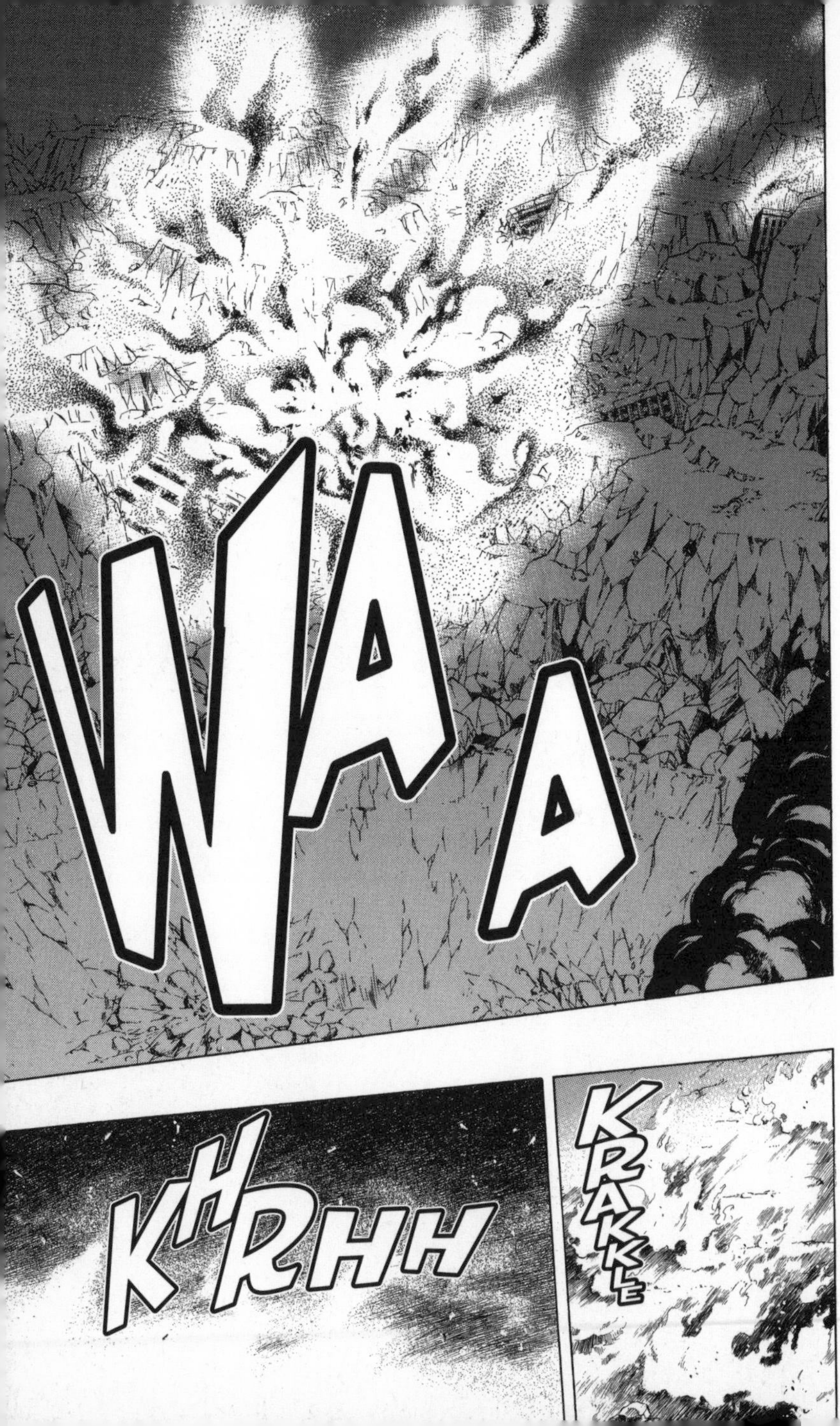
WAA
KRAKLE
KHRHH

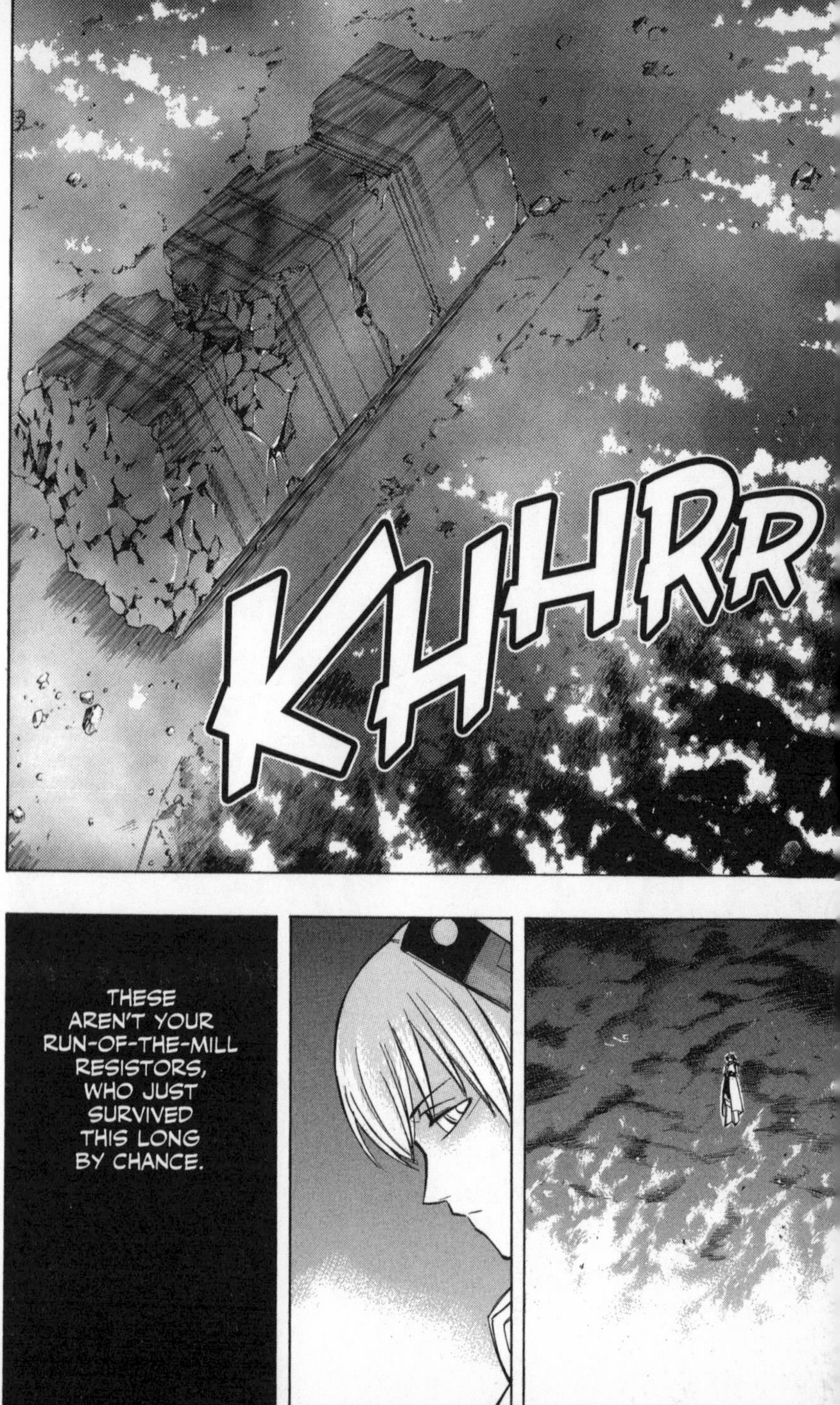
KHHRR
THESE AREN'T YOUR RUN-OF-THE-MILL RESISTORS, WHO JUST SURVIVED THIS LONG BY CHANCE.

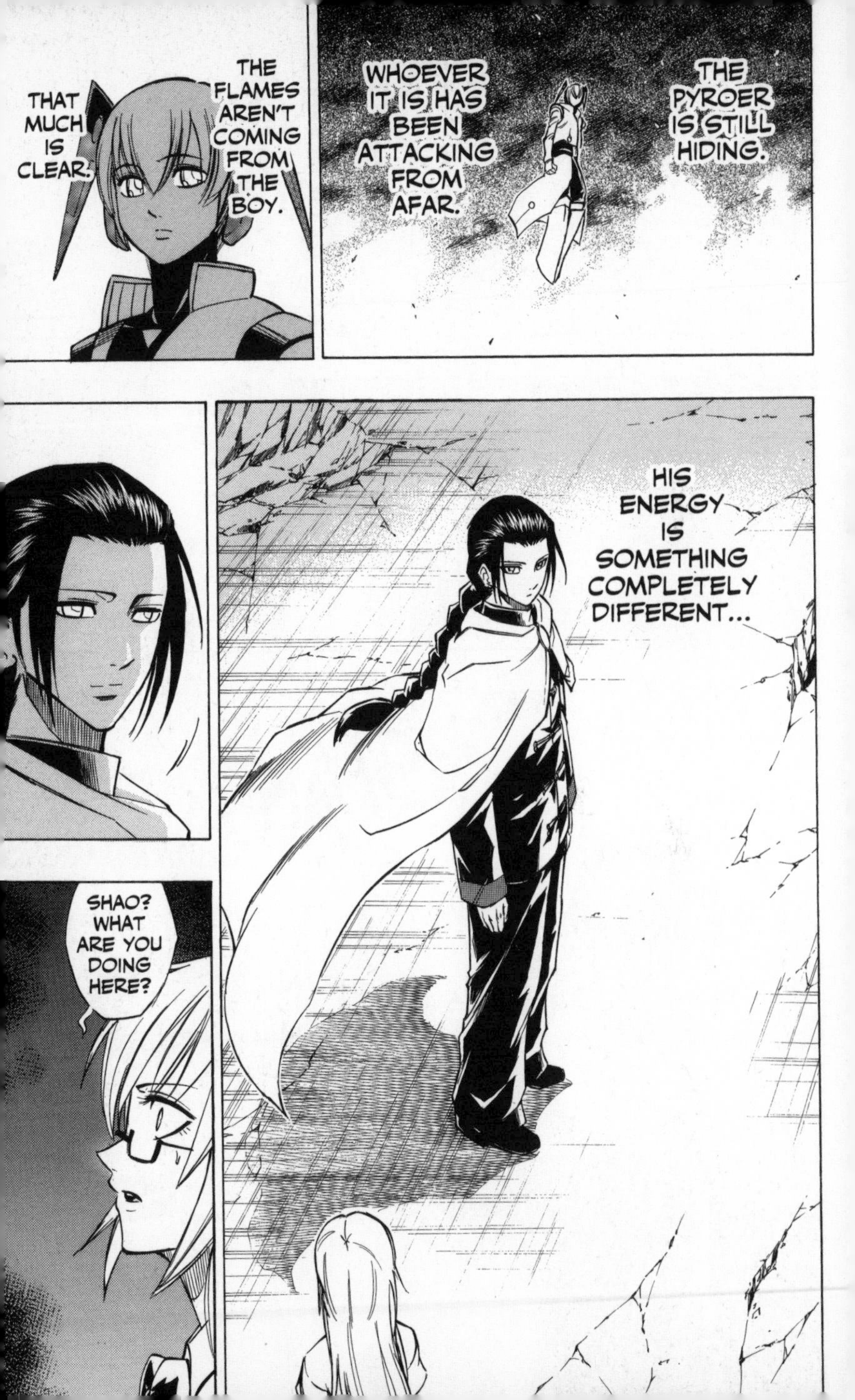
THE PYROER IS STILL HIDING.
WHOEVER IT IS HAS BEEN ATTACKING FROM AFAR.
THE FLAMES AREN'T COMING FROM THE BOY.
THAT MUCH IS CLEAR.
HIS ENERGY IS SOMETHING COMPLETELY DIFFERENT...
SHAO? WHAT ARE YOU DOING HERE?

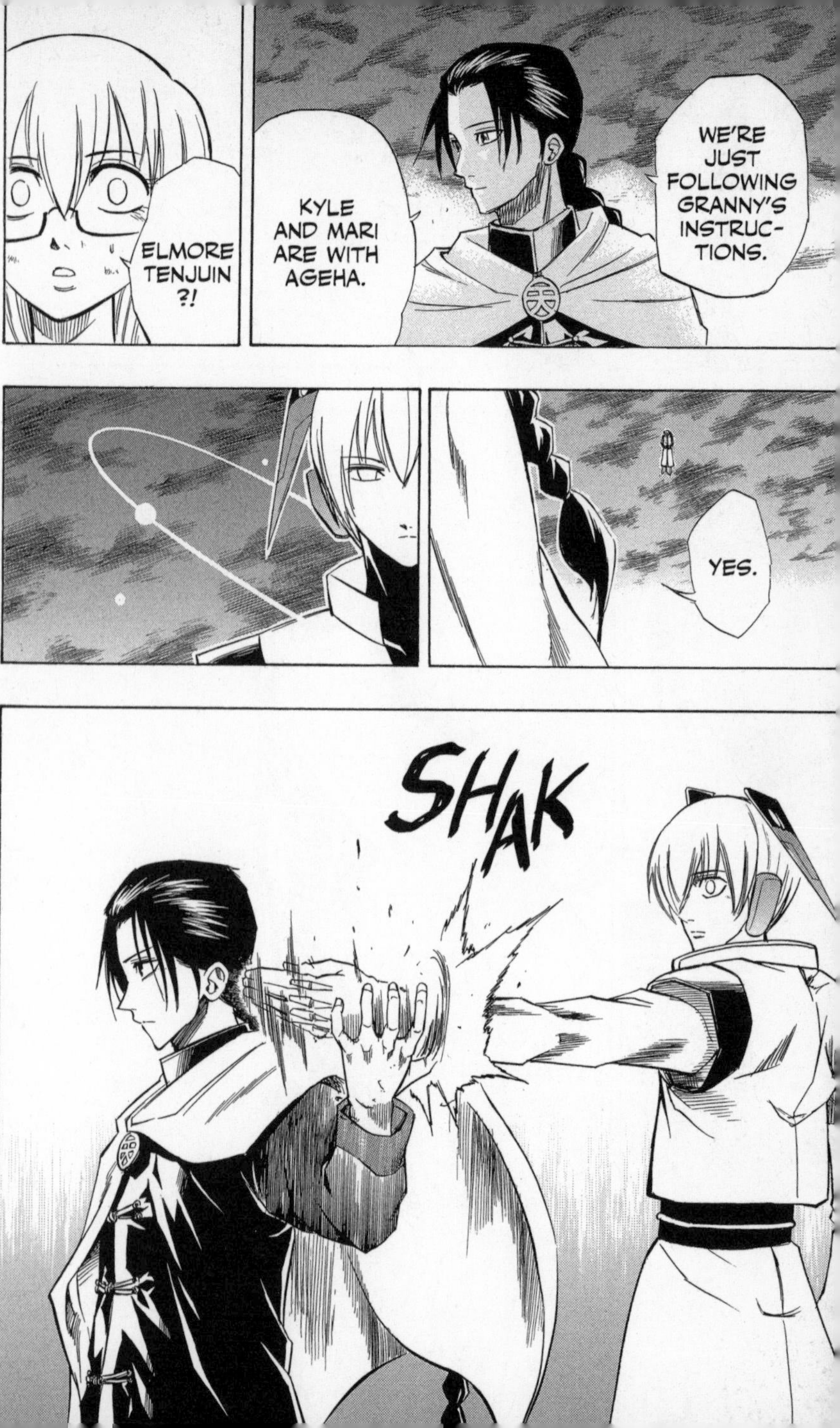
WE'RE JUST FOLLOWING GRANNY'S INSTRUC-TIONS.
KYLE AND MARI ARE WITH AGEHA.
ELMORE TENJUIN ?!
YES.
SHAK

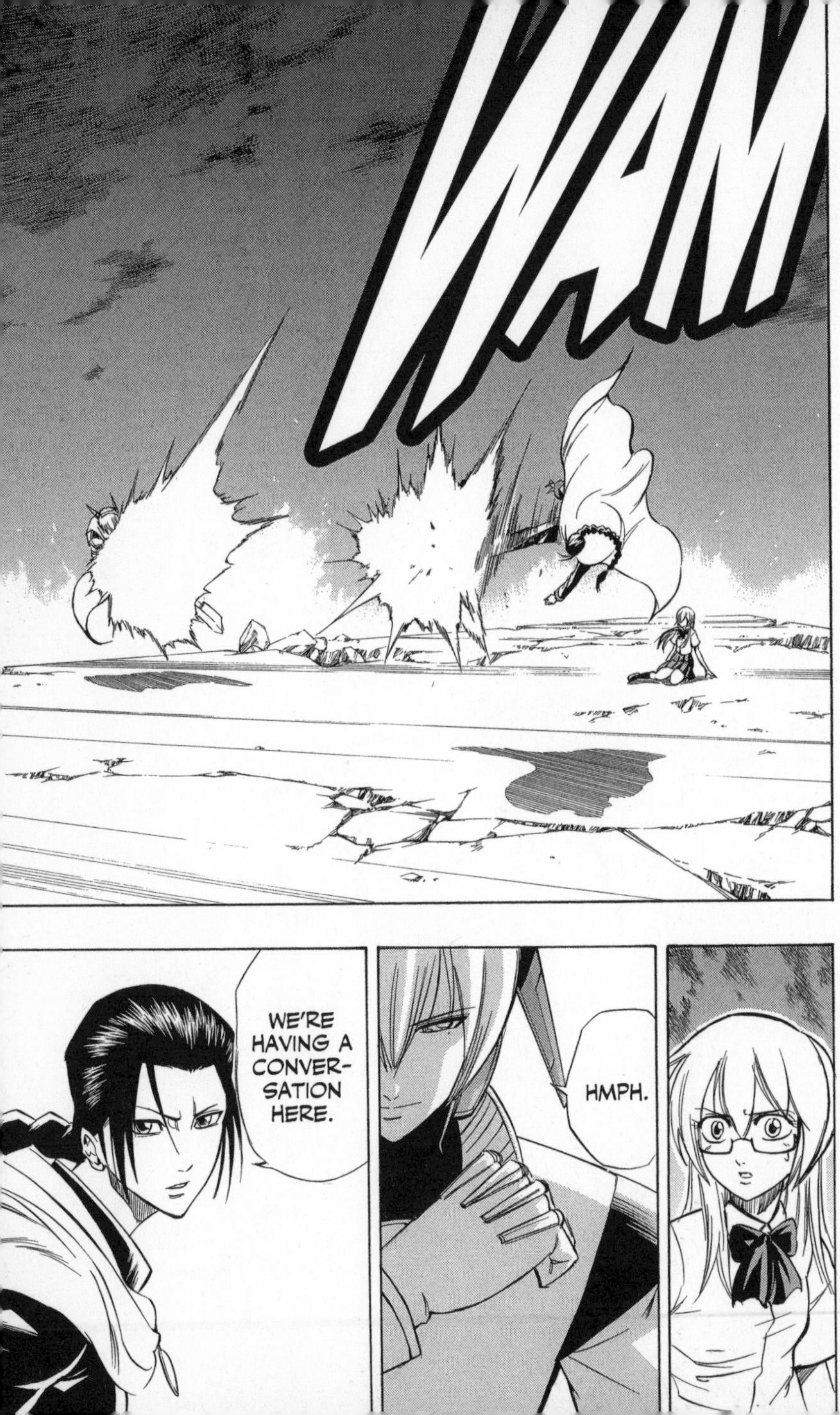
WAM
HMPH.
WE'RE HAVING A CONVER-SATION HERE.

CALL.66: WARRIORS

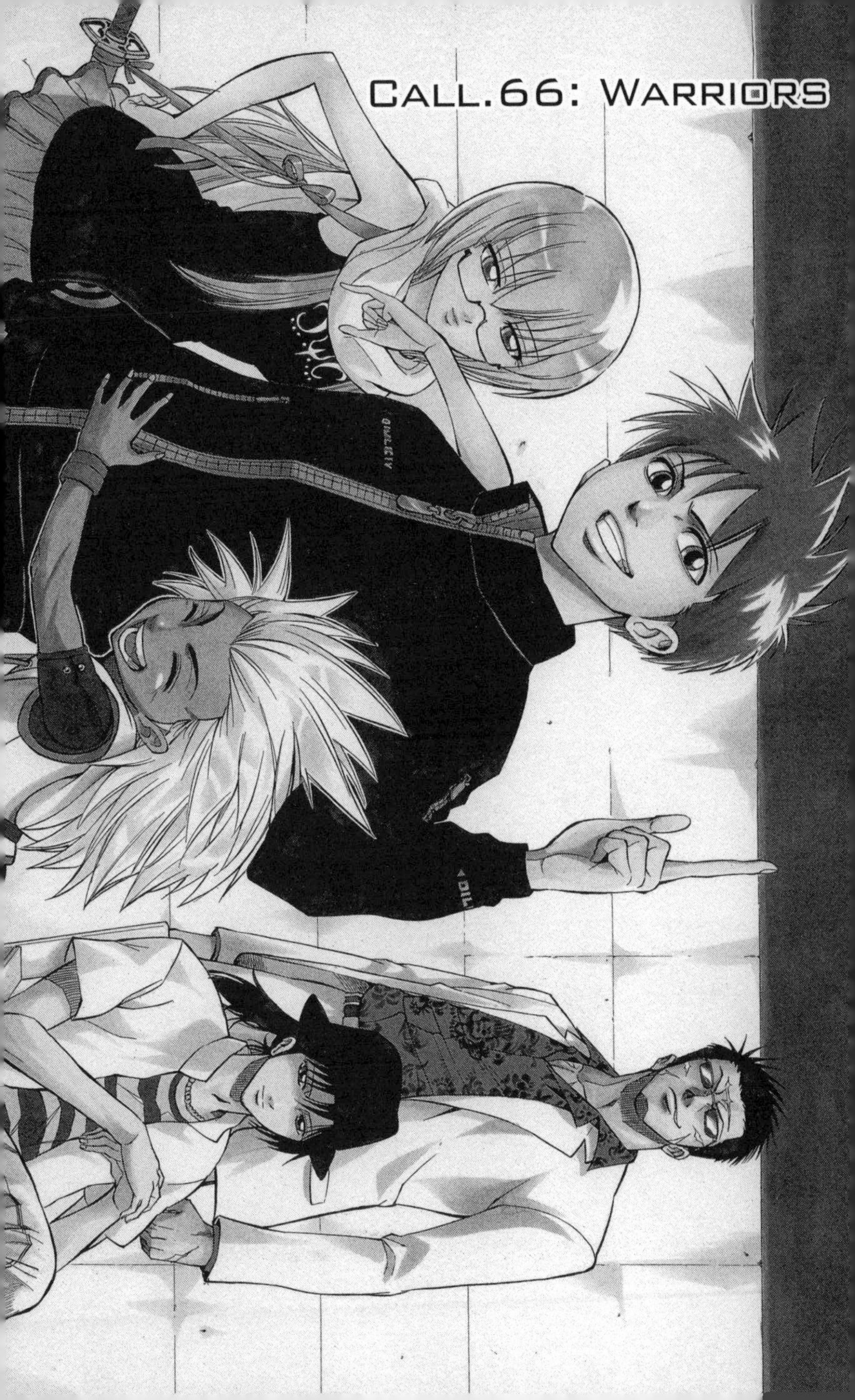

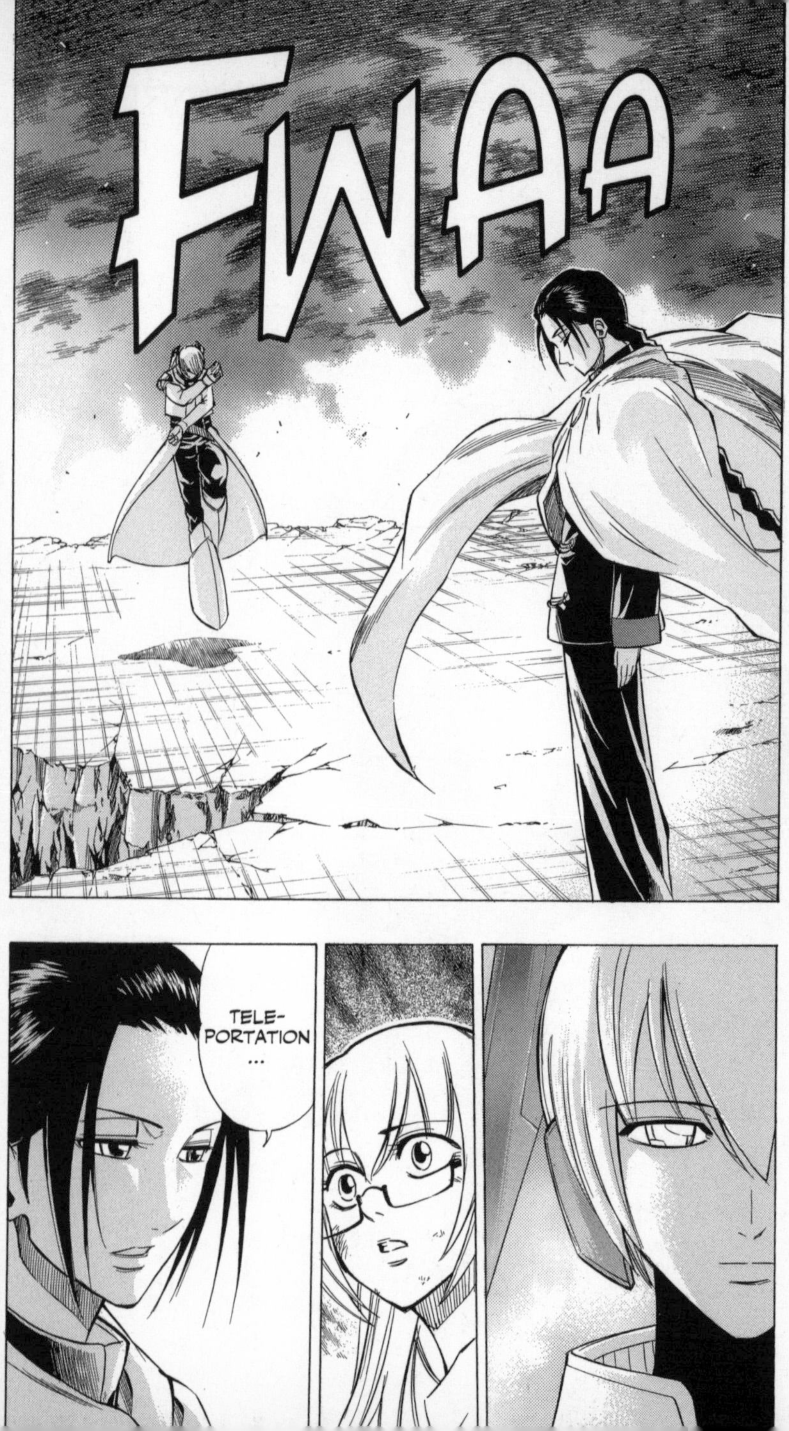
FWAA
TELE-PORTATION ...

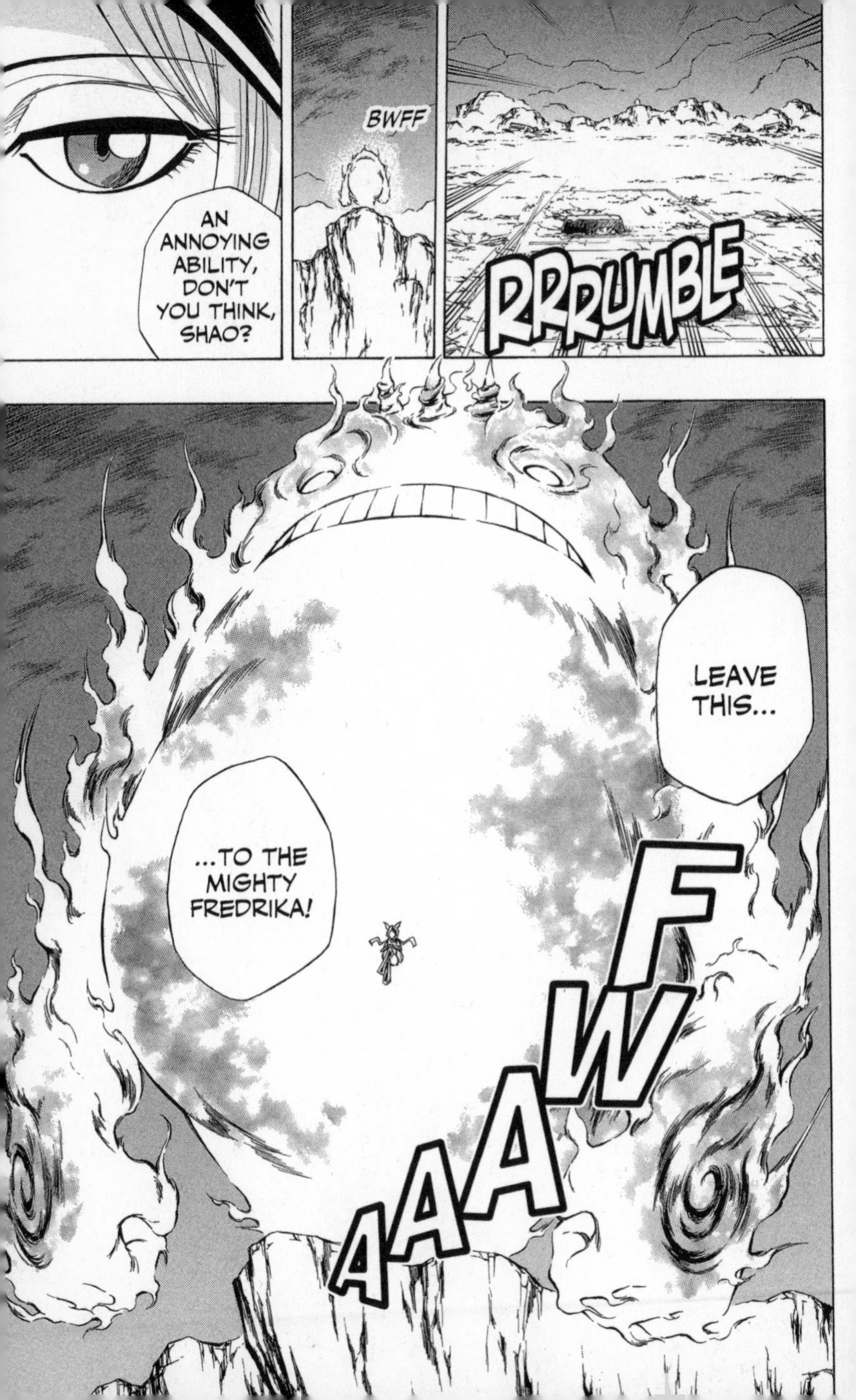
RRRUMBLE
BWFF
AN ANNOYING ABILITY, DON'T YOU THINK, SHAO?
LEAVE THIS...
...TO THE MIGHTY FREDRIKA!
FWAAA

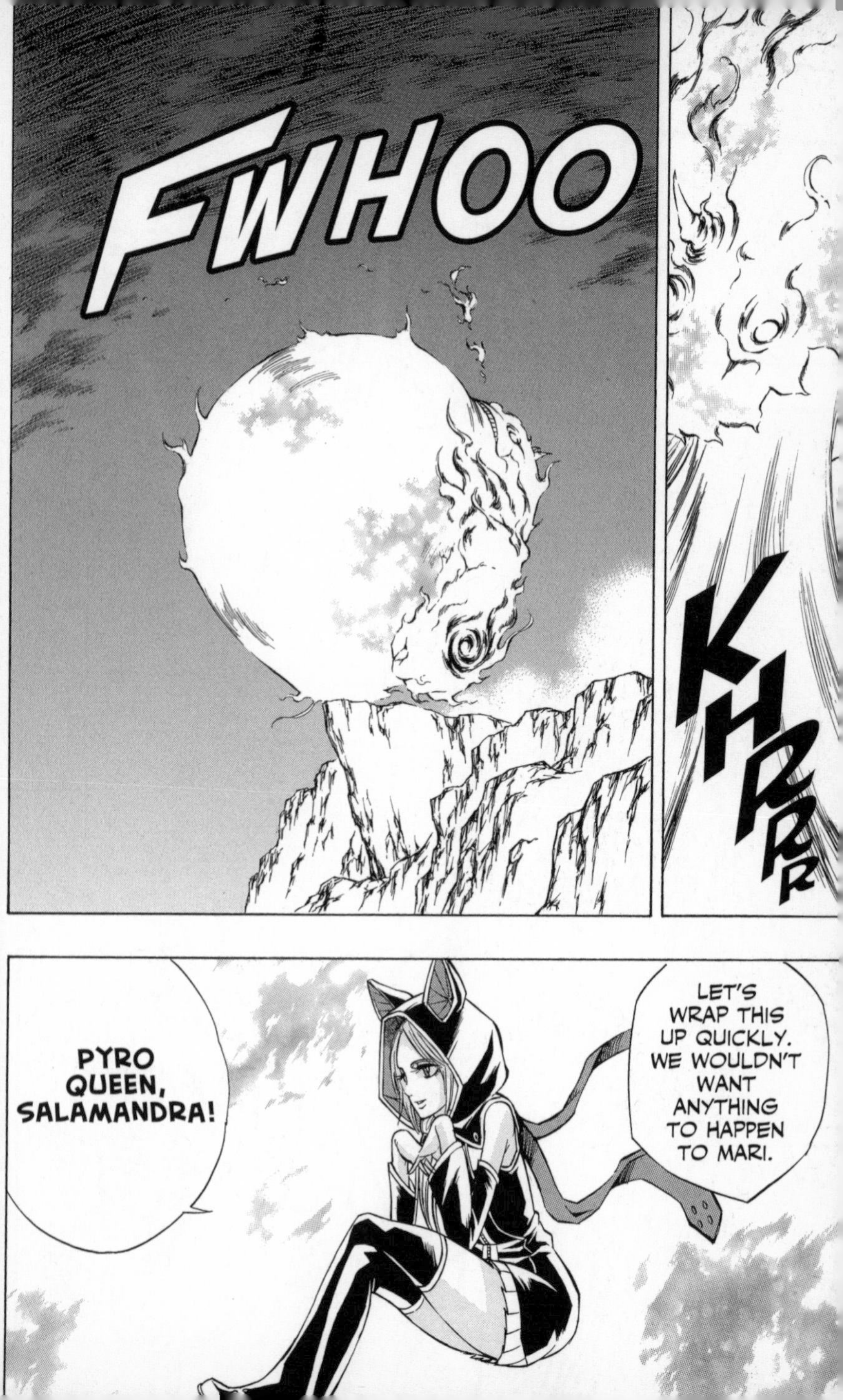
KHRRR
FWHOO
LET'S WRAP THIS UP QUICKLY. WE WOULDN'T WANT ANYTHING TO HAPPEN TO MARI.
PYRO QUEEN, SALAMANDRA!

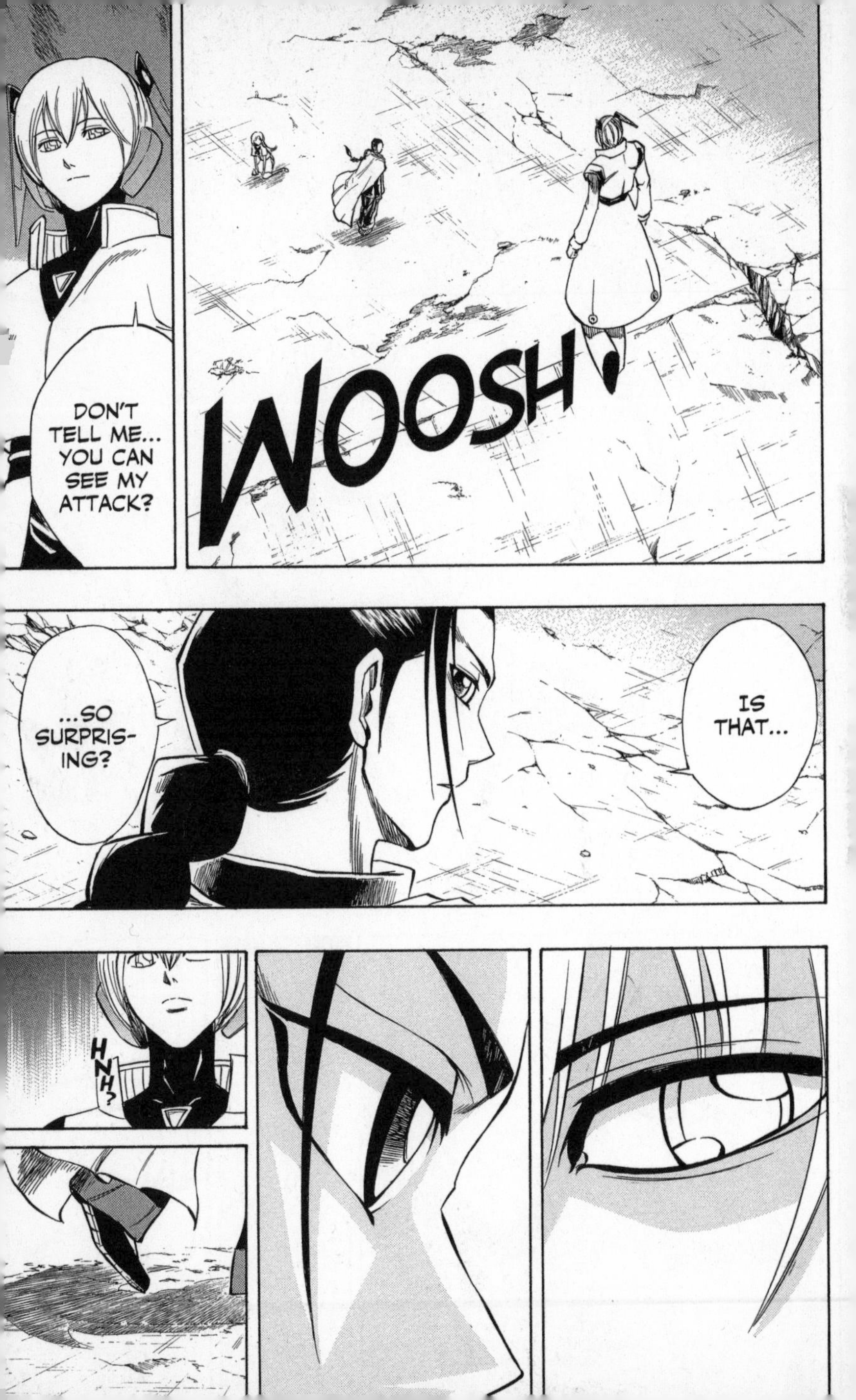
WOOSH
DON'T TELL ME... YOU CAN SEE MY ATTACK?
IS THAT...
...SO SURPRIS-ING?
HNH?

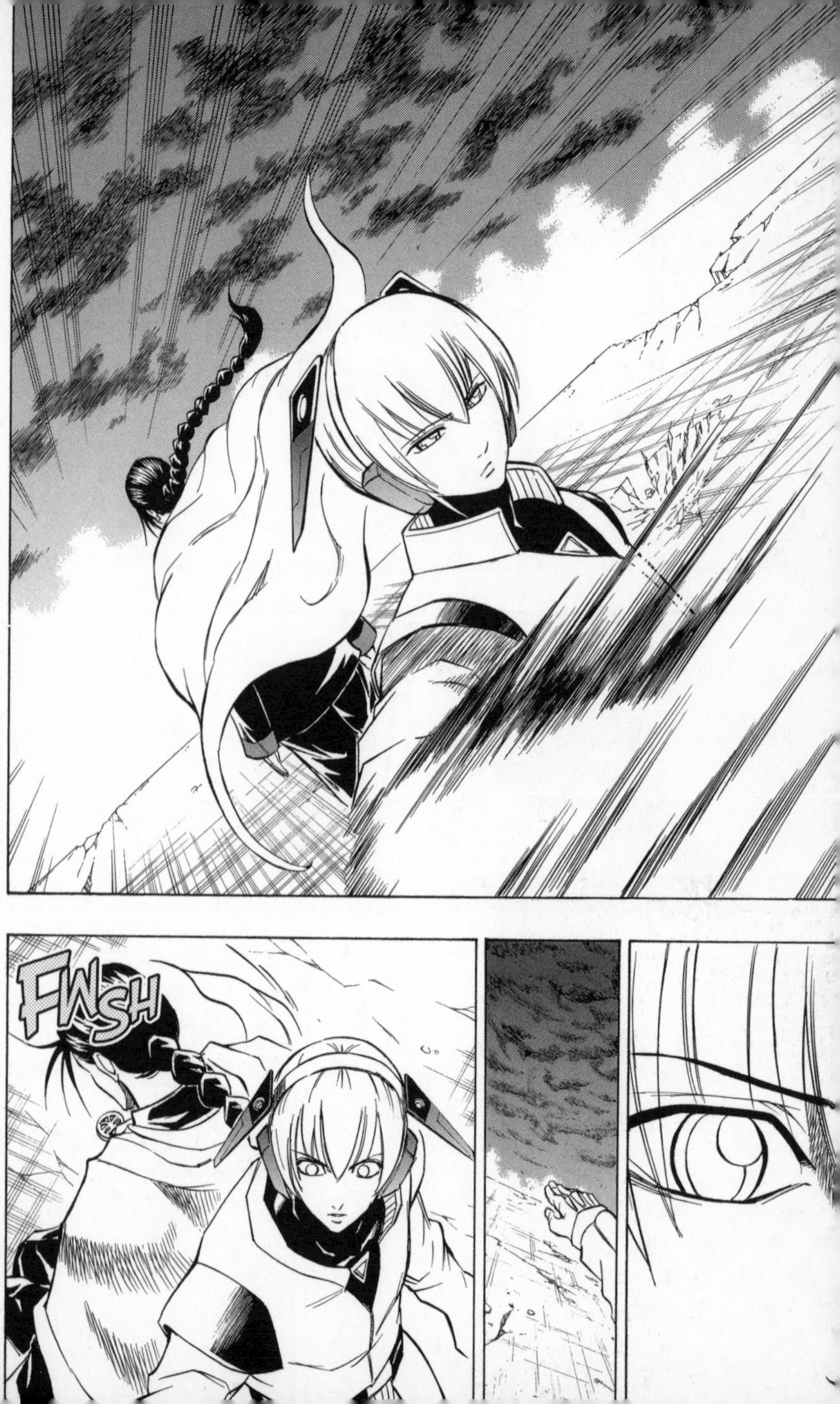
FWSH

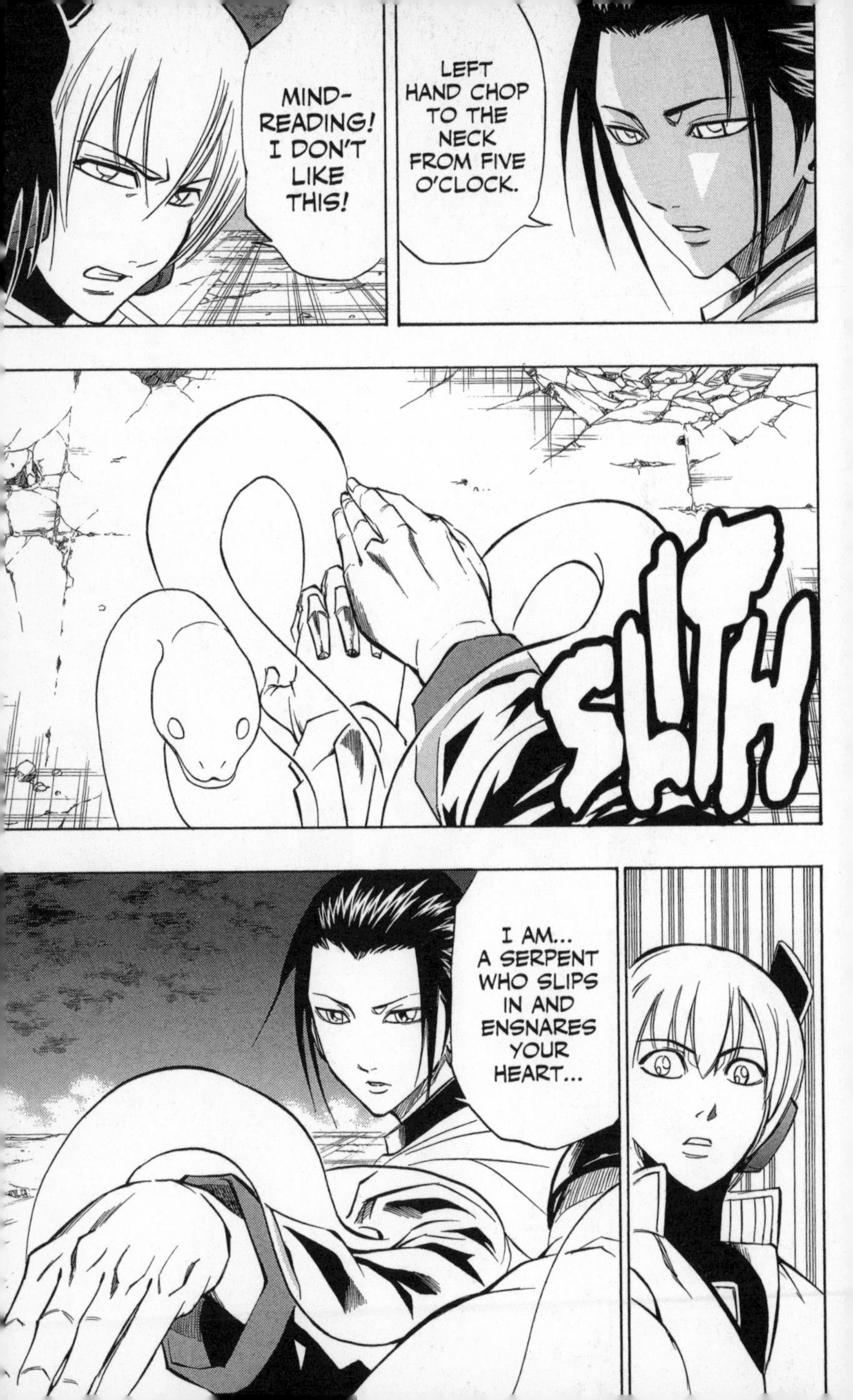
LEFT HAND CHOP TO THE NECK FROM FIVE O'CLOCK.
MIND-READING! I DON'T LIKE THIS!
SLITH
I AM... A SERPENT WHO SLIPS IN AND ENSNARES YOUR HEART...

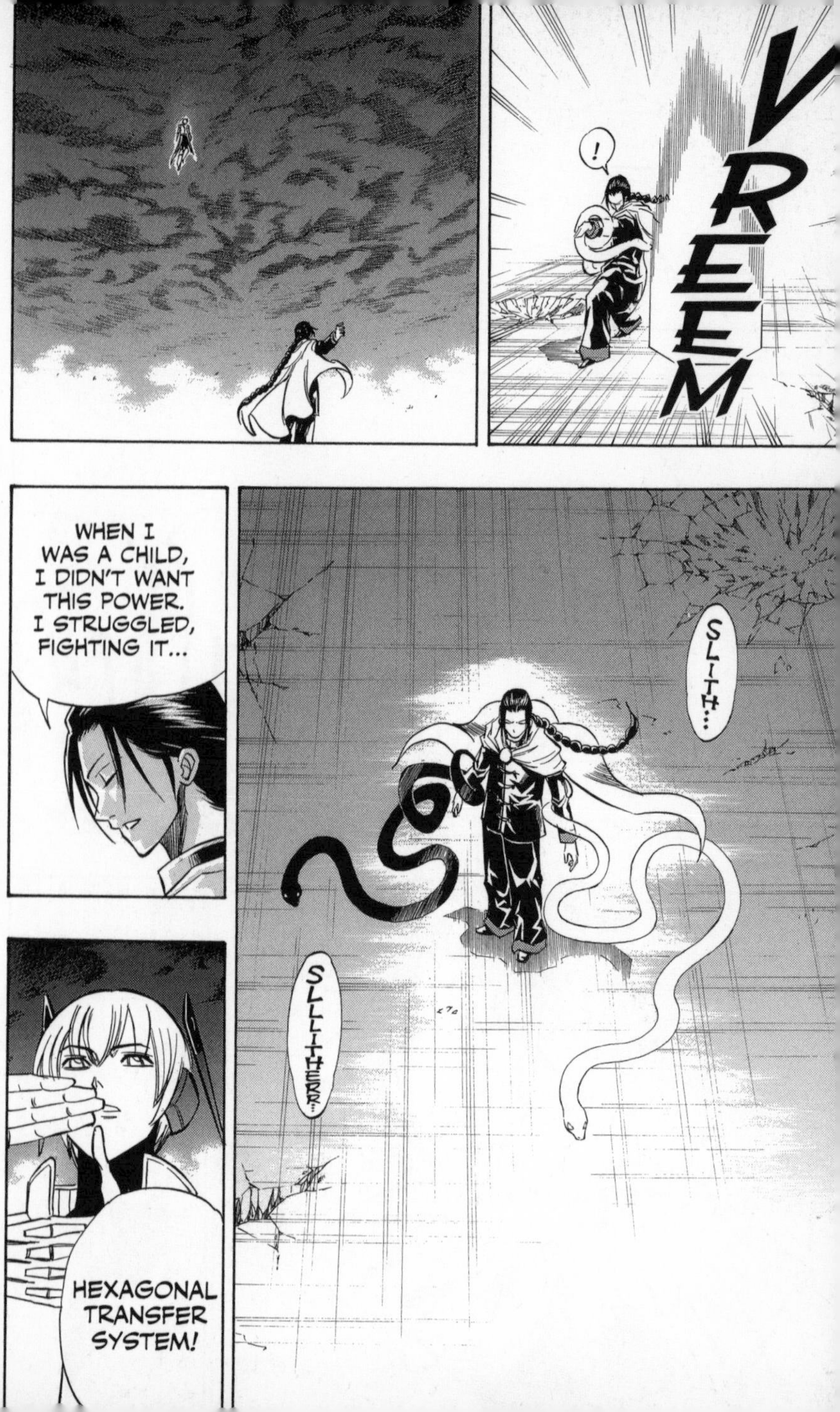
VREEM
!
SLITH...
SLLITHERR...
WHEN I WAS A CHILD, I DIDN'T WANT THIS POWER. I STRUGGLED, FIGHTING IT...
HEXAGONAL TRANSFER SYSTEM!

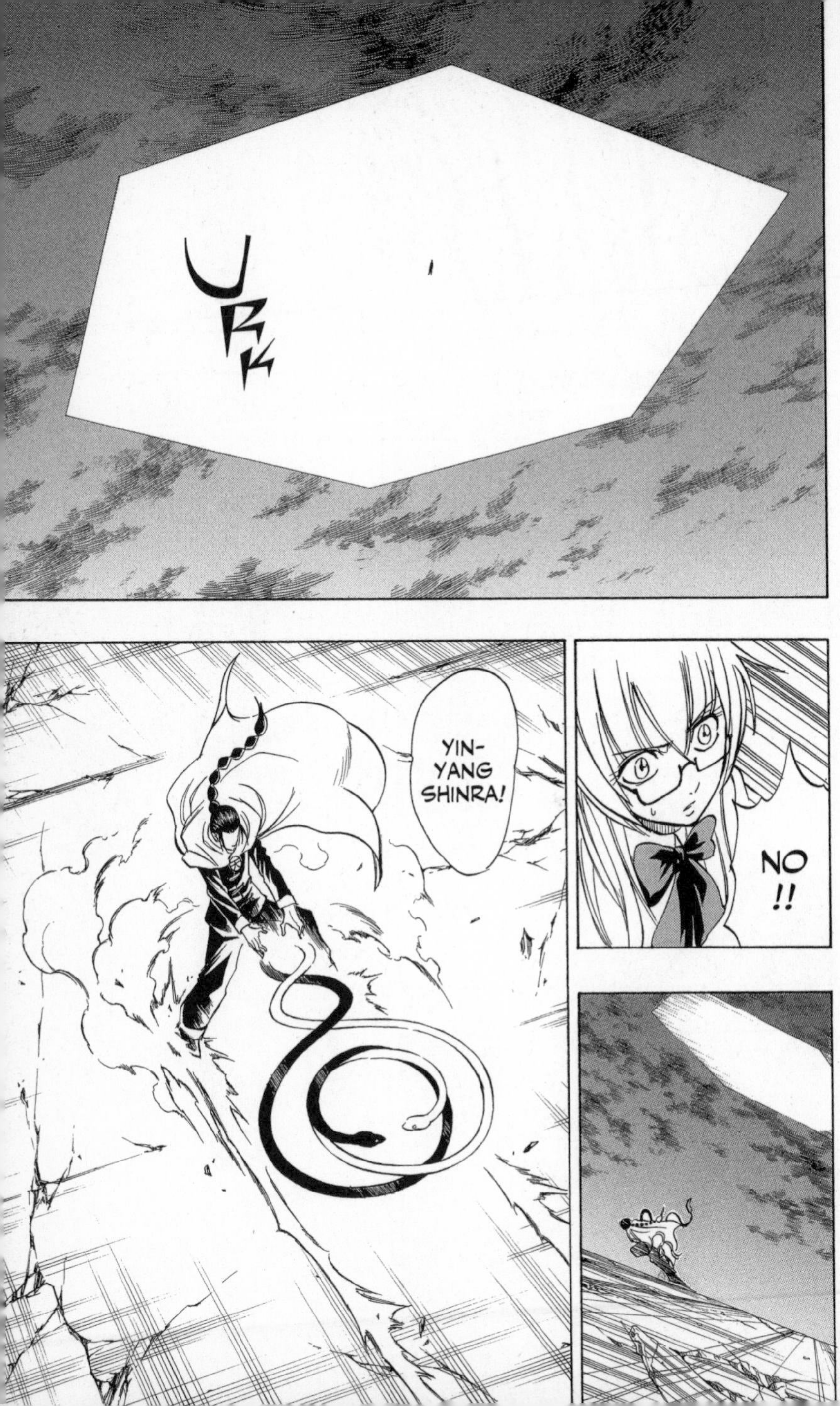
URK
NO !!
YIN-YANG SHINRA!

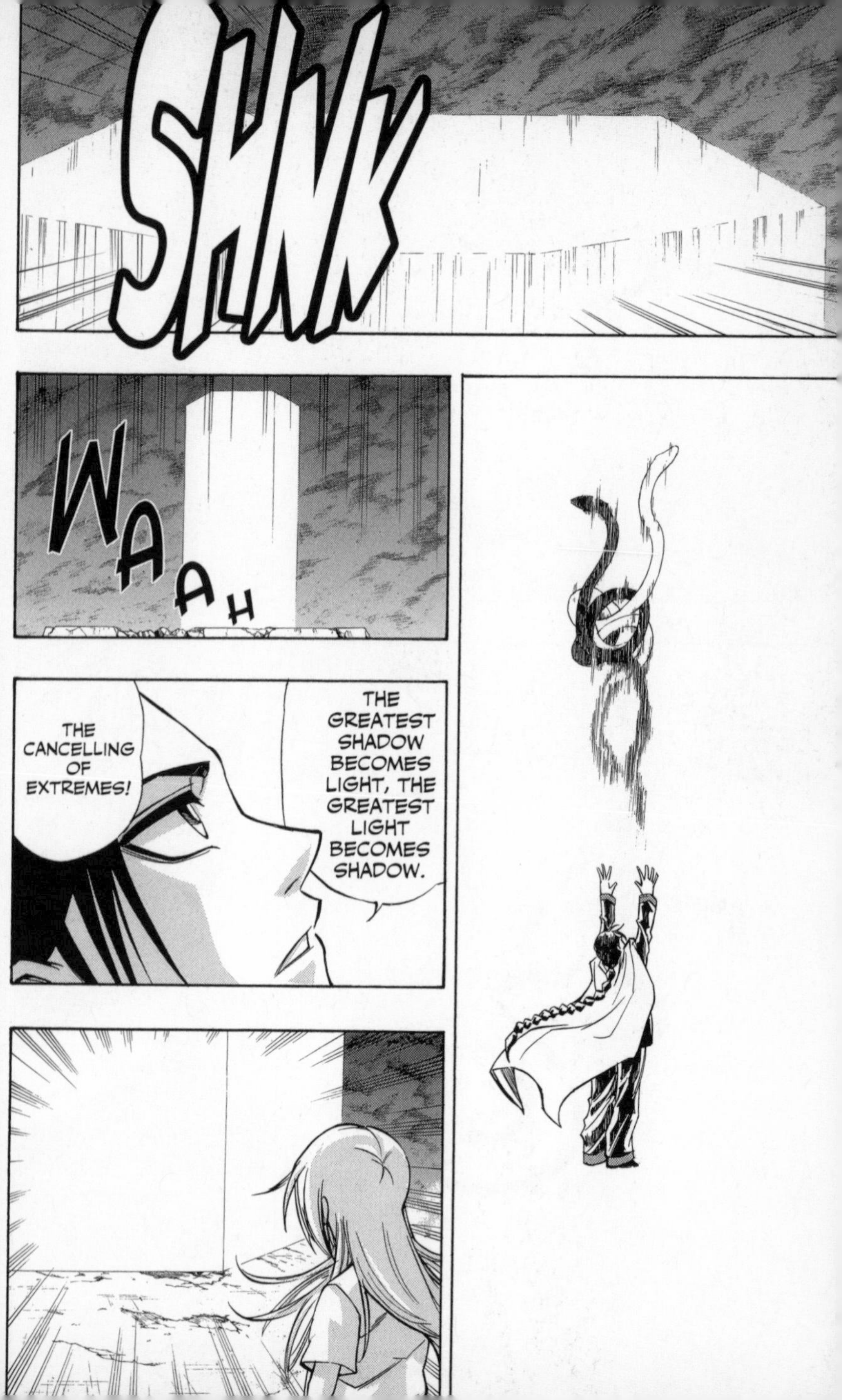
SHINK
WAAAH
THE GREATEST SHADOW BECOMES LIGHT, THE GREATEST LIGHT BECOMES SHADOW.
THE CANCELLING OF EXTREMES!

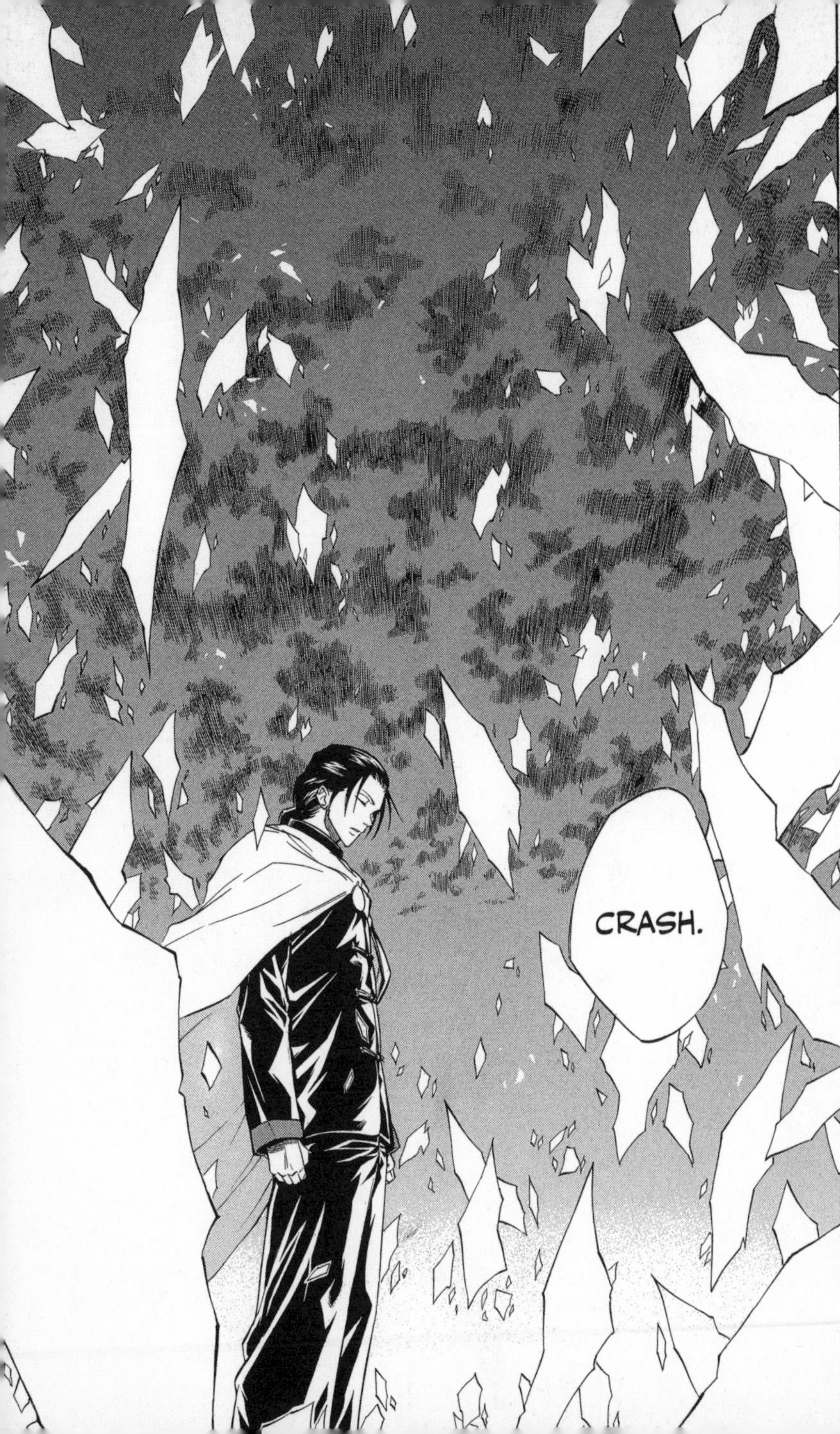
CRASH.

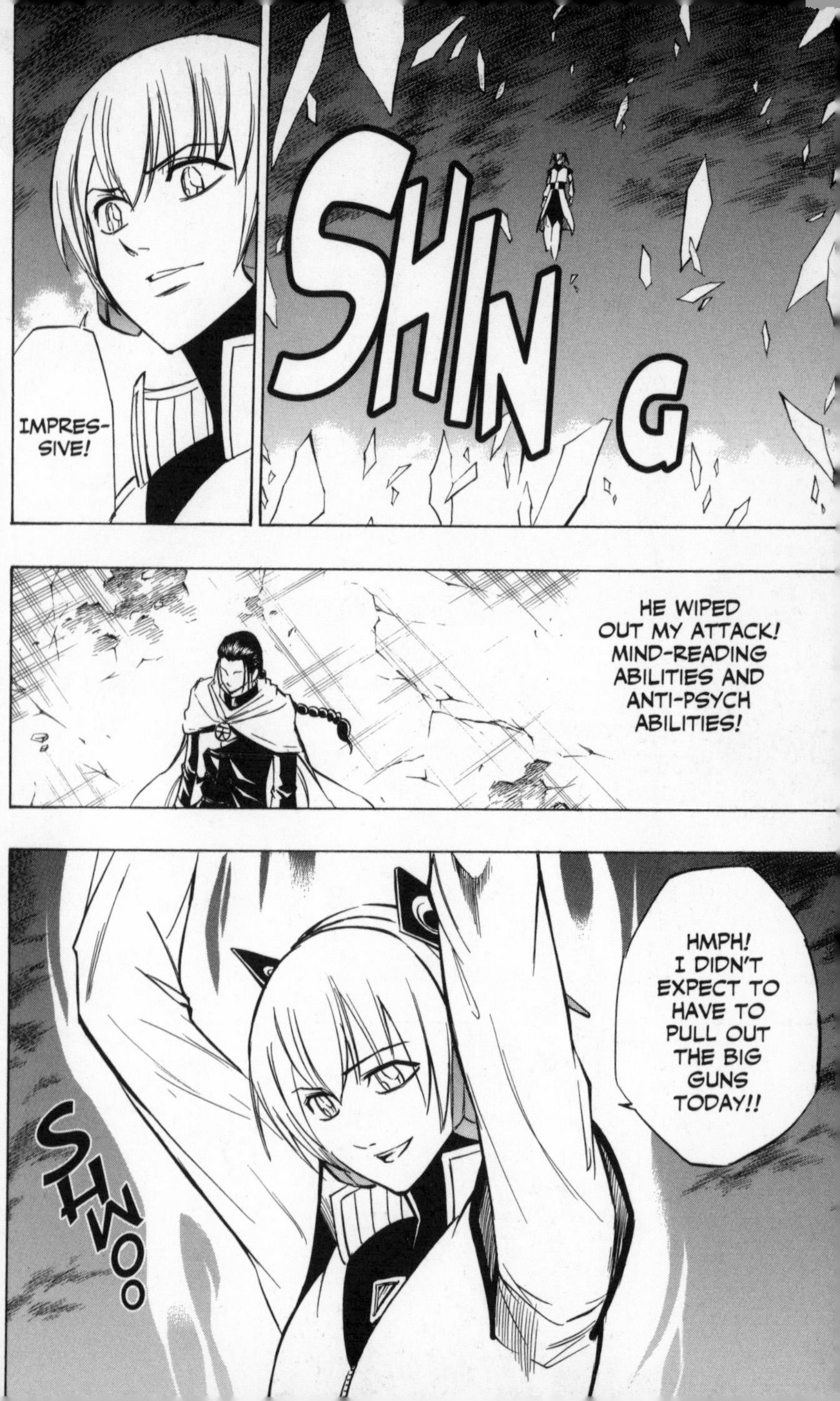
SHINNG
IMPRES-SIVE!
HE WIPED OUT MY ATTACK! MIND-READING ABILITIES AND ANTI-PSYCH ABILITIES!
HMPH! I DIDN'T EXPECT TO HAVE TO PULL OUT THE BIG GUNS TODAY!!
SHWOO

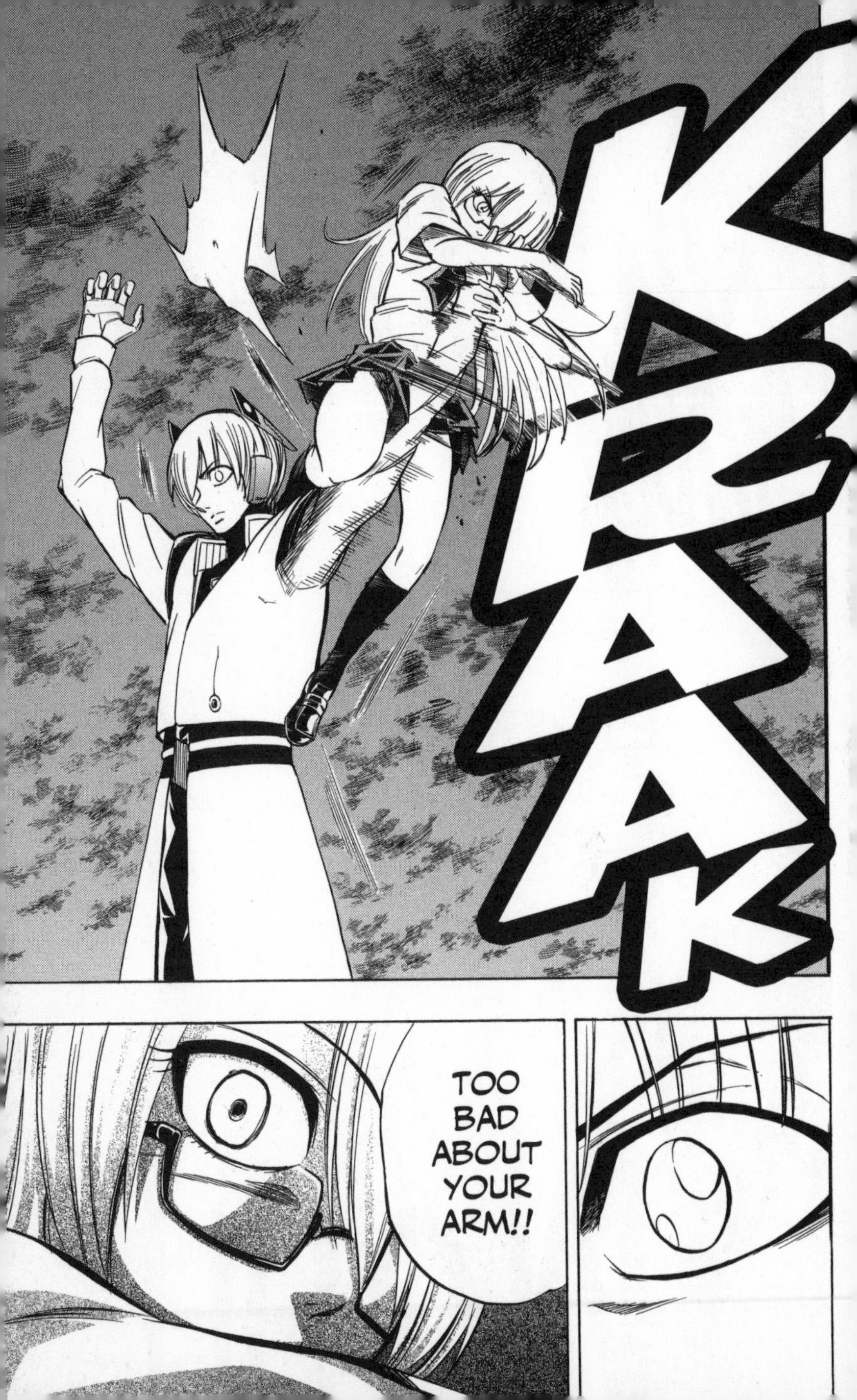
KRAK
TOO BAD ABOUT YOUR ARM!!

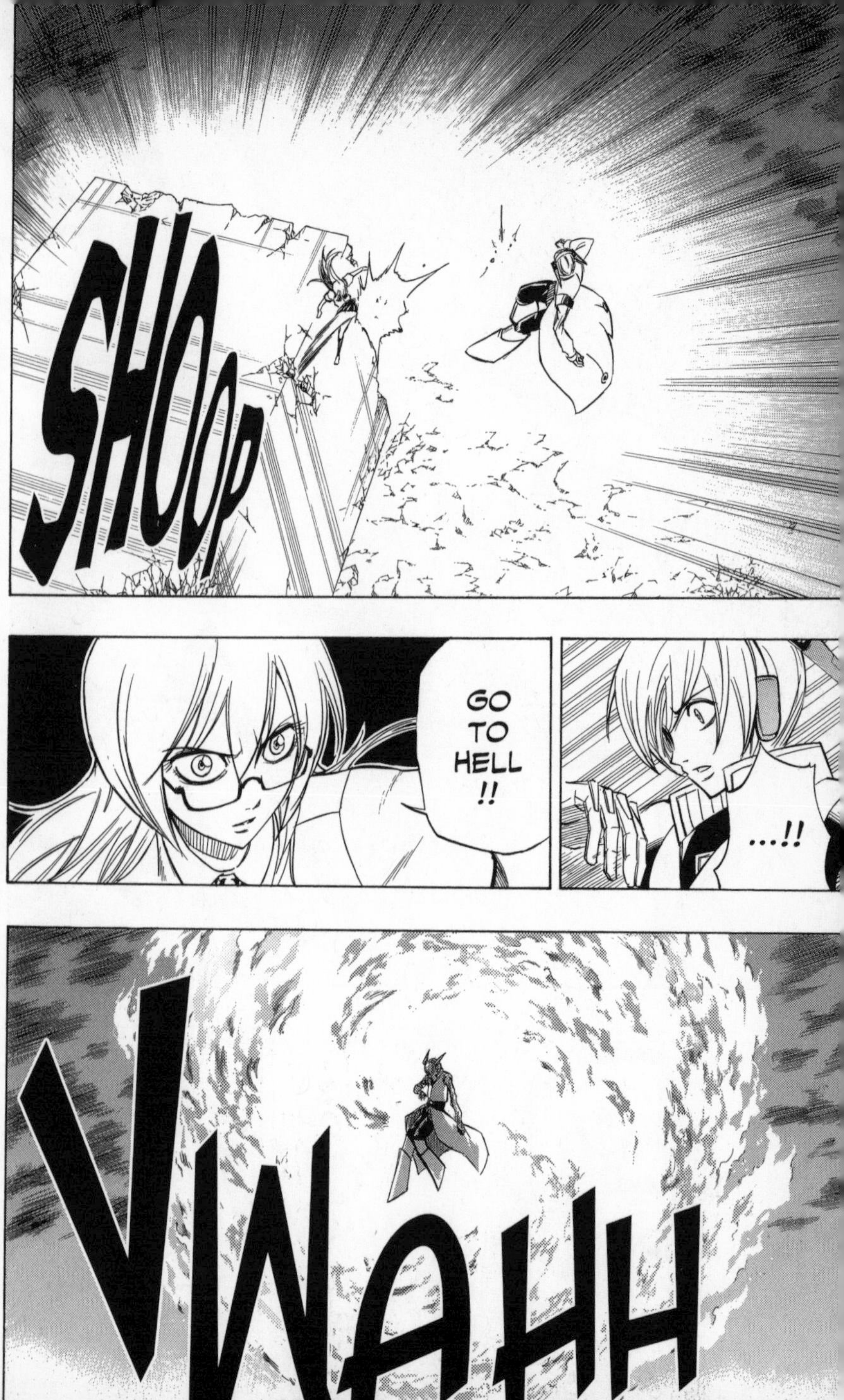
SHOOP
...!!
GO TO HELL !!
VWAHH

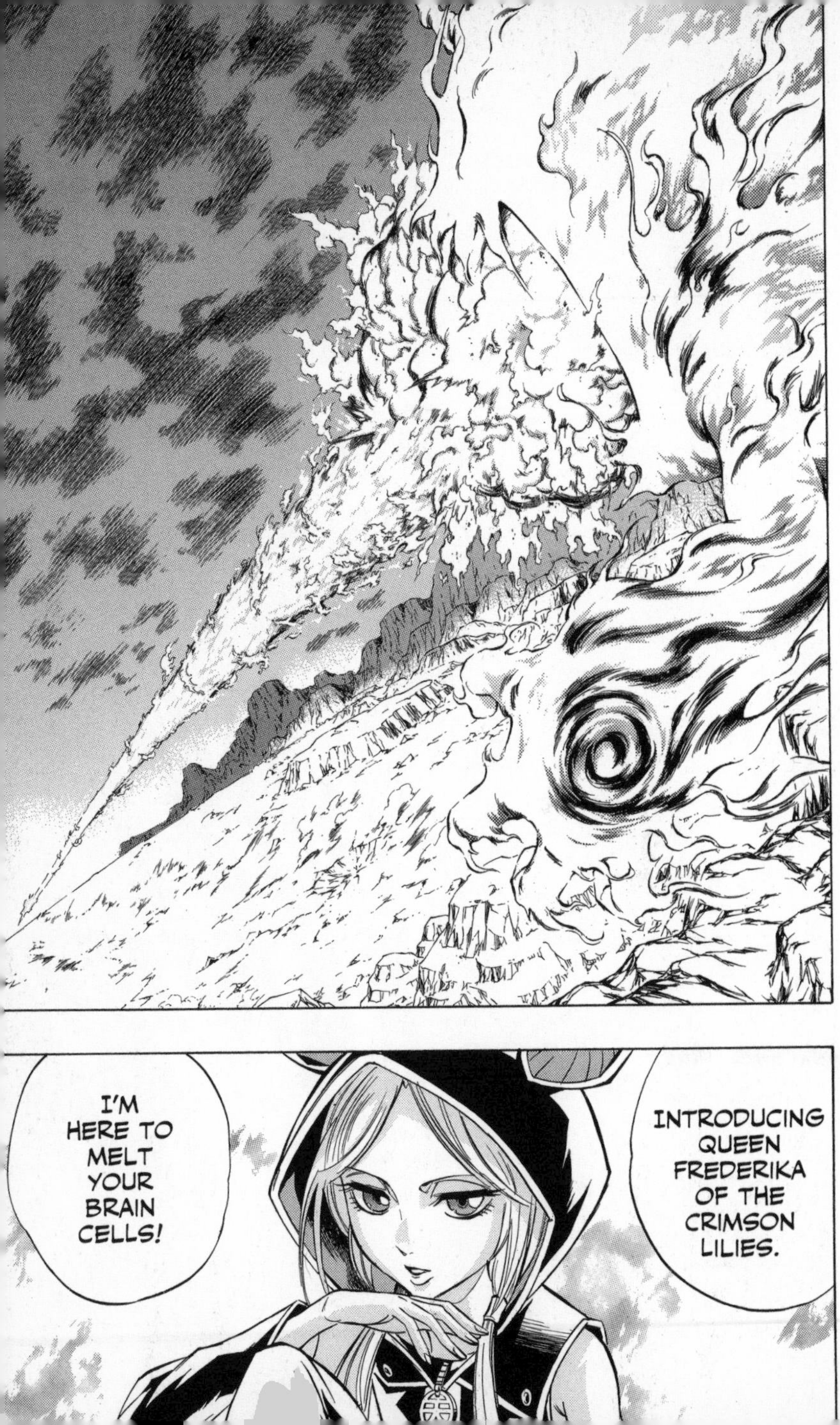
INTRODUCING QUEEN FREDERIKA OF THE CRIMSON LILIES.
I'M HERE TO MELT YOUR BRAIN CELLS!

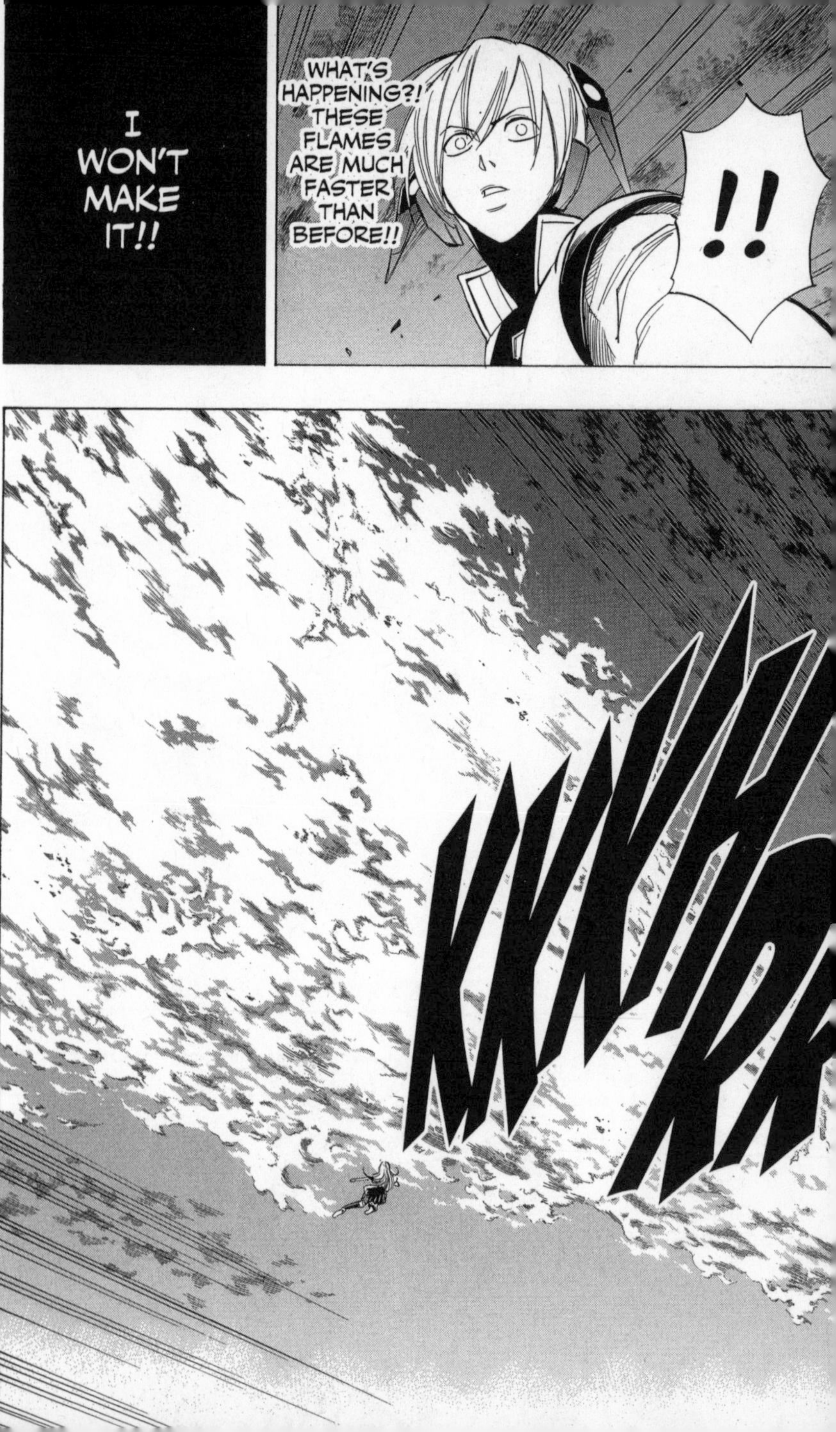
!!
WHAT'S HAPPENING?! THESE FLAMES ARE MUCH FASTER THAN BEFORE!!
I WON'T MAKE IT!!

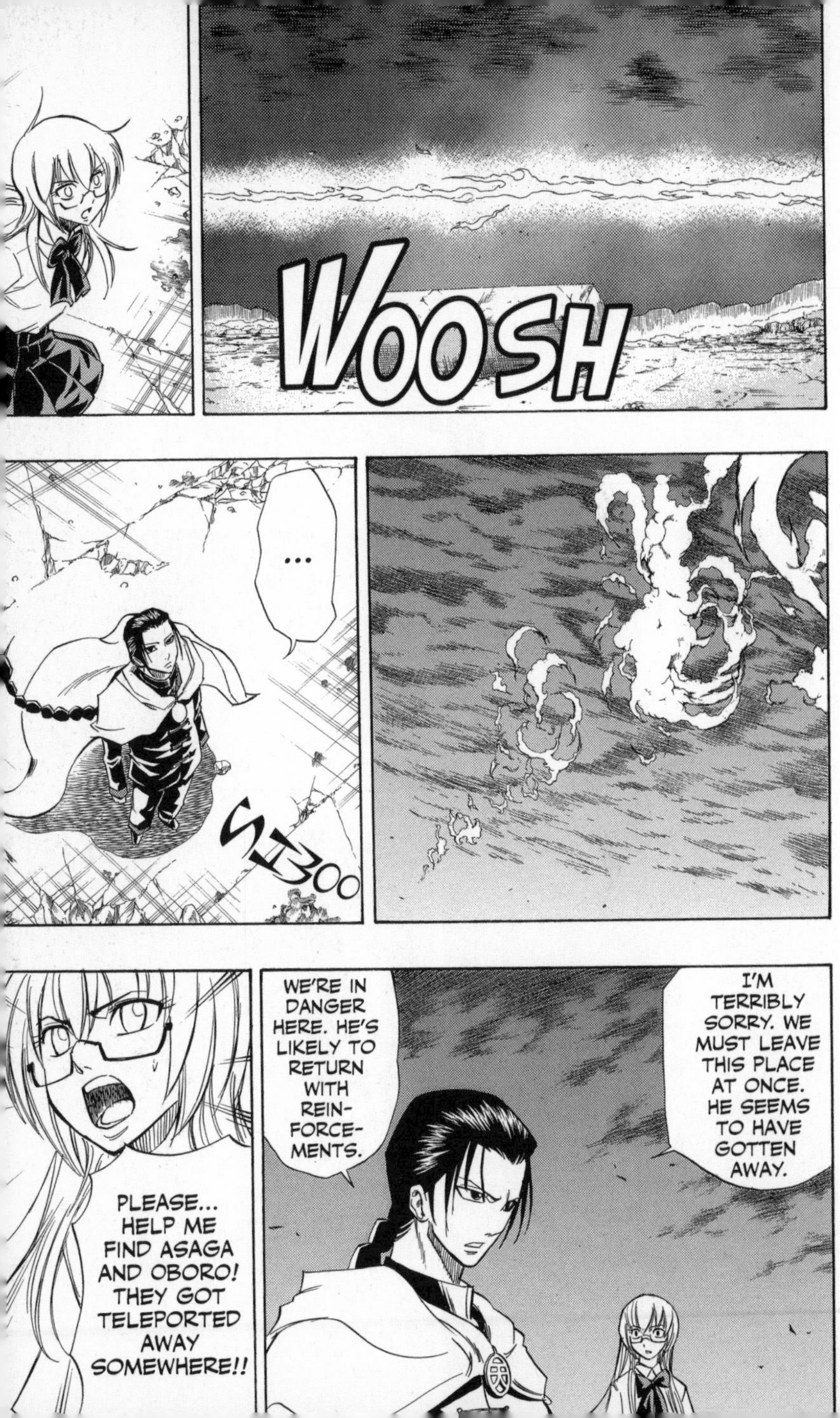
WOOSH
...
I'M TERRIBLY SORRY. WE MUST LEAVE THIS PLACE AT ONCE. HE SEEMS TO HAVE GOTTEN AWAY.
WE'RE IN DANGER HERE. HE'S LIKELY TO RETURN WITH REIN-FORCE-MENTS.
PLEASE... HELP ME FIND ASAGA AND OBORO! THEY GOT TELEPORTED AWAY SOMEWHERE!!

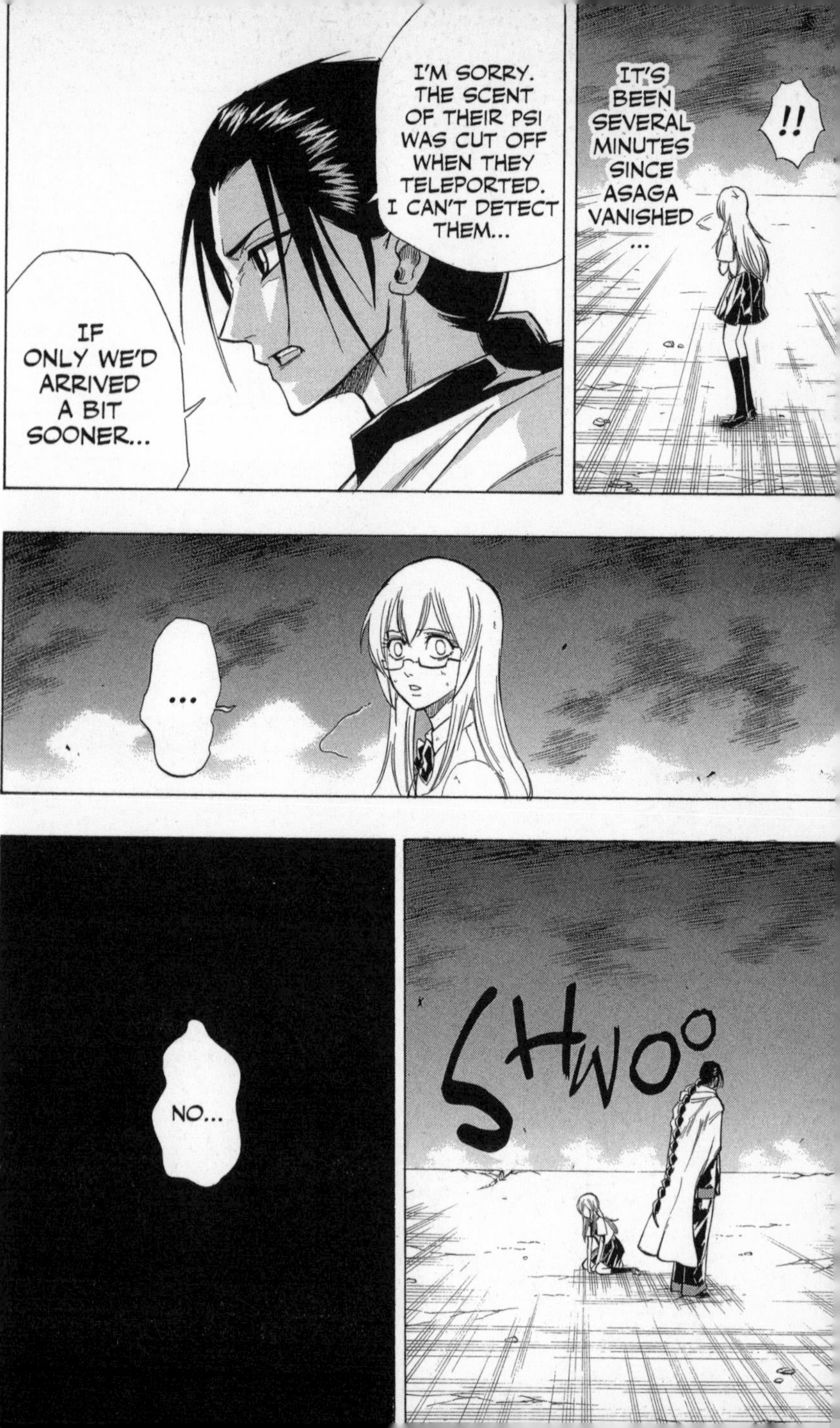

!!
IT'S BEEN SEVERAL MINUTES SINCE ASAGA VANISHED...
I'M SORRY. THE SCENT OF THEIR PSI WAS CUT OFF WHEN THEY TELEPORTED. I CAN'T DETECT THEM...
IF ONLY WE'D ARRIVED A BIT SOONER...
...
SHWOO
NO...

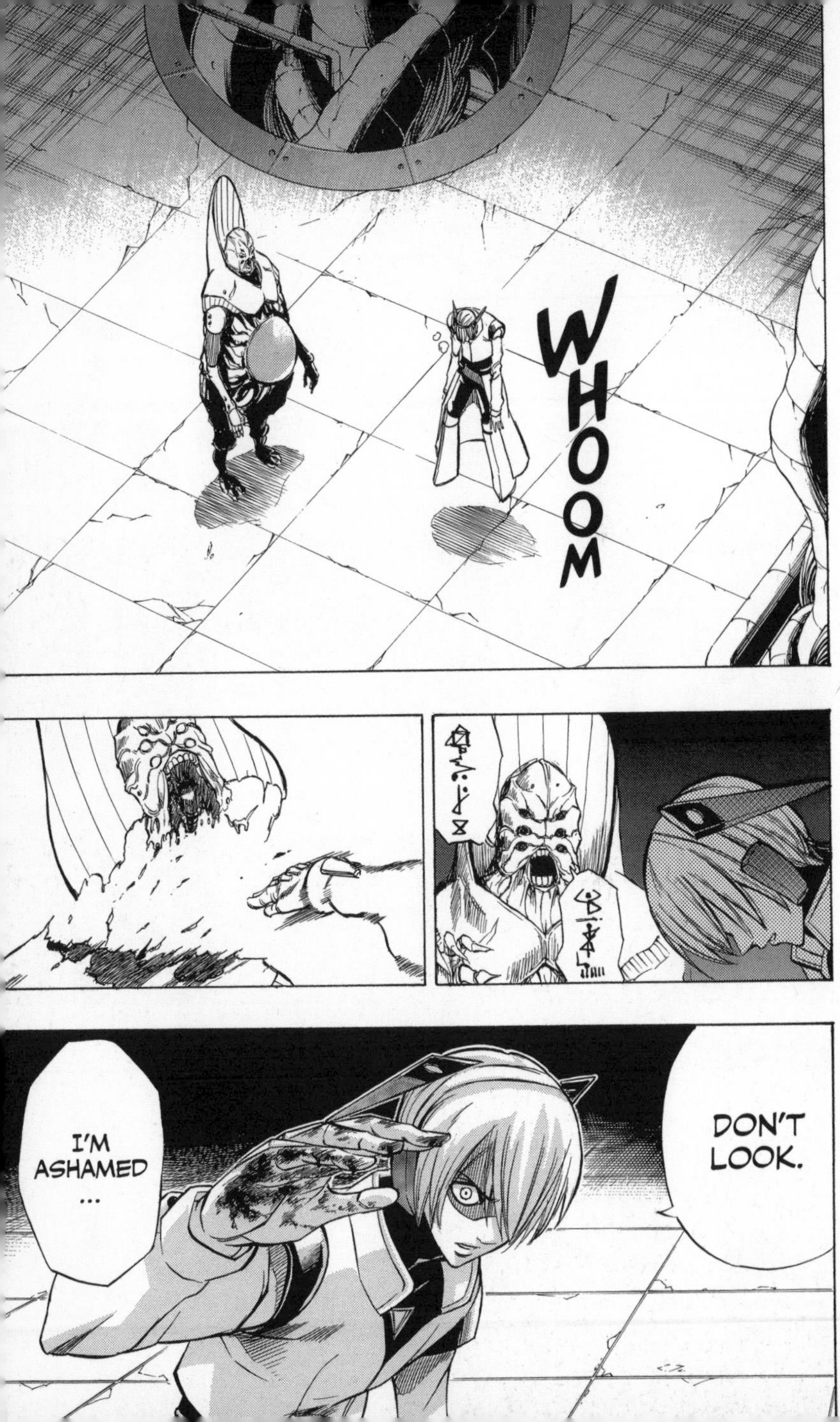
WHOOM
DON'T LOOK.
I'M ASHAMED ...

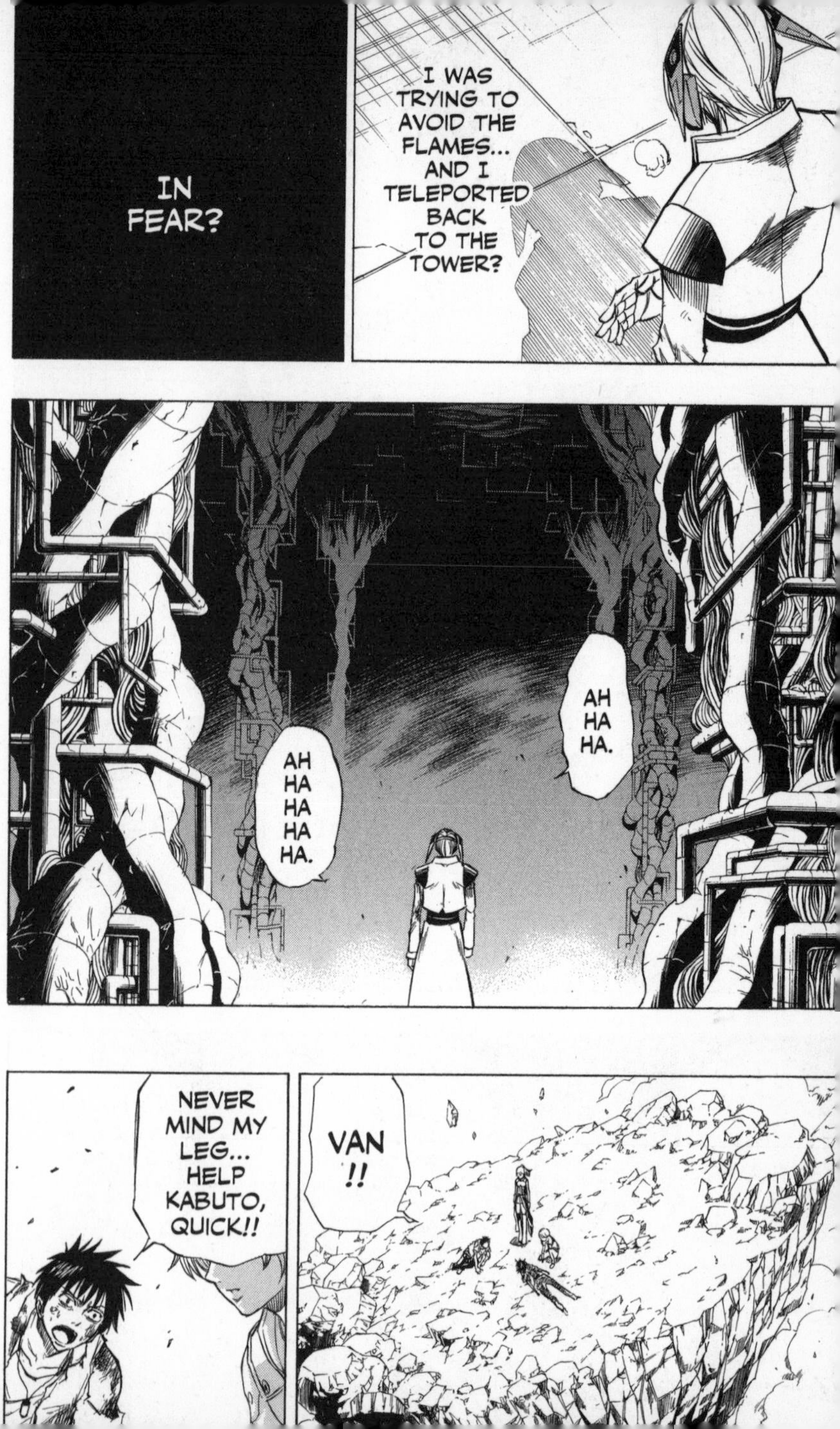
I WAS TRYING TO AVOID THE FLAMES... AND I TELEPORTED BACK TO THE TOWER?
IN FEAR?
AH HA HA.
AH HA HA HA HA.
VAN !!
NEVER MIND MY LEG... HELP KABUTO, QUICK!!

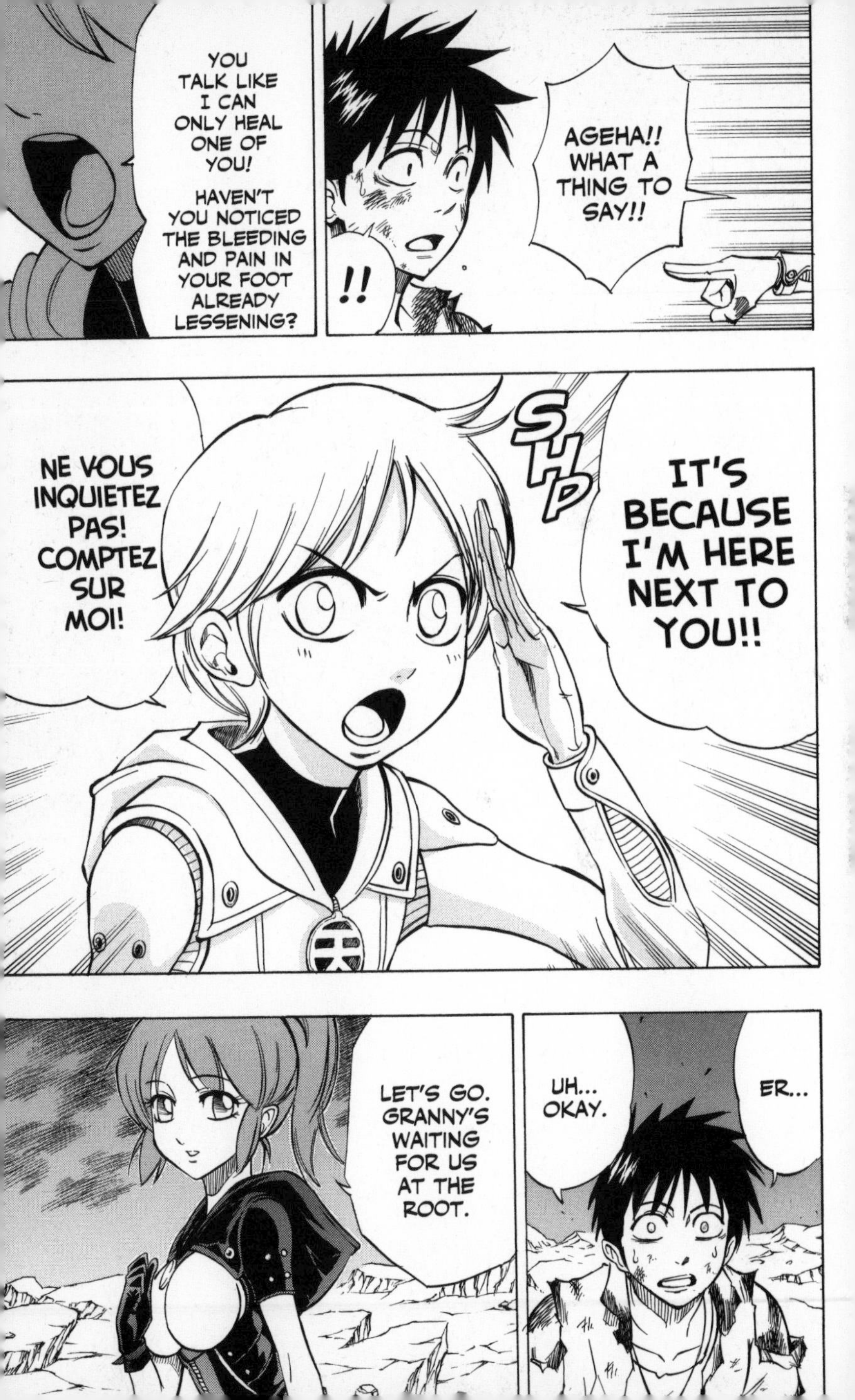
AGEHA!! WHAT A THING TO SAY!!
!!
YOU TALK LIKE I CAN ONLY HEAL ONE OF YOU!
HAVEN'T YOU NOTICED THE BLEEDING AND PAIN IN YOUR FOOT ALREADY LESSENING?
IT'S BECAUSE I'M HERE NEXT TO YOU!!
SHP
NE VOUS INQUIETEZ PAS! COMPTEZ SUR MOI!
ER...
UH... OKAY.
LET'S GO. GRANNY'S WAITING FOR US AT THE ROOT.

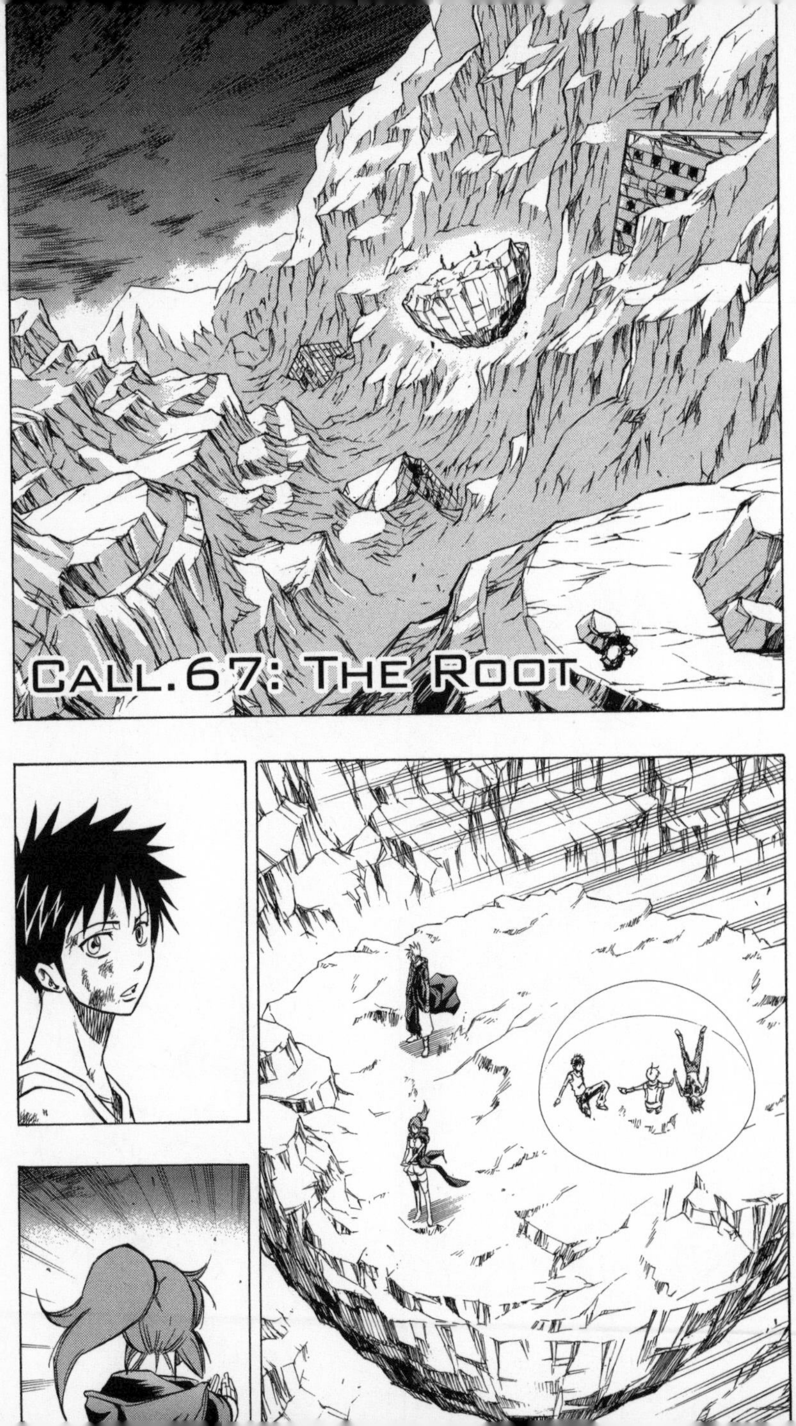
CALL.67: THE ROOT

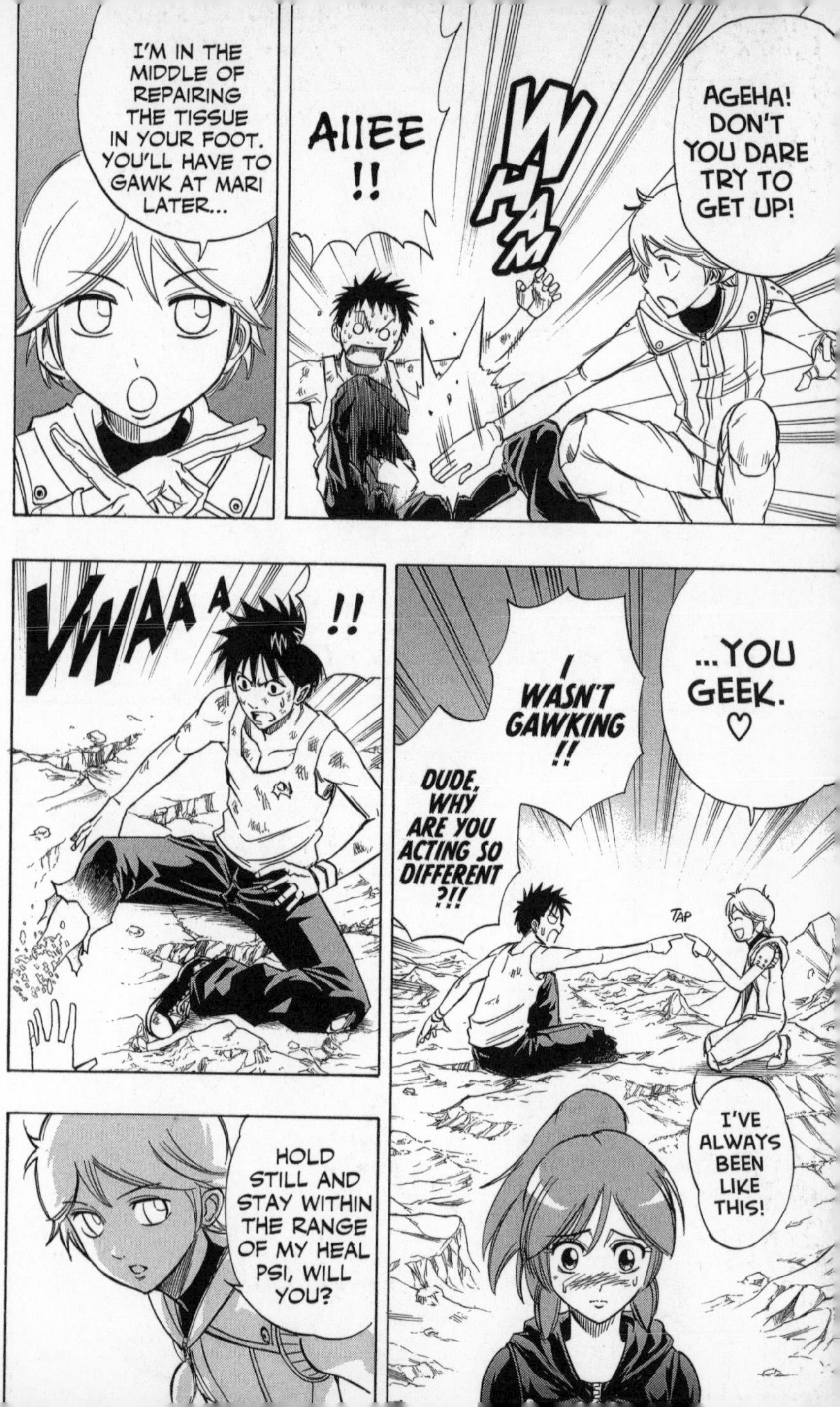
AGEHA! DON'T YOU DARE TRY TO GET UP!
WHAM
AIIEE !!
I'M IN THE MIDDLE OF REPAIRING THE TISSUE IN YOUR FOOT. YOU'LL HAVE TO GAWK AT MARI LATER...
...YOU GEEK. ♡
I WASN'T GAWKING !!
DUDE, WHY ARE YOU ACTING SO DIFFERENT ?!!
TAP
VWAAA !!
I'VE ALWAYS BEEN LIKE THIS!
HOLD STILL AND STAY WITHIN THE RANGE OF MY HEAL PSI, WILL YOU?

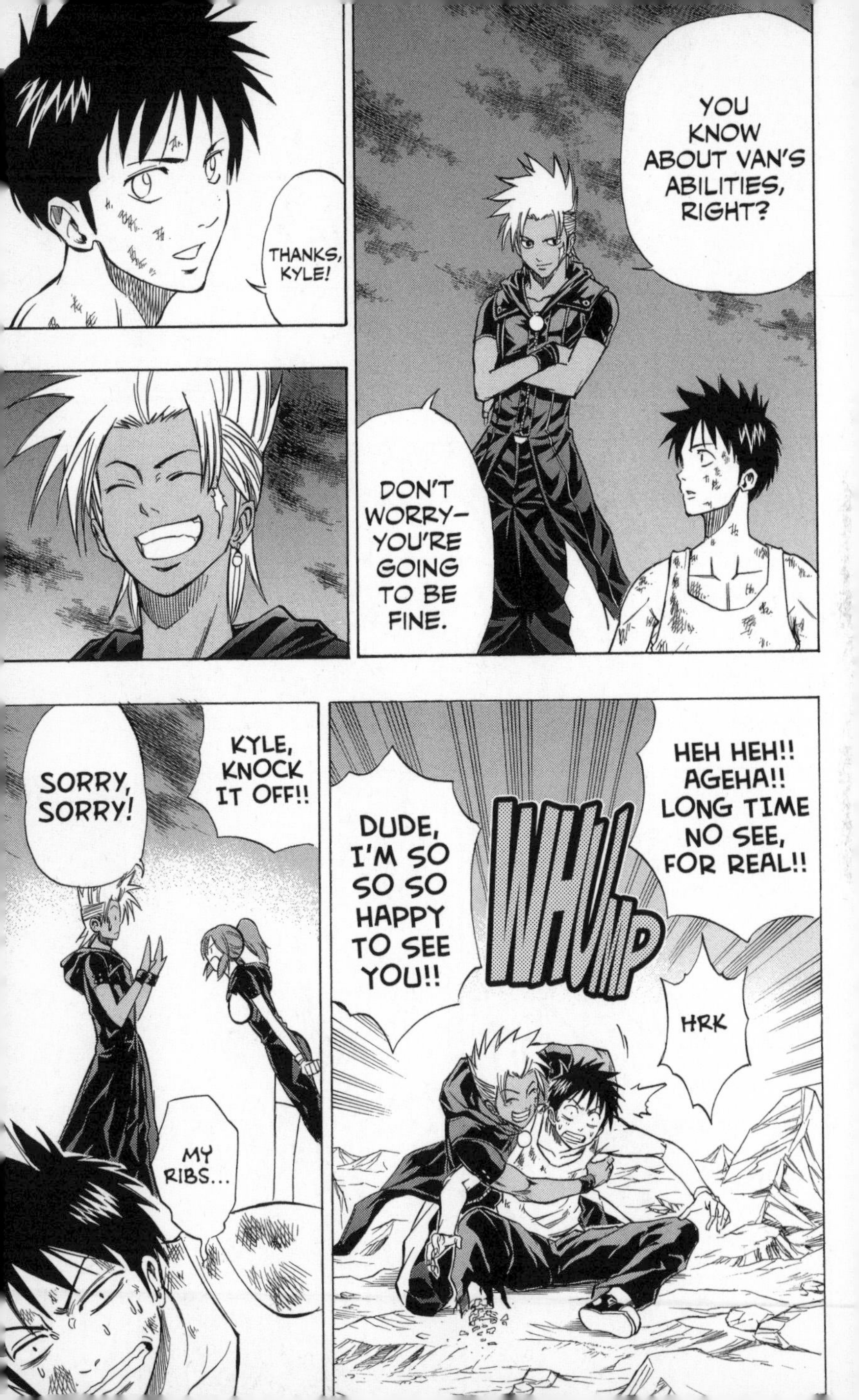

YOU KNOW ABOUT VAN'S ABILITIES, RIGHT?
DON'T WORRY— YOU'RE GOING TO BE FINE.
THANKS, KYLE!
HEH HEH!! AGEHA!! LONG TIME NO SEE, FOR REAL!!
WHUMP
DUDE, I'M SO SO SO HAPPY TO SEE YOU!!
HRK
KYLE, KNOCK IT OFF!!
SORRY, SORRY!
MY RIBS...

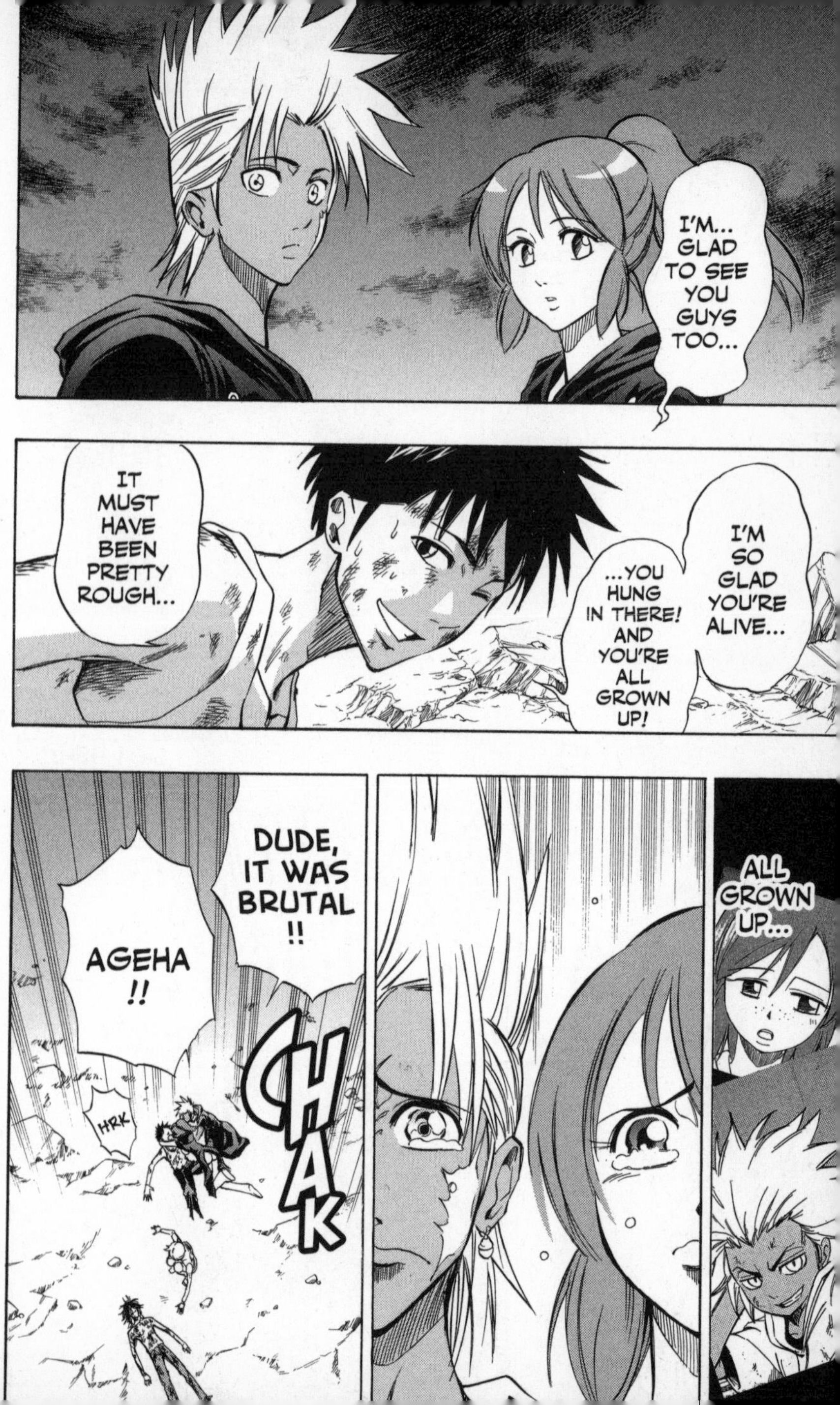
I'M... GLAD TO SEE YOU GUYS TOO...
I'M SO GLAD YOU'RE ALIVE...
...YOU HUNG IN THERE! AND YOU'RE ALL GROWN UP!
IT MUST HAVE BEEN PRETTY ROUGH...
ALL GROWN UP...
DUDE, IT WAS BRUTAL!!
AGEHA!!
CHAK
HRK

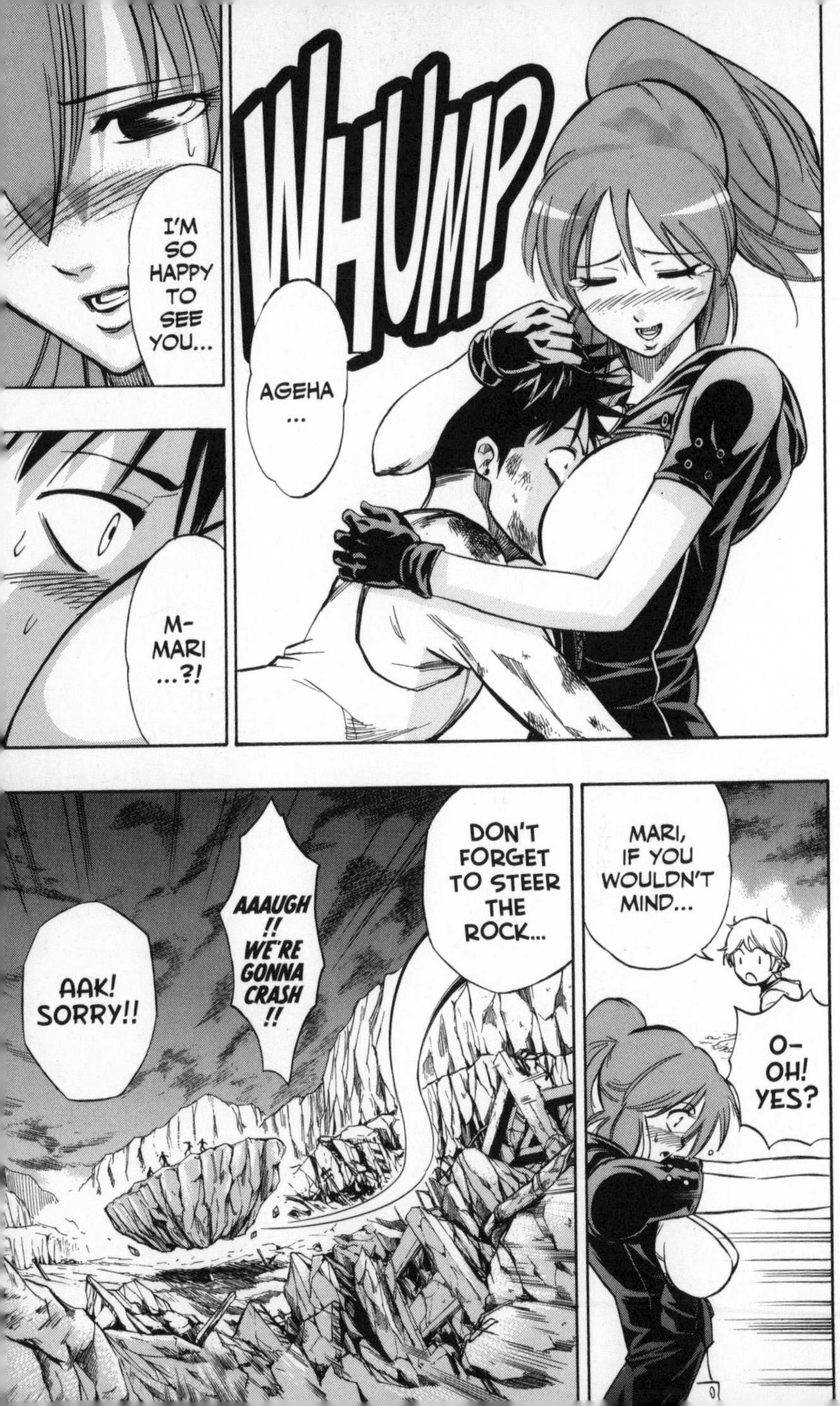
WHUMP
AGEHA...
I'M SO HAPPY TO SEE YOU...
M-MARI...?!
MARI, IF YOU WOULDN'T MIND...
O-OH! YES?
DON'T FORGET TO STEER THE ROCK...
AAAUGH!! WE'RE GONNA CRASH!!
AAK! SORRY!!

WHHHOO

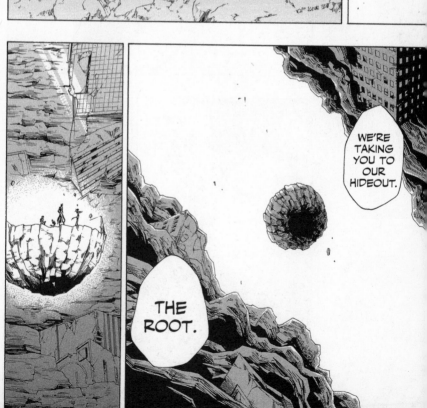

WE'RE TAKING YOU TO OUR HIDEOUT.

THE ROOT.

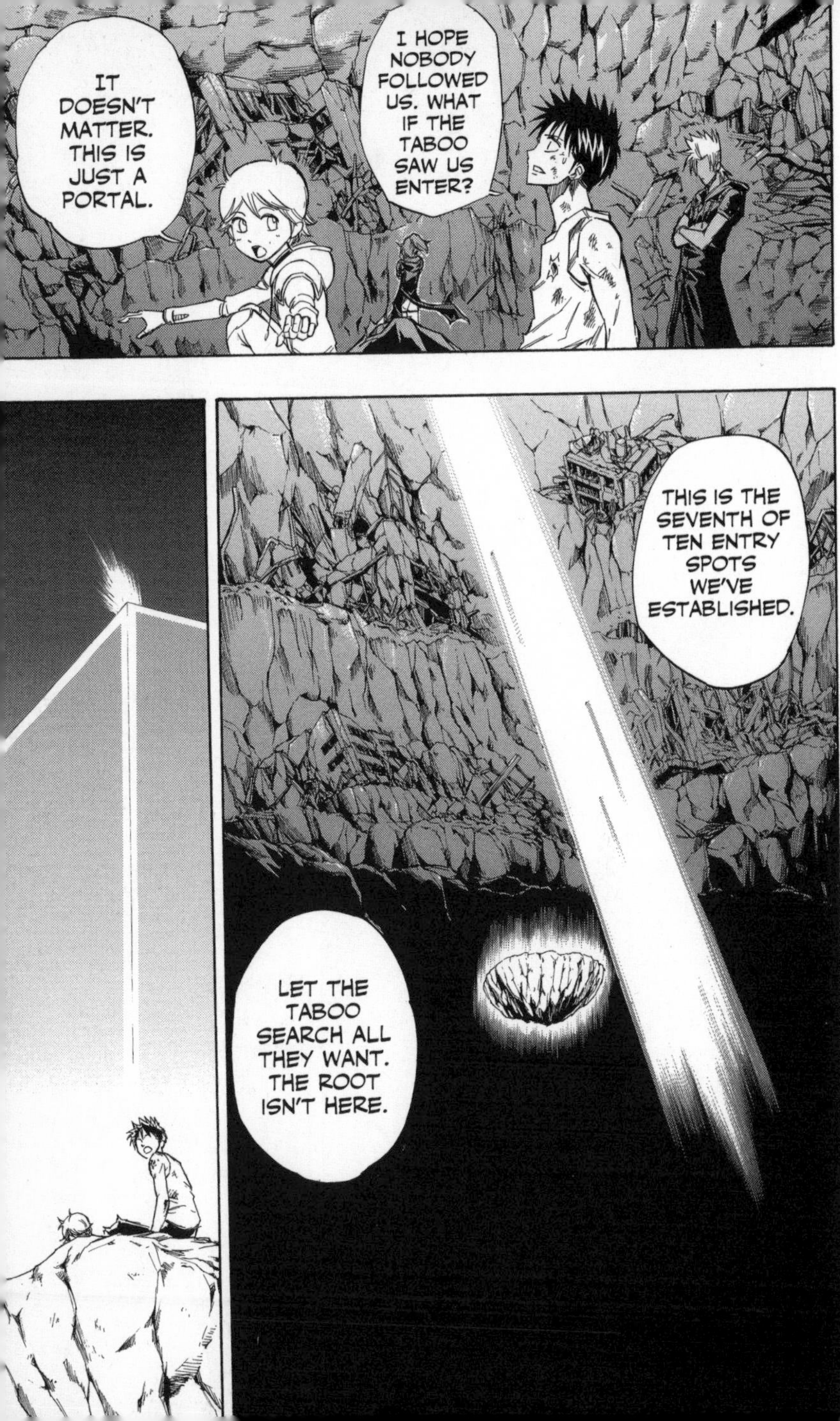
I HOPE NOBODY FOLLOWED US. WHAT IF THE TABOO SAW US ENTER?
IT DOESN'T MATTER. THIS IS JUST A PORTAL.
THIS IS THE SEVENTH OF TEN ENTRY SPOTS WE'VE ESTABLISHED.
LET THE TABOO SEARCH ALL THEY WANT. THE ROOT ISN'T HERE.

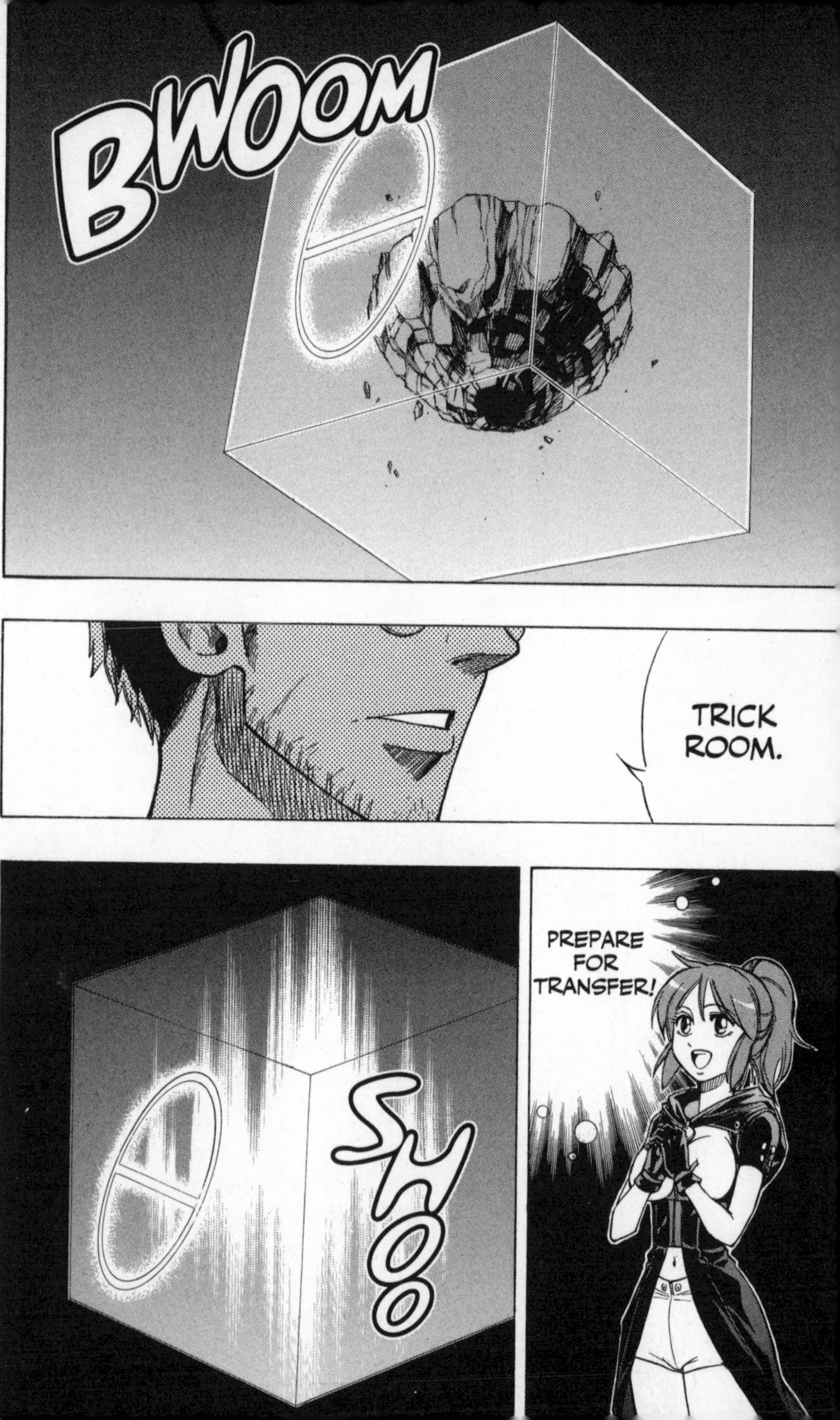
BWOOM
TRICK ROOM.
PREPARE FOR TRANSFER!
SHOO

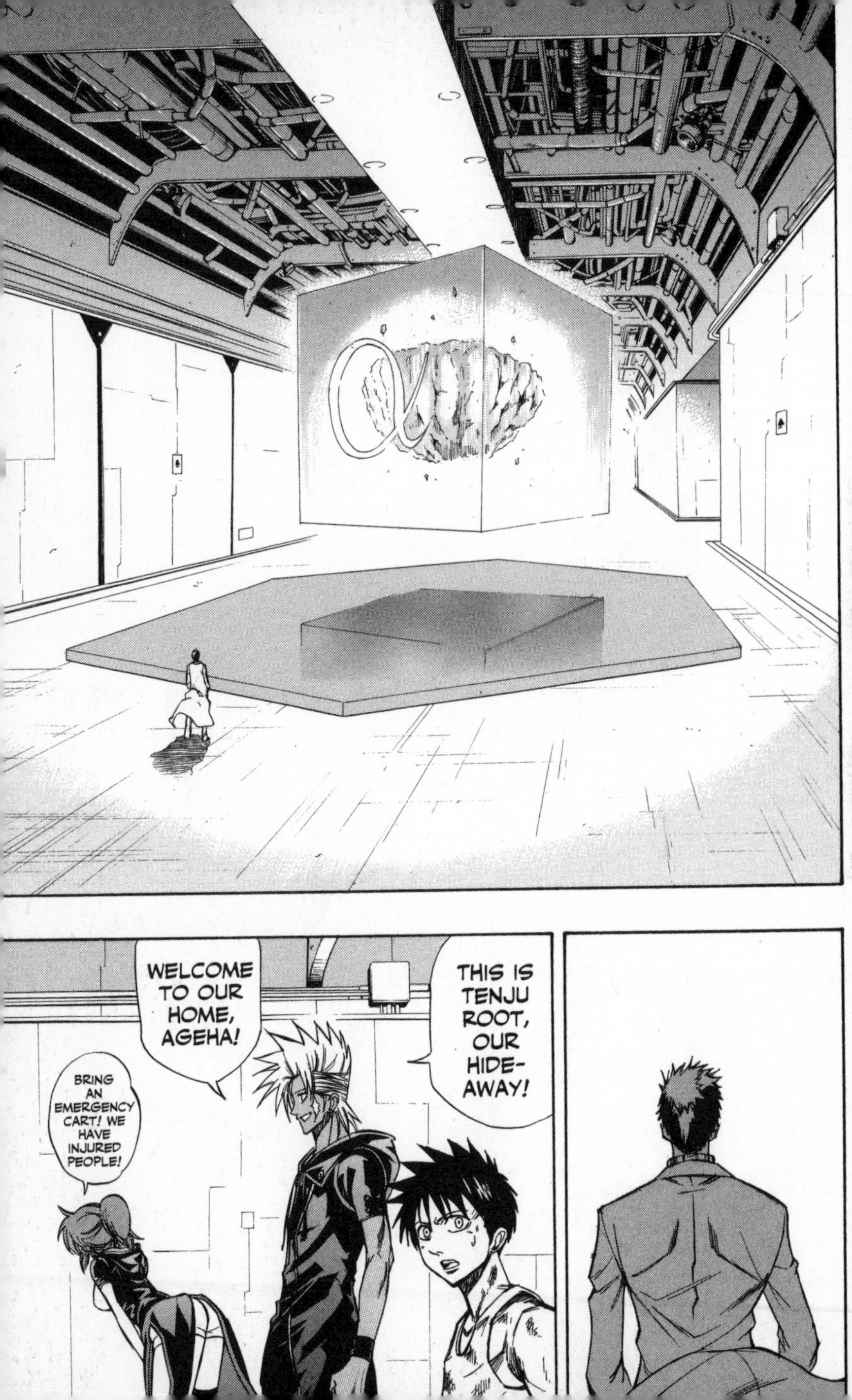
THIS IS TENJU ROOT, OUR HIDE-AWAY!
WELCOME TO OUR HOME, AGEHA!
BRING AN EMERGENCY CART! WE HAVE INJURED PEOPLE!

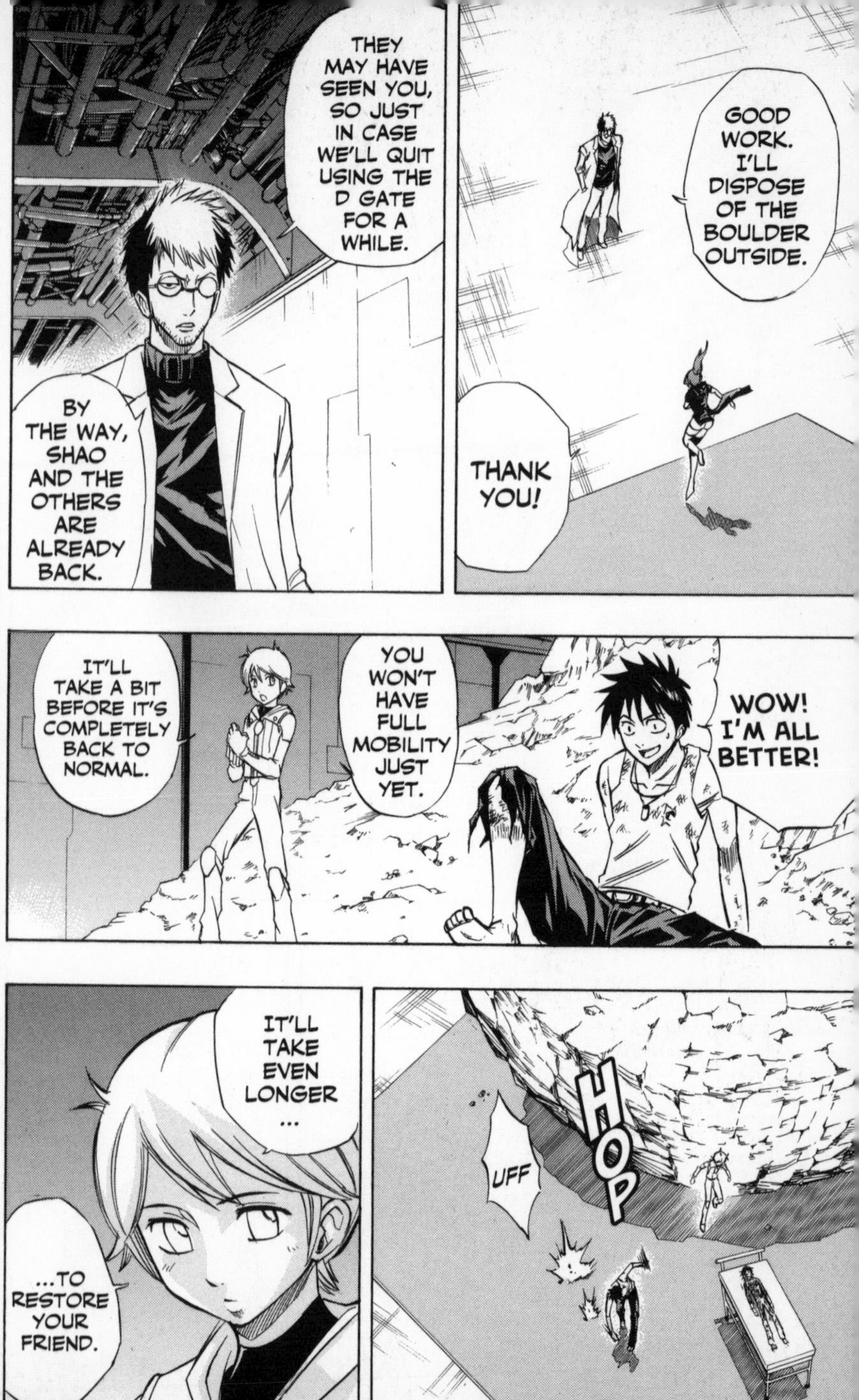
GOOD WORK. I'LL DISPOSE OF THE BOULDER OUTSIDE.
THANK YOU!
THEY MAY HAVE SEEN YOU, SO JUST IN CASE WE'LL QUIT USING THE D GATE FOR A WHILE.
BY THE WAY, SHAO AND THE OTHERS ARE ALREADY BACK.
WOW! I'M ALL BETTER!
YOU WON'T HAVE FULL MOBILITY JUST YET.
IT'LL TAKE A BIT BEFORE IT'S COMPLETELY BACK TO NORMAL.
HOP
UFF
IT'LL TAKE EVEN LONGER ...
...TO RESTORE YOUR FRIEND.

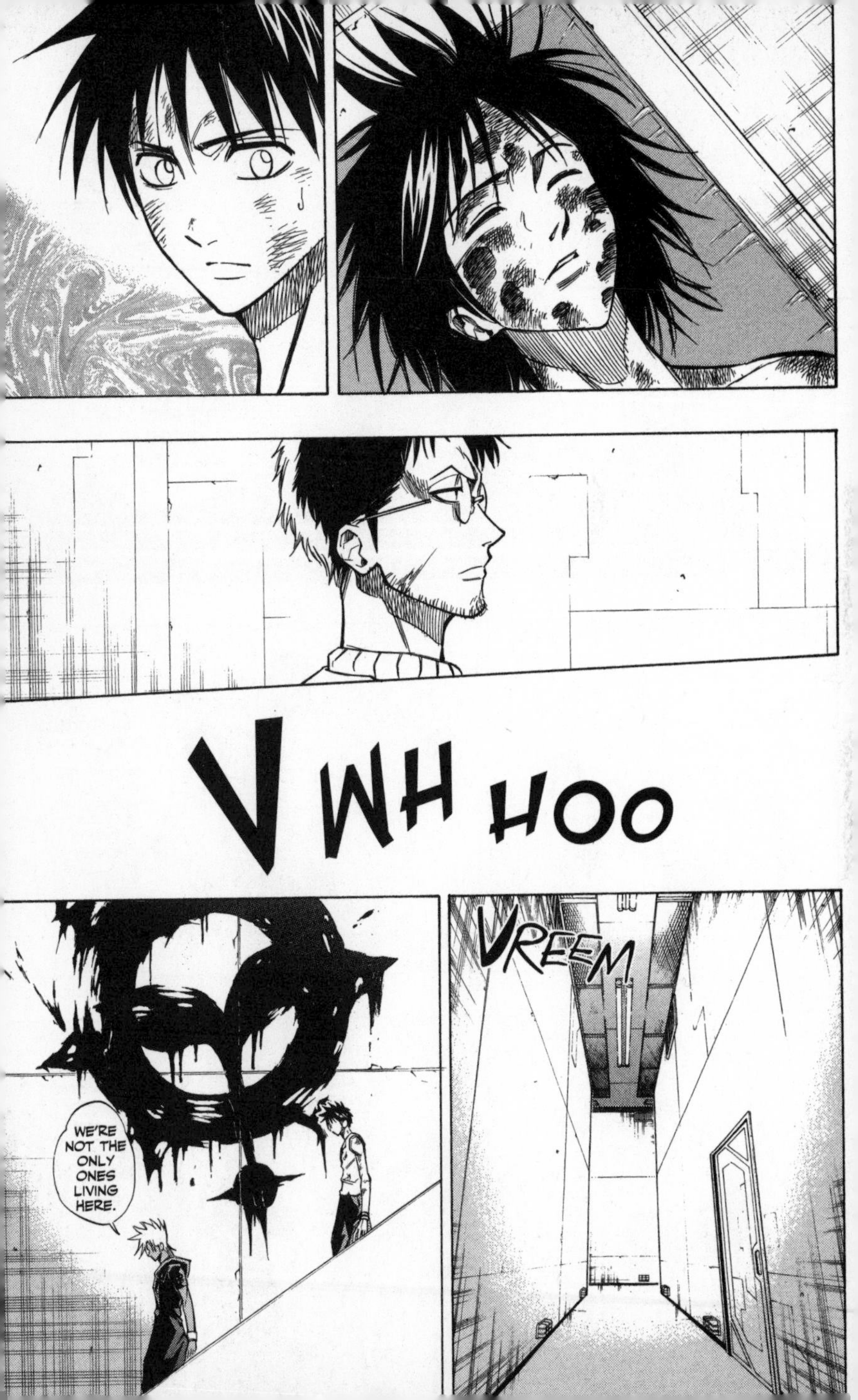
VWHHOO
VREEM
WE'RE NOT THE ONLY ONES LIVING HERE.

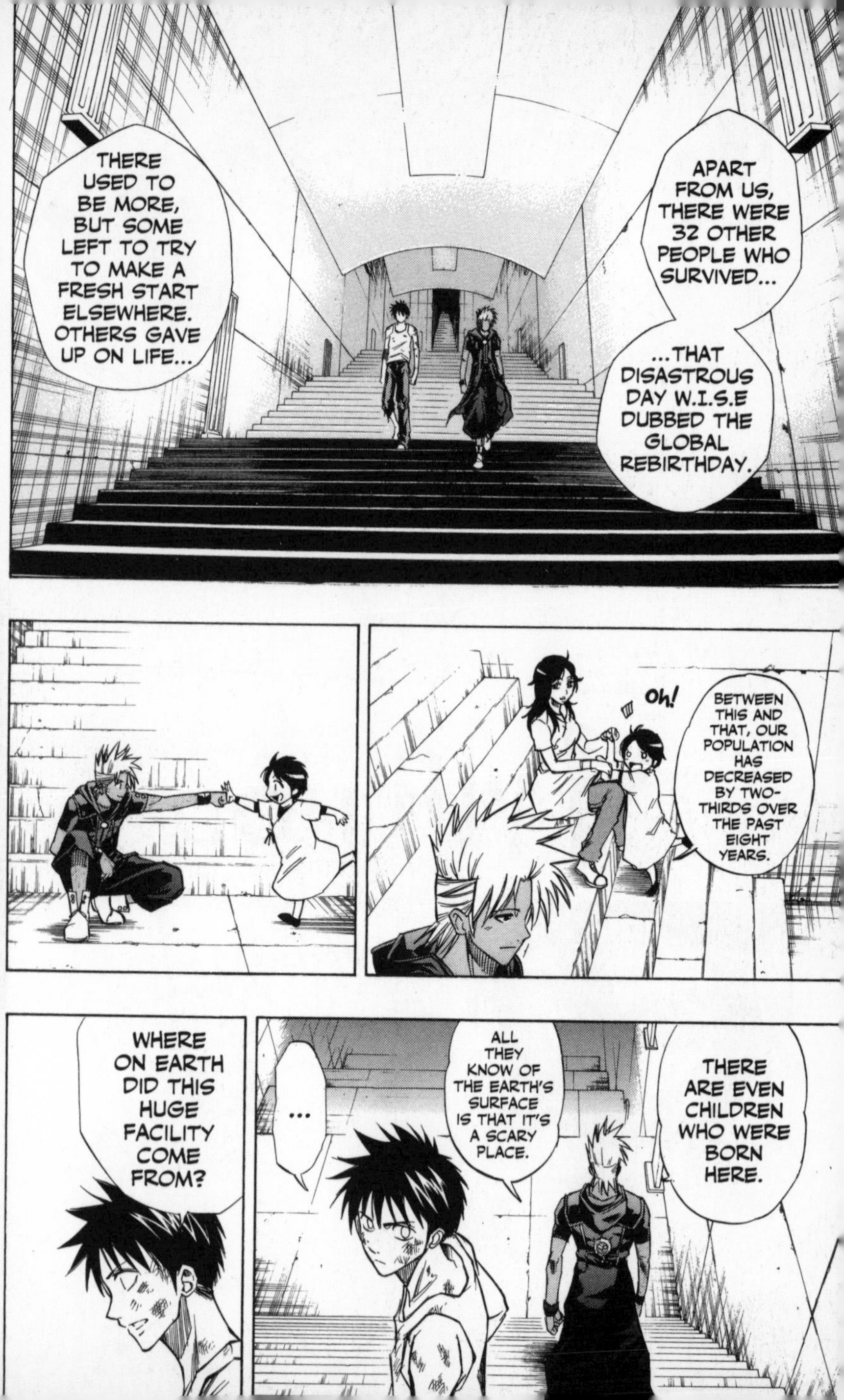
APART FROM US, THERE WERE 32 OTHER PEOPLE WHO SURVIVED...
...THAT DISASTROUS DAY W.I.S.E DUBBED THE GLOBAL REBIRTHDAY.
THERE USED TO BE MORE, BUT SOME LEFT TO TRY TO MAKE A FRESH START ELSEWHERE. OTHERS GAVE UP ON LIFE...
Oh!
BETWEEN THIS AND THAT, OUR POPULATION HAS DECREASED BY TWO-THIRDS OVER THE PAST EIGHT YEARS.
THERE ARE EVEN CHILDREN WHO WERE BORN HERE.
ALL THEY KNOW OF THE EARTH'S SURFACE IS THAT IT'S A SCARY PLACE.
...
WHERE ON EARTH DID THIS HUGE FACILITY COME FROM?

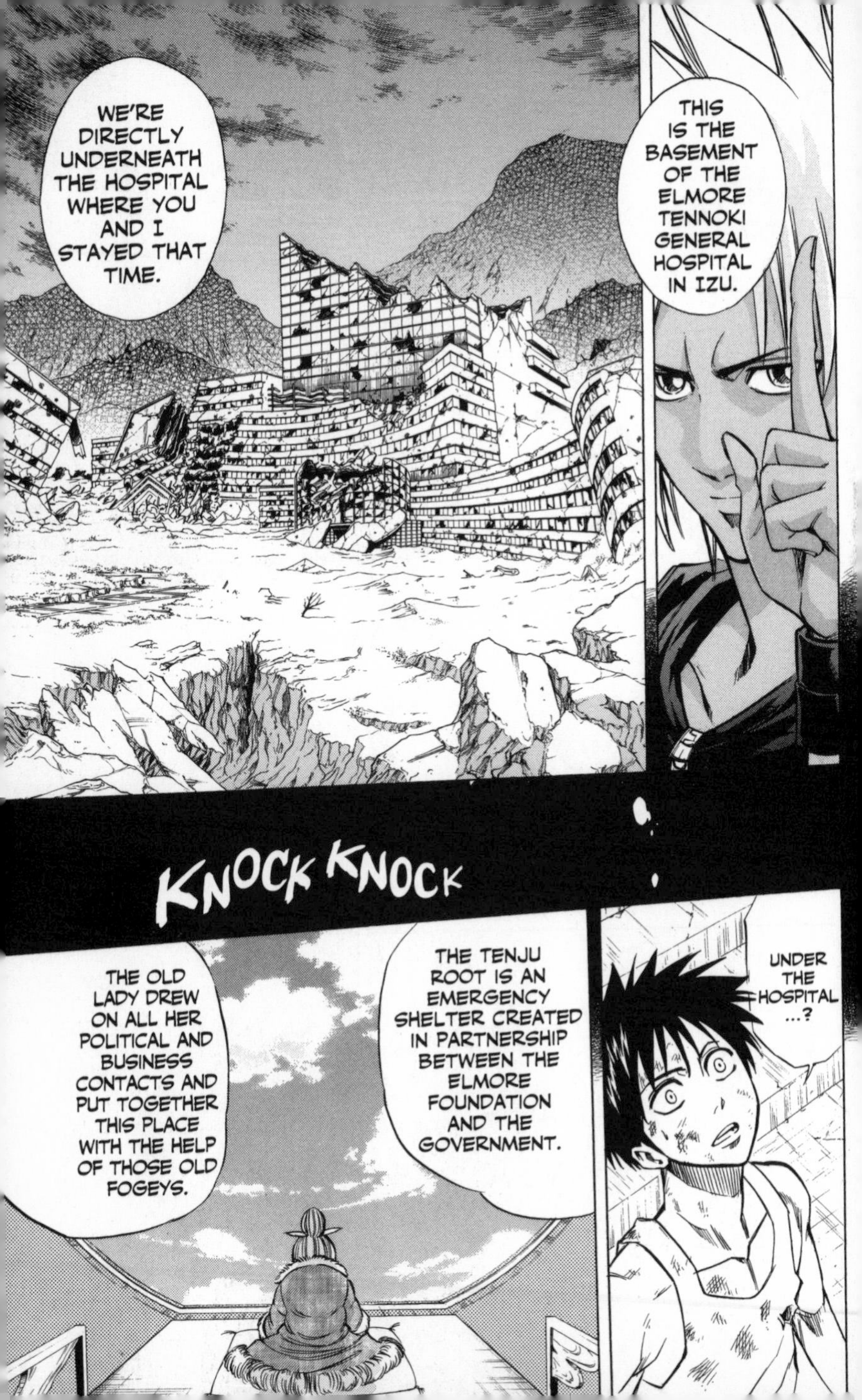
THIS IS THE BASEMENT OF THE ELMORE TENNOKI GENERAL HOSPITAL IN IZU.
WE'RE DIRECTLY UNDERNEATH THE HOSPITAL WHERE YOU AND I STAYED THAT TIME.
KNOCK KNOCK
UNDER THE HOSPITAL ...?
THE TENJU ROOT IS AN EMERGENCY SHELTER CREATED IN PARTNERSHIP BETWEEN THE ELMORE FOUNDATION AND THE GOVERNMENT.
THE OLD LADY DREW ON ALL HER POLITICAL AND BUSINESS CONTACTS AND PUT TOGETHER THIS PLACE WITH THE HELP OF THOSE OLD FOGEYS.

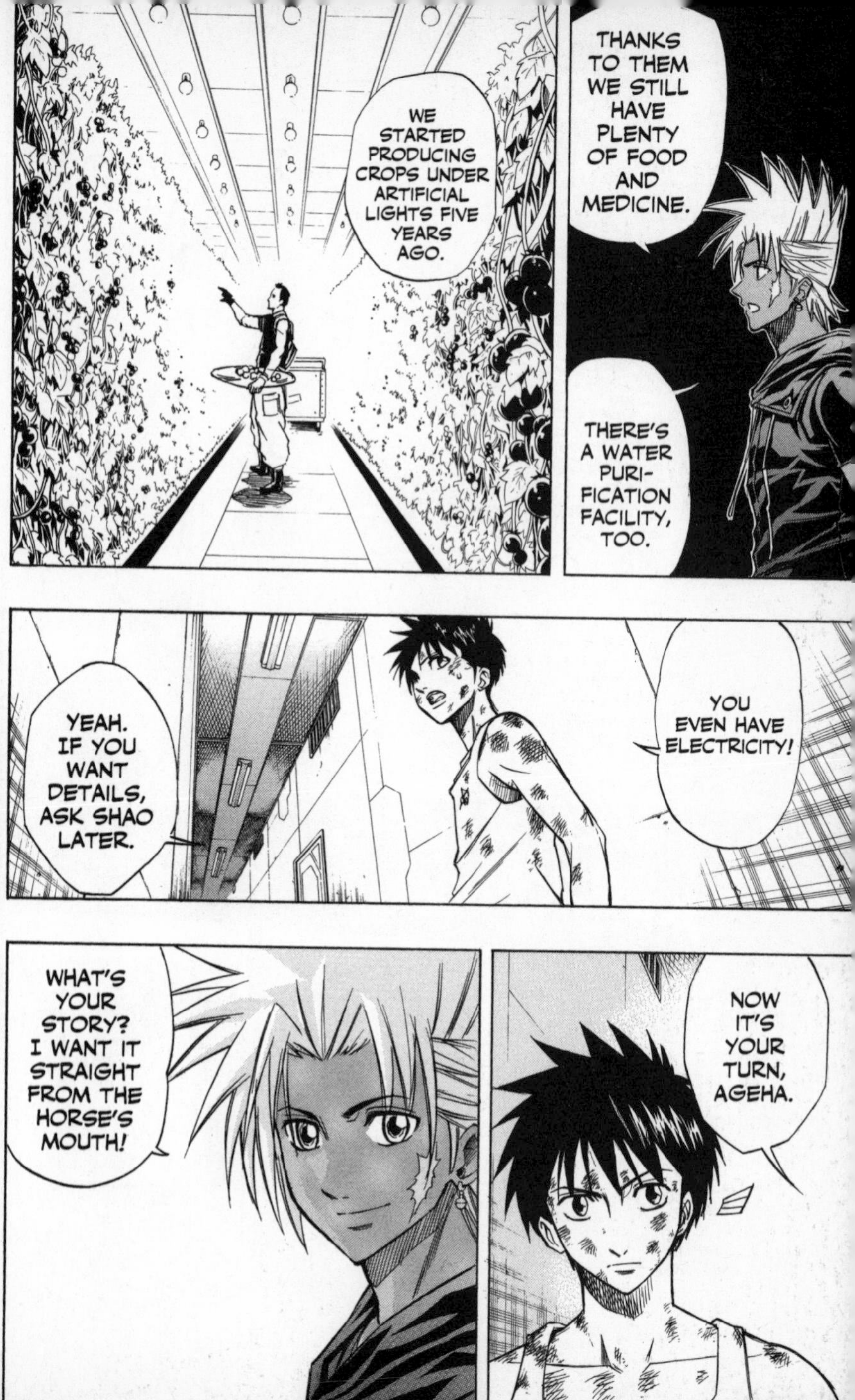
THANKS TO THEM WE STILL HAVE PLENTY OF FOOD AND MEDICINE.
THERE'S A WATER PURI-FICATION FACILITY, TOO.
WE STARTED PRODUCING CROPS UNDER ARTIFICIAL LIGHTS FIVE YEARS AGO.
YOU EVEN HAVE ELECTRICITY!
YEAH. IF YOU WANT DETAILS, ASK SHAO LATER.
NOW IT'S YOUR TURN, AGEHA.
WHAT'S YOUR STORY? I WANT IT STRAIGHT FROM THE HORSE'S MOUTH!

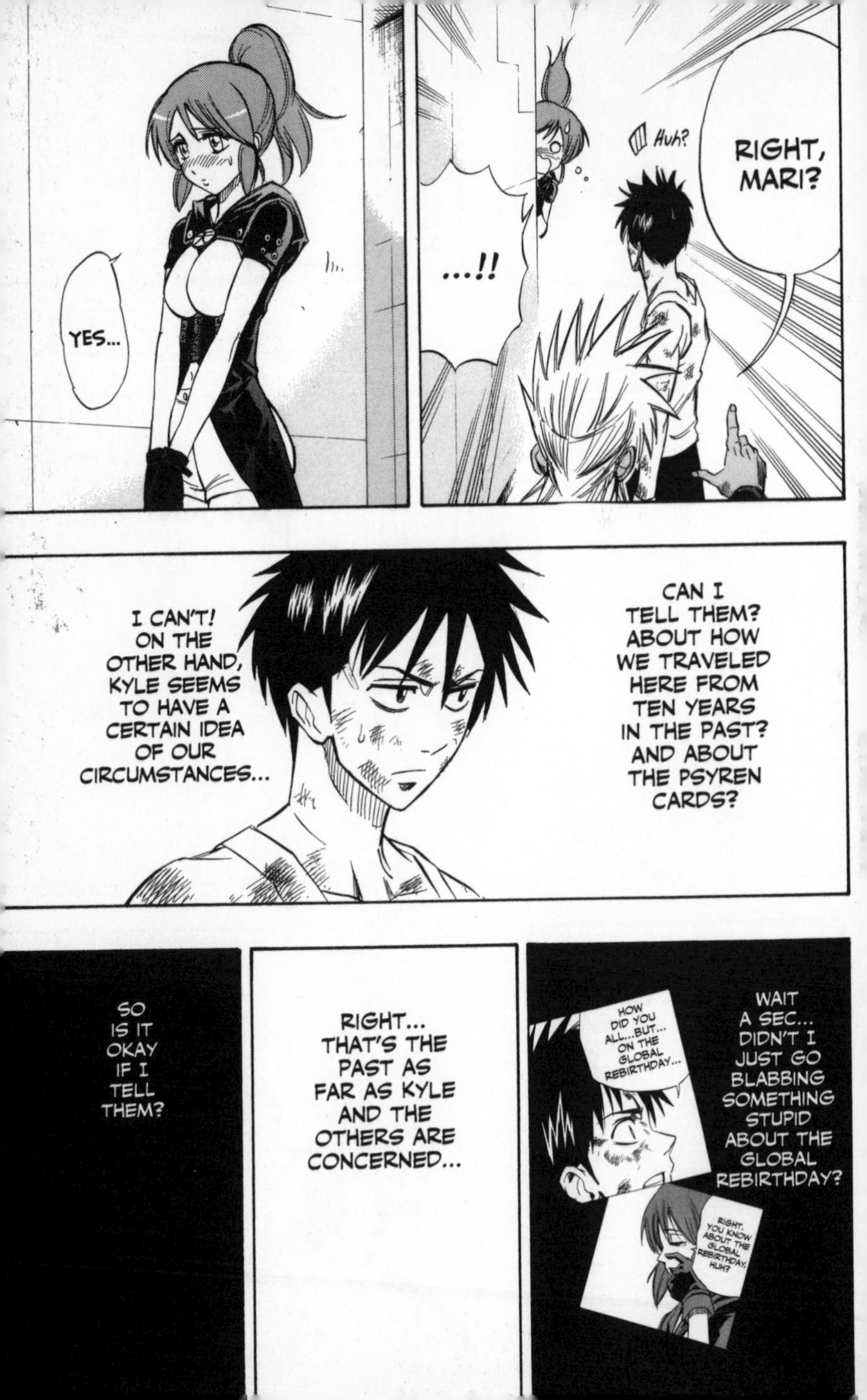

RIGHT, MARI?
Huh?
...!!
YES...
CAN I TELL THEM? ABOUT HOW WE TRAVELED HERE FROM TEN YEARS IN THE PAST? AND ABOUT THE PSYREN CARDS?
I CAN'T! ON THE OTHER HAND, KYLE SEEMS TO HAVE A CERTAIN IDEA OF OUR CIRCUMSTANCES...
WAIT A SEC... DIDN'T I JUST GO BLABBING SOMETHING STUPID ABOUT THE GLOBAL REBIRTHDAY?
HOW DID YOU ALL...BUT... ON THE GLOBAL REBIRTHDAY...
RIGHT. YOU KNOW ABOUT THE GLOBAL REBIRTHDAY, HUH?
RIGHT... THAT'S THE PAST AS FAR AS KYLE AND THE OTHERS ARE CONCERNED...
SO IS IT OKAY IF I TELL THEM?

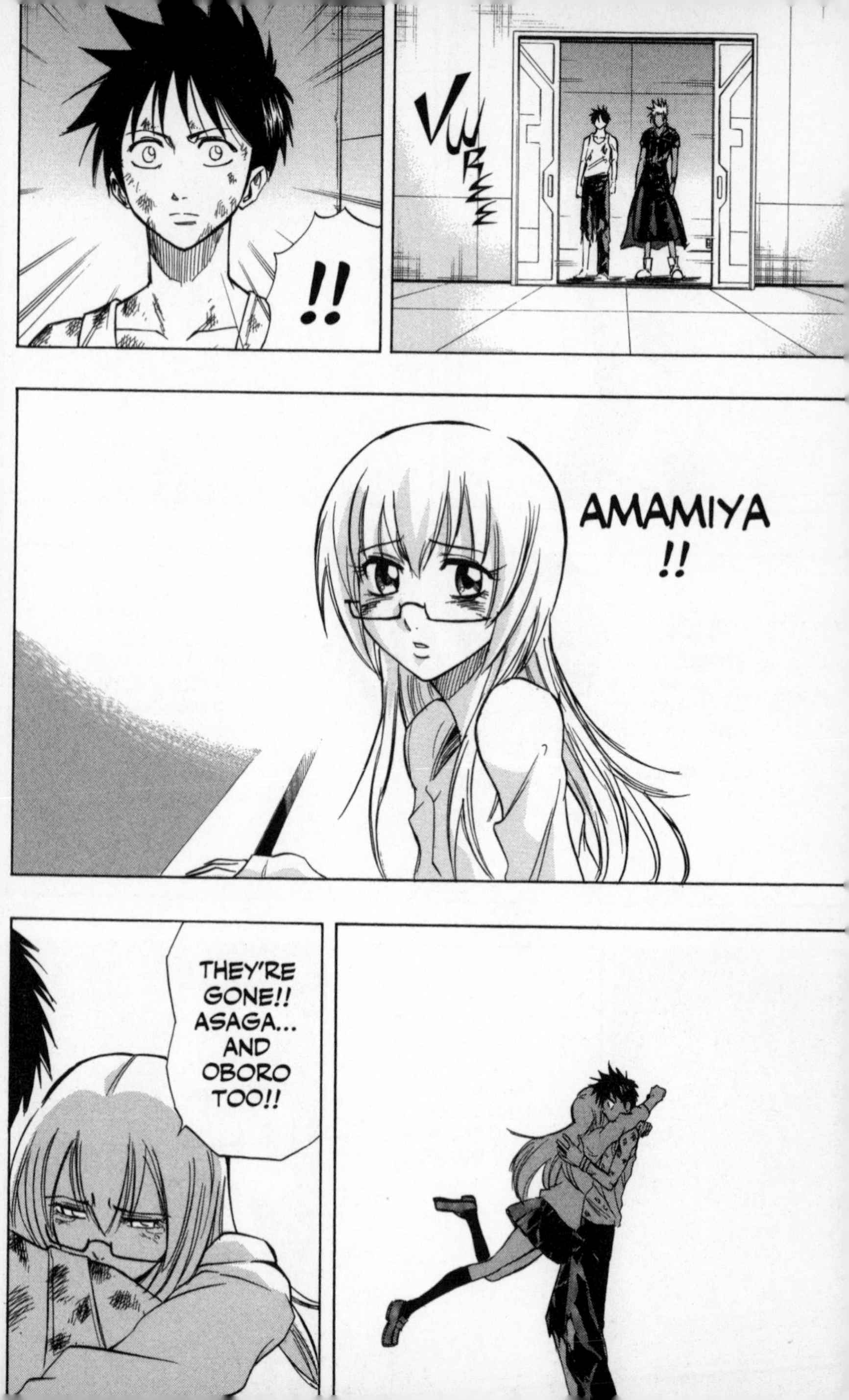
VWREE
!!
AMAMIYA !!
THEY'RE GONE!! ASAGA... AND OBORO TOO!!

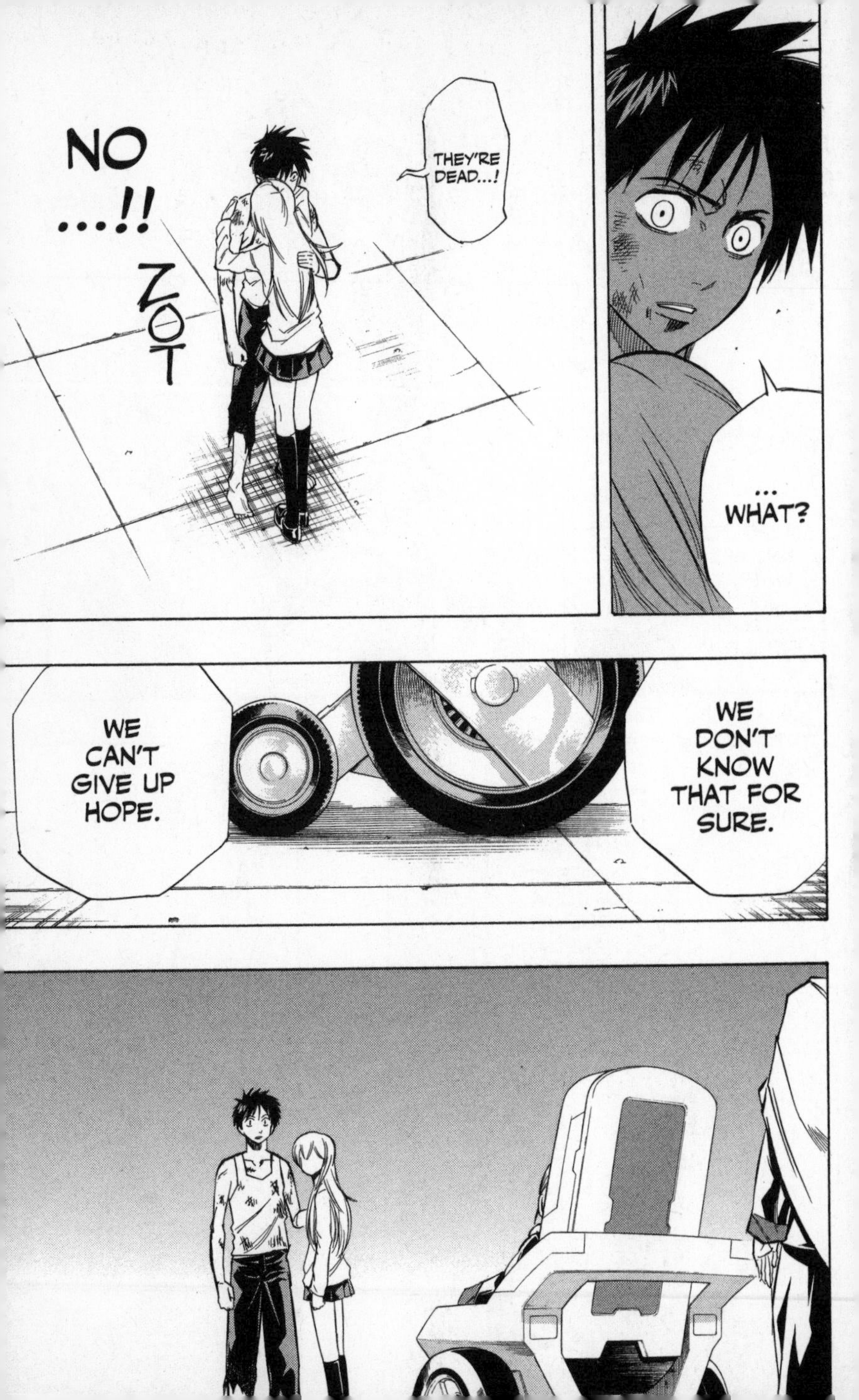
... WHAT?
THEY'RE DEAD...!
NO ...!!
ZOT
WE DON'T KNOW THAT FOR SURE.
WE CAN'T GIVE UP HOPE.

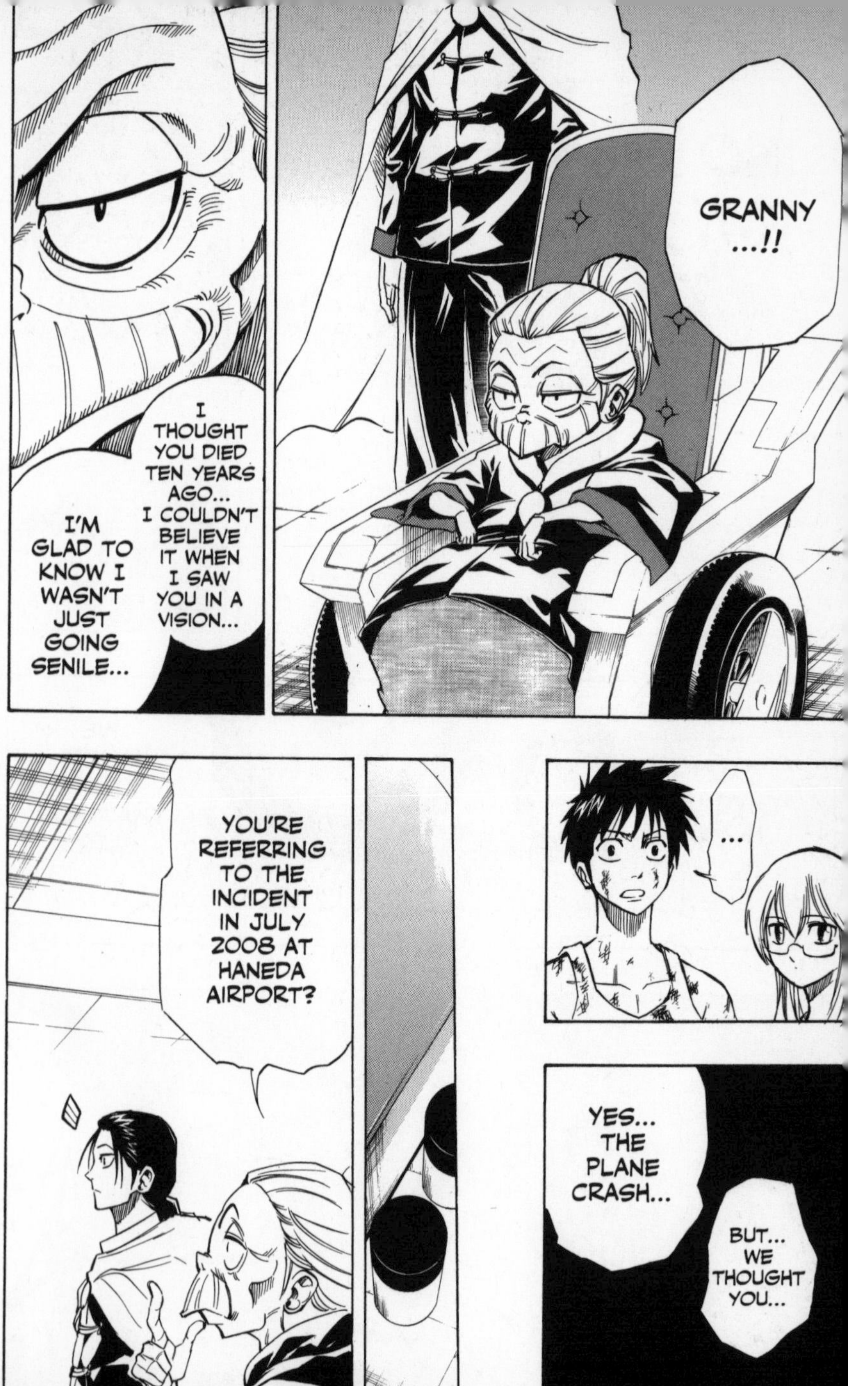
GRANNY ...!!
I THOUGHT YOU DIED TEN YEARS AGO... I COULDN'T BELIEVE IT WHEN I SAW YOU IN A VISION...
I'M GLAD TO KNOW I WASN'T JUST GOING SENILE...
...
YES... THE PLANE CRASH...
BUT... WE THOUGHT YOU...
YOU'RE REFERRING TO THE INCIDENT IN JULY 2008 AT HANEDA AIRPORT?

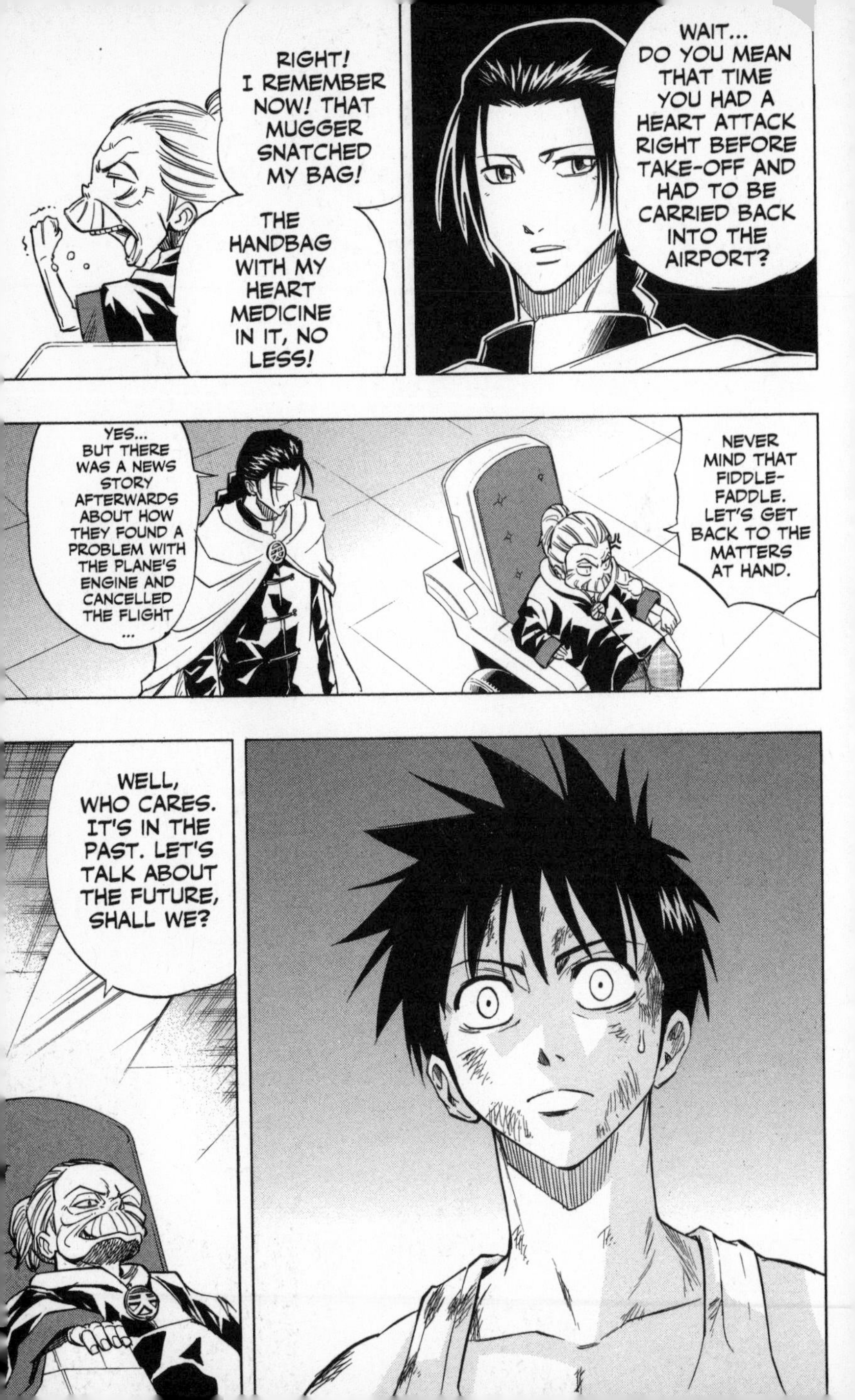
WAIT... DO YOU MEAN THAT TIME YOU HAD A HEART ATTACK RIGHT BEFORE TAKE-OFF AND HAD TO BE CARRIED BACK INTO THE AIRPORT?
RIGHT! I REMEMBER NOW! THAT MUGGER SNATCHED MY BAG!
THE HANDBAG WITH MY HEART MEDICINE IN IT, NO LESS!
NEVER MIND THAT FIDDLE-FADDLE. LET'S GET BACK TO THE MATTERS AT HAND.
YES... BUT THERE WAS A NEWS STORY AFTERWARDS ABOUT HOW THEY FOUND A PROBLEM WITH THE PLANE'S ENGINE AND CANCELLED THE FLIGHT ...
WELL, WHO CARES. IT'S IN THE PAST. LET'S TALK ABOUT THE FUTURE, SHALL WE?

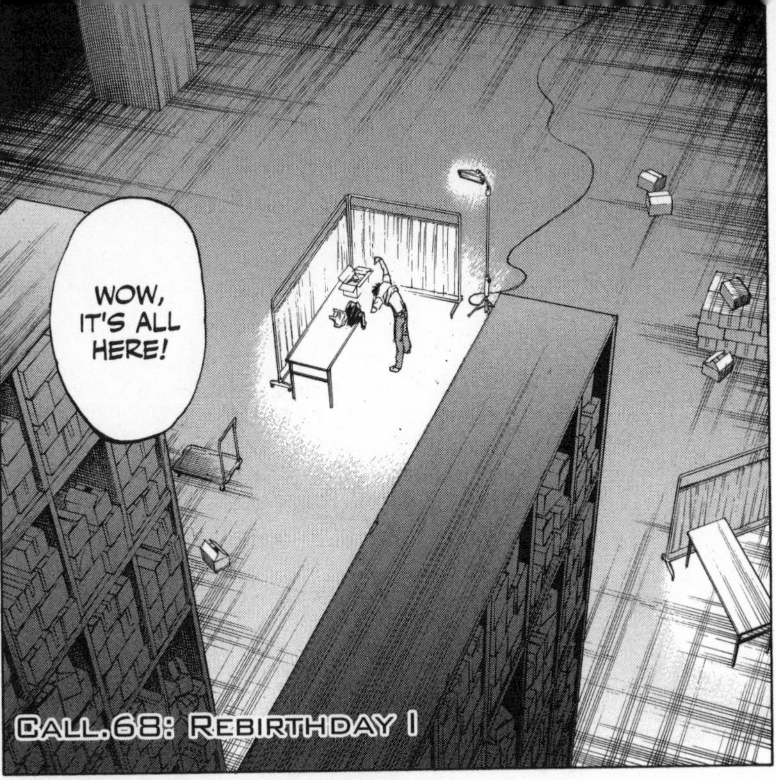
WOW, IT'S ALL HERE!
CALL.68: REBIRTHDAY 1

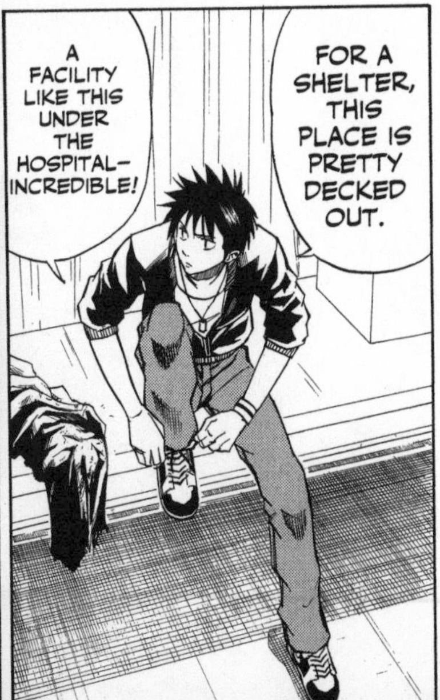
FOR A SHELTER, THIS PLACE IS PRETTY DECKED OUT.
A FACILITY LIKE THIS UNDER THE HOSPITAL—INCREDIBLE!

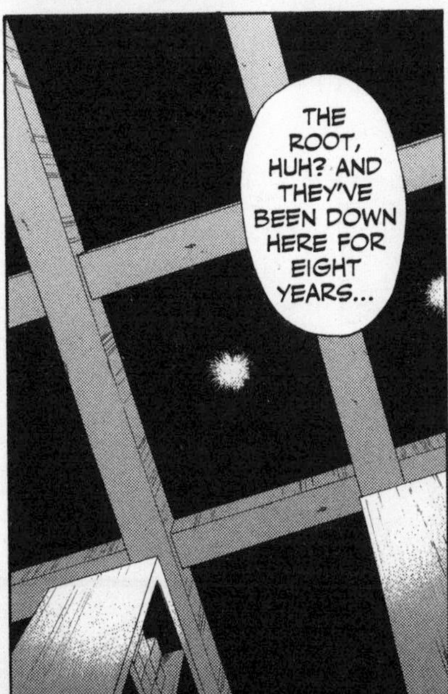
THE ROOT, HUH? AND THEY'VE BEEN DOWN HERE FOR EIGHT YEARS...

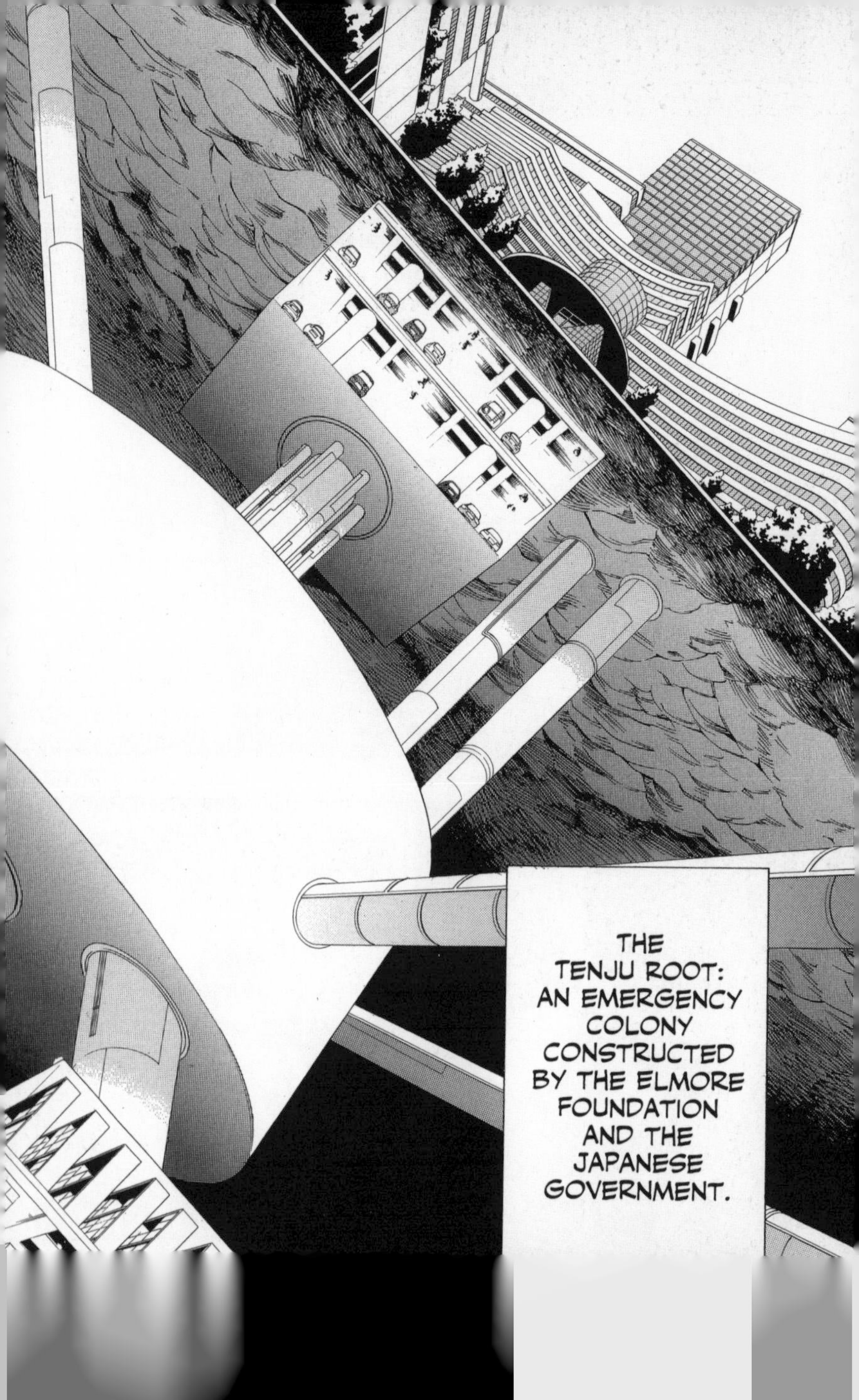
THE TENJU ROOT: AN EMERGENCY COLONY CONSTRUCTED BY THE ELMORE FOUNDATION AND THE JAPANESE GOVERNMENT.

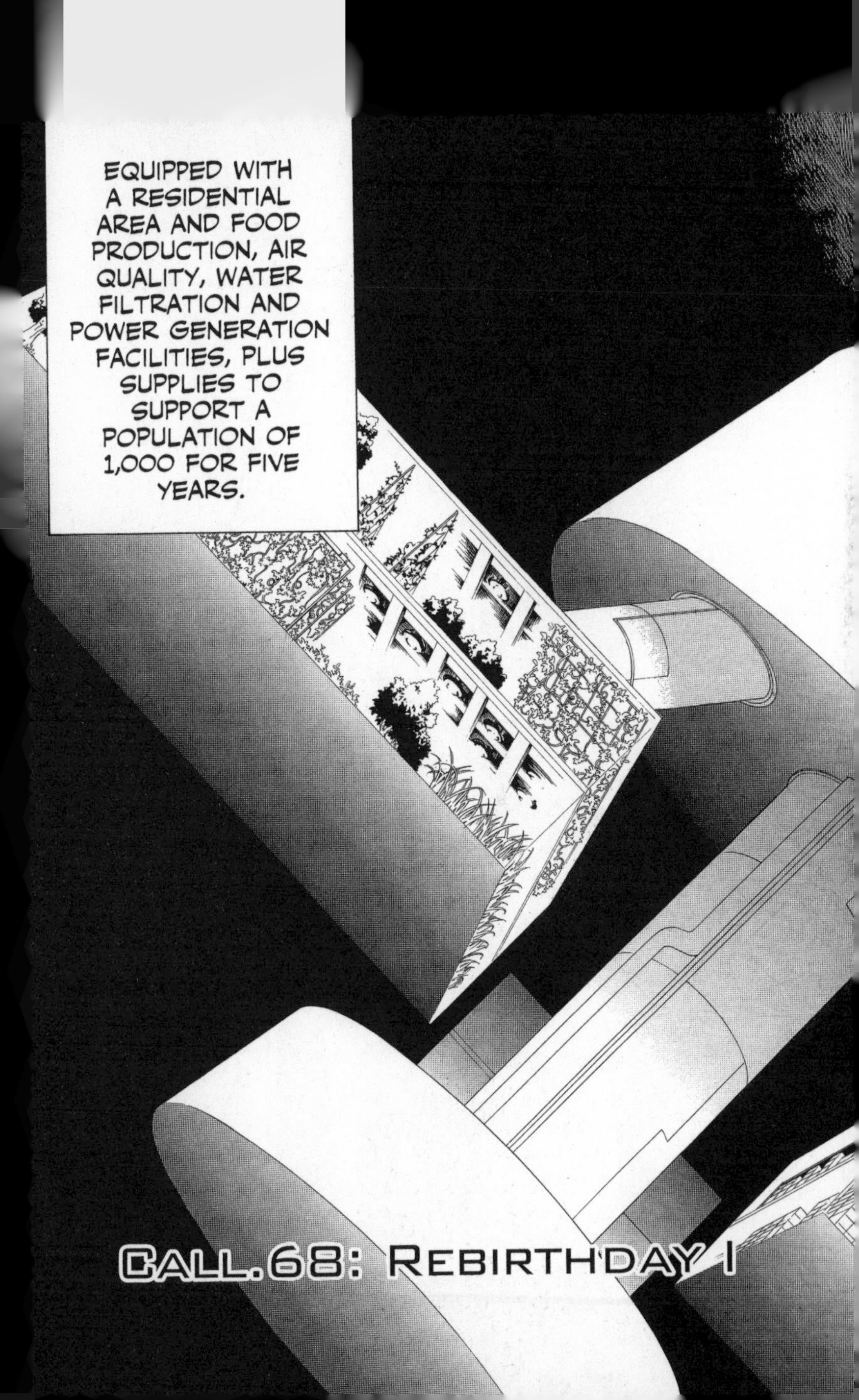
EQUIPPED WITH A RESIDENTIAL AREA AND FOOD PRODUCTION, AIR QUALITY, WATER FILTRATION AND POWER GENERATION FACILITIES, PLUS SUPPLIES TO SUPPORT A POPULATION OF 1,000 FOR FIVE YEARS.
CALL.68: REBIRTHDAY I

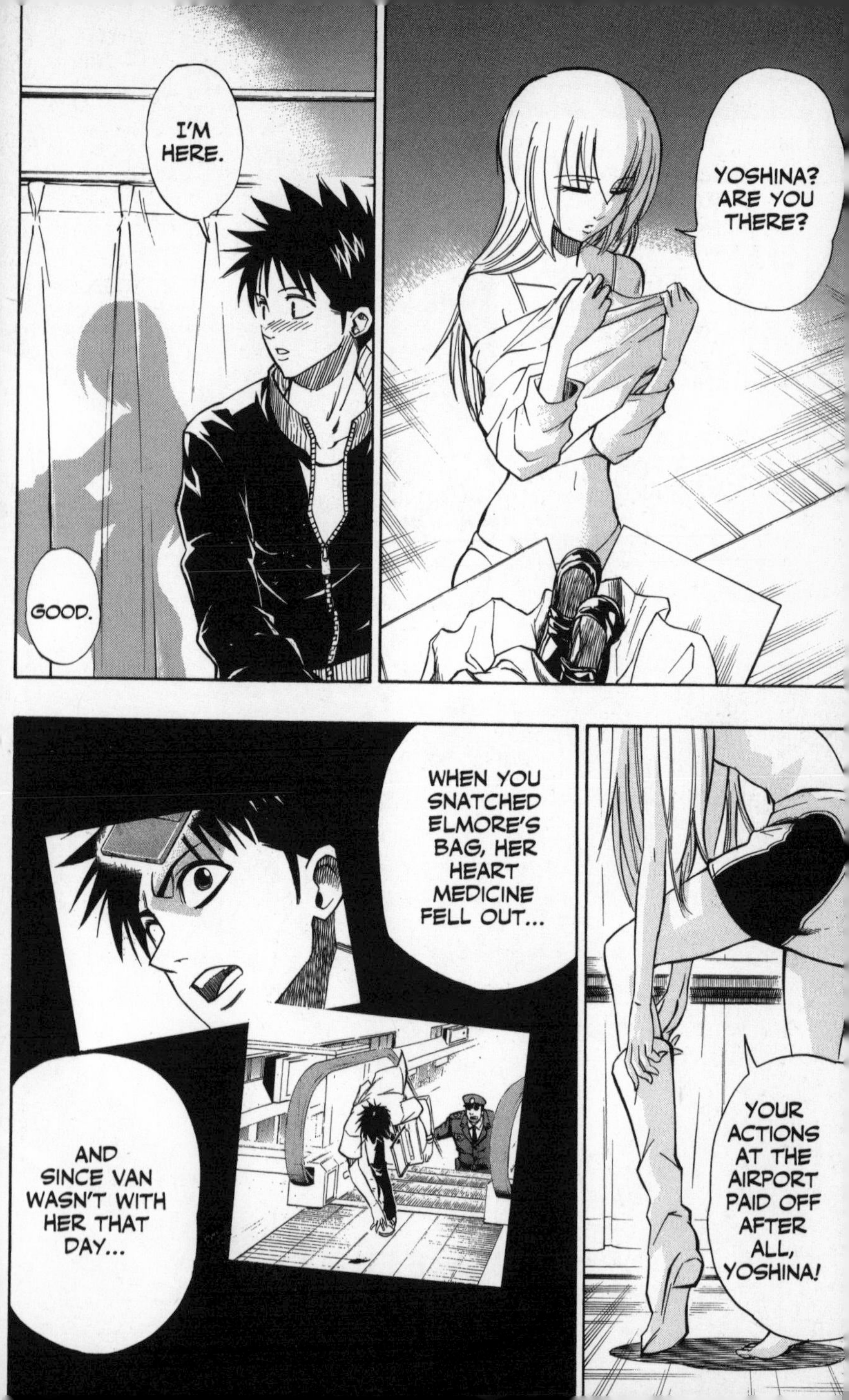
YOSHINA? ARE YOU THERE?
I'M HERE.
GOOD.
YOUR ACTIONS AT THE AIRPORT PAID OFF AFTER ALL, YOSHINA!
WHEN YOU SNATCHED ELMORE'S BAG, HER HEART MEDICINE FELL OUT...
AND SINCE VAN WASN'T WITH HER THAT DAY...

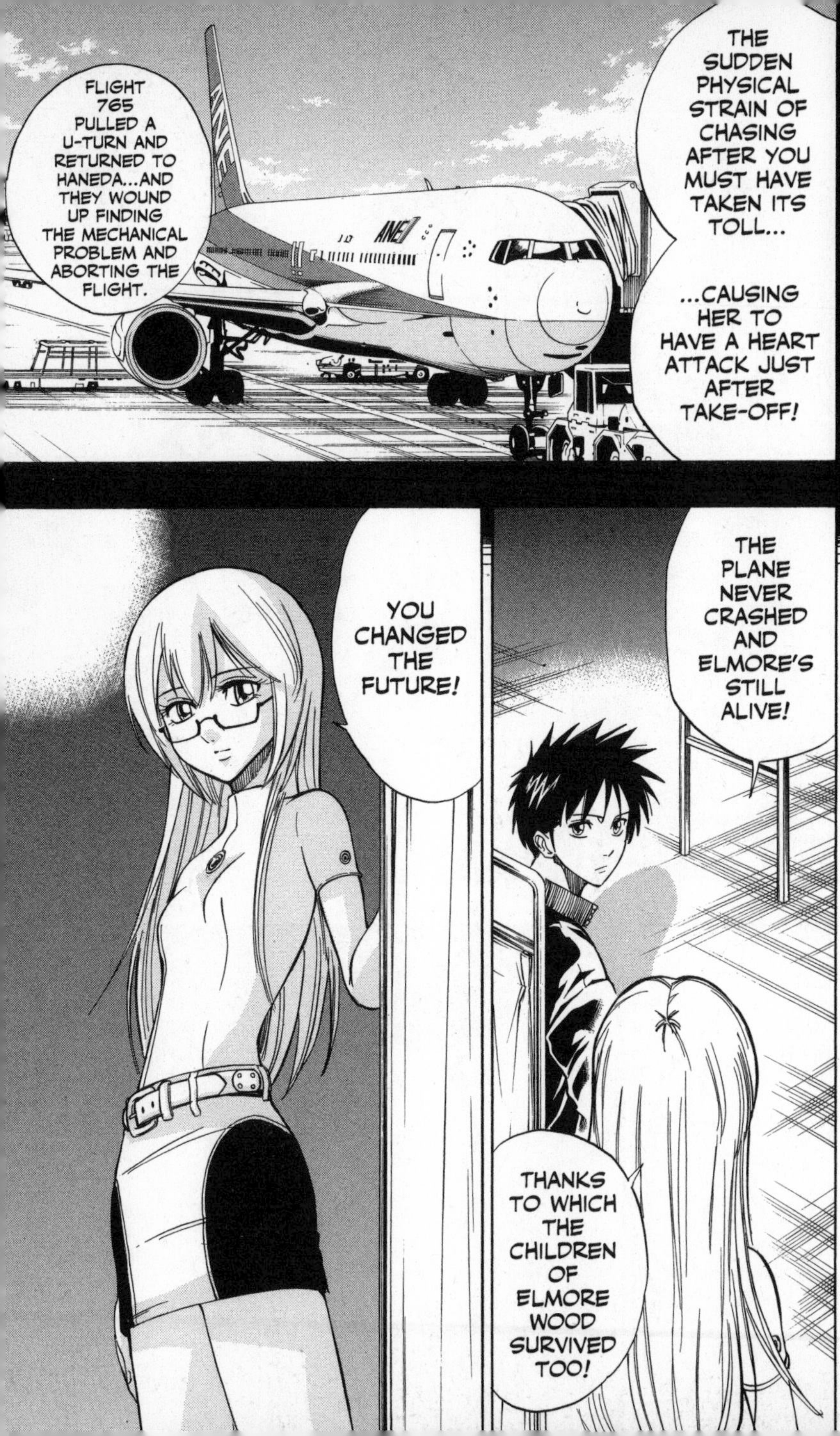
THE SUDDEN PHYSICAL STRAIN OF CHASING AFTER YOU MUST HAVE TAKEN ITS TOLL...
...CAUSING HER TO HAVE A HEART ATTACK JUST AFTER TAKE-OFF!
FLIGHT 765 PULLED A U-TURN AND RETURNED TO HANEDA...AND THEY WOUND UP FINDING THE MECHANICAL PROBLEM AND ABORTING THE FLIGHT.
THE PLANE NEVER CRASHED AND ELMORE'S STILL ALIVE!
THANKS TO WHICH THE CHILDREN OF ELMORE WOOD SURVIVED TOO!
YOU CHANGED THE FUTURE!

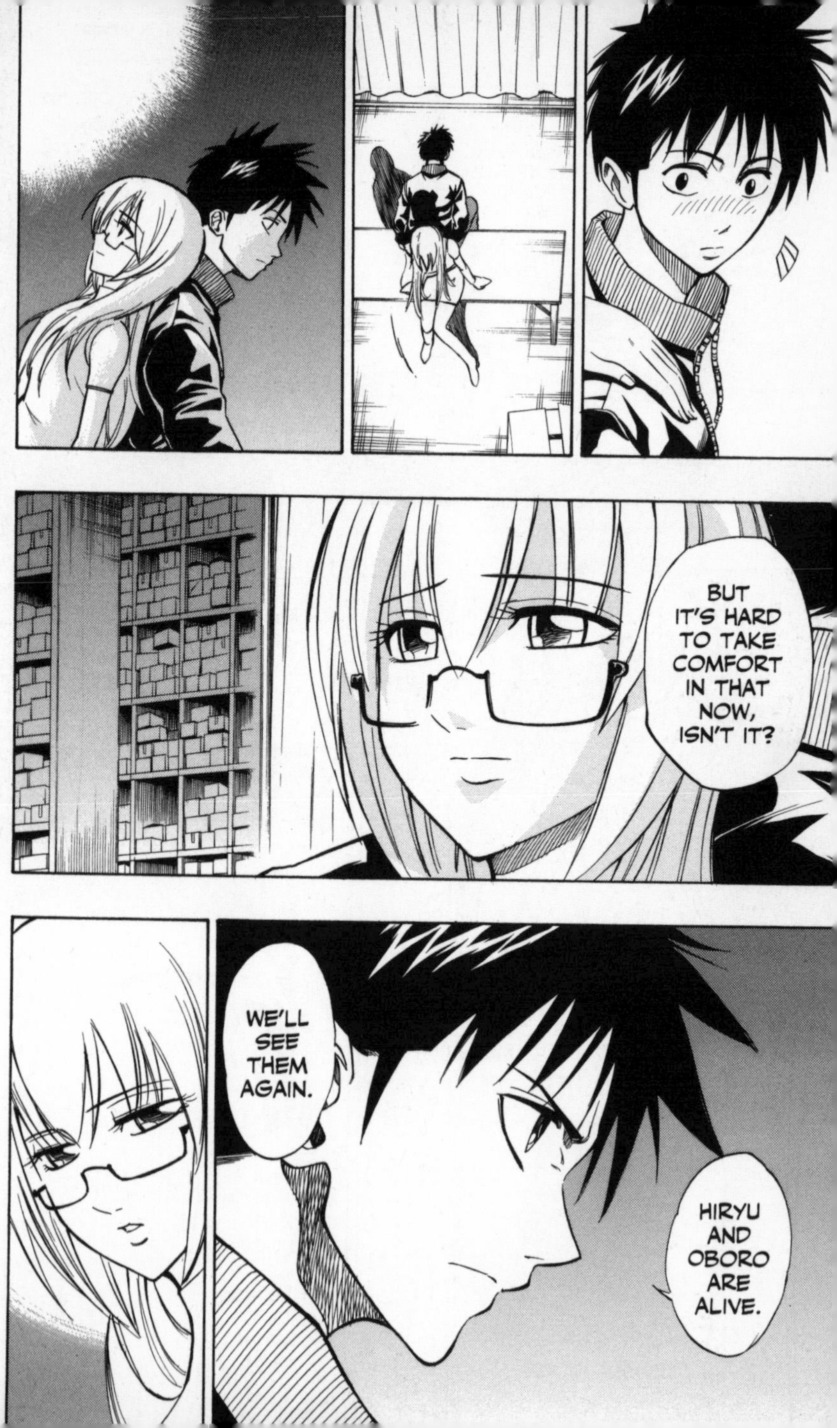
BUT IT'S HARD TO TAKE COMFORT IN THAT NOW, ISN'T IT?
HIRYU AND OBORO ARE ALIVE.
WE'LL SEE THEM AGAIN.

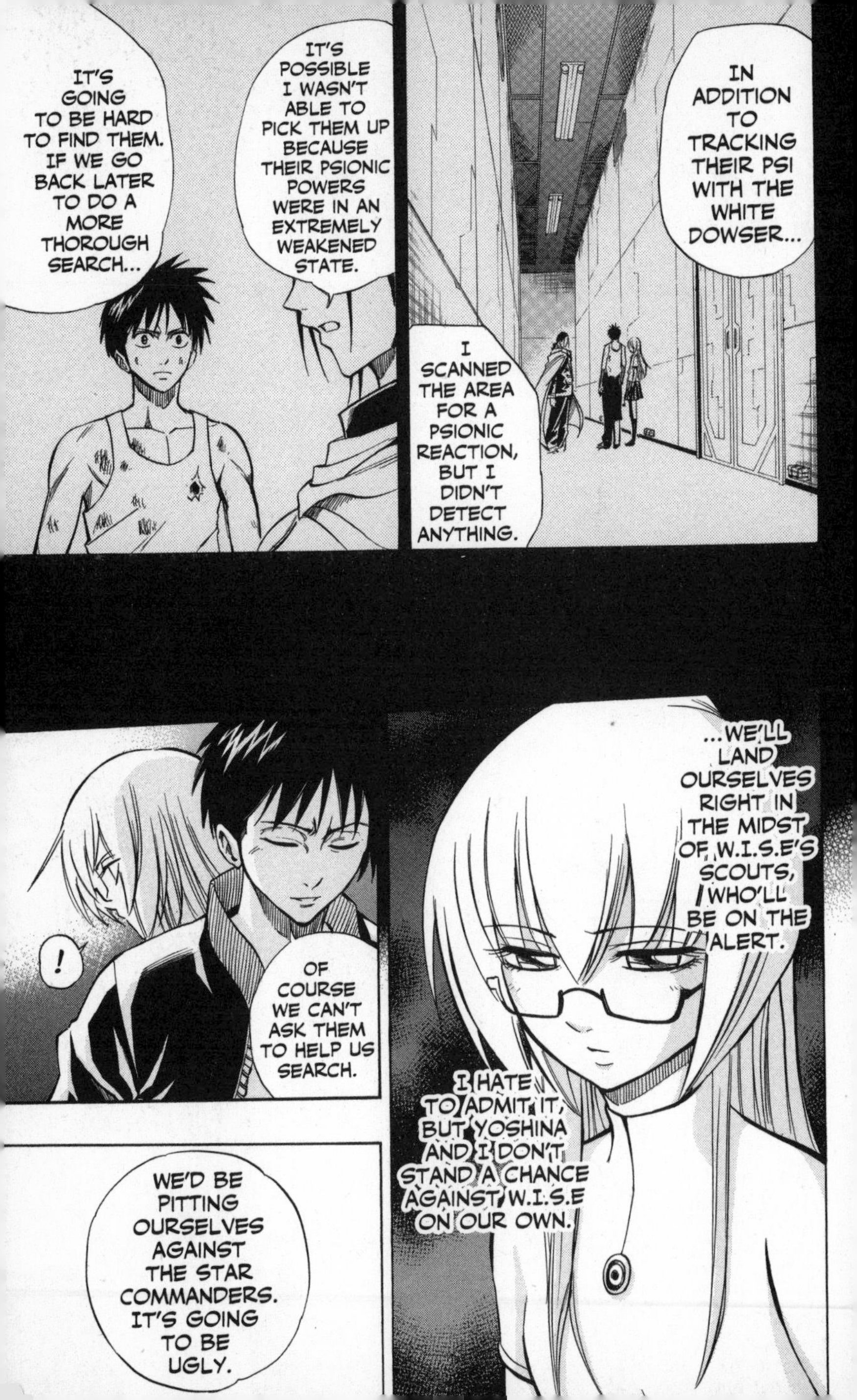
IN ADDITION TO TRACKING THEIR PSI WITH THE WHITE DOWSER...
I SCANNED THE AREA FOR A PSIONIC REACTION, BUT I DIDN'T DETECT ANYTHING.
IT'S POSSIBLE I WASN'T ABLE TO PICK THEM UP BECAUSE THEIR PSIONIC POWERS WERE IN AN EXTREMELY WEAKENED STATE.
IT'S GOING TO BE HARD TO FIND THEM. IF WE GO BACK LATER TO DO A MORE THOROUGH SEARCH...
...WE'LL LAND OURSELVES RIGHT IN THE MIDST OF W.I.S.E'S SCOUTS, WHO'LL BE ON THE ALERT.
I HATE TO ADMIT IT, BUT YOSHINA AND I DON'T STAND A CHANCE AGAINST W.I.S.E ON OUR OWN.
!
OF COURSE WE CAN'T ASK THEM TO HELP US SEARCH.
WE'D BE PITTING OURSELVES AGAINST THE STAR COMMANDERS. IT'S GOING TO BE UGLY.

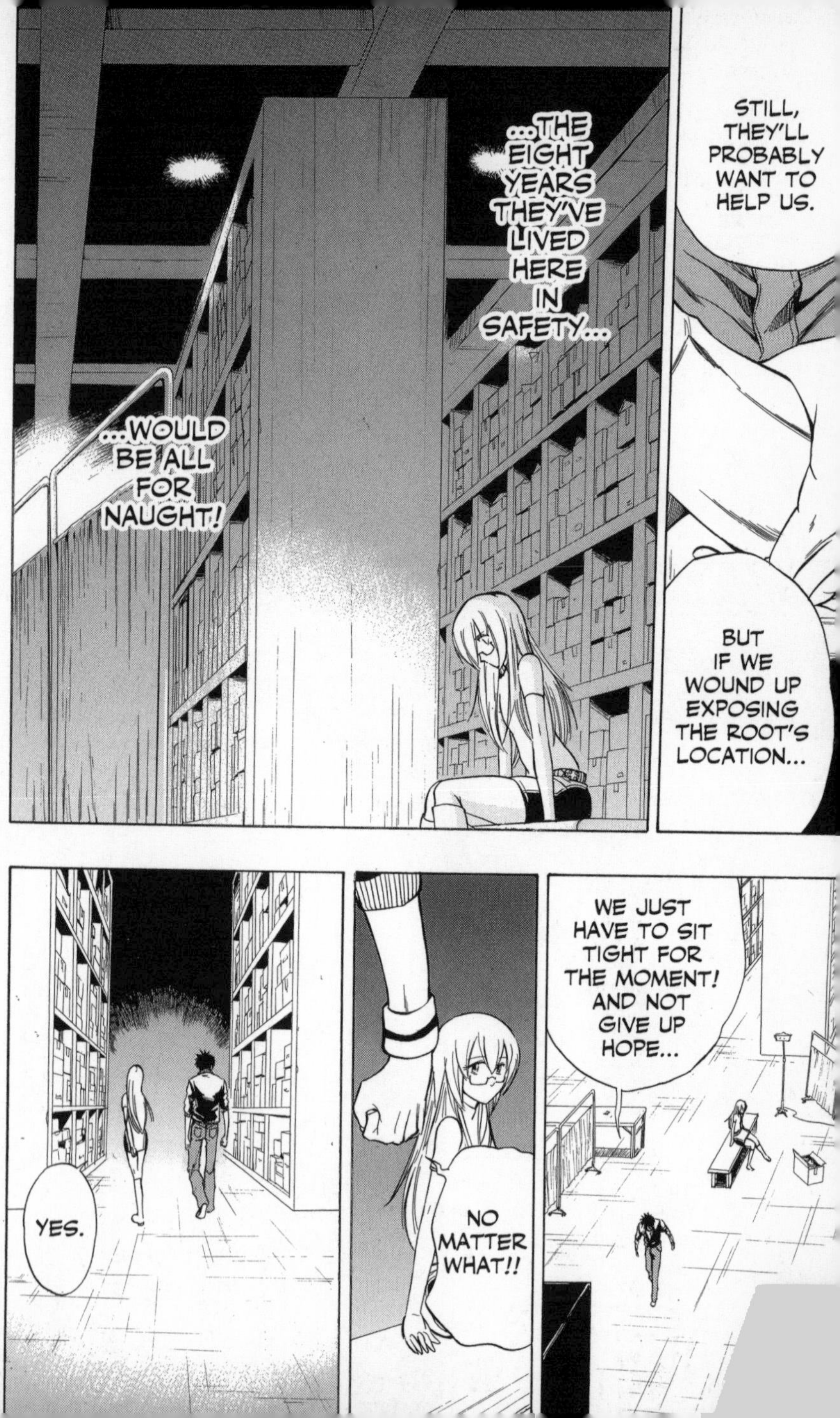
STILL, THEY'LL PROBABLY WANT TO HELP US.
BUT IF WE WOUND UP EXPOSING THE ROOT'S LOCATION...
...THE EIGHT YEARS THEY'VE LIVED HERE IN SAFETY...
...WOULD BE ALL FOR NAUGHT!
WE JUST HAVE TO SIT TIGHT FOR THE MOMENT! AND NOT GIVE UP HOPE...
NO MATTER WHAT!!
YES.

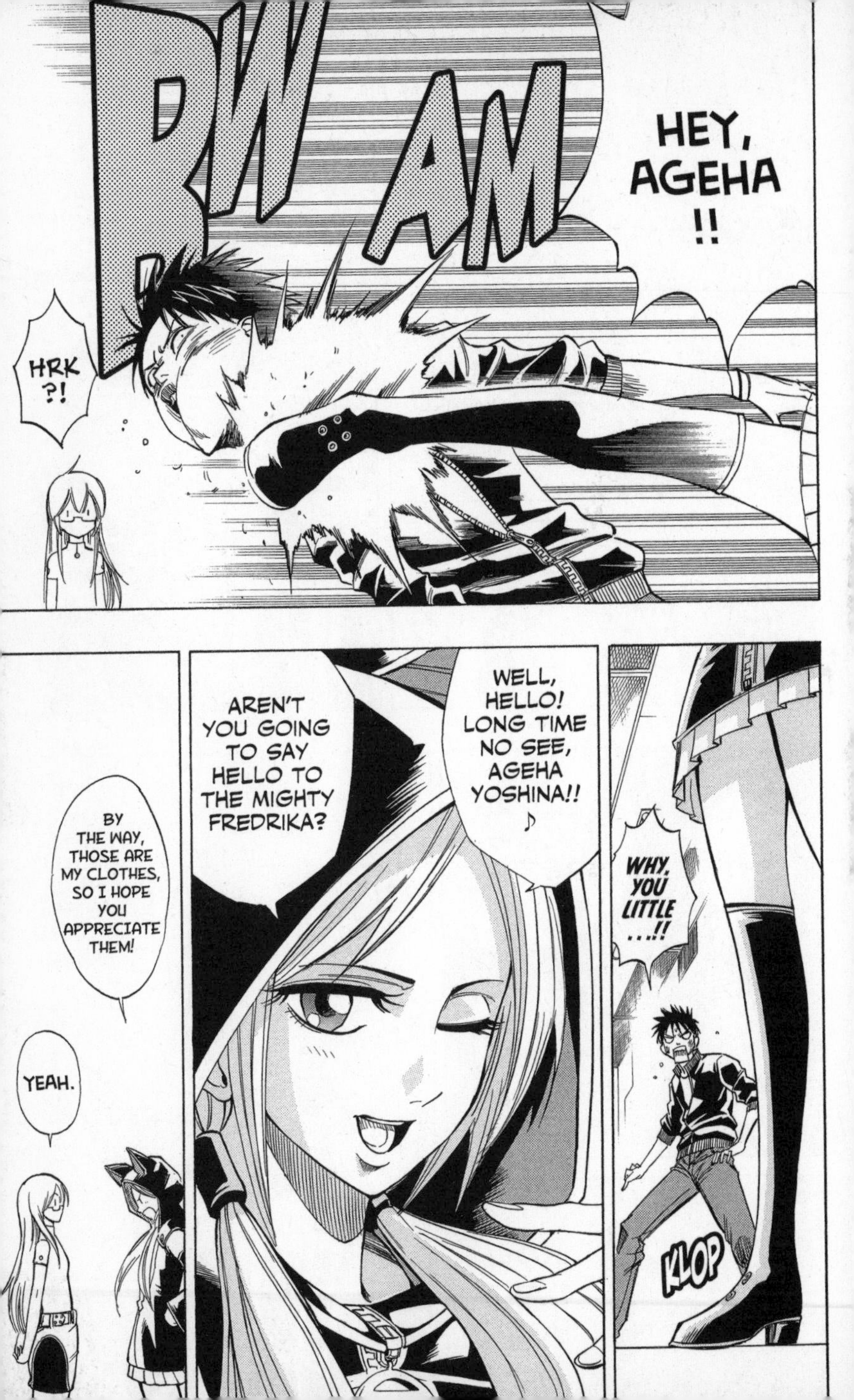
HEY, AGEHA!!
BWAM
HRK?!
WHY, YOU LITTLE...!!
KLOP
WELL, HELLO! LONG TIME NO SEE, AGEHA YOSHINA!! ♪
AREN'T YOU GOING TO SAY HELLO TO THE MIGHTY FREDRIKA?
BY THE WAY, THOSE ARE MY CLOTHES, SO I HOPE YOU APPRECIATE THEM!
YEAH.

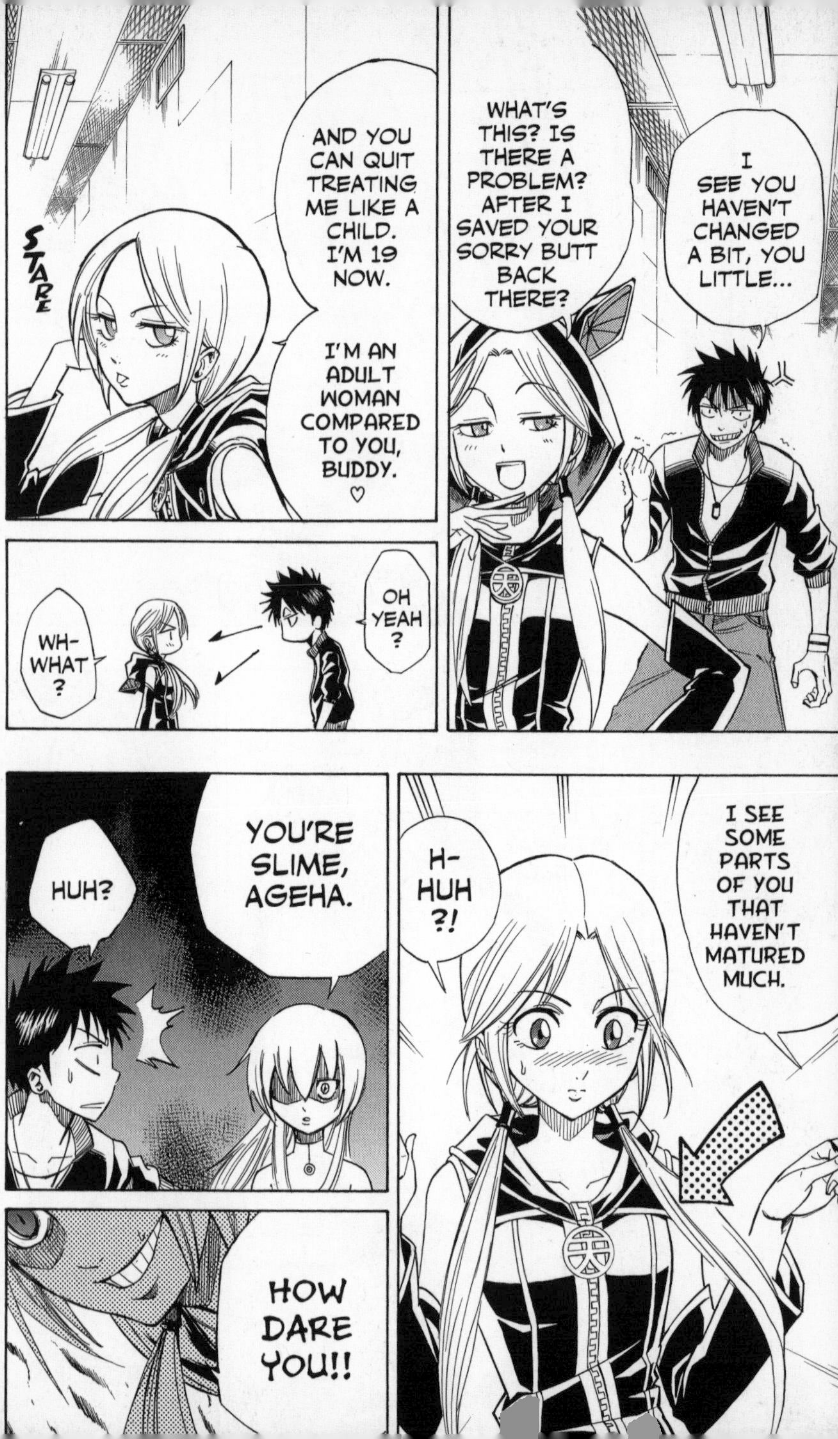
I SEE YOU HAVEN'T CHANGED A BIT, YOU LITTLE...
WHAT'S THIS? IS THERE A PROBLEM? AFTER I SAVED YOUR SORRY BUTT BACK THERE?
STARE
AND YOU CAN QUIT TREATING ME LIKE A CHILD. I'M 19 NOW.
I'M AN ADULT WOMAN COMPARED TO YOU, BUDDY. ♡
OH YEAH?
WH-WHAT?
I SEE SOME PARTS OF YOU THAT HAVEN'T MATURED MUCH.
H-HUH?!
YOU'RE SLIME, AGEHA.
HUH?
HOW DARE YOU!!

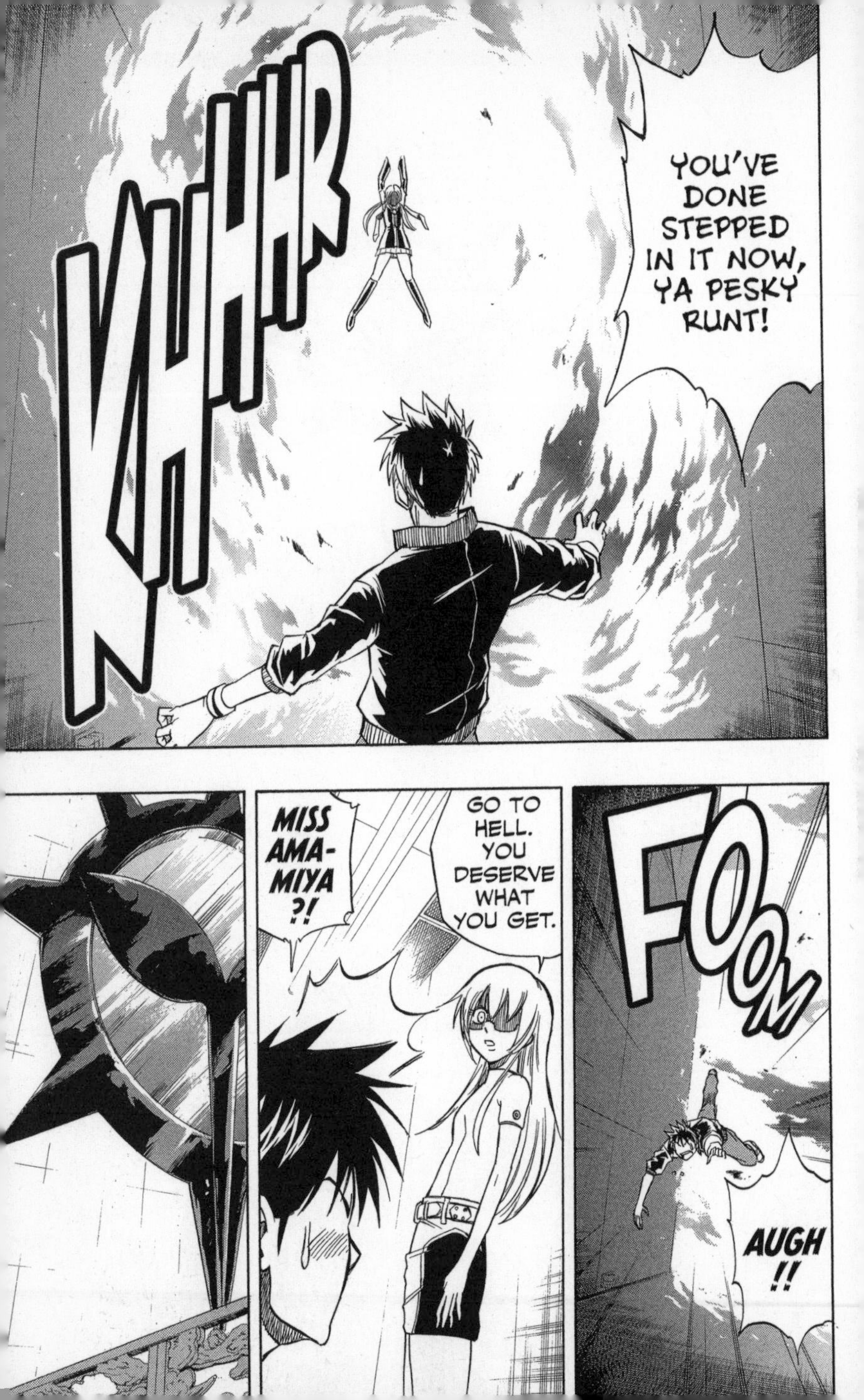
YOU'VE DONE STEPPED IN IT NOW, YA PESKY RUNT!
KHHHR
FOOOM
AUGH !!
GO TO HELL. YOU DESERVE WHAT YOU GET.
MISS AMA-MIYA ?!

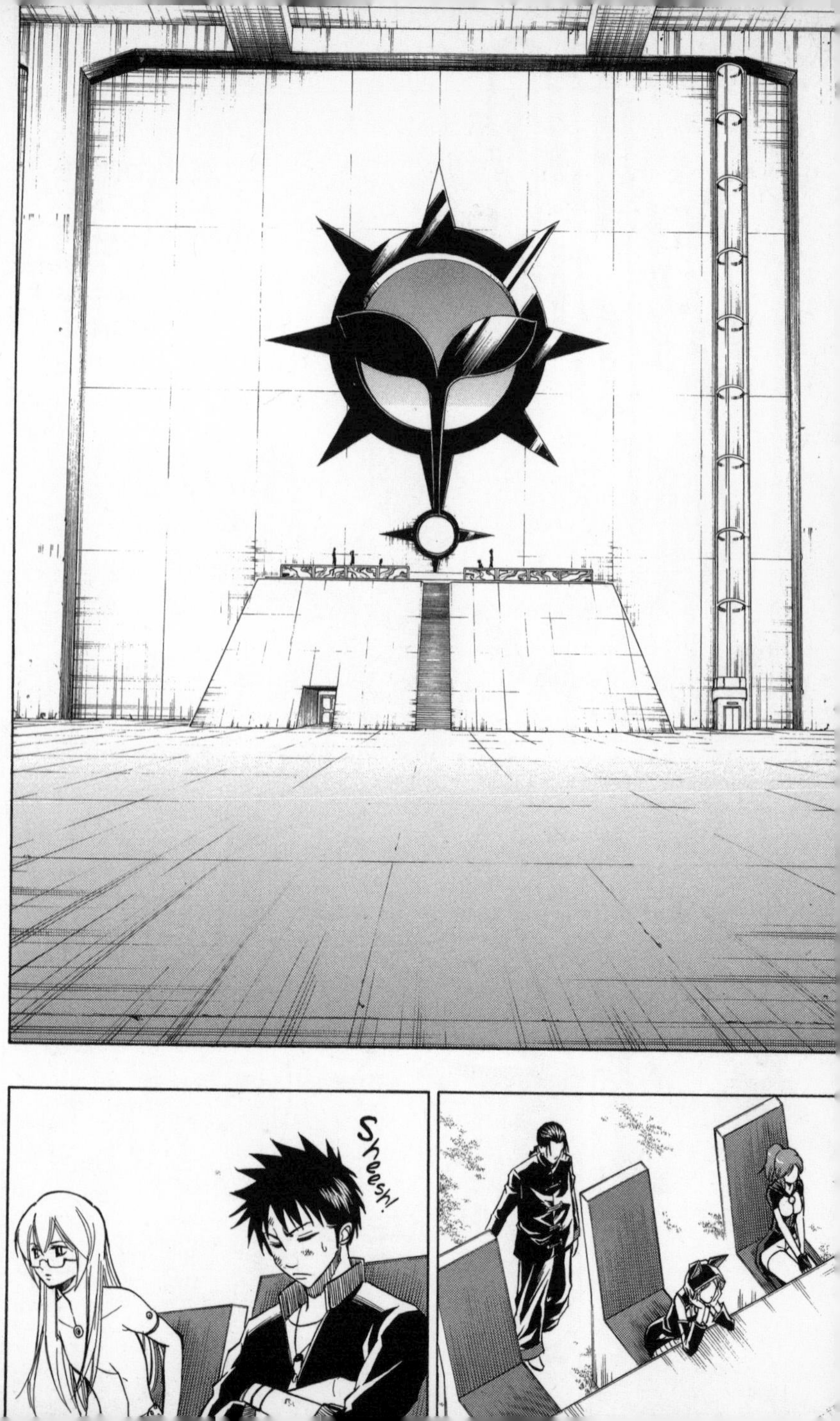
Sheesh!

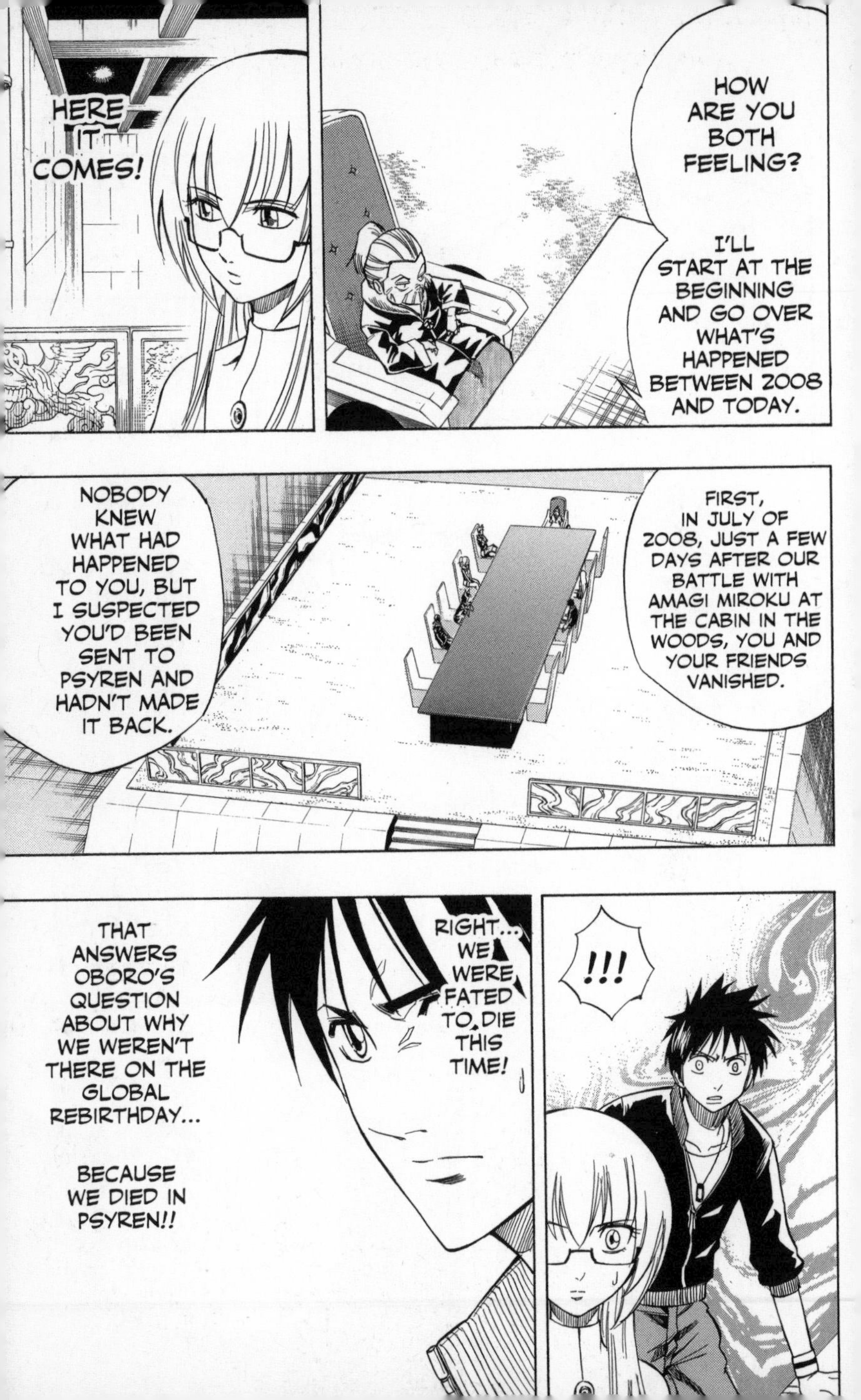
HOW ARE YOU BOTH FEELING?
I'LL START AT THE BEGINNING AND GO OVER WHAT'S HAPPENED BETWEEN 2008 AND TODAY.
HERE IT COMES!
FIRST, IN JULY OF 2008, JUST A FEW DAYS AFTER OUR BATTLE WITH AMAGI MIROKU AT THE CABIN IN THE WOODS, YOU AND YOUR FRIENDS VANISHED.
NOBODY KNEW WHAT HAD HAPPENED TO YOU, BUT I SUSPECTED YOU'D BEEN SENT TO PSYREN AND HADN'T MADE IT BACK.
!!!
RIGHT... WE WERE FATED TO DIE THIS TIME!
THAT ANSWERS OBORO'S QUESTION ABOUT WHY WE WEREN'T THERE ON THE GLOBAL REBIRTHDAY...
BECAUSE WE DIED IN PSYREN!!

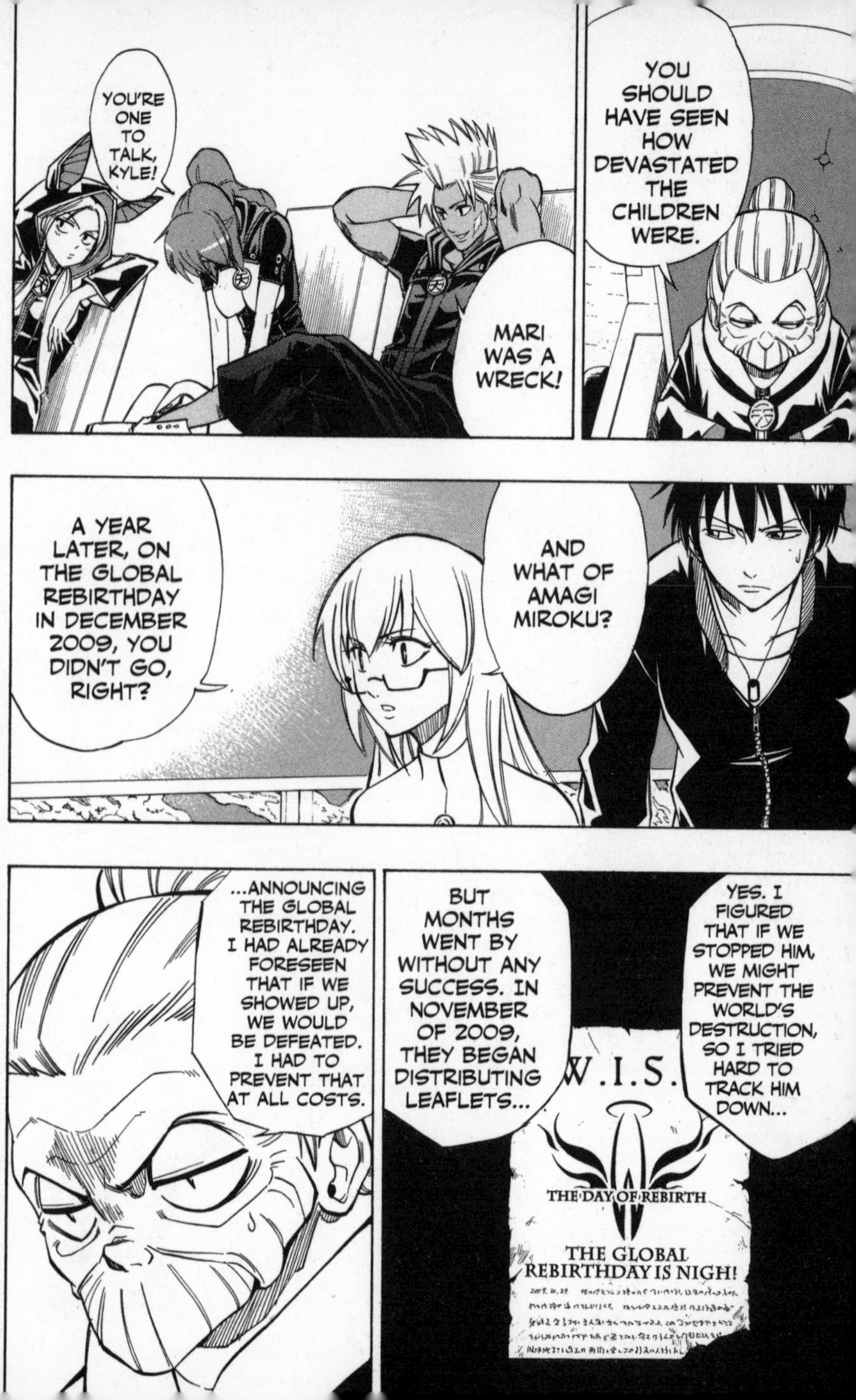
YOU SHOULD HAVE SEEN HOW DEVASTATED THE CHILDREN WERE.
MARI WAS A WRECK!
YOU'RE ONE TO TALK, KYLE!
AND WHAT OF AMAGI MIROKU?
A YEAR LATER, ON THE GLOBAL REBIRTHDAY IN DECEMBER 2009, YOU DIDN'T GO, RIGHT?
YES. I FIGURED THAT IF WE STOPPED HIM, WE MIGHT PREVENT THE WORLD'S DESTRUCTION, SO I TRIED HARD TO TRACK HIM DOWN...
BUT MONTHS WENT BY WITHOUT ANY SUCCESS. IN NOVEMBER OF 2009, THEY BEGAN DISTRIBUTING LEAFLETS...
W.I.S.
THE DAY OF REBIRTH
THE GLOBAL REBIRTHDAY IS NIGH!
...ANNOUNCING THE GLOBAL REBIRTHDAY. I HAD ALREADY FORESEEN THAT IF WE SHOWED UP, WE WOULD BE DEFEATED. I HAD TO PREVENT THAT AT ALL COSTS.

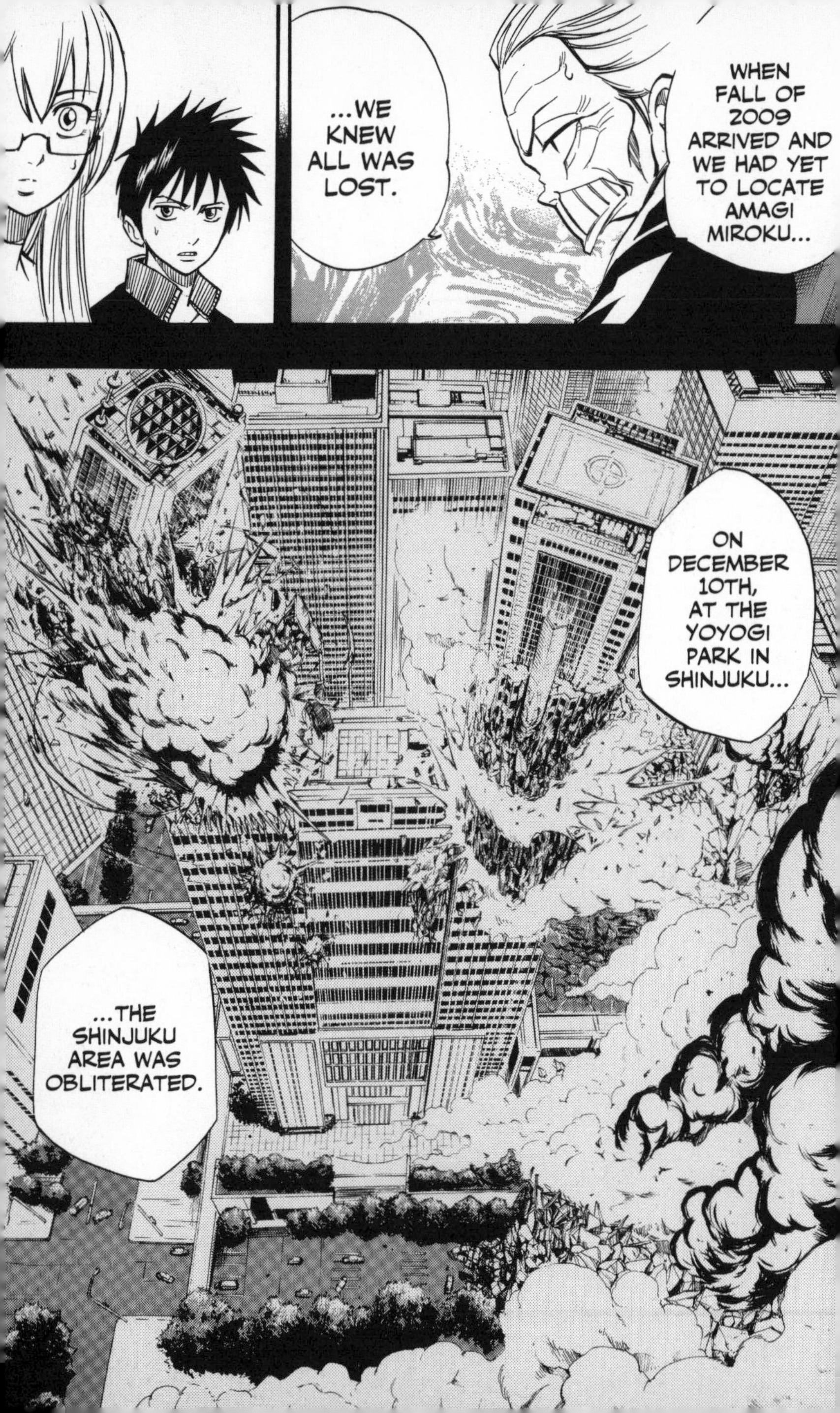
WHEN FALL OF 2009 ARRIVED AND WE HAD YET TO LOCATE AMAGI MIROKU...
...WE KNEW ALL WAS LOST.
ON DECEMBER 10TH, AT THE YOYOGI PARK IN SHINJUKU...
...THE SHINJUKU AREA WAS OBLITERATED.

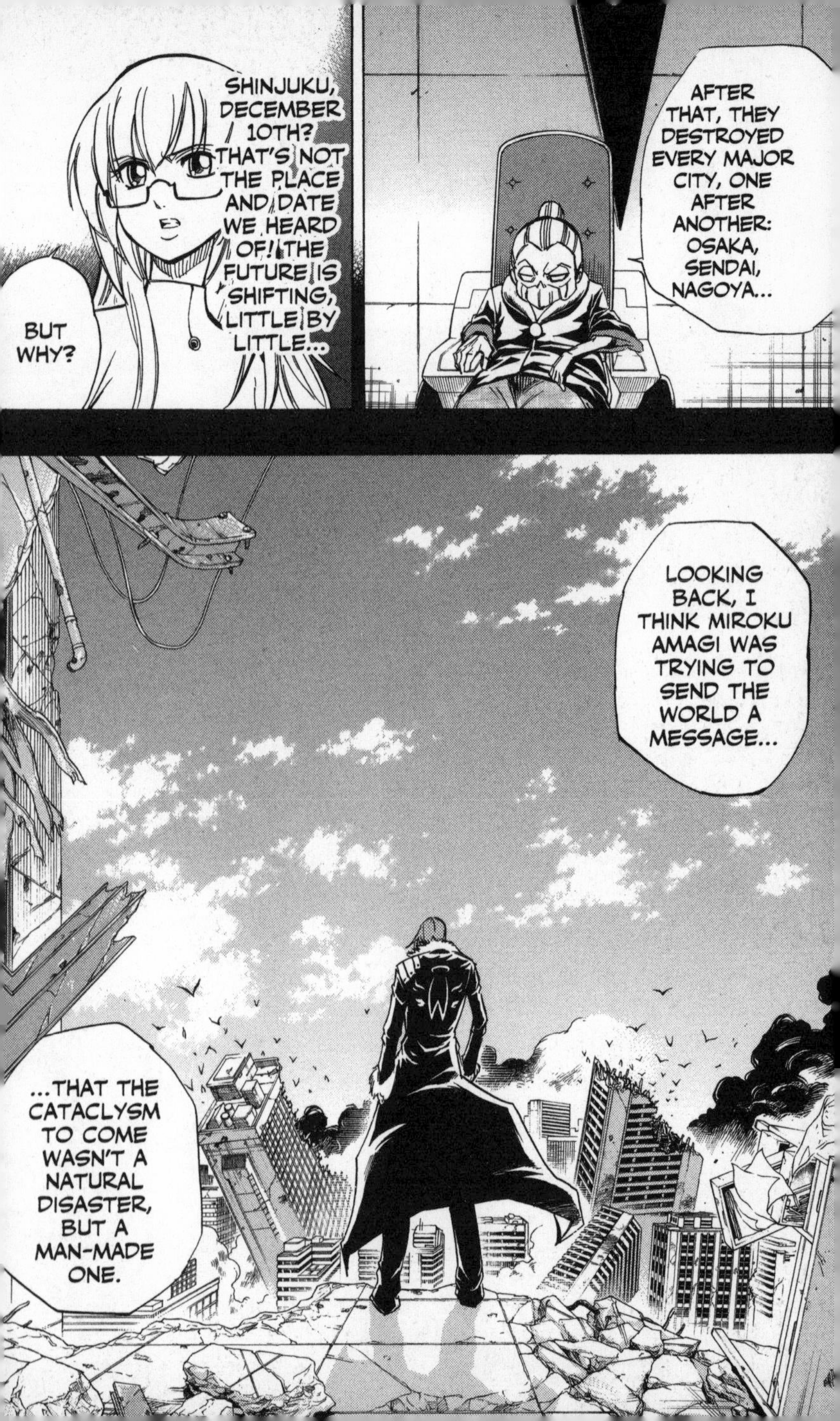
AFTER THAT, THEY DESTROYED EVERY MAJOR CITY, ONE AFTER ANOTHER: OSAKA, SENDAI, NAGOYA...
SHINJUKU, DECEMBER 10TH? THAT'S NOT THE PLACE AND DATE WE HEARD OF! THE FUTURE IS SHIFTING, LITTLE BY LITTLE...
BUT WHY?
LOOKING BACK, I THINK MIROKU AMAGI WAS TRYING TO SEND THE WORLD A MESSAGE...
...THAT THE CATACLYSM TO COME WASN'T A NATURAL DISASTER, BUT A MAN-MADE ONE.

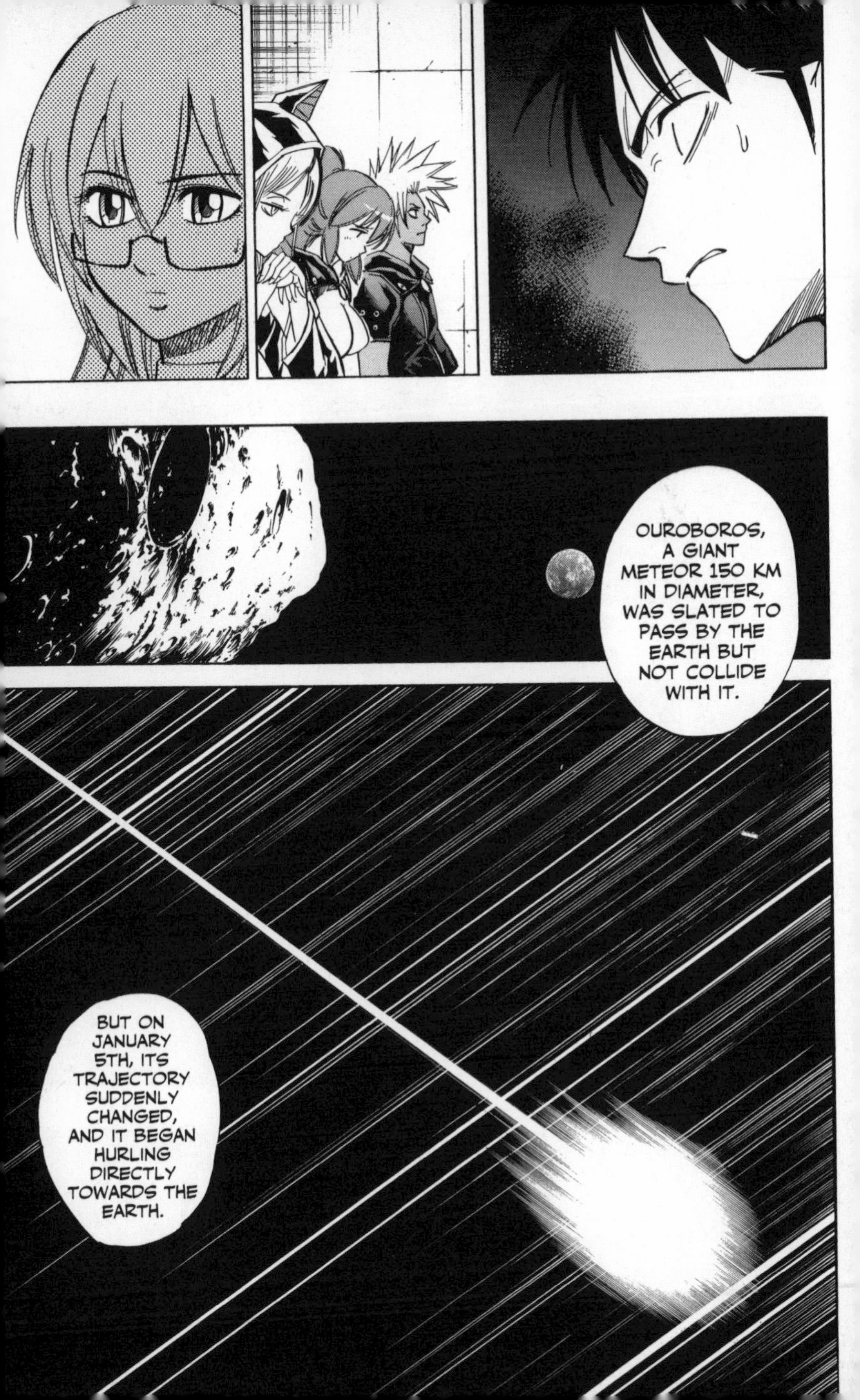
OUROBOROS, A GIANT METEOR 150 KM IN DIAMETER, WAS SLATED TO PASS BY THE EARTH BUT NOT COLLIDE WITH IT.
BUT ON JANUARY 5TH, ITS TRAJECTORY SUDDENLY CHANGED, AND IT BEGAN HURLING DIRECTLY TOWARDS THE EARTH.

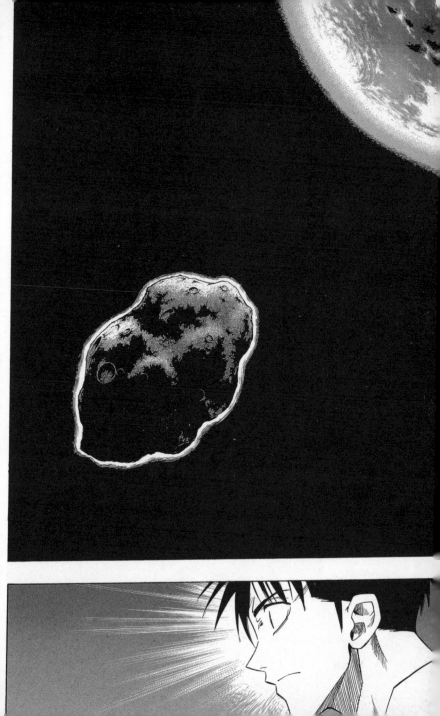

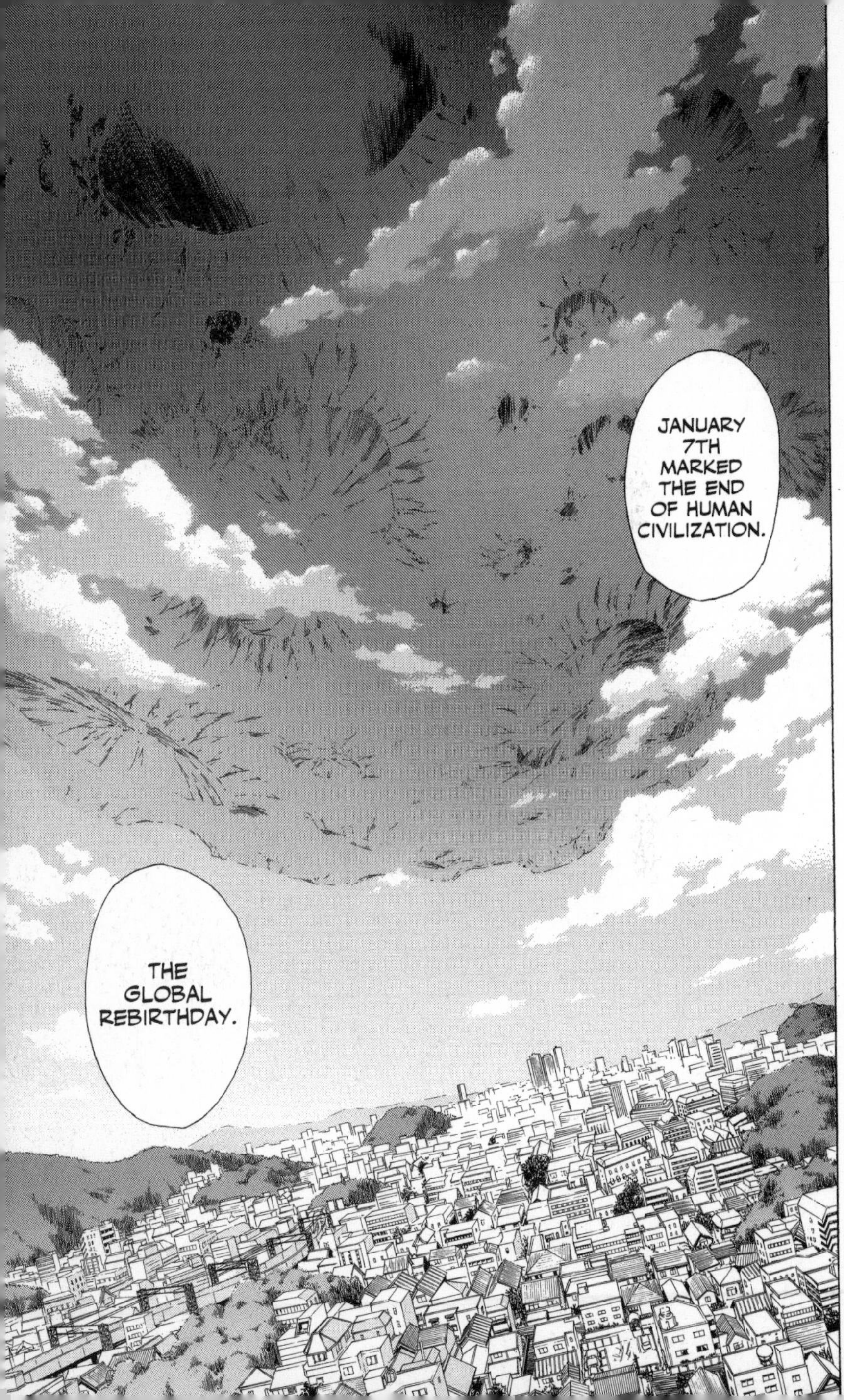
JANUARY 7TH MARKED THE END OF HUMAN CIVILIZATION.
THE GLOBAL REBIRTHDAY.

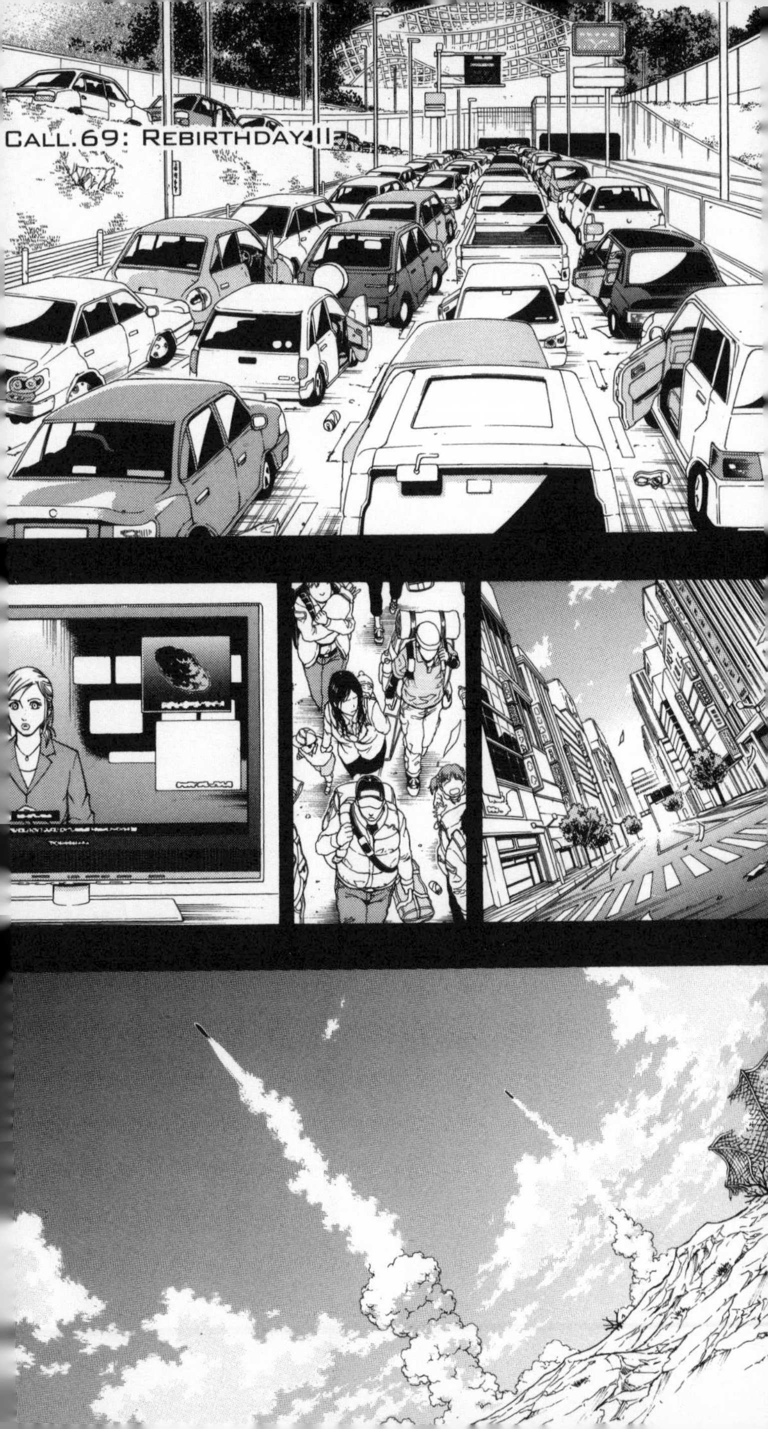
CALL.69: REBIRTHDAY II

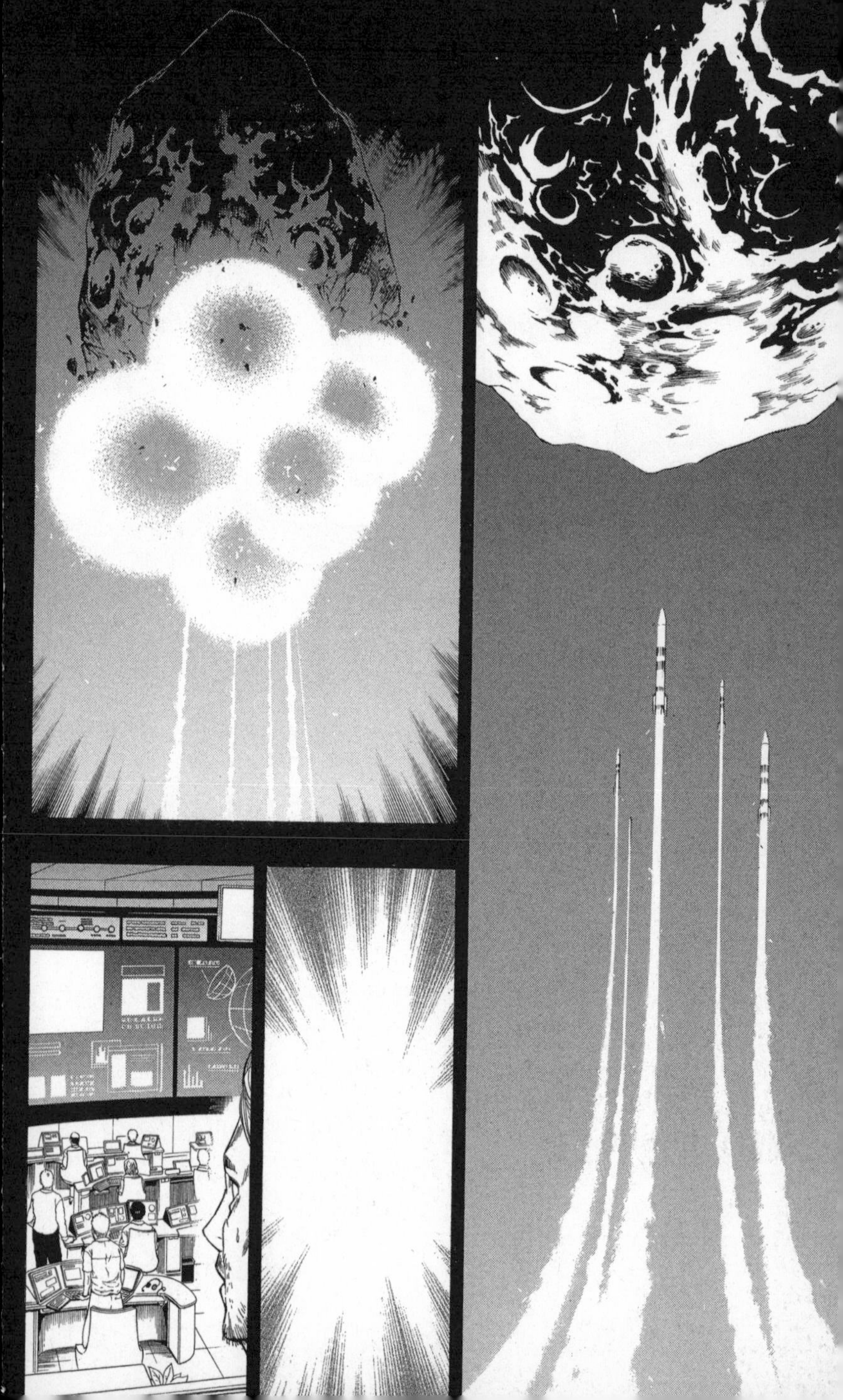

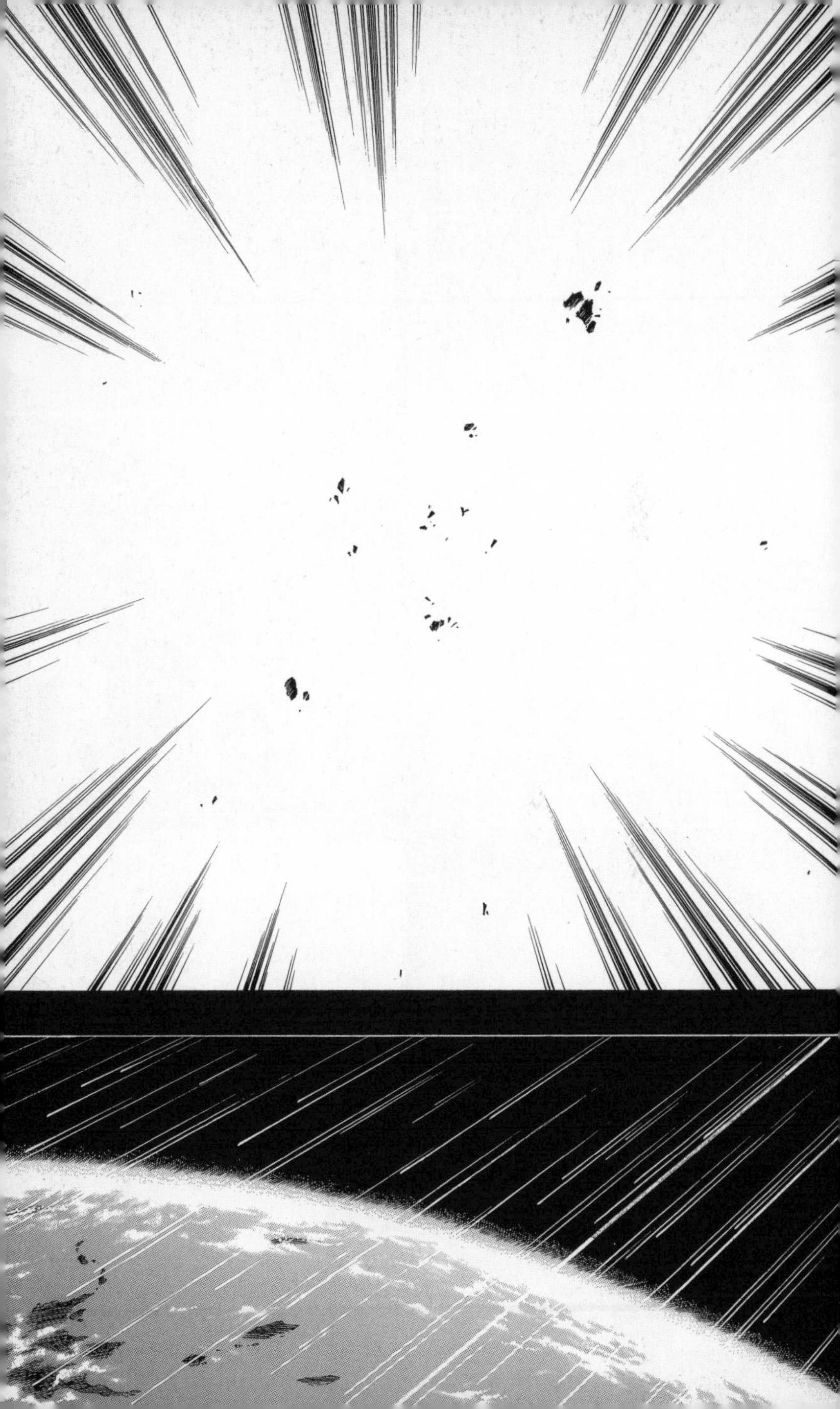

JANUARY
7, 2010:
THE GLOBAL
REBIRTHDAY.

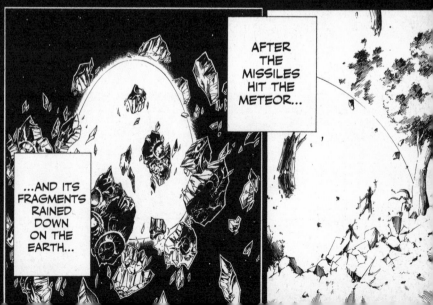

AFTER
THE
MISSILES
HIT THE
METEOR...

...AND ITS
FRAGMENTS
RAINED
DOWN
ON THE
EARTH...

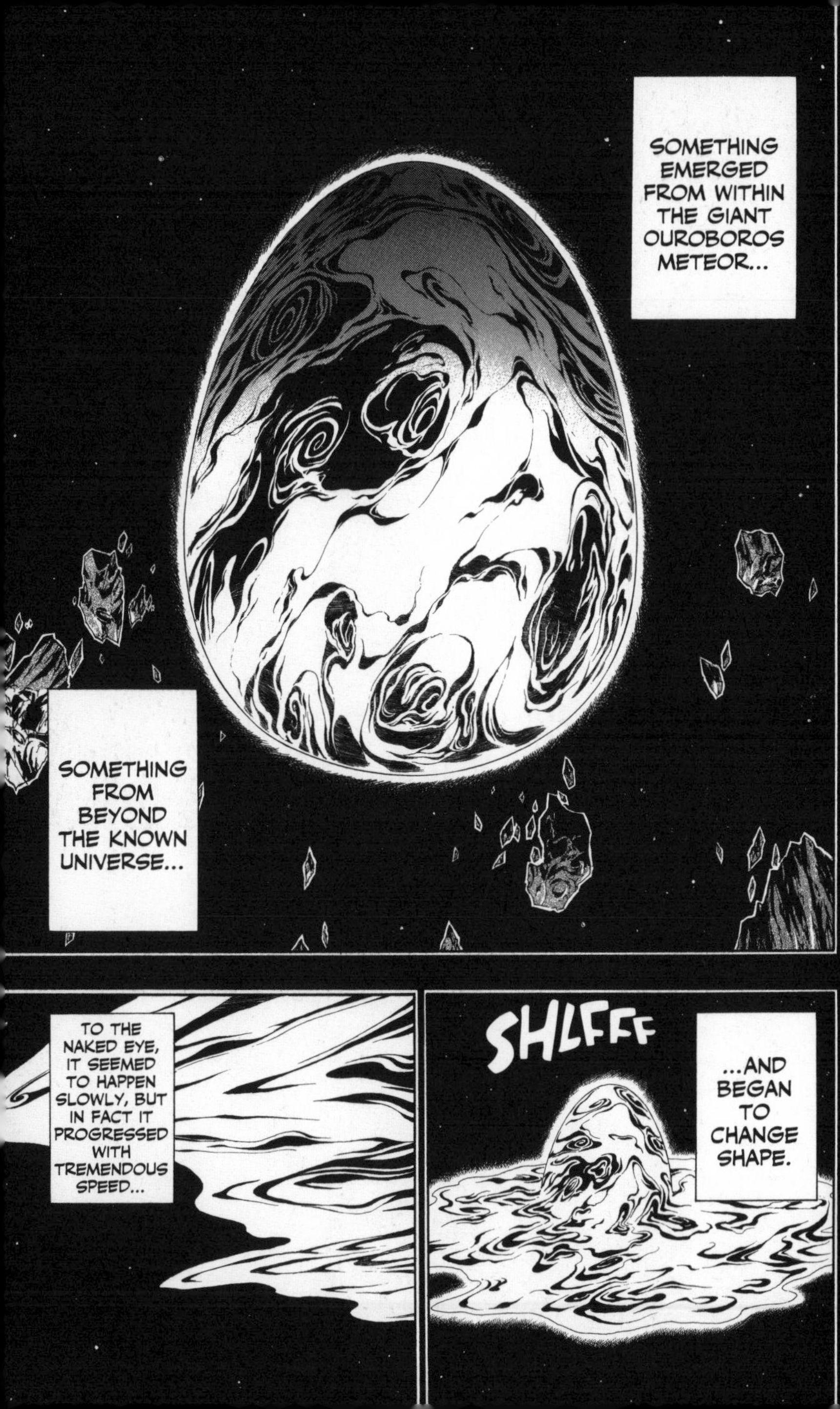
SOMETHING EMERGED FROM WITHIN THE GIANT OUROBOROS METEOR...
SOMETHING FROM BEYOND THE KNOWN UNIVERSE...
SHLFFF
...AND BEGAN TO CHANGE SHAPE.
TO THE NAKED EYE, IT SEEMED TO HAPPEN SLOWLY, BUT IN FACT IT PROGRESSED WITH TREMENDOUS SPEED...

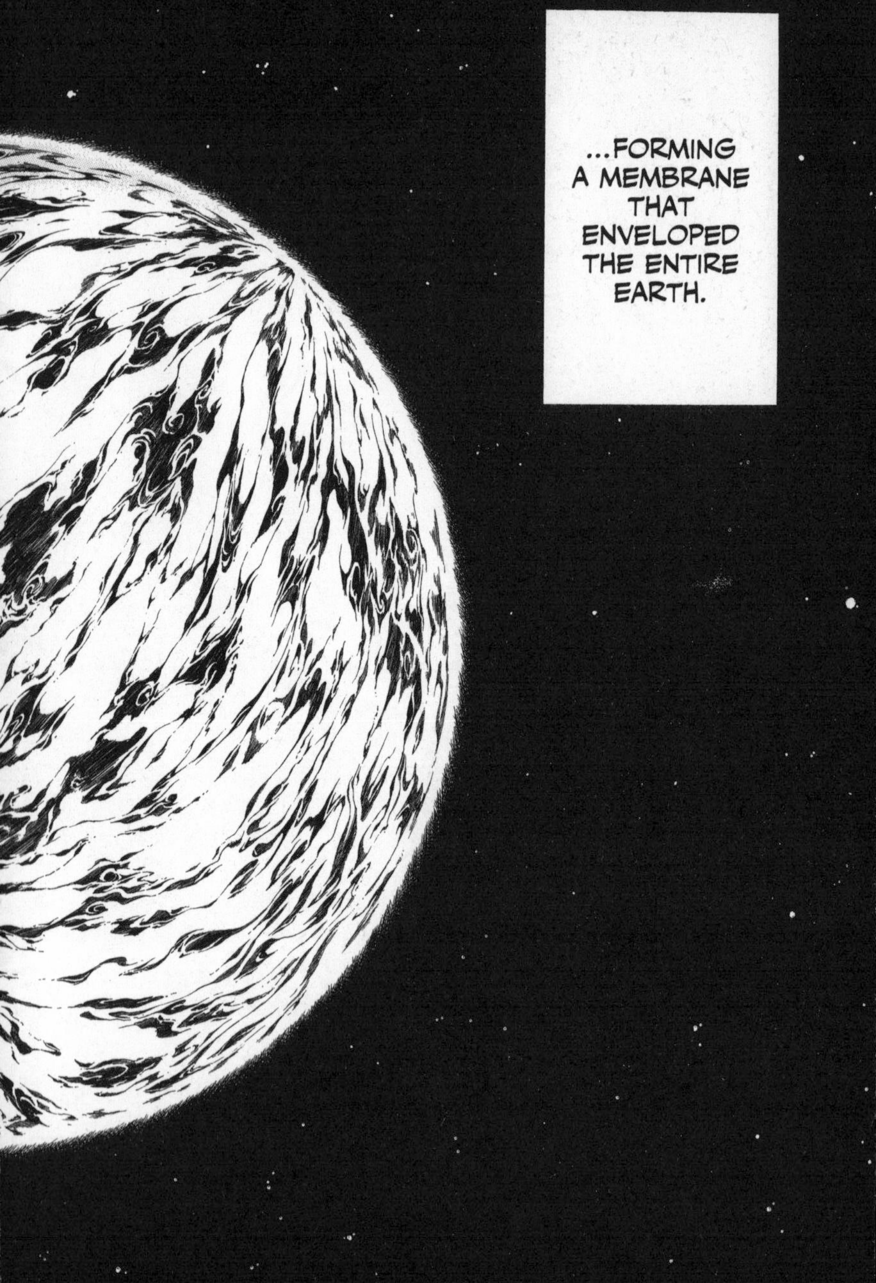
...FORMING A MEMBRANE THAT ENVELOPED THE ENTIRE EARTH.

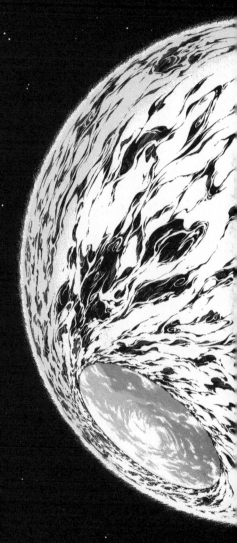

CALL.69: REBIRTHDAY II

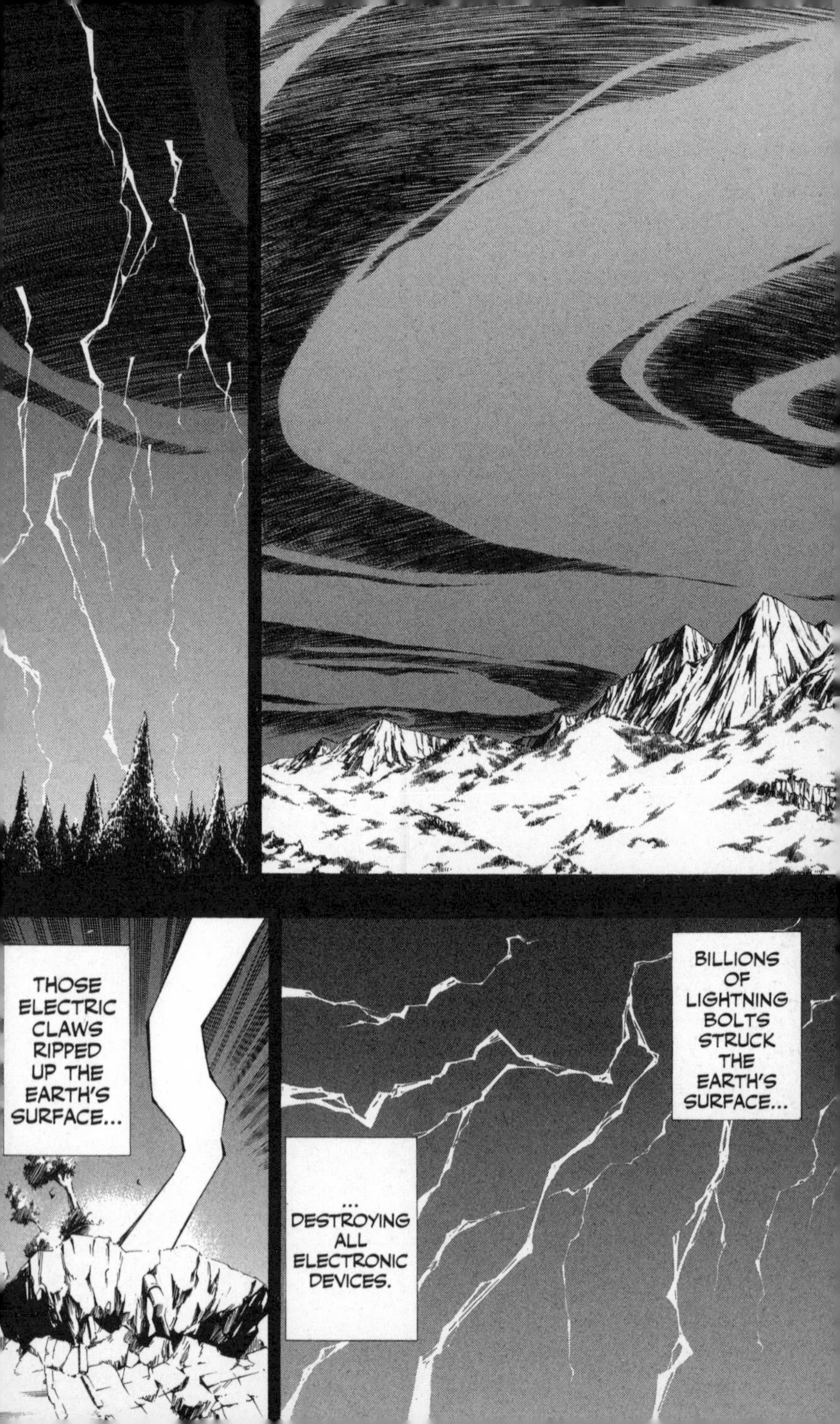
BILLIONS OF LIGHTNING BOLTS STRUCK THE EARTH'S SURFACE...
...DESTROYING ALL ELECTRONIC DEVICES.
THOSE ELECTRIC CLAWS RIPPED UP THE EARTH'S SURFACE...

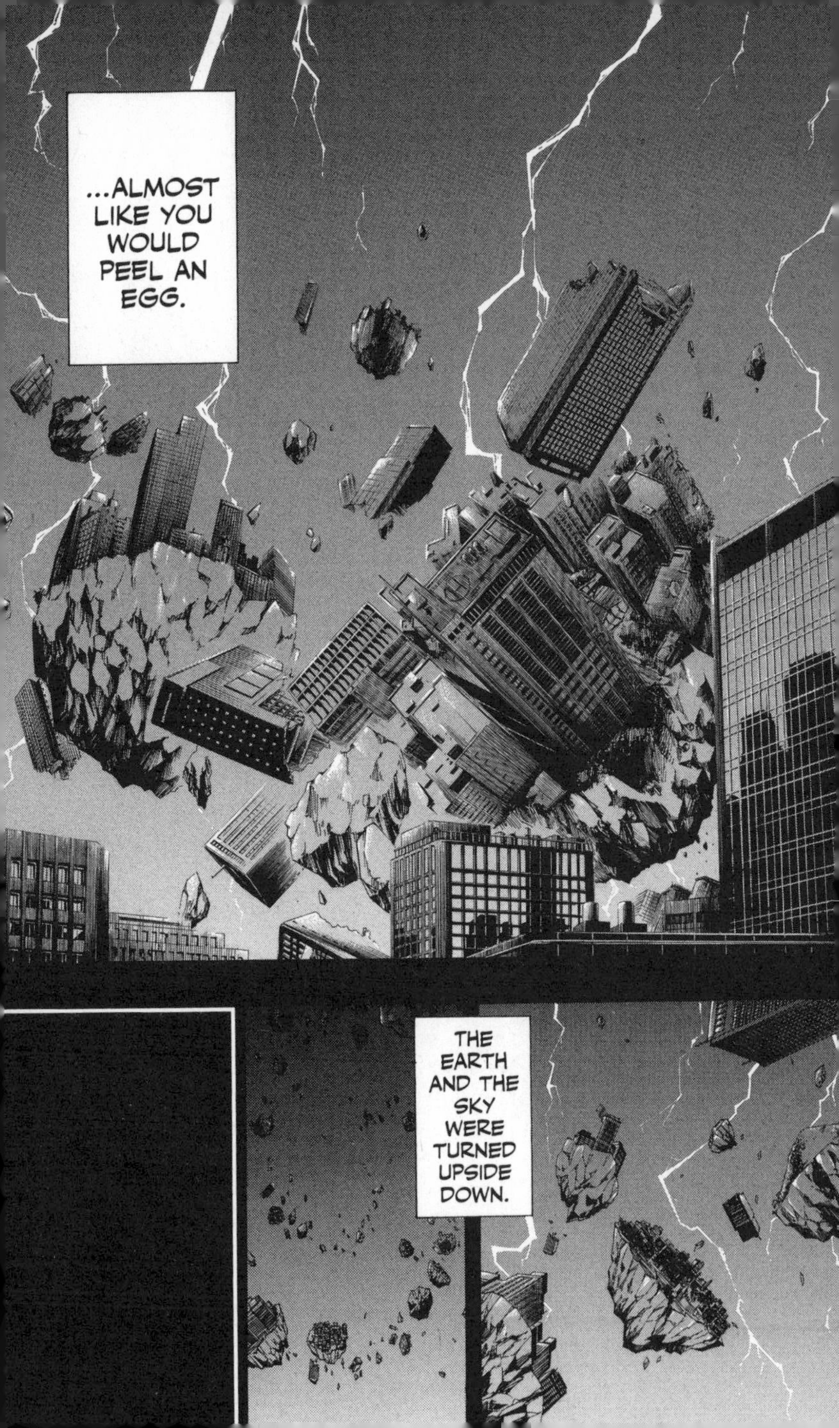
...ALMOST LIKE YOU WOULD PEEL AN EGG.
THE EARTH AND THE SKY WERE TURNED UPSIDE DOWN.

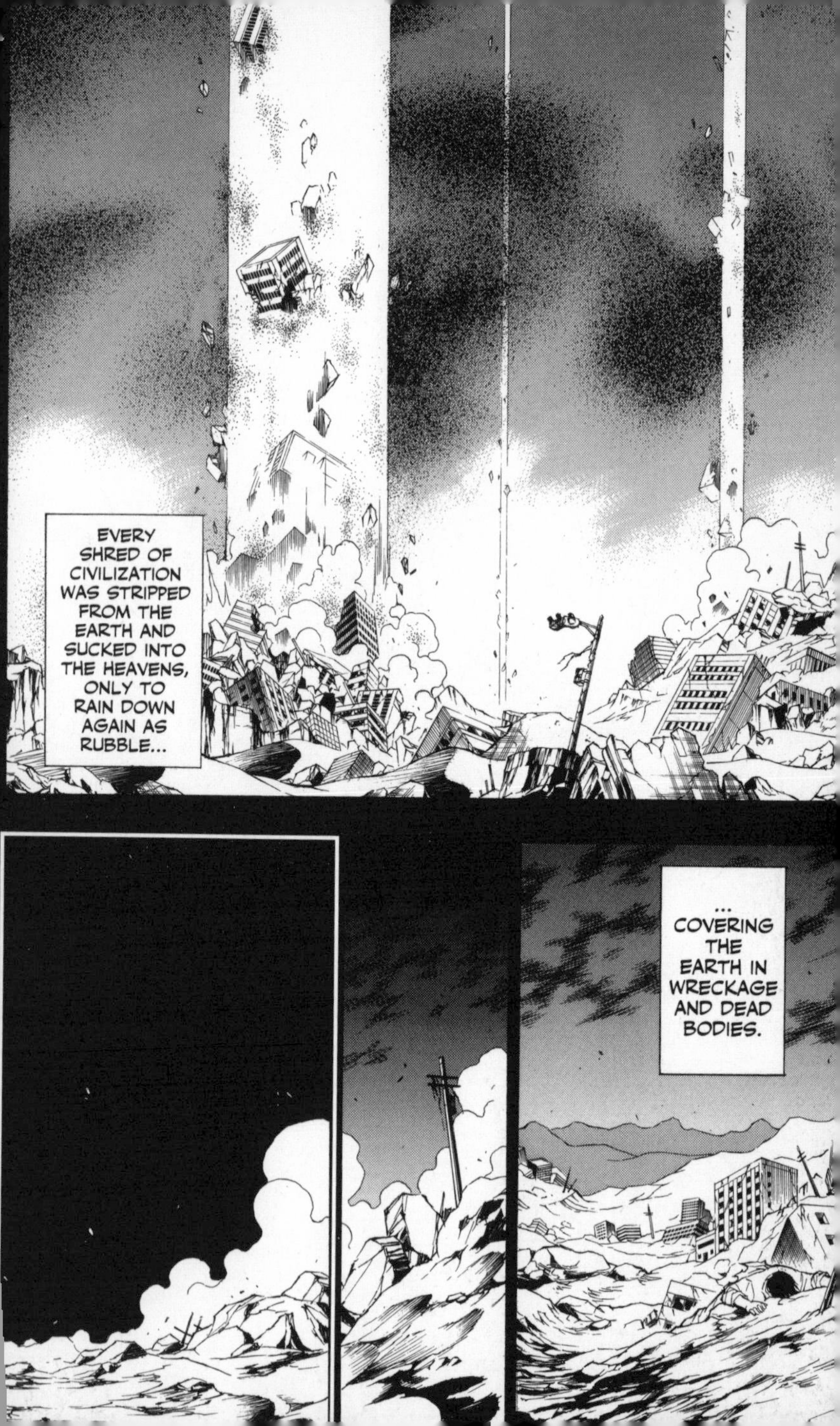
EVERY SHRED OF CIVILIZATION WAS STRIPPED FROM THE EARTH AND SUCKED INTO THE HEAVENS, ONLY TO RAIN DOWN AGAIN AS RUBBLE...
...COVERING THE EARTH IN WRECKAGE AND DEAD BODIES.

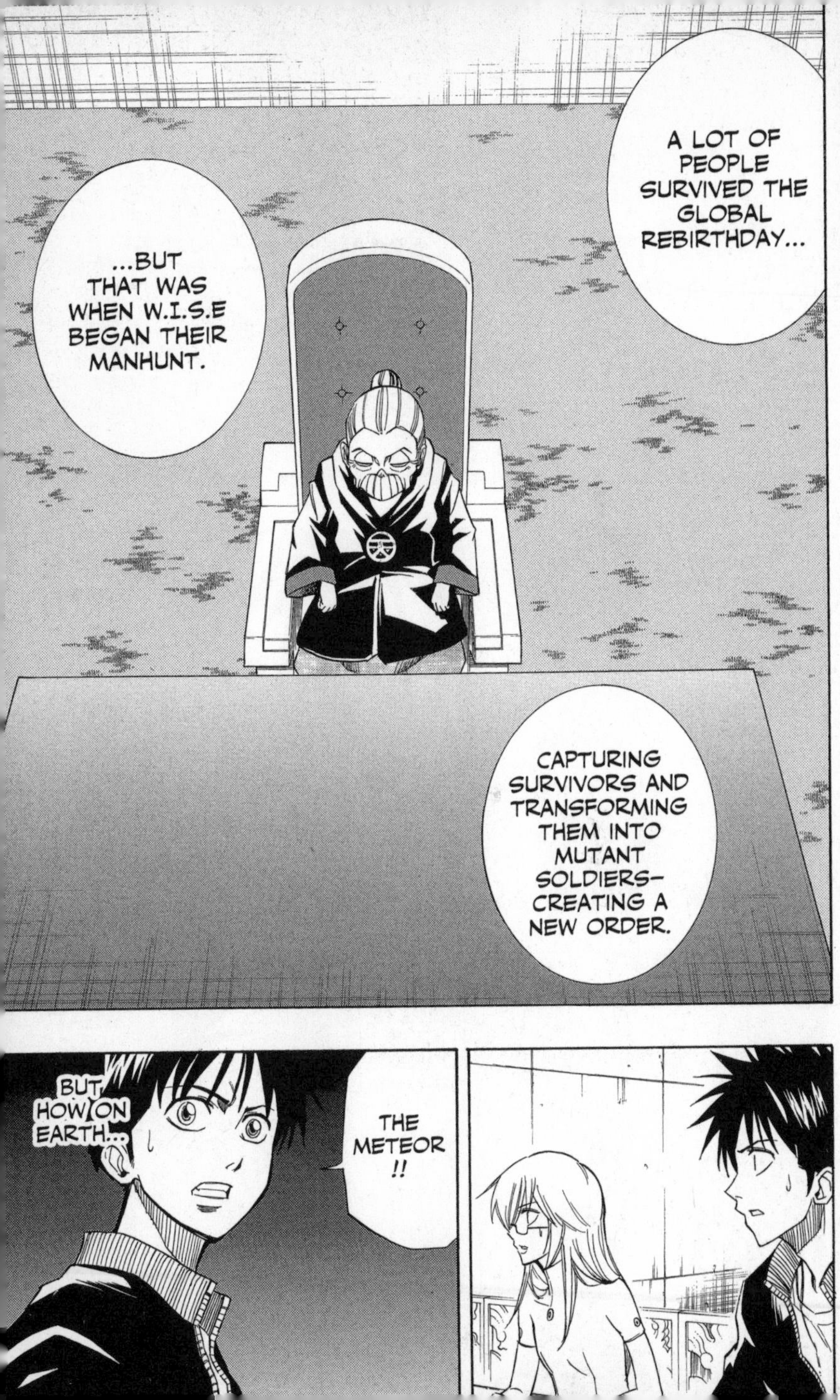
A LOT OF PEOPLE SURVIVED THE GLOBAL REBIRTHDAY...
...BUT THAT WAS WHEN W.I.S.E BEGAN THEIR MANHUNT.
CAPTURING SURVIVORS AND TRANSFORMING THEM INTO MUTANT SOLDIERS– CREATING A NEW ORDER.
THE METEOR !!
BUT HOW ON EARTH...

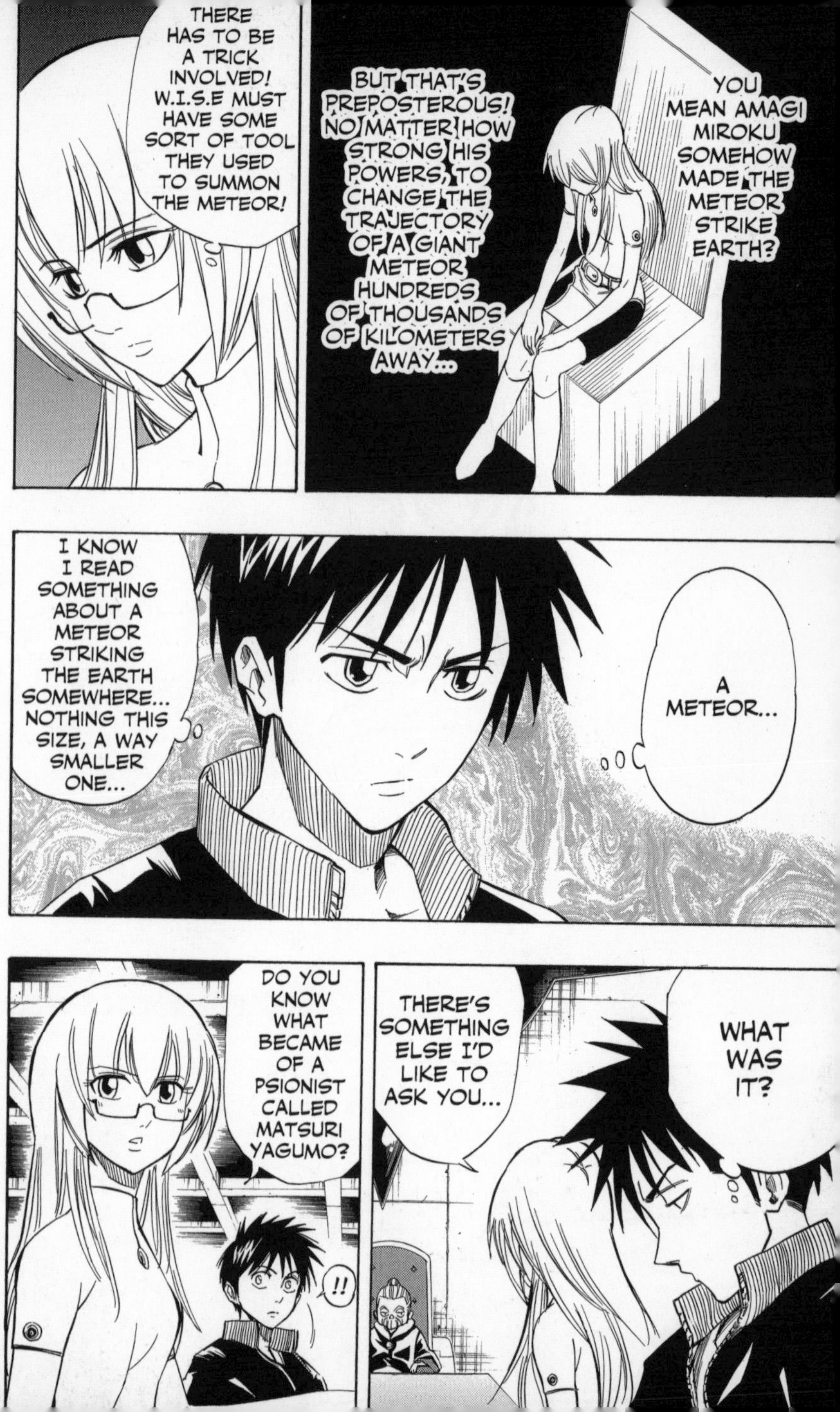
YOU MEAN AMAGI MIROKU SOMEHOW MADE THE METEOR STRIKE EARTH?
BUT THAT'S PREPOSTEROUS! NO MATTER HOW STRONG HIS POWERS, TO CHANGE THE TRAJECTORY OF A GIANT METEOR HUNDREDS OF THOUSANDS OF KILOMETERS AWAY...
THERE HAS TO BE A TRICK INVOLVED! W.I.S.E MUST HAVE SOME SORT OF TOOL THEY USED TO SUMMON THE METEOR!
A METEOR...
I KNOW I READ SOMETHING ABOUT A METEOR STRIKING THE EARTH SOMEWHERE... NOTHING THIS SIZE, A WAY SMALLER ONE...
WHAT WAS IT?
THERE'S SOMETHING ELSE I'D LIKE TO ASK YOU...
DO YOU KNOW WHAT BECAME OF A PSIONIST CALLED MATSURI YAGUMO?
!!

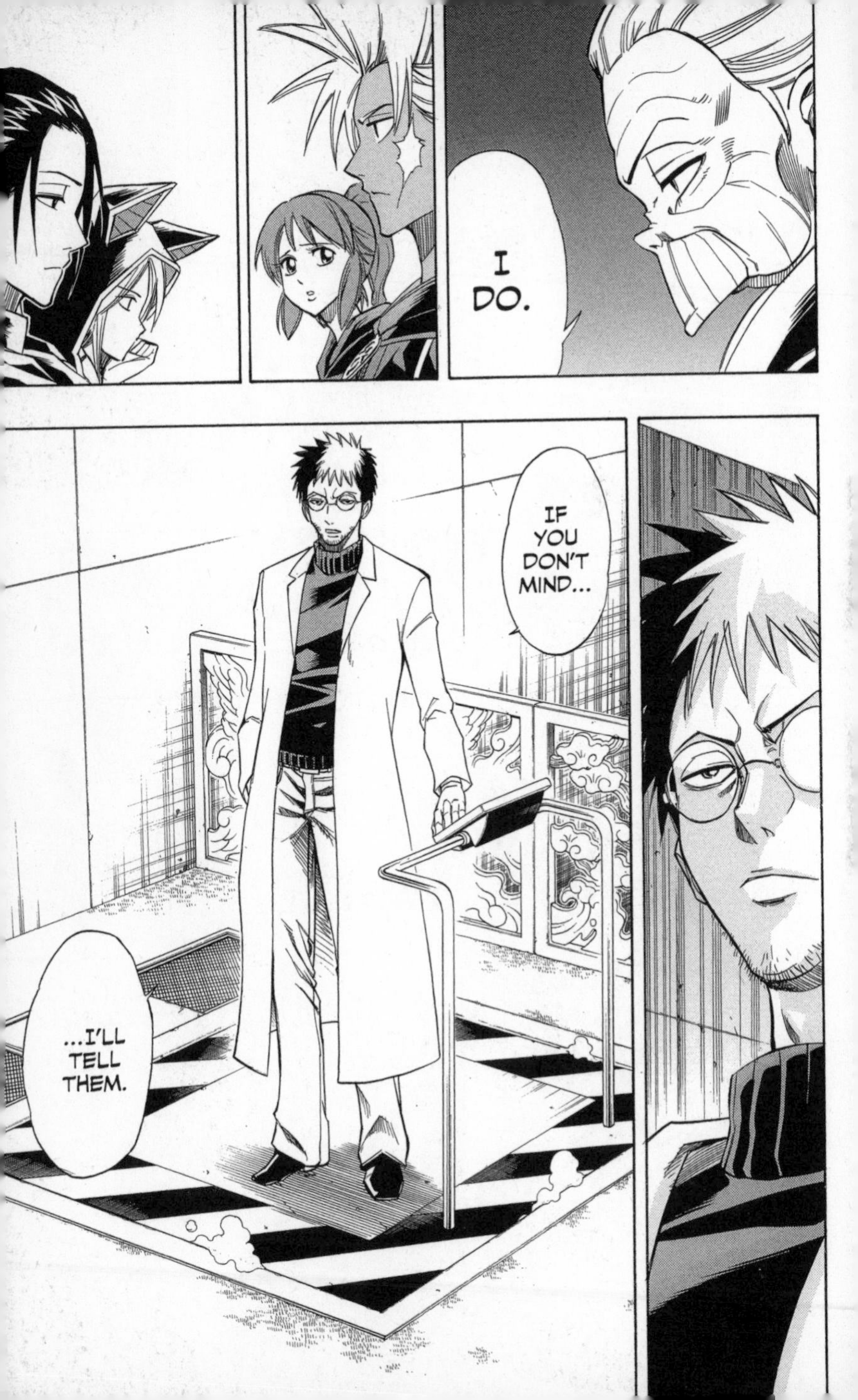
I DO.
IF YOU DON'T MIND...
...I'LL TELL THEM.

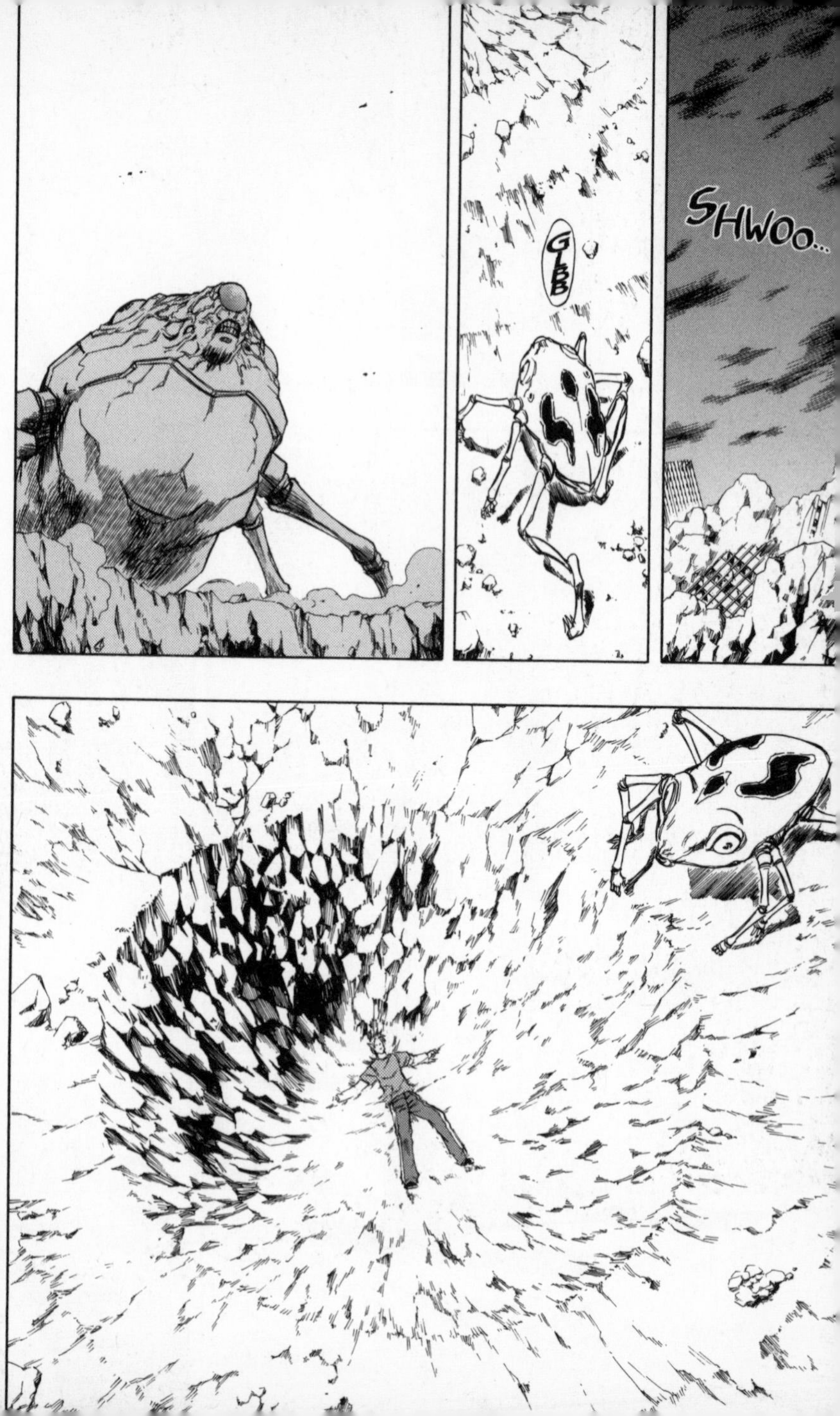
SHWOO...
GLBB

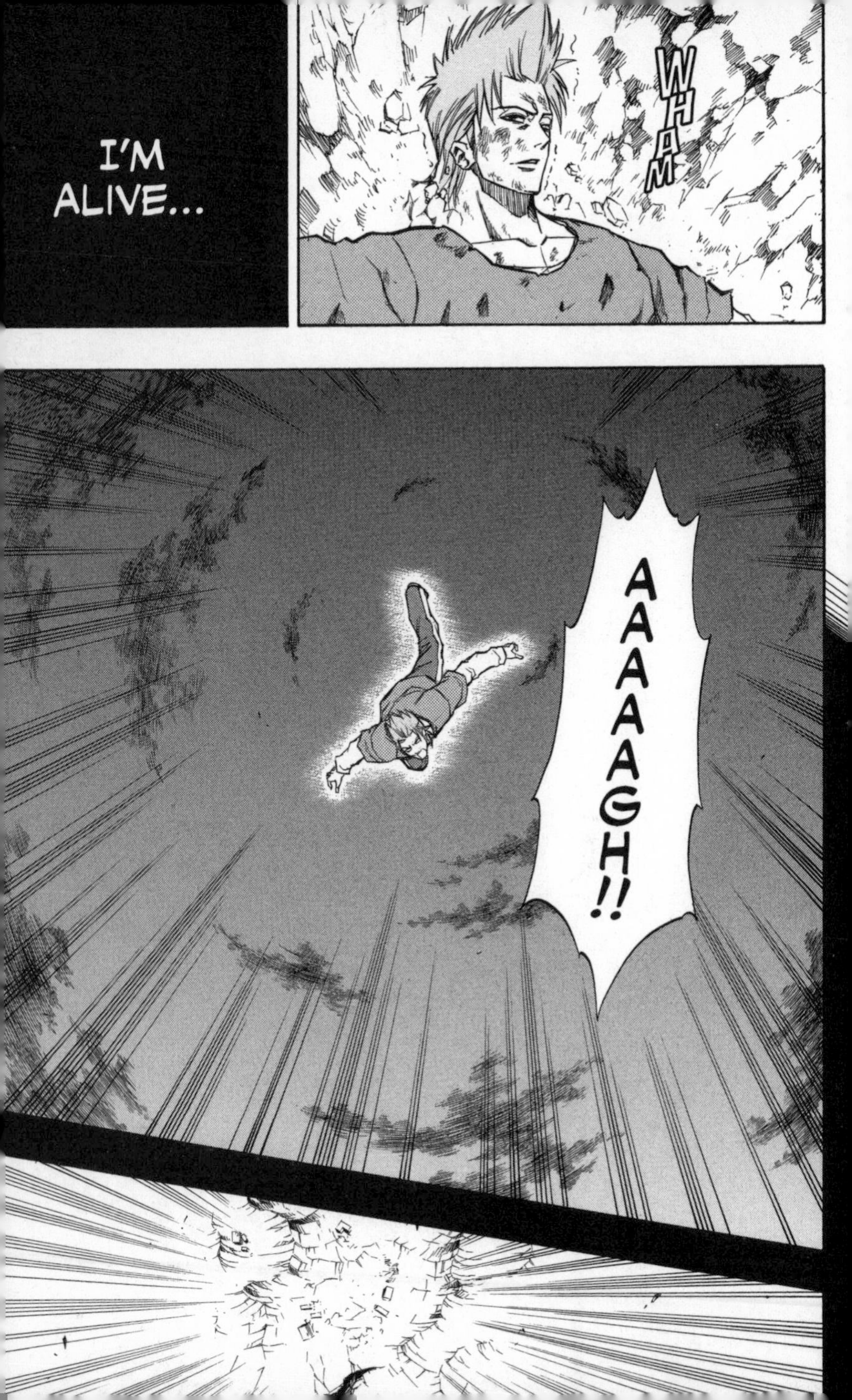
WHAM
I'M ALIVE...
AAAAAGH!!

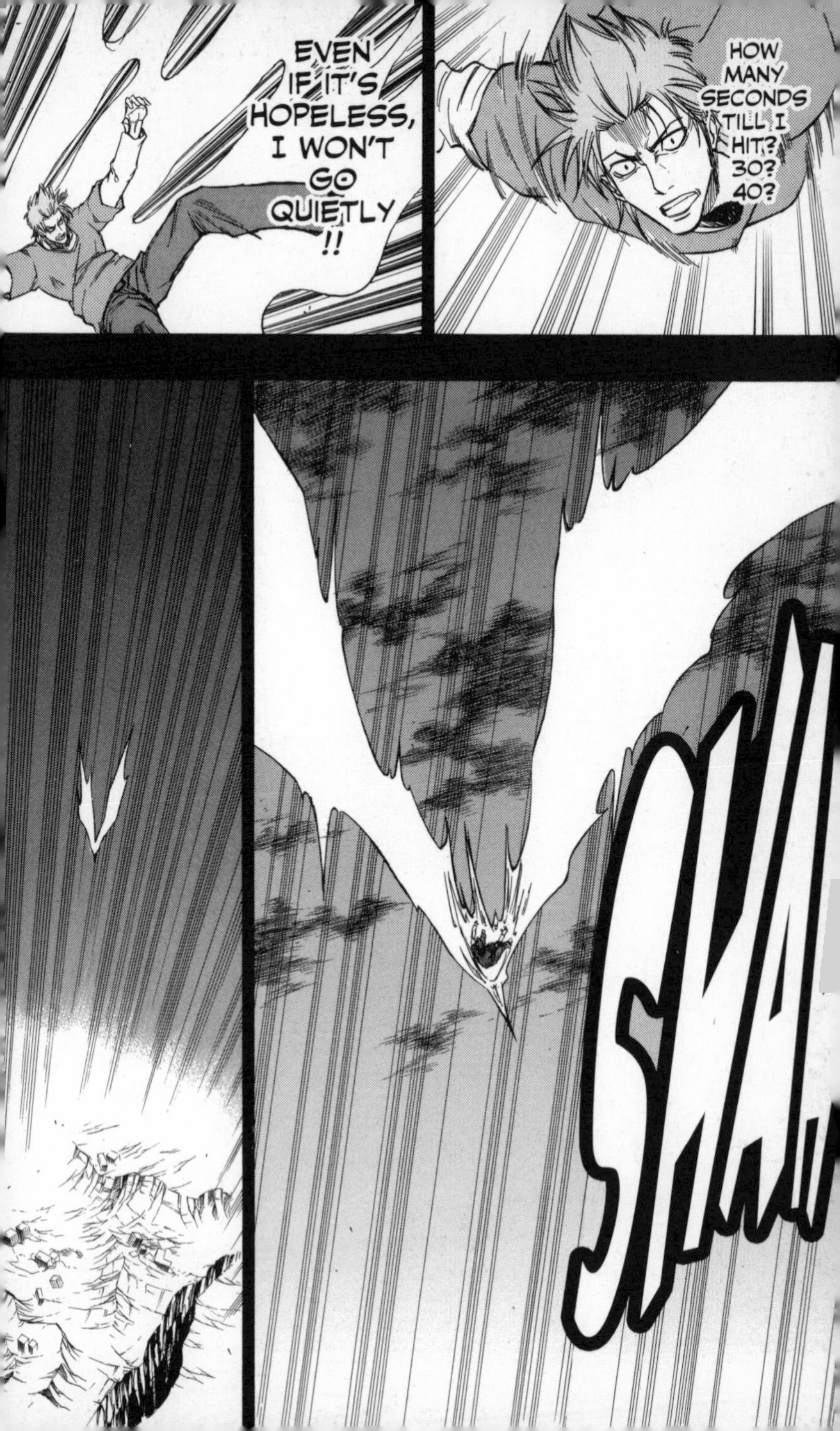
HOW MANY SECONDS TILL I HIT? 30? 40?
EVEN IF IT'S HOPELESS, I WON'T GO QUIETLY!!
SHA

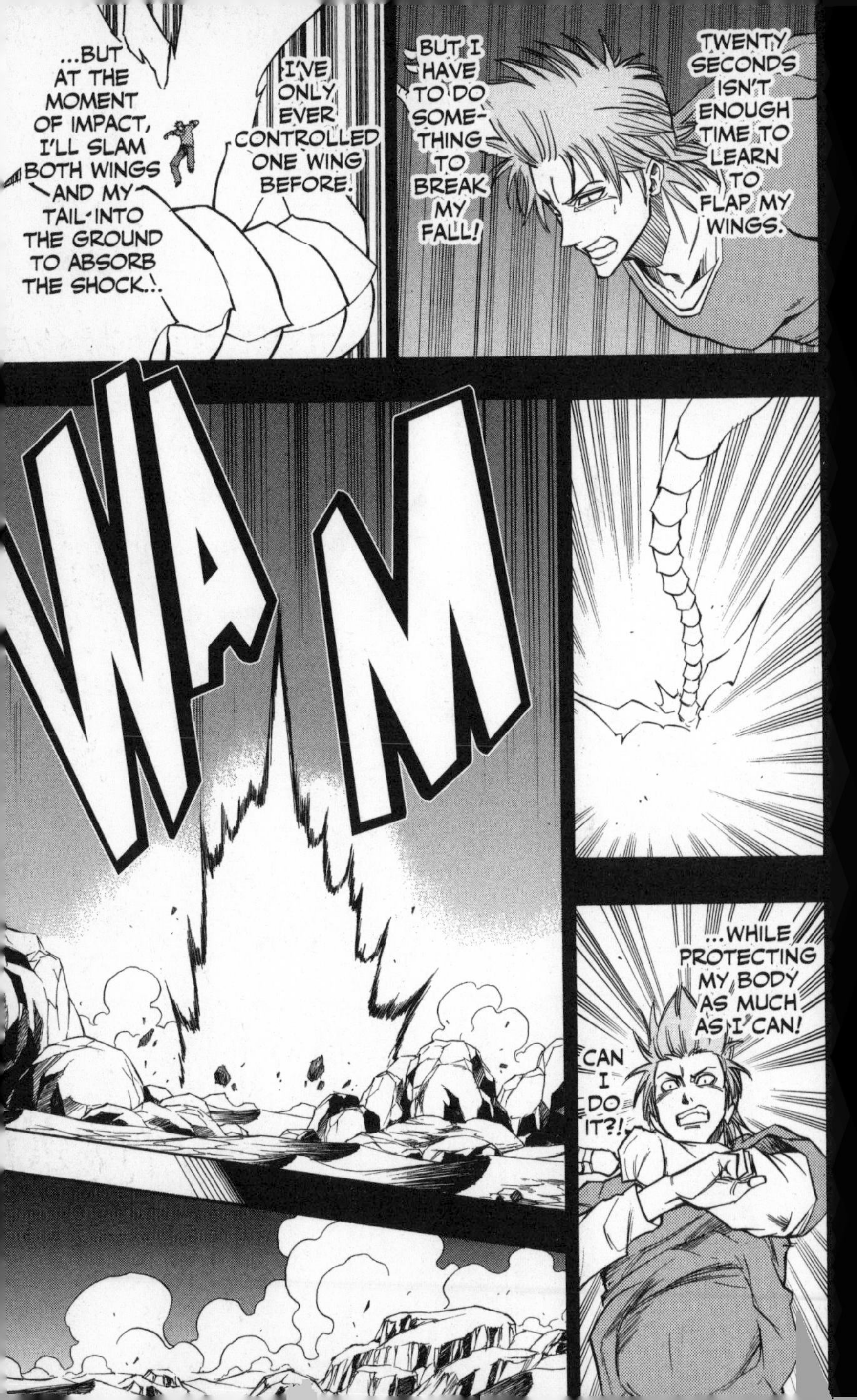
TWENTY SECONDS ISN'T ENOUGH TIME TO LEARN TO FLAP MY WINGS.
BUT I HAVE TO DO SOME-THING TO BREAK MY FALL!
I'VE ONLY EVER CONTROLLED ONE WING BEFORE.
...BUT AT THE MOMENT OF IMPACT, I'LL SLAM BOTH WINGS AND MY TAIL INTO THE GROUND TO ABSORB THE SHOCK...
...WHILE PROTECTING MY BODY AS MUCH AS I CAN!
CAN I DO IT?!
WAM

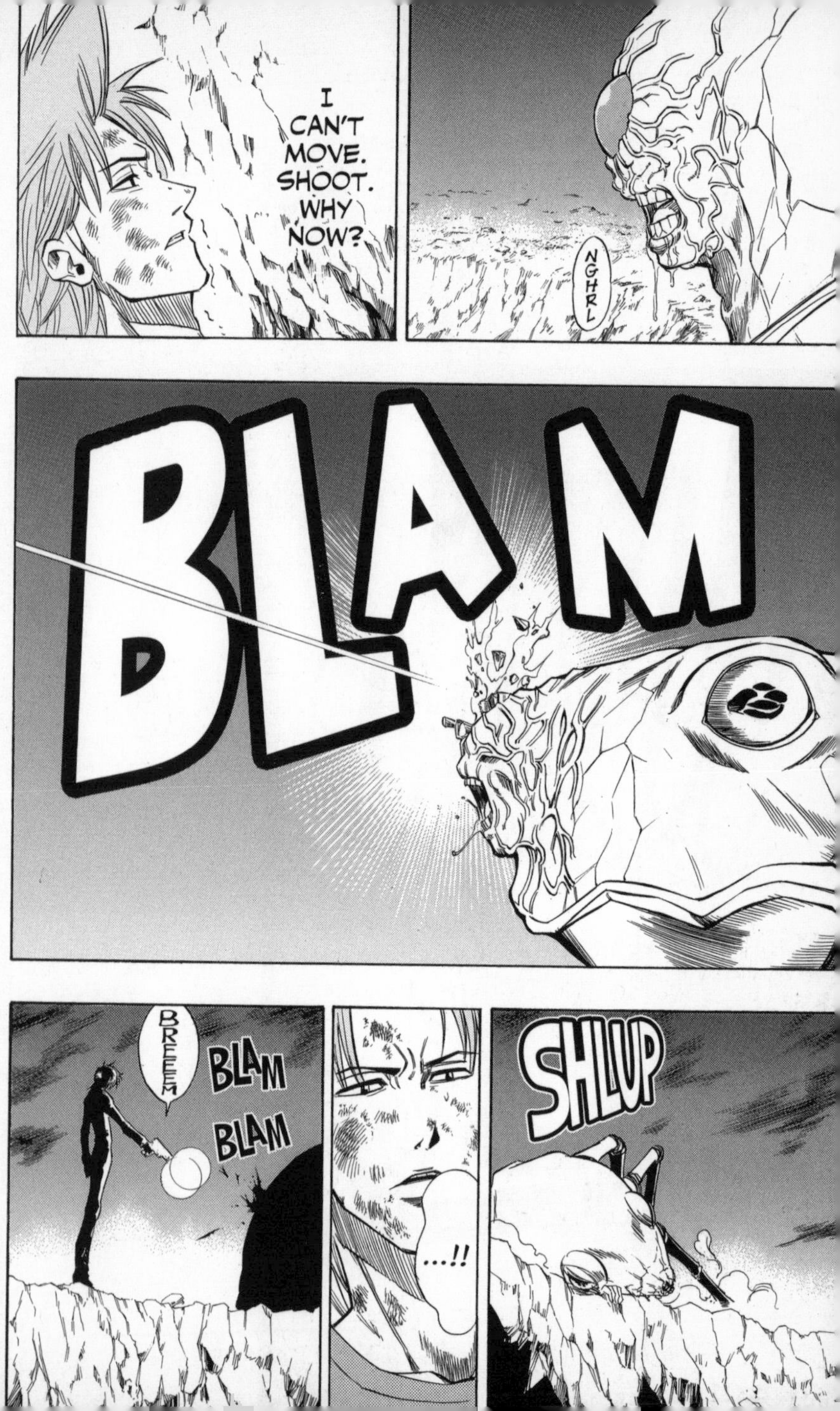
NGHRL
I CAN'T MOVE. SHOOT. WHY NOW?
BLAM
SHLUP
...!!
BREEEM
BLAM
BLAM

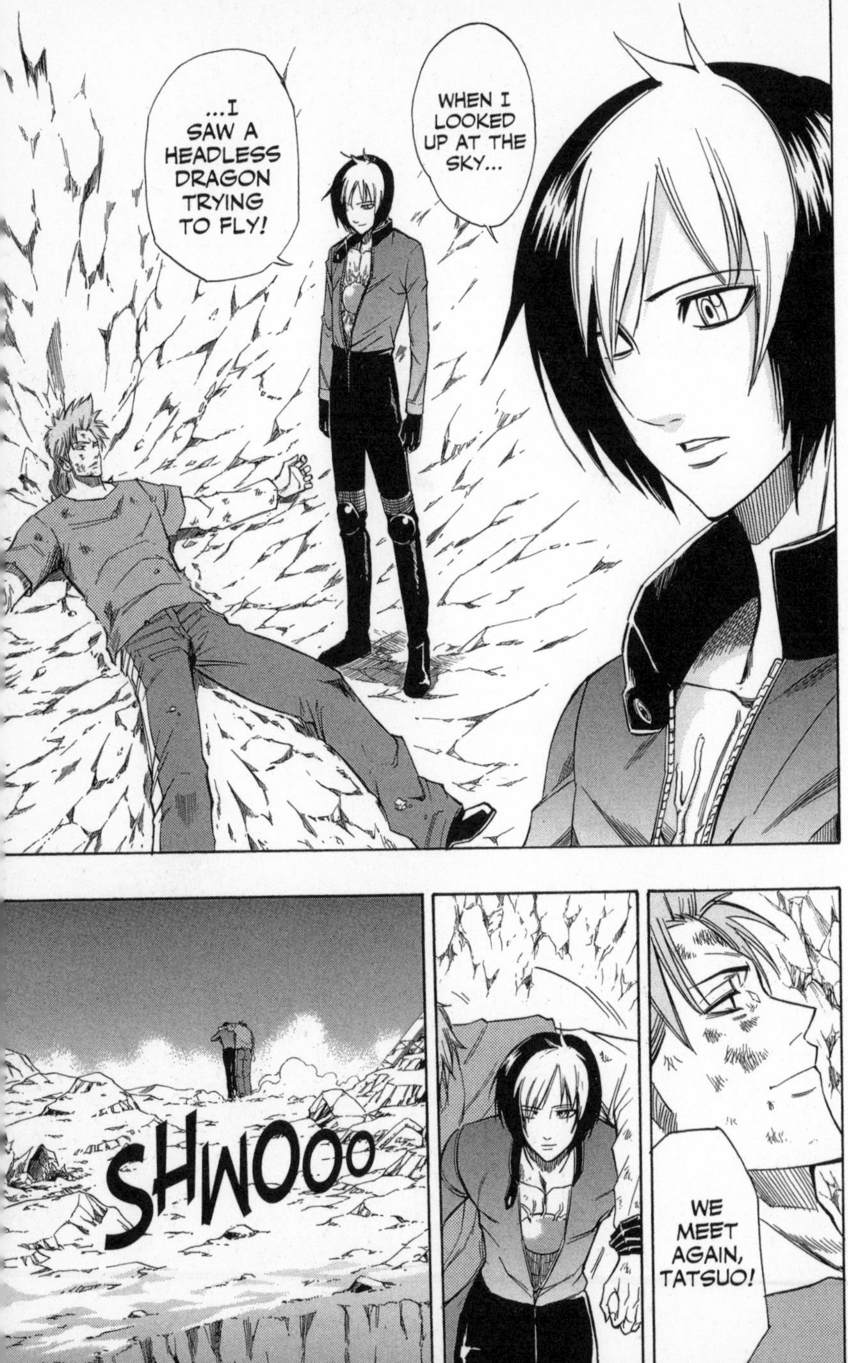
WHEN I LOOKED UP AT THE SKY...
...I SAW A HEADLESS DRAGON TRYING TO FLY!
WE MEET AGAIN, TATSUO!
SHWOOO

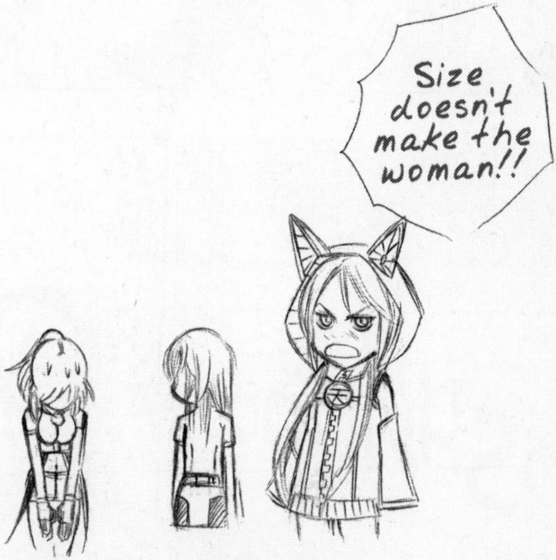
Size doesn't make the woman!!

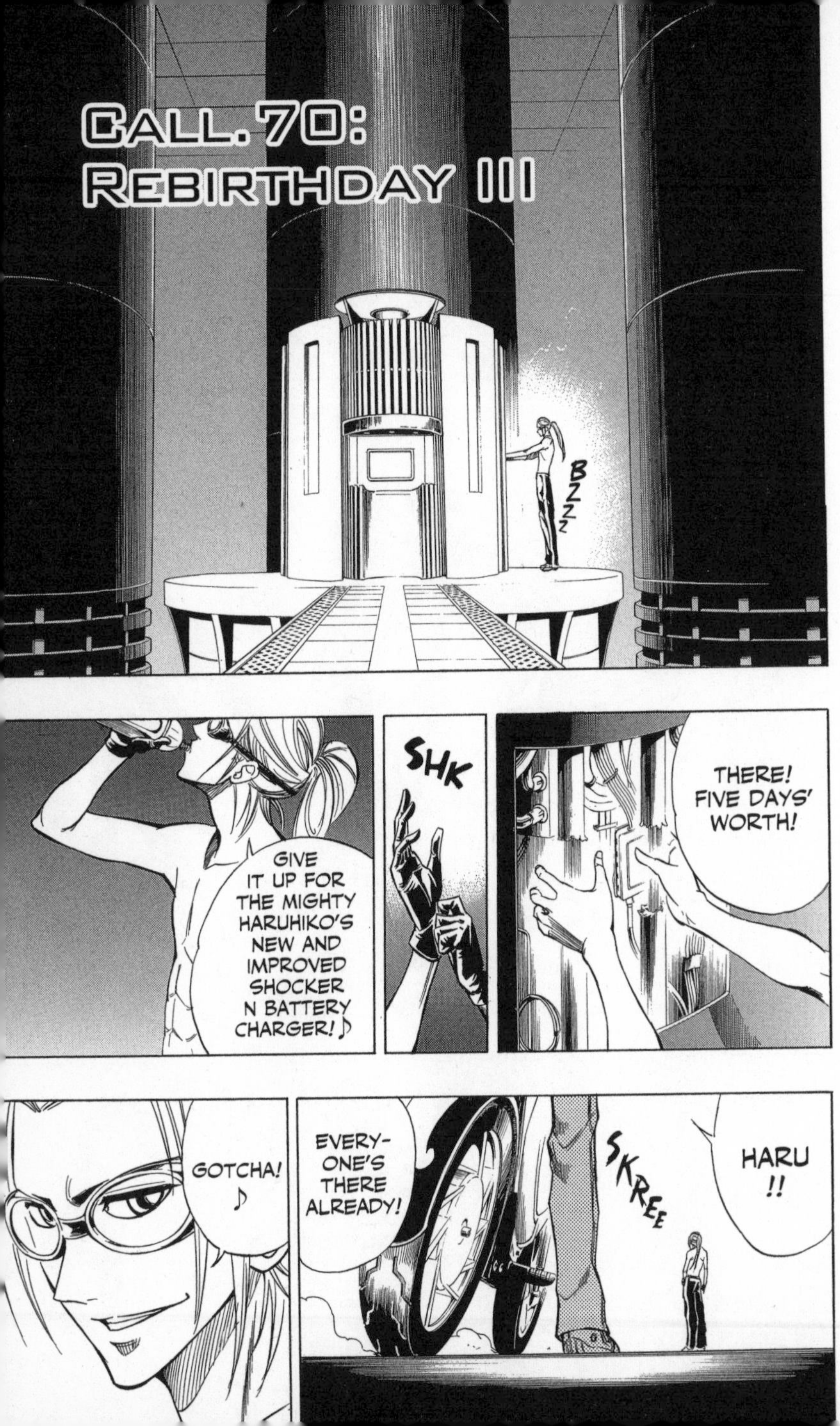
CALL. 70: REBIRTHDAY III
BZZZZ
THERE! FIVE DAYS' WORTH!
SHK
GIVE IT UP FOR THE MIGHTY HARUHIKO'S NEW AND IMPROVED SHOCKER N BATTERY CHARGER! ♪
HARU !!
SKREE
EVERY-ONE'S THERE ALREADY!
GOTCHA! ♪

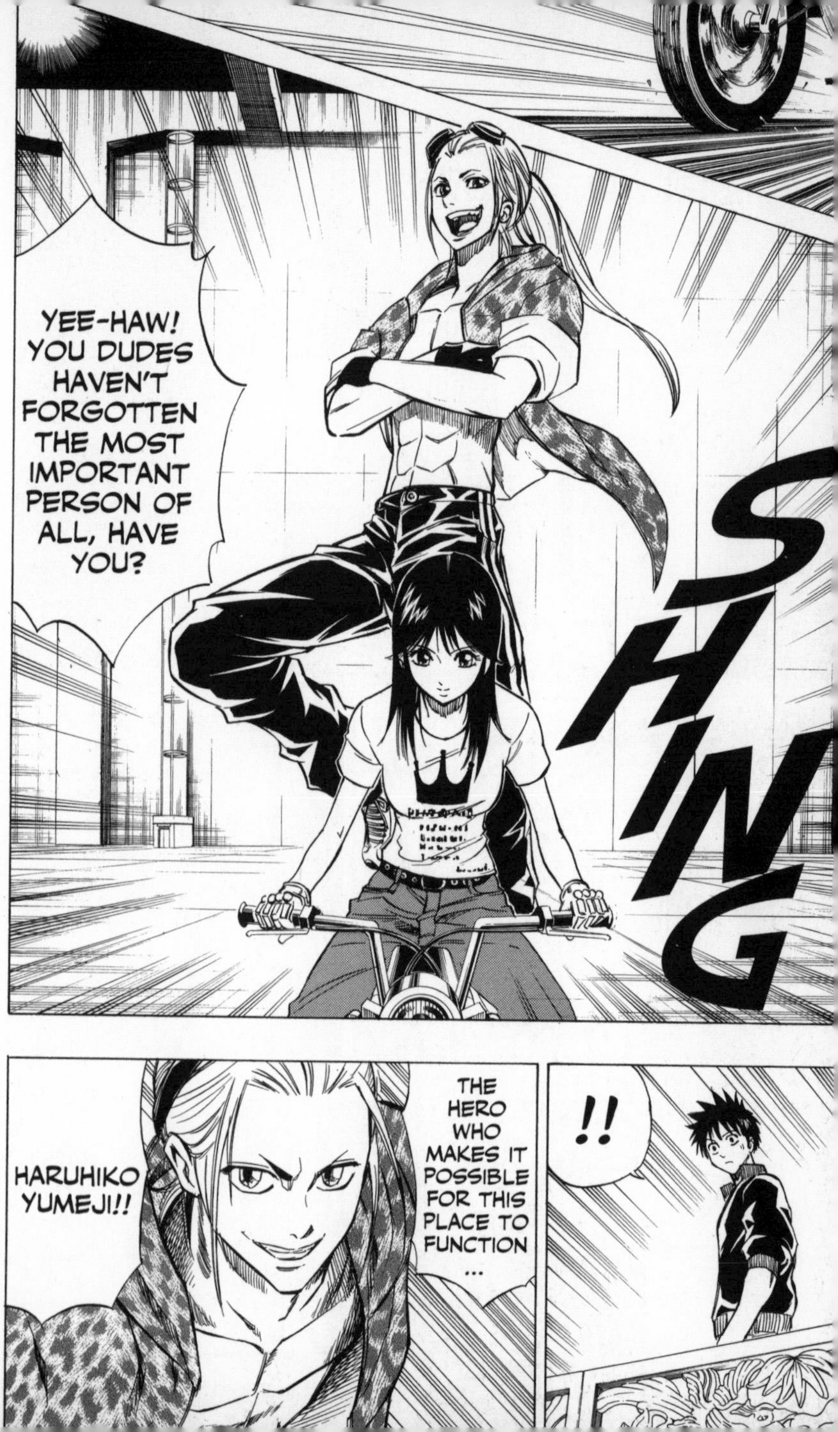
YEE-HAW! YOU DUDES HAVEN'T FORGOTTEN THE MOST IMPORTANT PERSON OF ALL, HAVE YOU?
SHING
!!
THE HERO WHO MAKES IT POSSIBLE FOR THIS PLACE TO FUNCTION ...
HARUHIKO YUMEJI!!

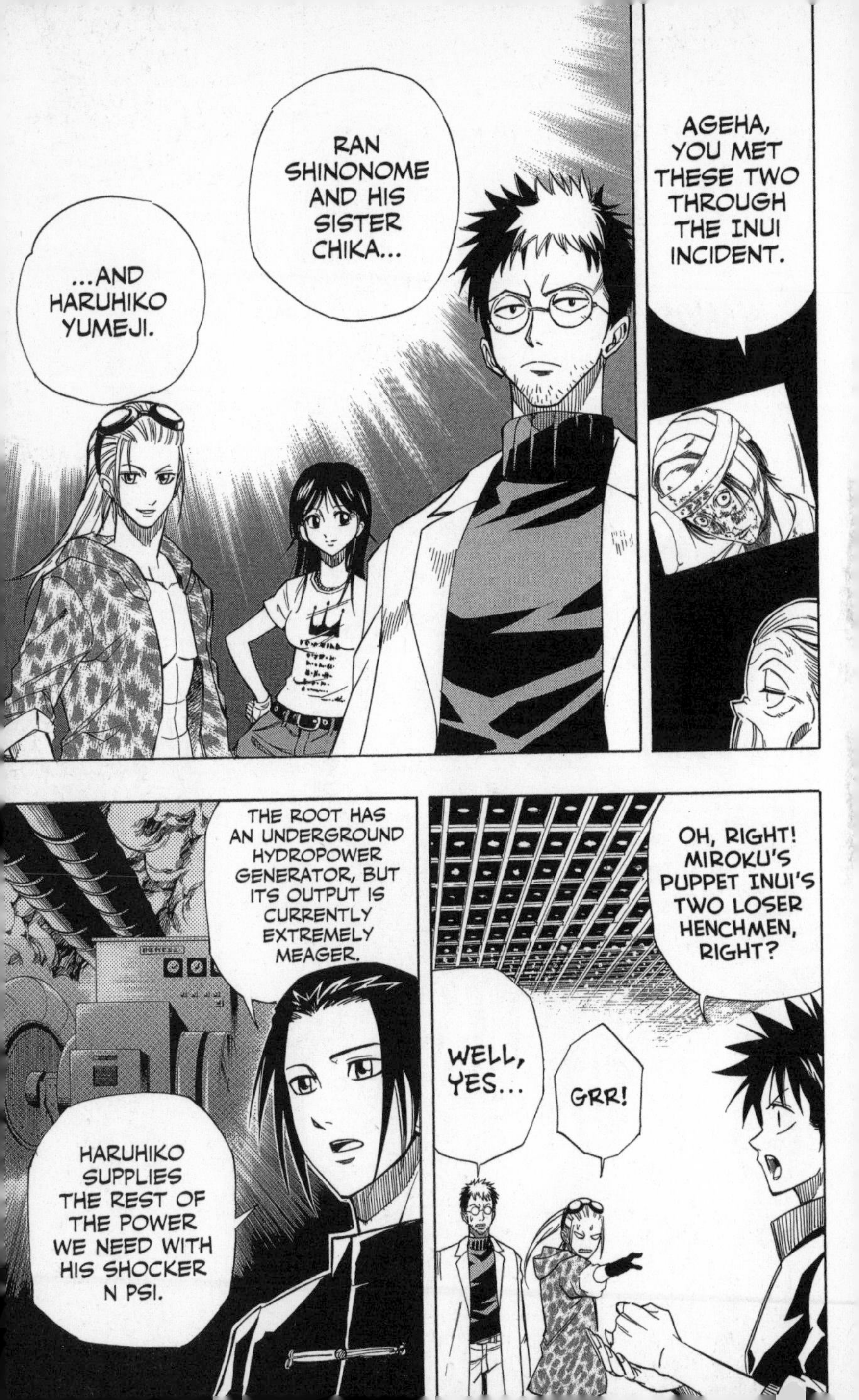
AGEHA, YOU MET THESE TWO THROUGH THE INUI INCIDENT.
RAN SHINONOME AND HIS SISTER CHIKA...
...AND HARUHIKO YUMEJI.
OH, RIGHT! MIROKU'S PUPPET INUI'S TWO LOSER HENCHMEN, RIGHT?
WELL, YES...
GRR!
THE ROOT HAS AN UNDERGROUND HYDROPOWER GENERATOR, BUT ITS OUTPUT IS CURRENTLY EXTREMELY MEAGER.
HARUHIKO SUPPLIES THE REST OF THE POWER WE NEED WITH HIS SHOCKER N PSI.

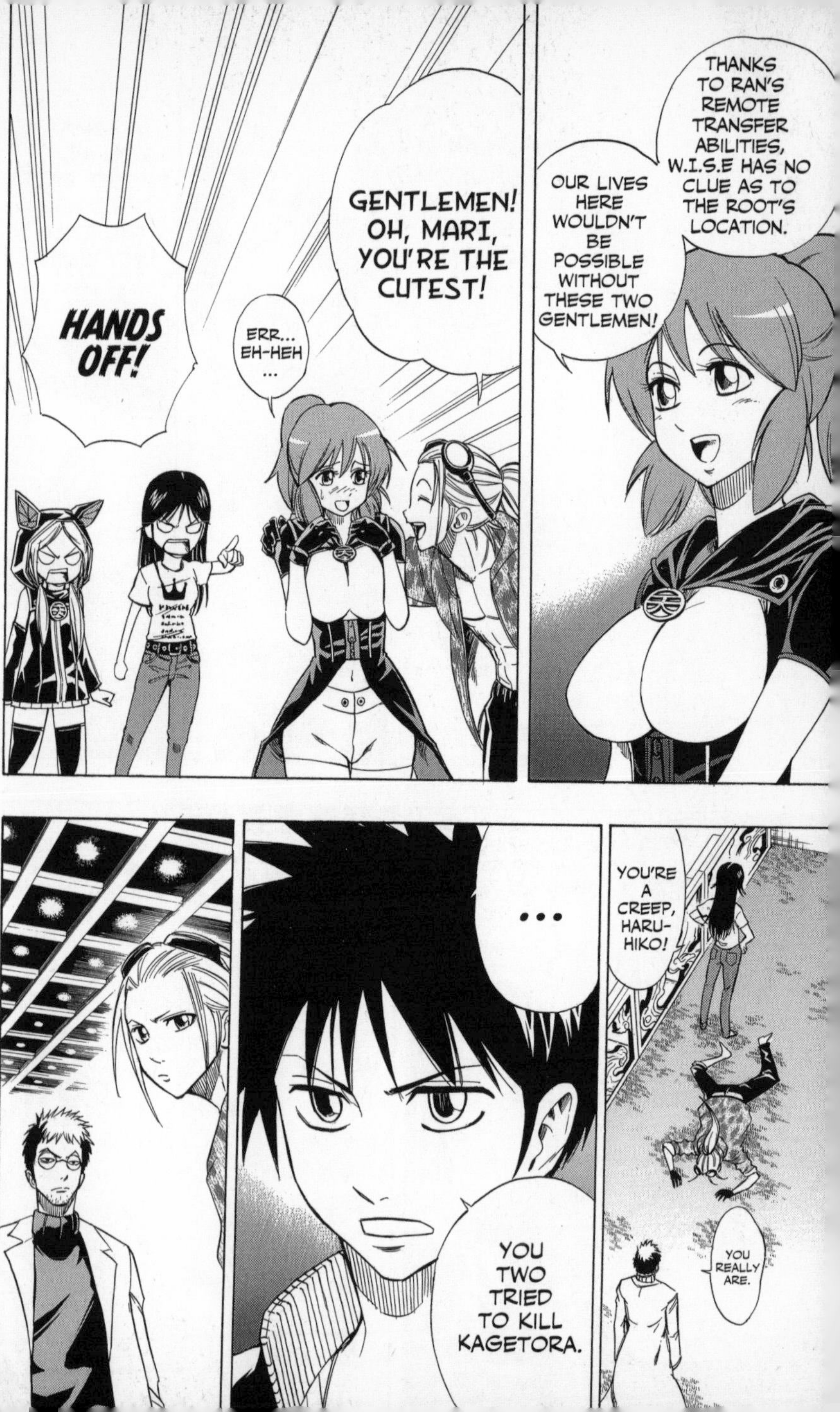
THANKS TO RAN'S REMOTE TRANSFER ABILITIES, W.I.S.E HAS NO CLUE AS TO THE ROOT'S LOCATION.
OUR LIVES HERE WOULDN'T BE POSSIBLE WITHOUT THESE TWO GENTLEMEN!
GENTLEMEN! OH, MARI, YOU'RE THE CUTEST!
ERR... EH-HEH ...
HANDS OFF!
YOU'RE A CREEP, HARU-HIKO!
YOU REALLY ARE.
...
YOU TWO TRIED TO KILL KAGETORA.

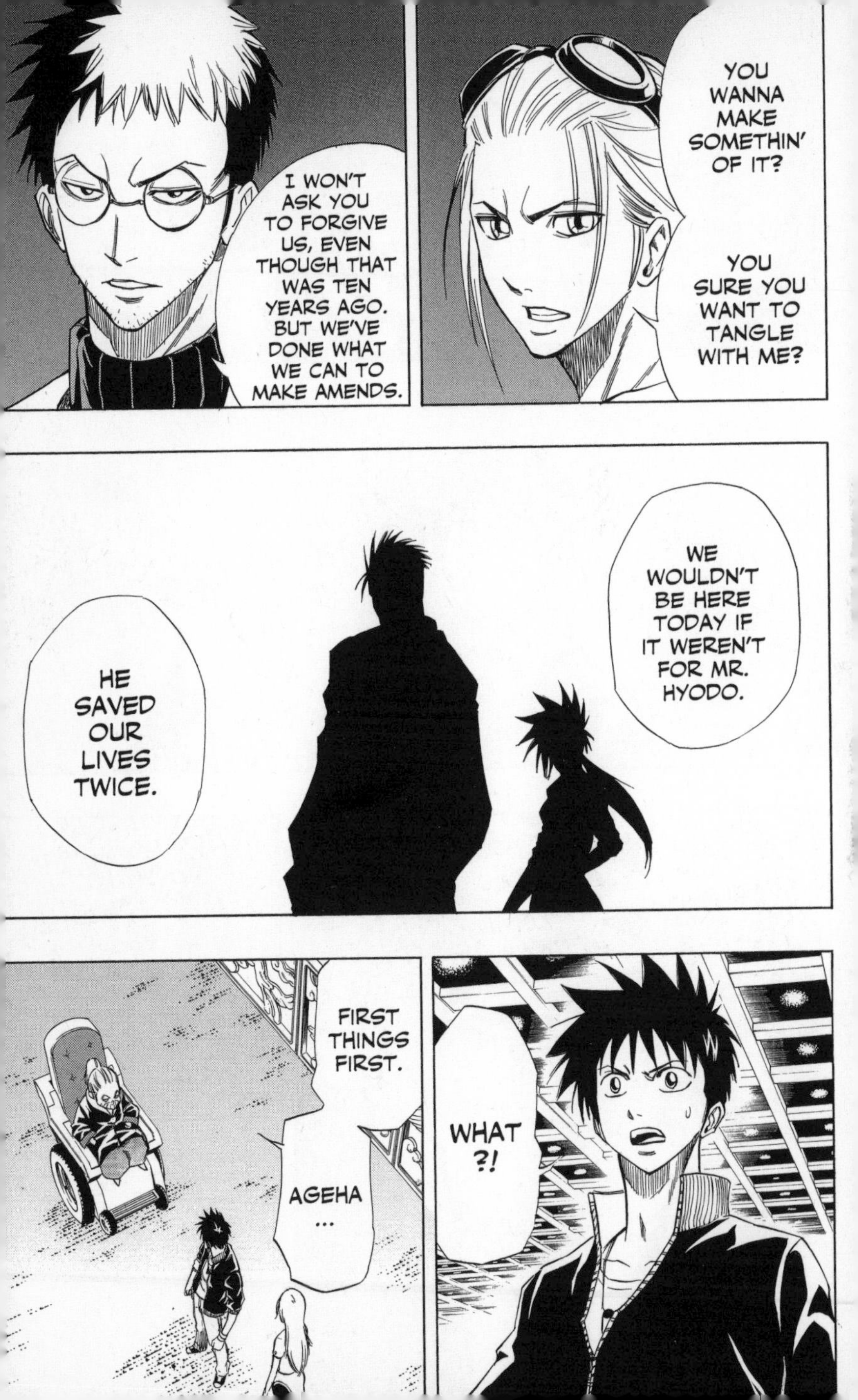
YOU WANNA MAKE SOMETHIN' OF IT?
YOU SURE YOU WANT TO TANGLE WITH ME?
I WON'T ASK YOU TO FORGIVE US, EVEN THOUGH THAT WAS TEN YEARS AGO. BUT WE'VE DONE WHAT WE CAN TO MAKE AMENDS.
WE WOULDN'T BE HERE TODAY IF IT WEREN'T FOR MR. HYODO.
HE SAVED OUR LIVES TWICE.
WHAT ?!
FIRST THINGS FIRST.
AGEHA ...

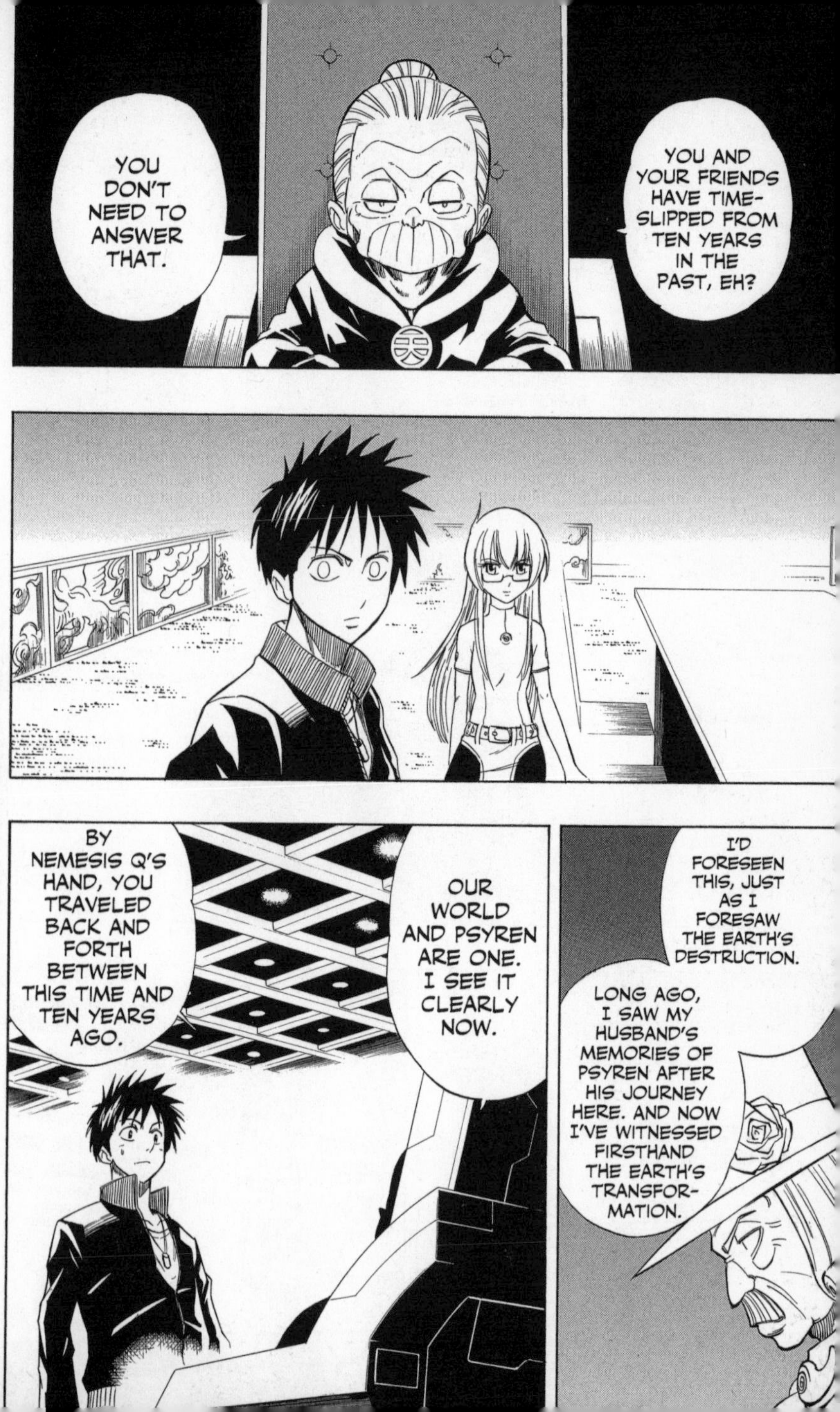
YOU AND YOUR FRIENDS HAVE TIME-SLIPPED FROM TEN YEARS IN THE PAST, EH?
YOU DON'T NEED TO ANSWER THAT.
I'D FORESEEN THIS, JUST AS I FORESAW THE EARTH'S DESTRUCTION.
LONG AGO, I SAW MY HUSBAND'S MEMORIES OF PSYREN AFTER HIS JOURNEY HERE. AND NOW I'VE WITNESSED FIRSTHAND THE EARTH'S TRANSFORMATION.
OUR WORLD AND PSYREN ARE ONE. I SEE IT CLEARLY NOW.
BY NEMESIS Q'S HAND, YOU TRAVELED BACK AND FORTH BETWEEN THIS TIME AND TEN YEARS AGO.

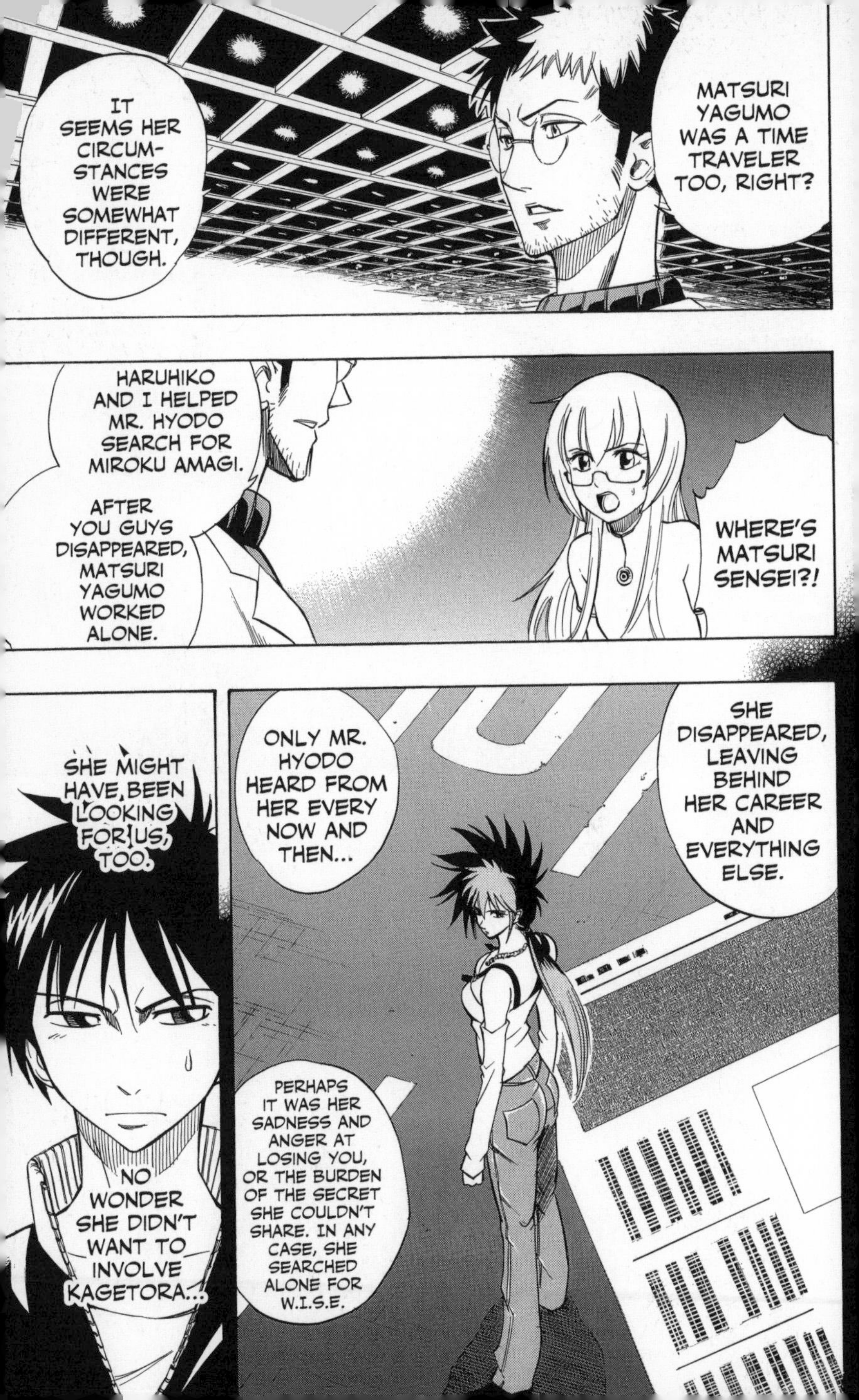
MATSURI YAGUMO WAS A TIME TRAVELER TOO, RIGHT?
IT SEEMS HER CIRCUM-STANCES WERE SOMEWHAT DIFFERENT, THOUGH.
WHERE'S MATSURI SENSEI?!
HARUHIKO AND I HELPED MR. HYODO SEARCH FOR MIROKU AMAGI.
AFTER YOU GUYS DISAPPEARED, MATSURI YAGUMO WORKED ALONE.
SHE DISAPPEARED, LEAVING BEHIND HER CAREER AND EVERYTHING ELSE.
ONLY MR. HYODO HEARD FROM HER EVERY NOW AND THEN...
PERHAPS IT WAS HER SADNESS AND ANGER AT LOSING YOU, OR THE BURDEN OF THE SECRET SHE COULDN'T SHARE. IN ANY CASE, SHE SEARCHED ALONE FOR W.I.S.E.
SHE MIGHT HAVE BEEN LOOKING FOR US, TOO.
NO WONDER SHE DIDN'T WANT TO INVOLVE KAGETORA...

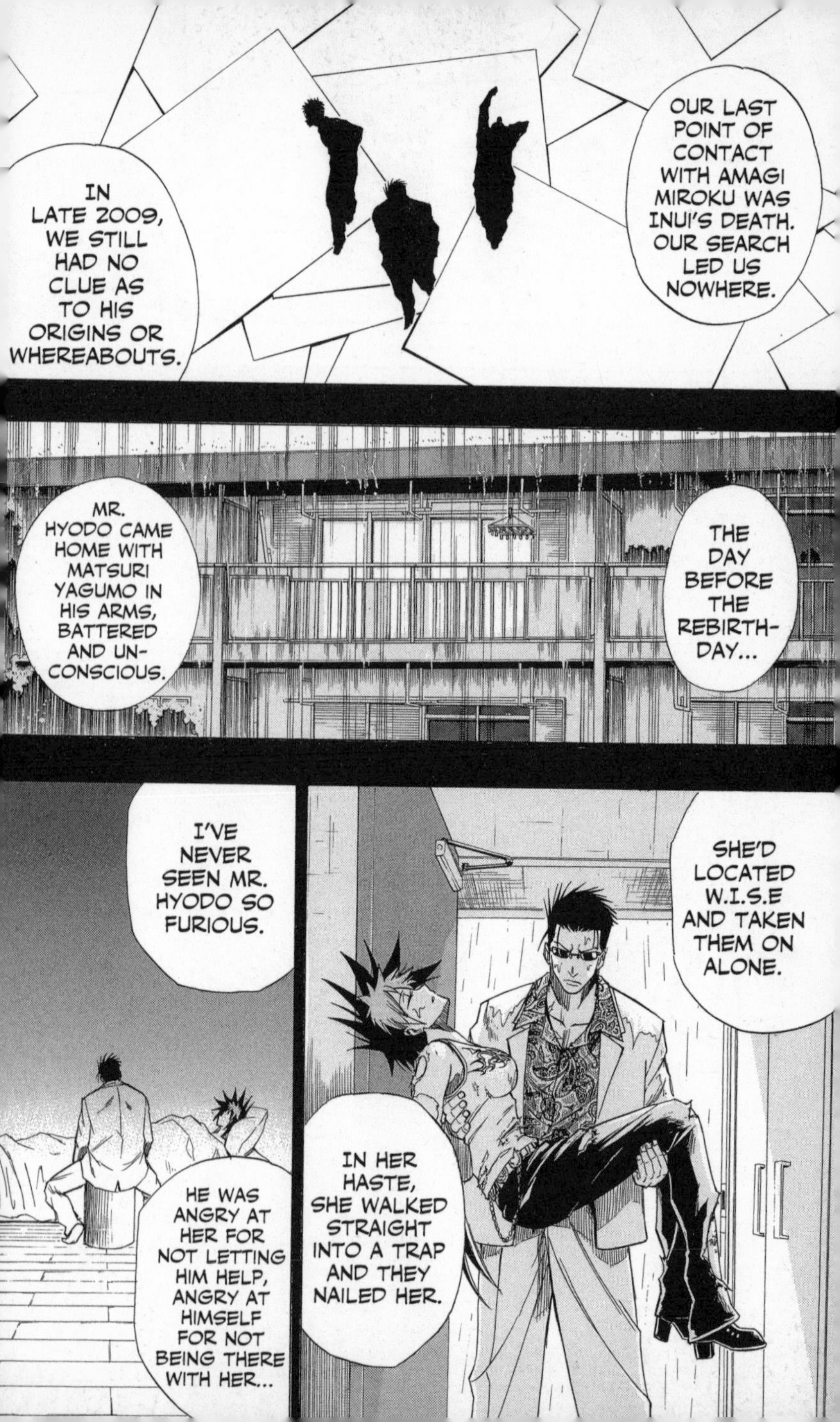
OUR LAST POINT OF CONTACT WITH AMAGI MIROKU WAS INUI'S DEATH. OUR SEARCH LED US NOWHERE.
IN LATE 2009, WE STILL HAD NO CLUE AS TO HIS ORIGINS OR WHEREABOUTS.
THE DAY BEFORE THE REBIRTH-DAY...
MR. HYODO CAME HOME WITH MATSURI YAGUMO IN HIS ARMS, BATTERED AND UN-CONSCIOUS.
SHE'D LOCATED W.I.S.E AND TAKEN THEM ON ALONE.
IN HER HASTE, SHE WALKED STRAIGHT INTO A TRAP AND THEY NAILED HER.
I'VE NEVER SEEN MR. HYODO SO FURIOUS.
HE WAS ANGRY AT HER FOR NOT LETTING HIM HELP, ANGRY AT HIMSELF FOR NOT BEING THERE WITH HER...

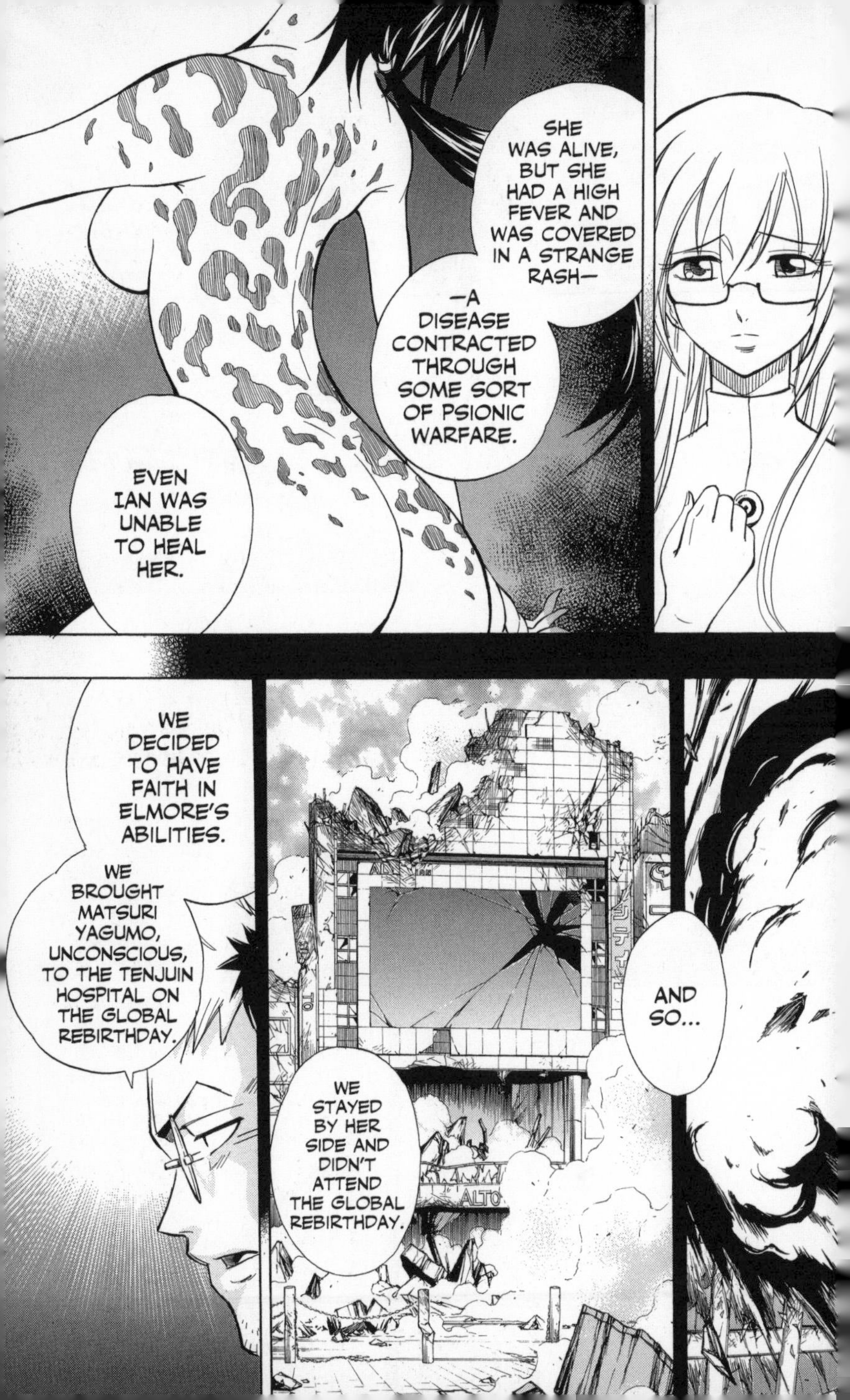
SHE WAS ALIVE, BUT SHE HAD A HIGH FEVER AND WAS COVERED IN A STRANGE RASH—
—A DISEASE CONTRACTED THROUGH SOME SORT OF PSIONIC WARFARE.
EVEN IAN WAS UNABLE TO HEAL HER.
AND SO...
WE STAYED BY HER SIDE AND DIDN'T ATTEND THE GLOBAL REBIRTHDAY.
WE DECIDED TO HAVE FAITH IN ELMORE'S ABILITIES.
WE BROUGHT MATSURI YAGUMO, UNCONSCIOUS, TO THE TENJUIN HOSPITAL ON THE GLOBAL REBIRTHDAY.

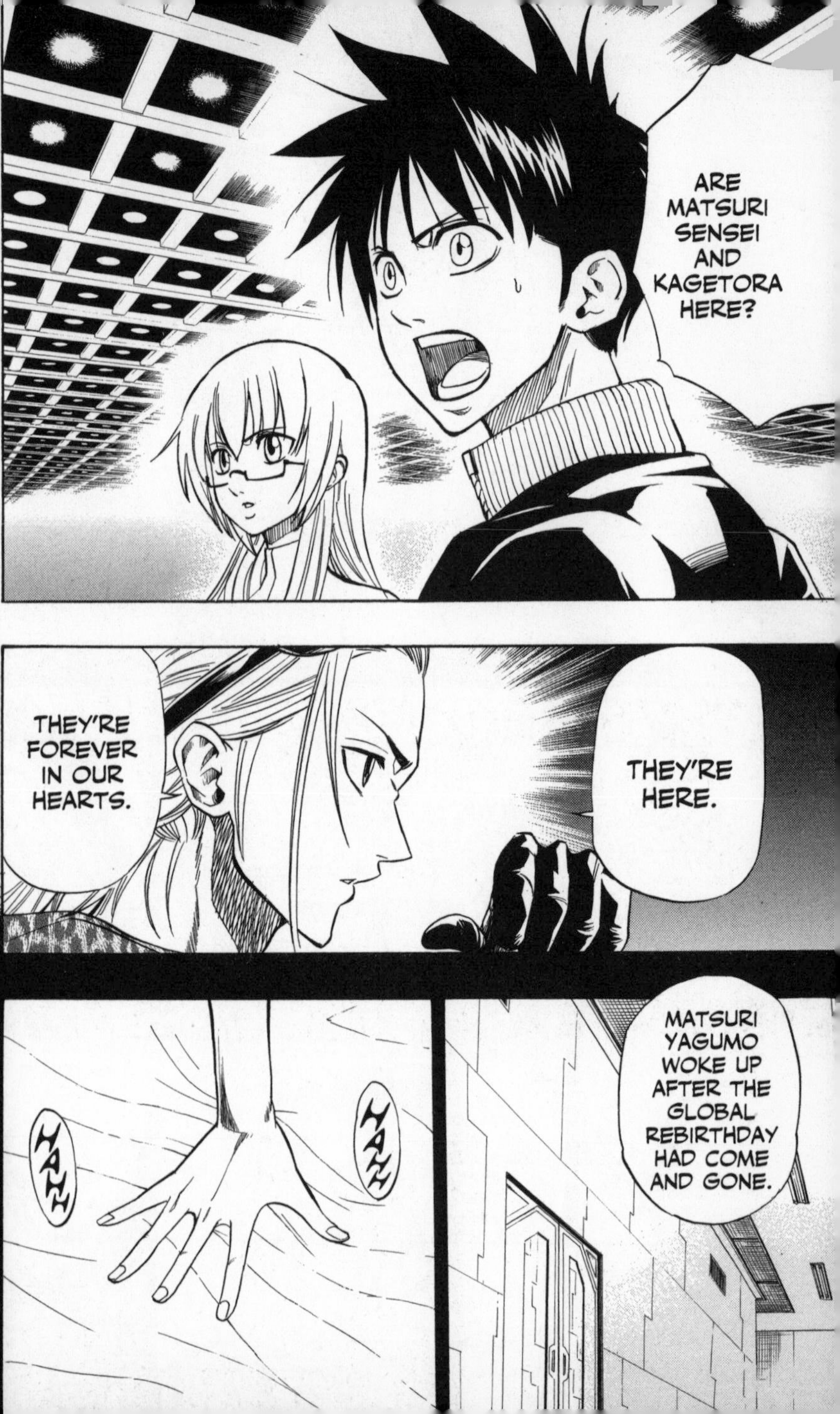
ARE MATSURI SENSEI AND KAGETORA HERE?
THEY'RE HERE.
THEY'RE FOREVER IN OUR HEARTS.
MATSURI YAGUMO WOKE UP AFTER THE GLOBAL REBIRTHDAY HAD COME AND GONE.
HAH
HAH

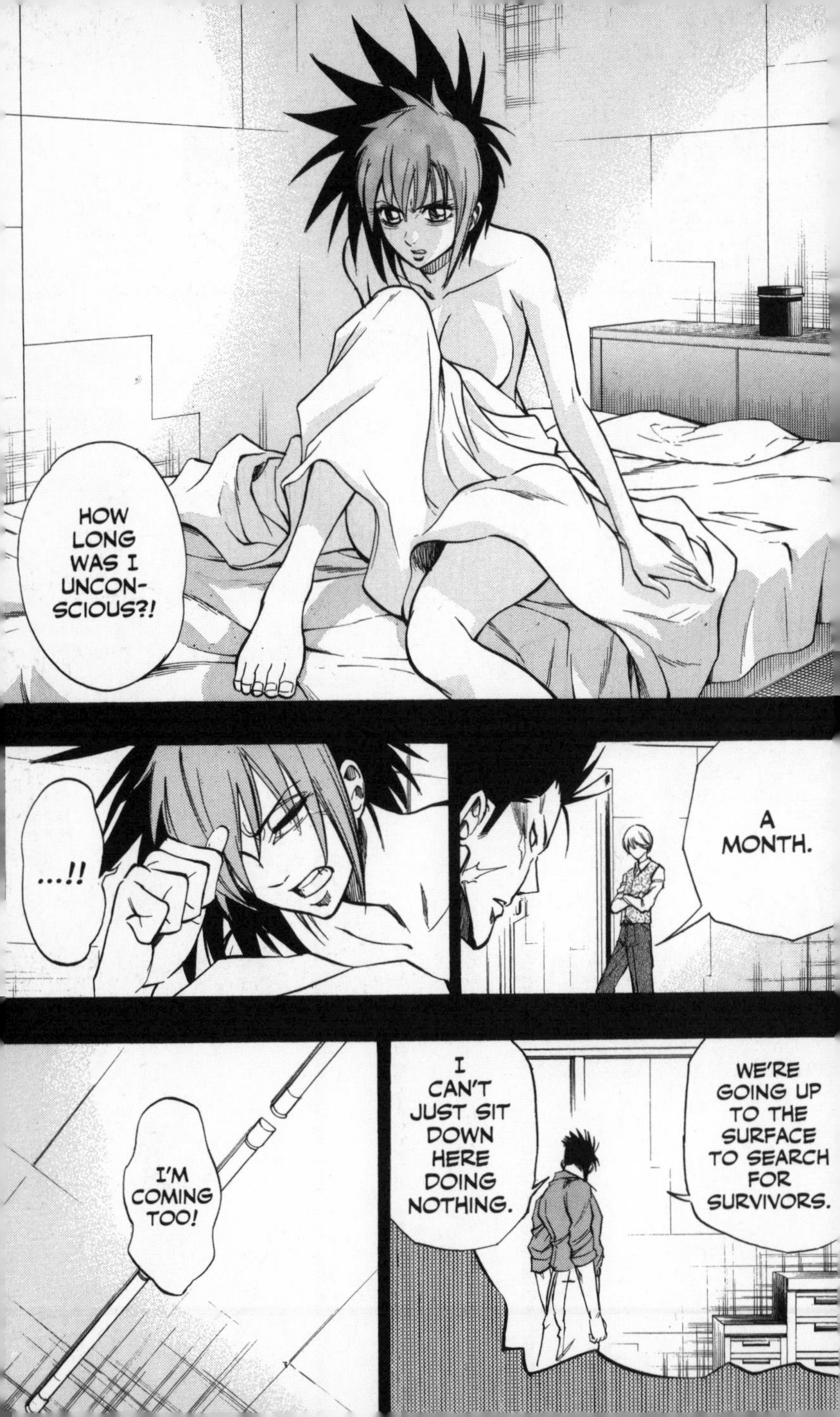
HOW LONG WAS I UNCONSCIOUS?!
A MONTH.
...!!
WE'RE GOING UP TO THE SURFACE TO SEARCH FOR SURVIVORS.
I CAN'T JUST SIT DOWN HERE DOING NOTHING.
I'M COMING TOO!

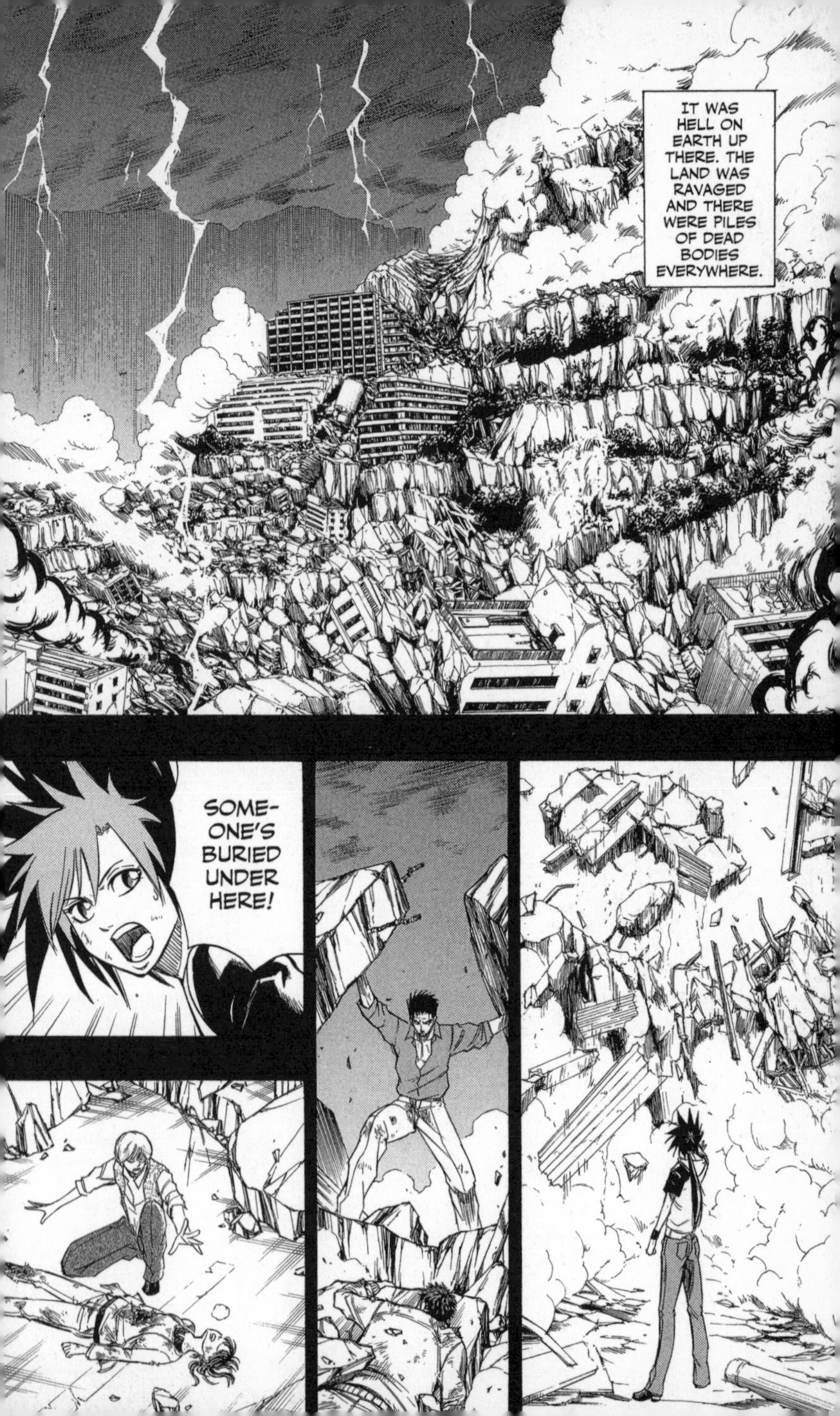
IT WAS HELL ON EARTH UP THERE. THE LAND WAS RAVAGED AND THERE WERE PILES OF DEAD BODIES EVERYWHERE.
SOME-ONE'S BURIED UNDER HERE!

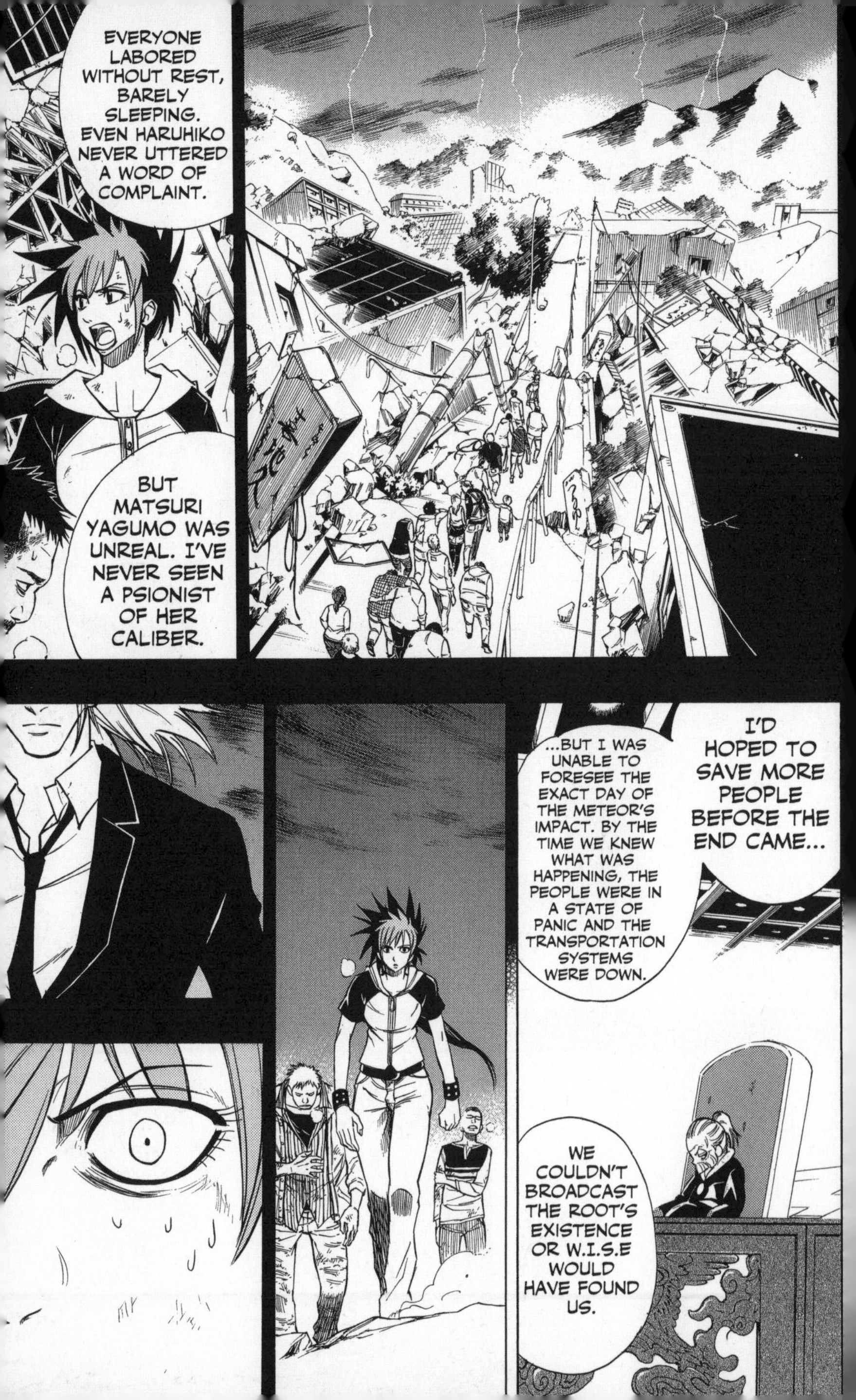
EVERYONE LABORED WITHOUT REST, BARELY SLEEPING. EVEN HARUHIKO NEVER UTTERED A WORD OF COMPLAINT.
BUT MATSURI YAGUMO WAS UNREAL. I'VE NEVER SEEN A PSIONIST OF HER CALIBER.
I'D HOPED TO SAVE MORE PEOPLE BEFORE THE END CAME...
...BUT I WAS UNABLE TO FORESEE THE EXACT DAY OF THE METEOR'S IMPACT. BY THE TIME WE KNEW WHAT WAS HAPPENING, THE PEOPLE WERE IN A STATE OF PANIC AND THE TRANSPORTATION SYSTEMS WERE DOWN.
WE COULDN'T BROADCAST THE ROOT'S EXISTENCE OR W.I.S.E WOULD HAVE FOUND US.

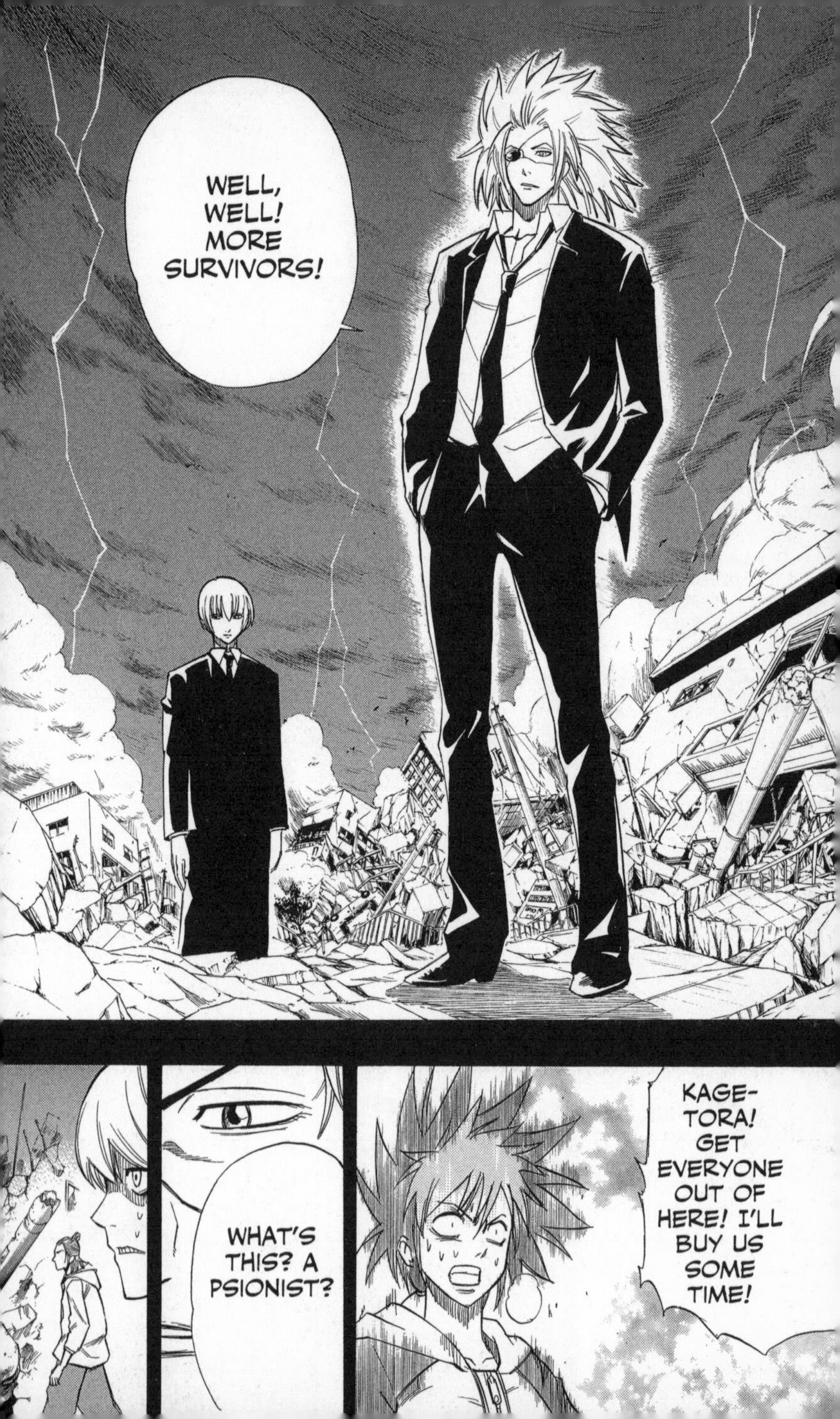
WELL, WELL! MORE SURVIVORS!
KAGE-TORA! GET EVERYONE OUT OF HERE! I'LL BUY US SOME TIME!
WHAT'S THIS? A PSIONIST?

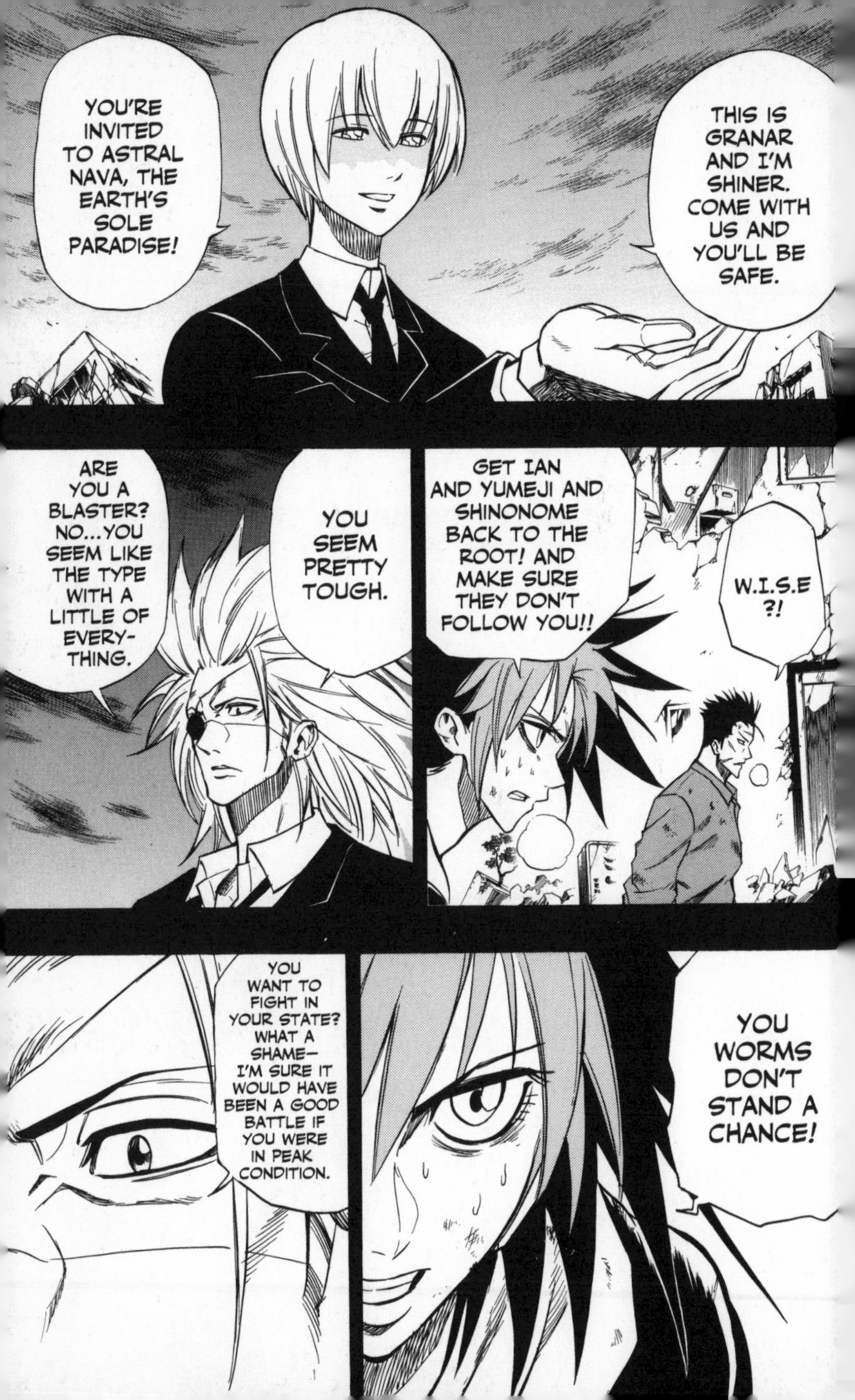
THIS IS GRANAR AND I'M SHINER. COME WITH US AND YOU'LL BE SAFE.
YOU'RE INVITED TO ASTRAL NAVA, THE EARTH'S SOLE PARADISE!
W.I.S.E ?!
GET IAN AND YUMEJI AND SHINONOME BACK TO THE ROOT! AND MAKE SURE THEY DON'T FOLLOW YOU!!
YOU SEEM PRETTY TOUGH.
ARE YOU A BLASTER? NO...YOU SEEM LIKE THE TYPE WITH A LITTLE OF EVERY-THING.
YOU WORMS DON'T STAND A CHANCE!
YOU WANT TO FIGHT IN YOUR STATE? WHAT A SHAME— I'M SURE IT WOULD HAVE BEEN A GOOD BATTLE IF YOU WERE IN PEAK CONDITION.

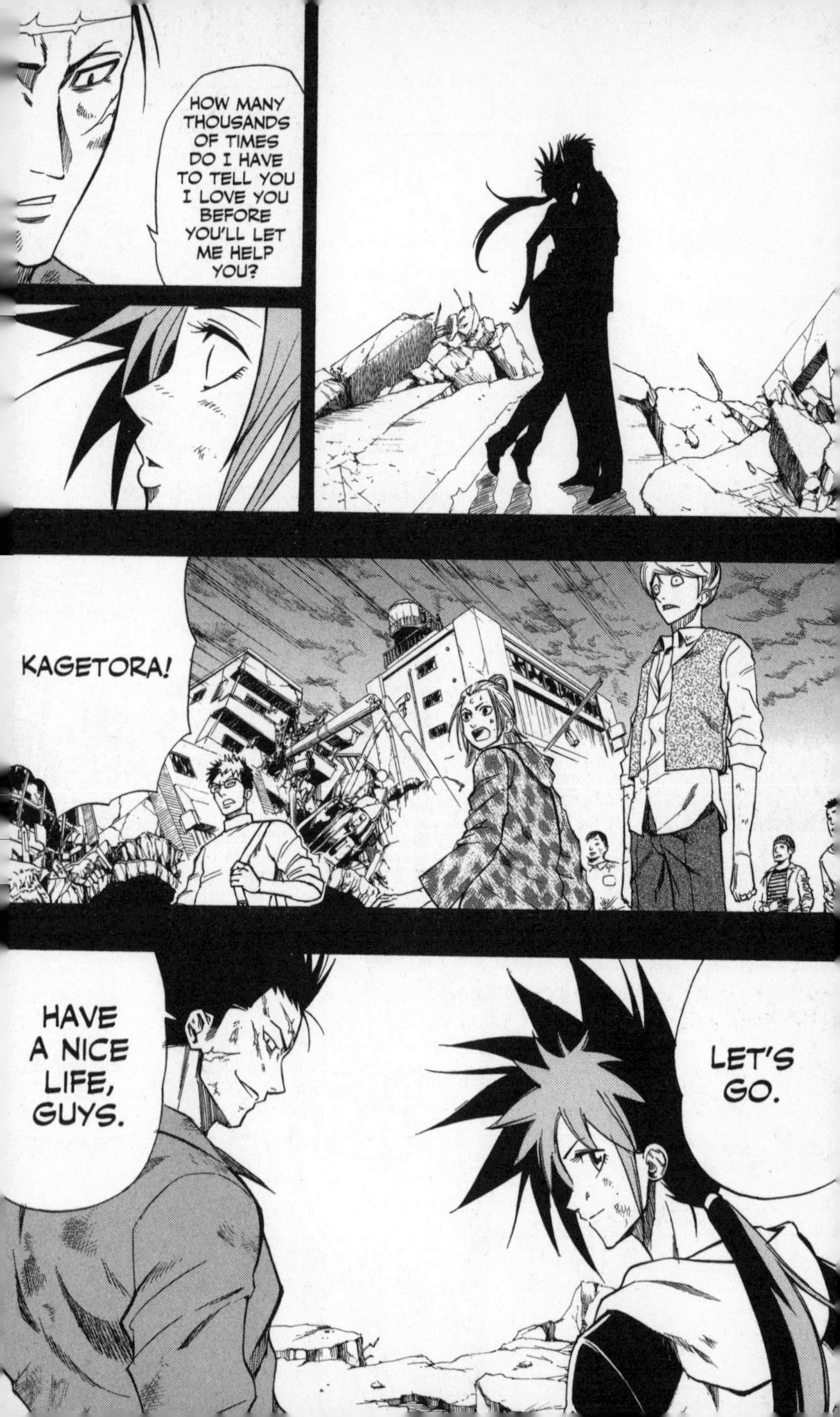
HOW MANY THOUSANDS OF TIMES DO I HAVE TO TELL YOU I LOVE YOU BEFORE YOU'LL LET ME HELP YOU?
KAGETORA!
LET'S GO.
HAVE A NICE LIFE, GUYS.

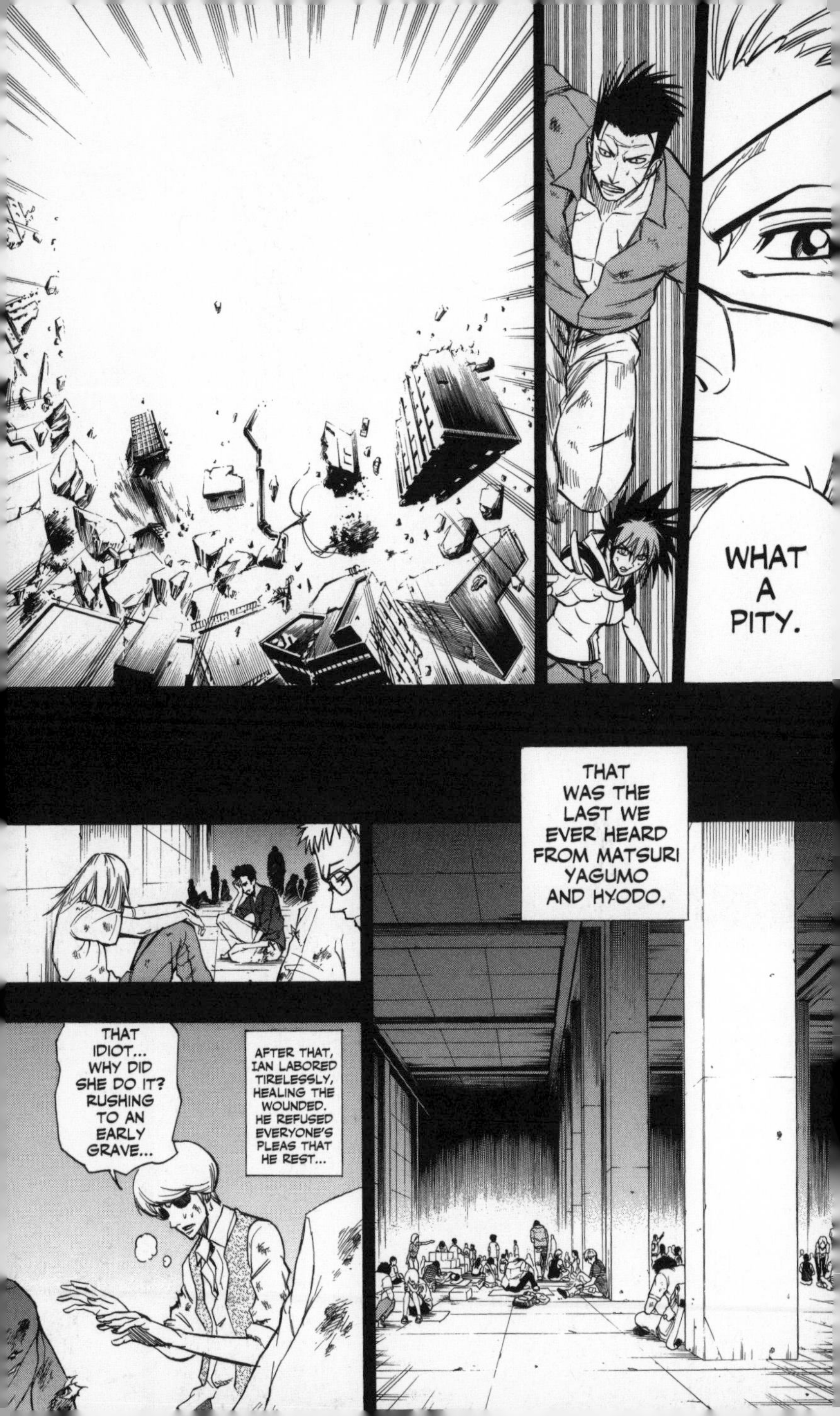
WHAT A PITY.
THAT WAS THE LAST WE EVER HEARD FROM MATSURI YAGUMO AND HYODO.
AFTER THAT, IAN LABORED TIRELESSLY, HEALING THE WOUNDED. HE REFUSED EVERYONE'S PLEAS THAT HE REST...
THAT IDIOT... WHY DID SHE DO IT? RUSHING TO AN EARLY GRAVE...

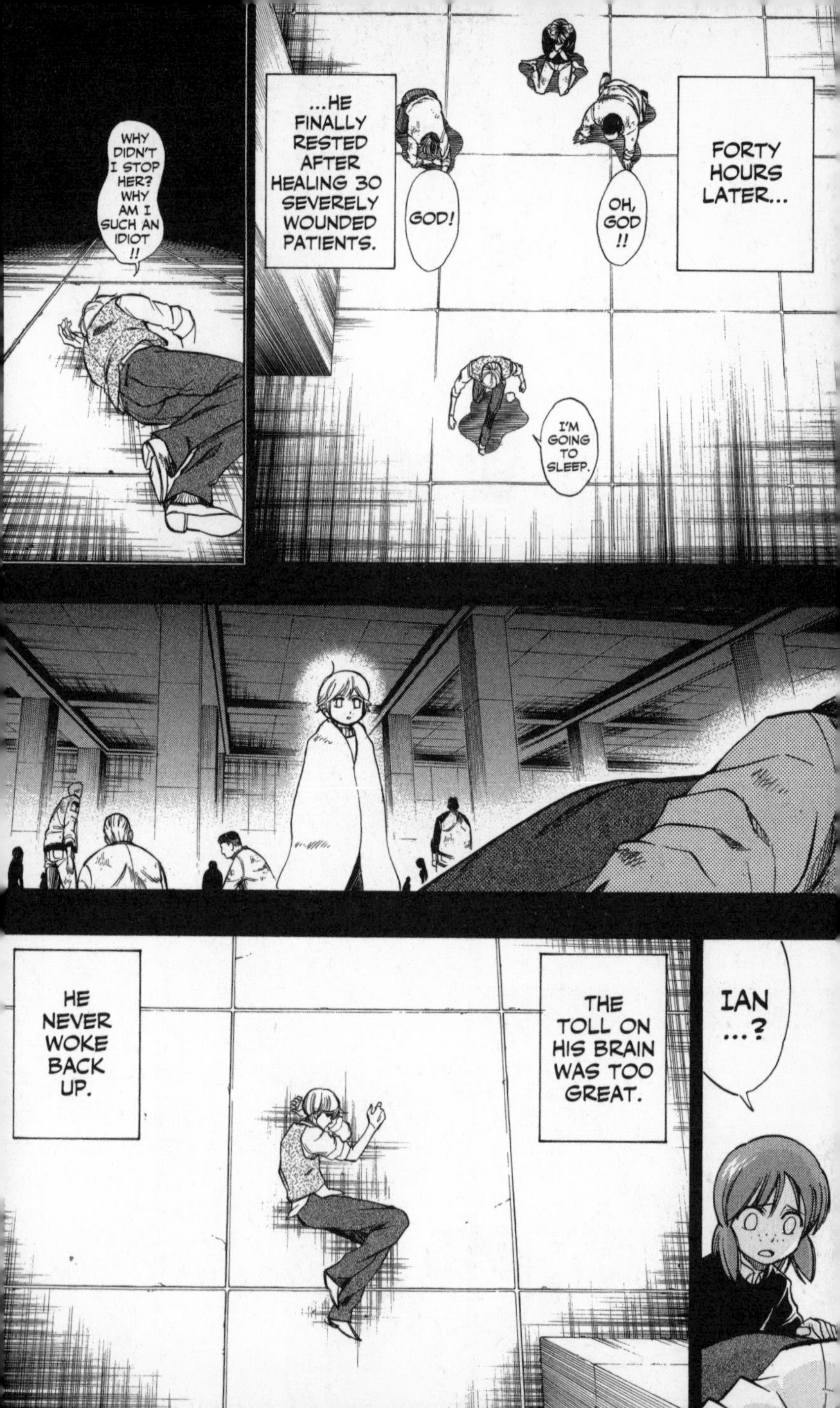
FORTY HOURS LATER...
OH, GOD !!
GOD!
...HE FINALLY RESTED AFTER HEALING 30 SEVERELY WOUNDED PATIENTS.
I'M GOING TO SLEEP.
WHY DIDN'T I STOP HER? WHY AM I SUCH AN IDIOT !!
IAN ...?
THE TOLL ON HIS BRAIN WAS TOO GREAT.
HE NEVER WOKE BACK UP.

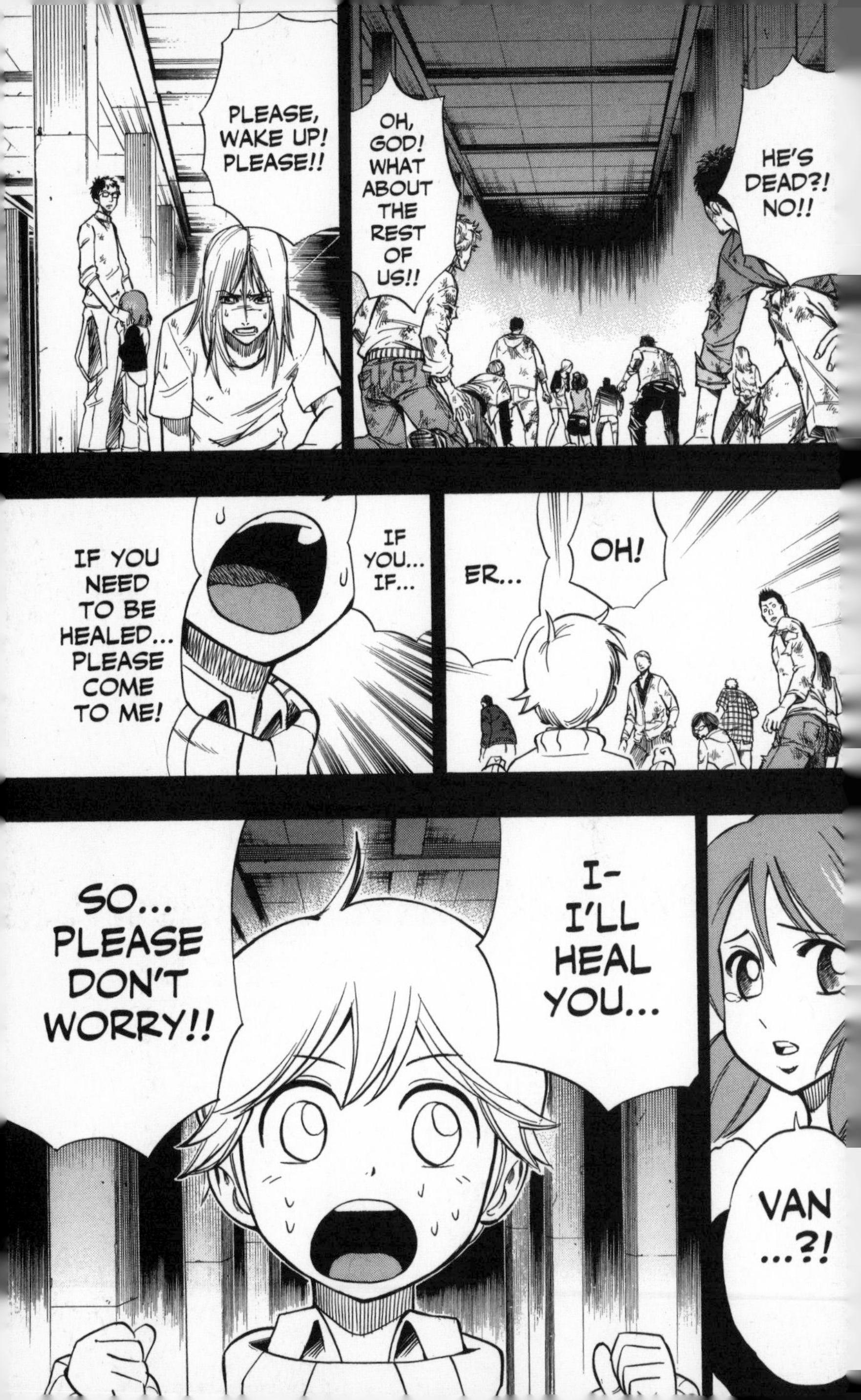
HE'S DEAD?! NO!!
OH, GOD! WHAT ABOUT THE REST OF US!!
PLEASE, WAKE UP! PLEASE!!
OH!
ER...
IF YOU... IF...
IF YOU NEED TO BE HEALED... PLEASE COME TO ME!
VAN ...?!
I- I'LL HEAL YOU...
SO... PLEASE DON'T WORRY!!

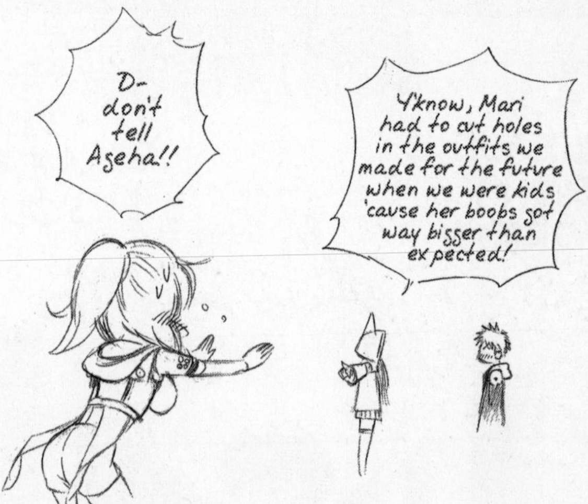
Y'know, Mari had to cut holes in the outfits we made for the future when we were kids 'cause her boobs got way bigger than expected!
D-don't tell Ageha!!

CALL.71: SOS

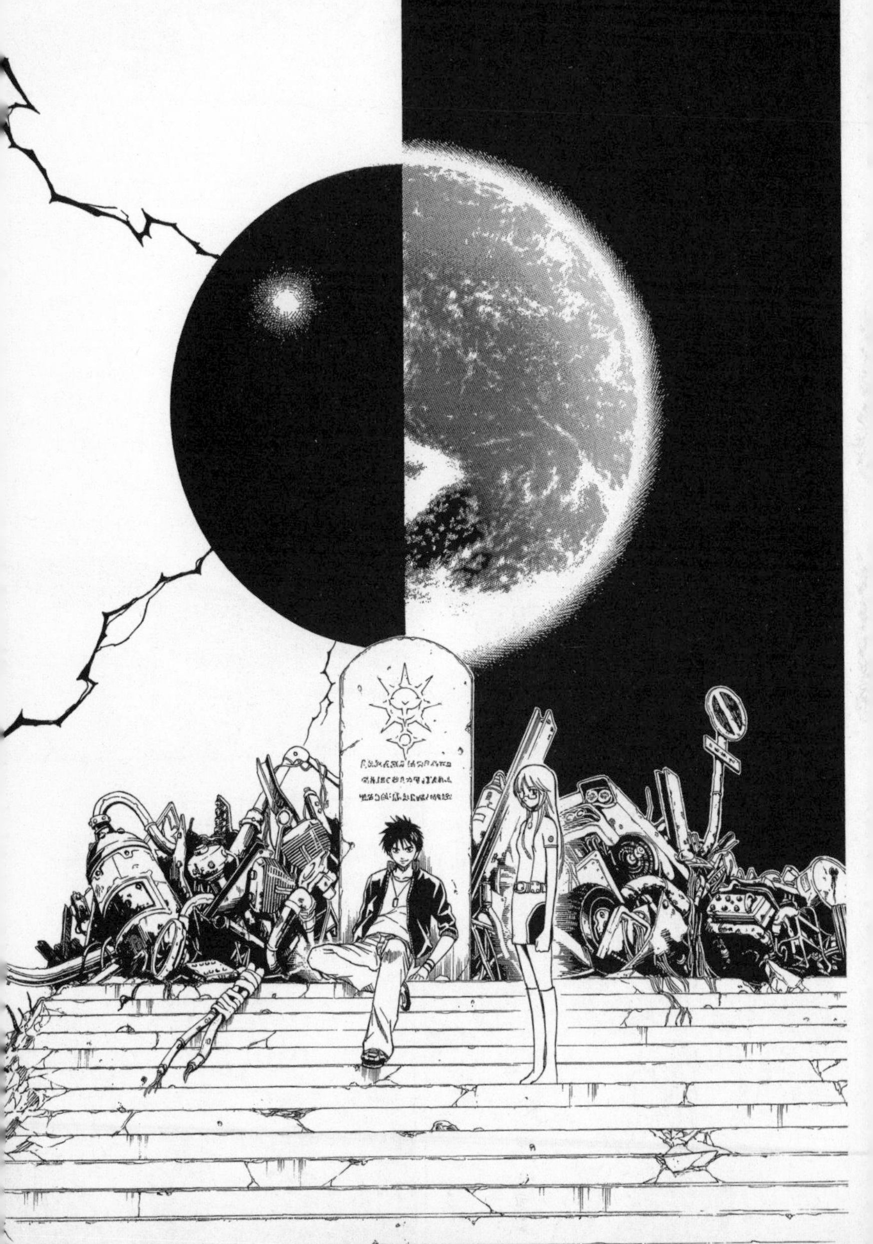

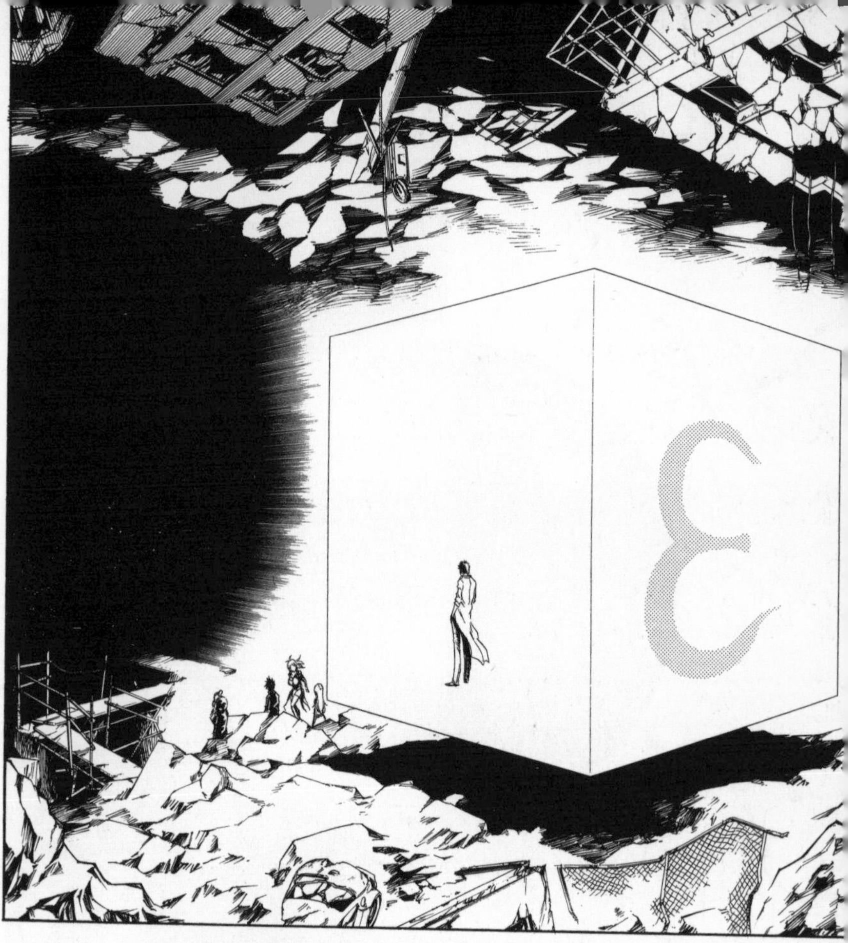
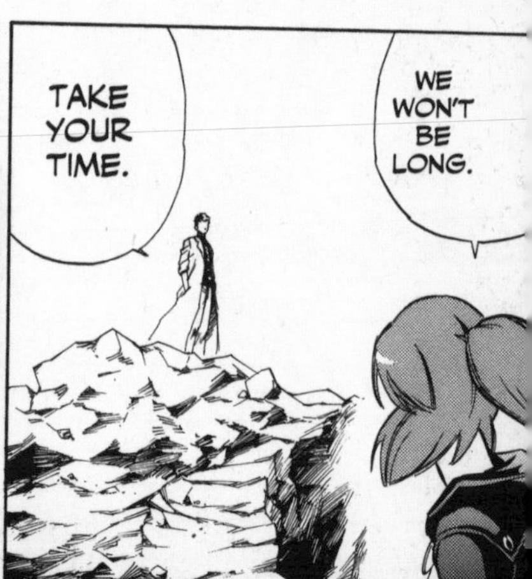
WE WON'T BE LONG.
TAKE YOUR TIME.
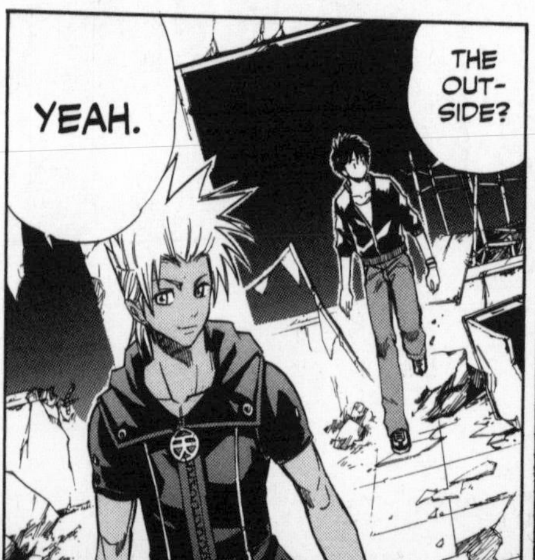
THE OUT-SIDE?
YEAH.

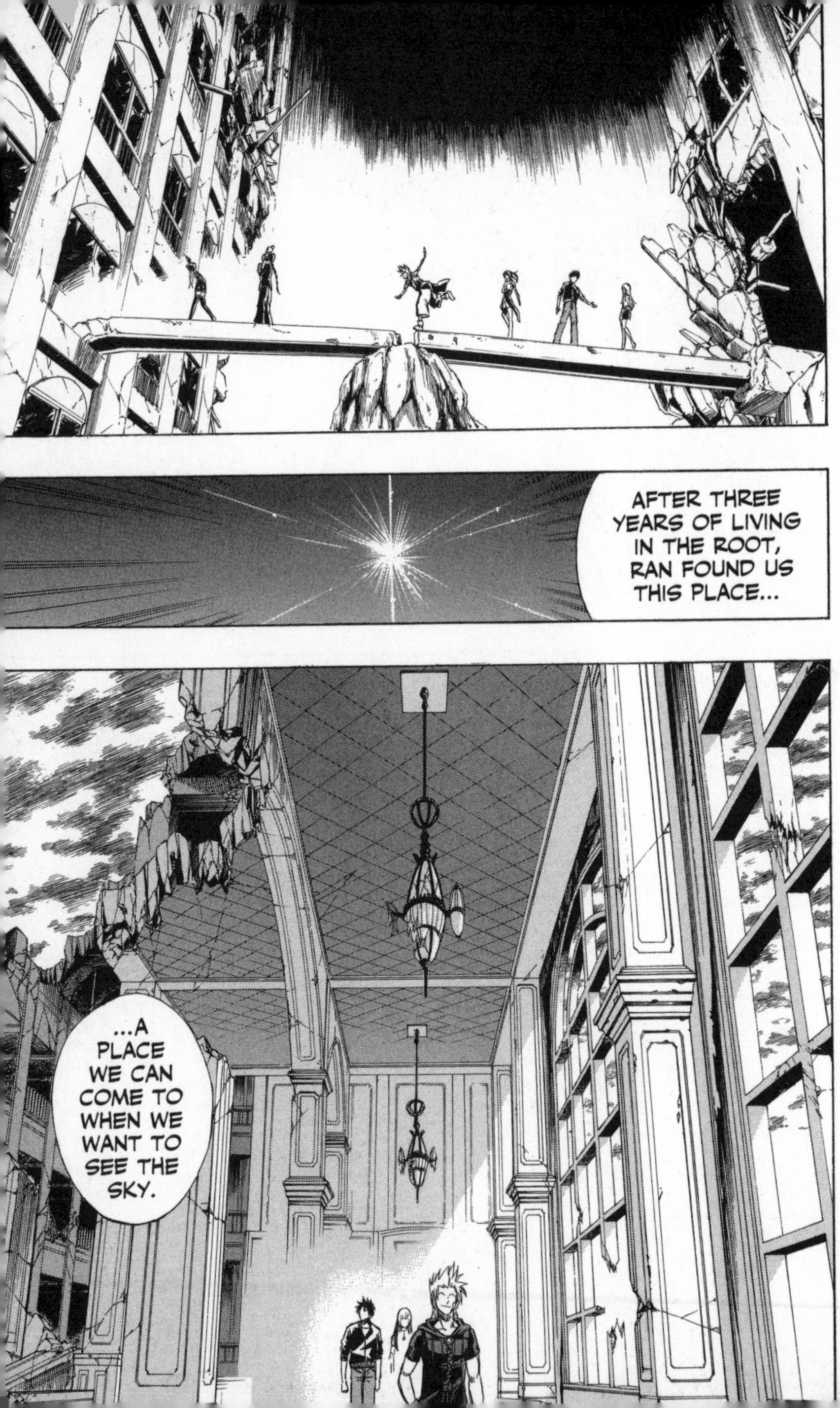
AFTER THREE YEARS OF LIVING IN THE ROOT, RAN FOUND US THIS PLACE...
...A PLACE WE CAN COME TO WHEN WE WANT TO SEE THE SKY.

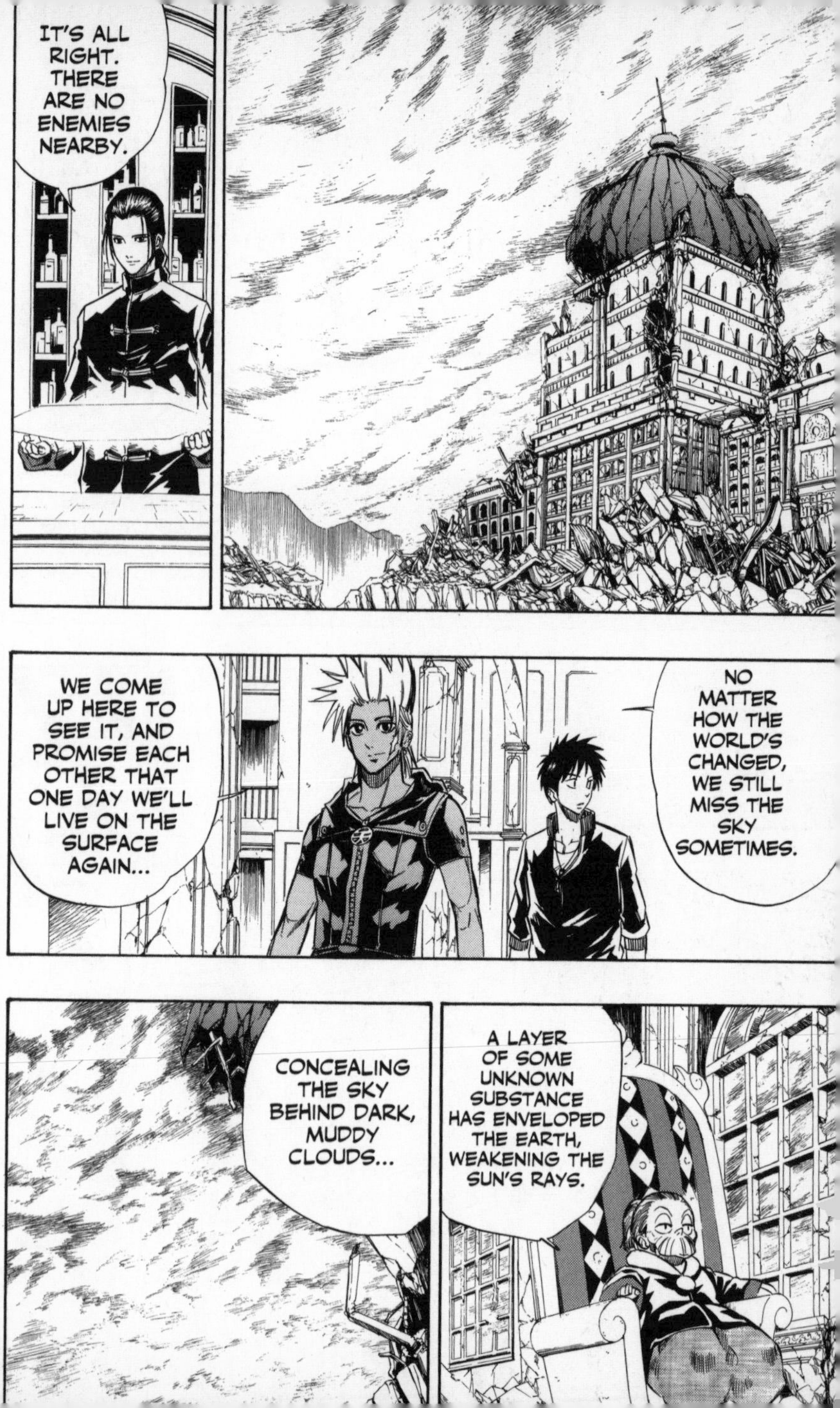
IT'S ALL RIGHT. THERE ARE NO ENEMIES NEARBY.
NO MATTER HOW THE WORLD'S CHANGED, WE STILL MISS THE SKY SOMETIMES.
WE COME UP HERE TO SEE IT, AND PROMISE EACH OTHER THAT ONE DAY WE'LL LIVE ON THE SURFACE AGAIN...
A LAYER OF SOME UNKNOWN SUBSTANCE HAS ENVELOPED THE EARTH, WEAKENING THE SUN'S RAYS.
CONCEALING THE SKY BEHIND DARK, MUDDY CLOUDS...

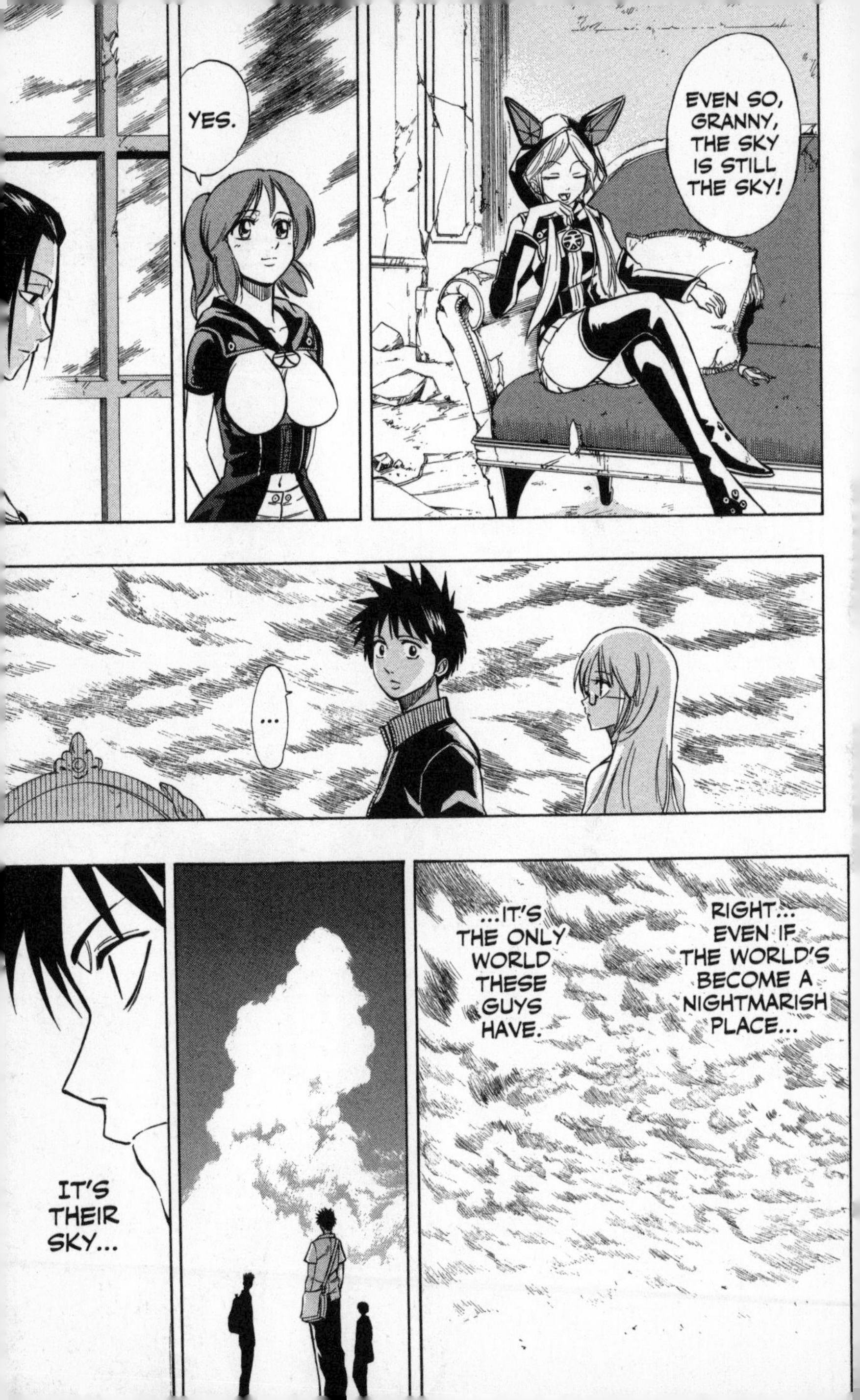
EVEN SO, GRANNY, THE SKY IS STILL THE SKY!
YES.
...
RIGHT... EVEN IF THE WORLD'S BECOME A NIGHTMARISH PLACE...
...IT'S THE ONLY WORLD THESE GUYS HAVE.
IT'S THEIR SKY...

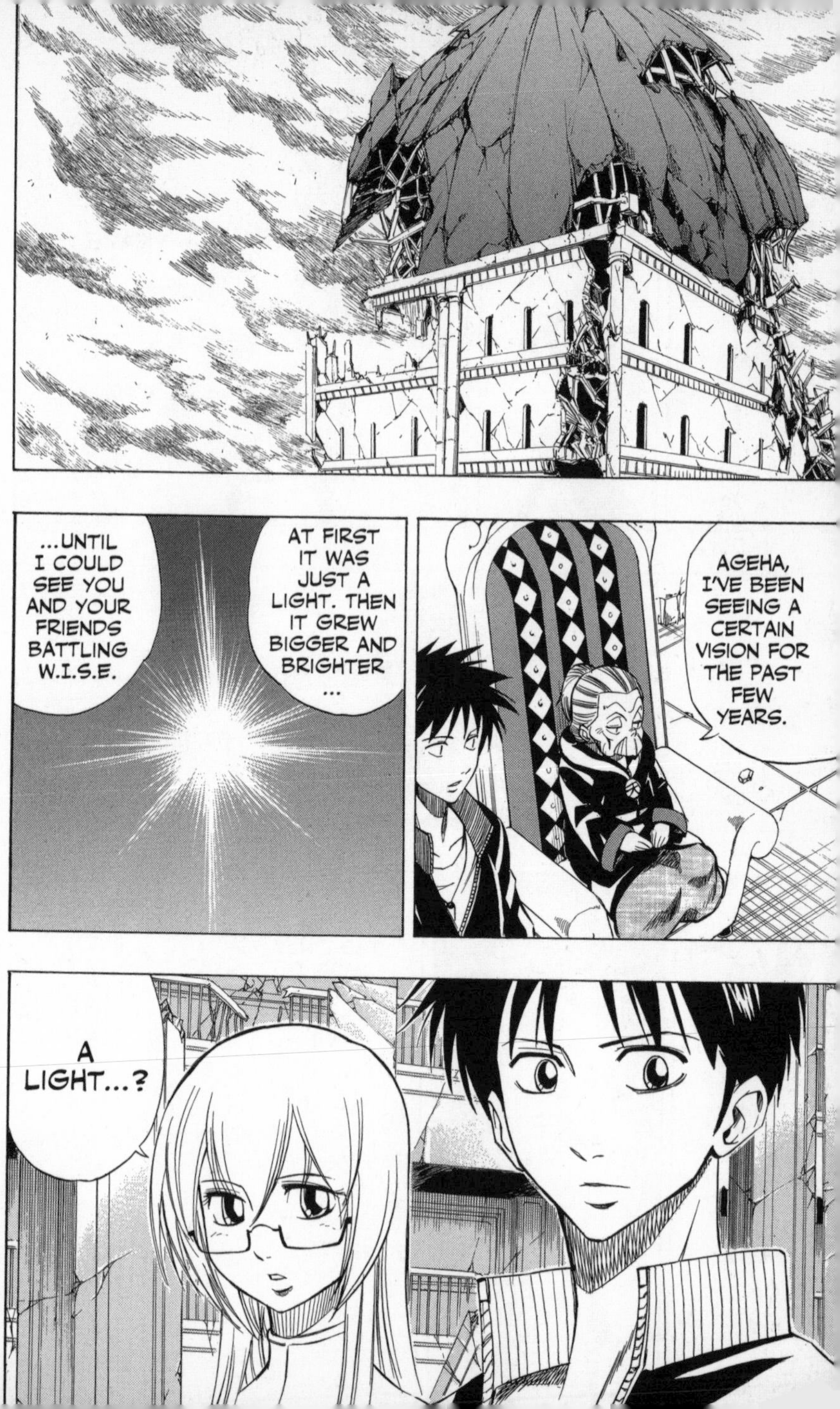
AGEHA, I'VE BEEN SEEING A CERTAIN VISION FOR THE PAST FEW YEARS.
AT FIRST IT WAS JUST A LIGHT. THEN IT GREW BIGGER AND BRIGHTER ...
...UNTIL I COULD SEE YOU AND YOUR FRIENDS BATTLING W.I.S.E.
A LIGHT...?

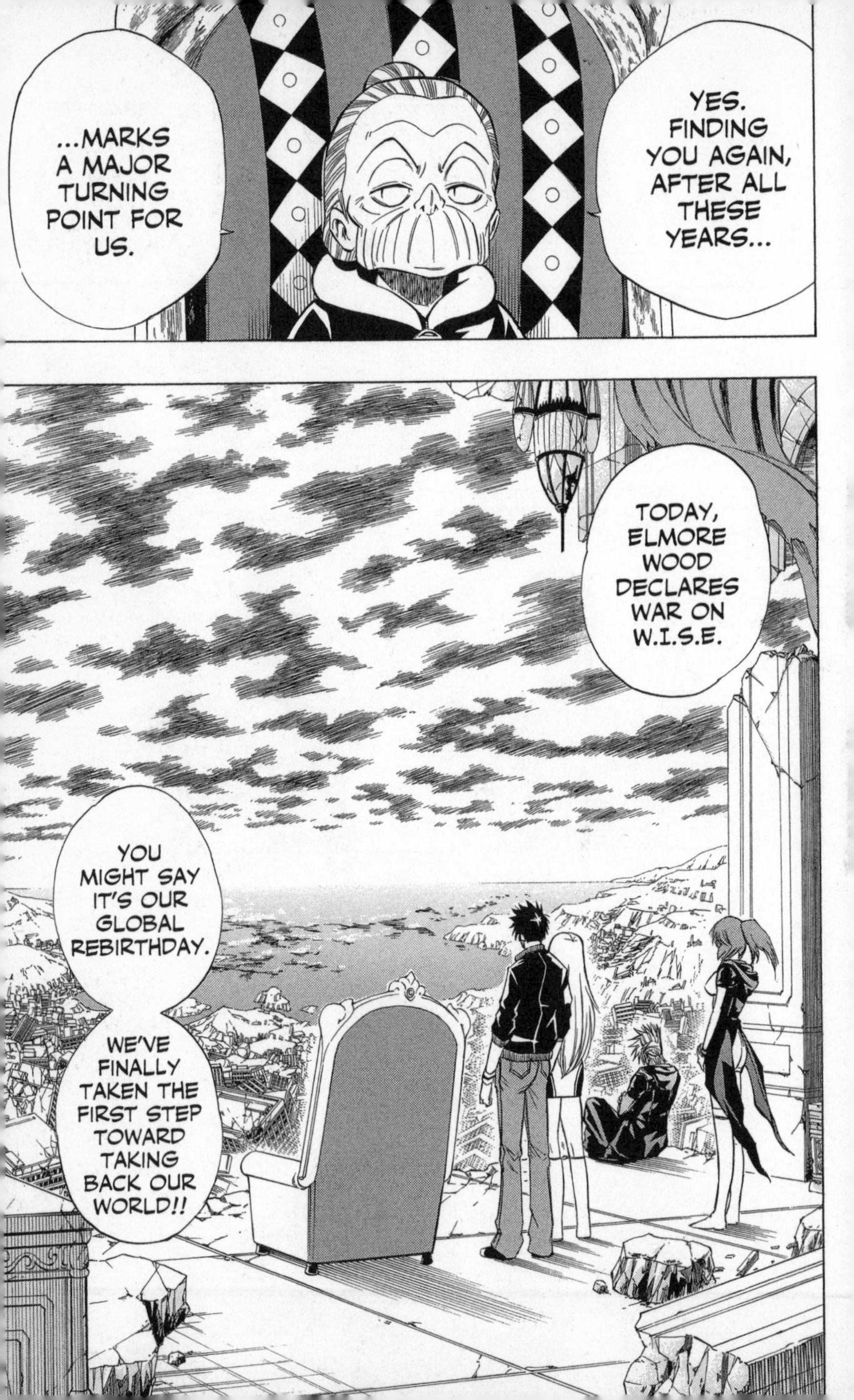
YES. FINDING YOU AGAIN, AFTER ALL THESE YEARS...
...MARKS A MAJOR TURNING POINT FOR US.
TODAY, ELMORE WOOD DECLARES WAR ON W.I.S.E.
YOU MIGHT SAY IT'S OUR GLOBAL REBIRTHDAY.
WE'VE FINALLY TAKEN THE FIRST STEP TOWARD TAKING BACK OUR WORLD!!

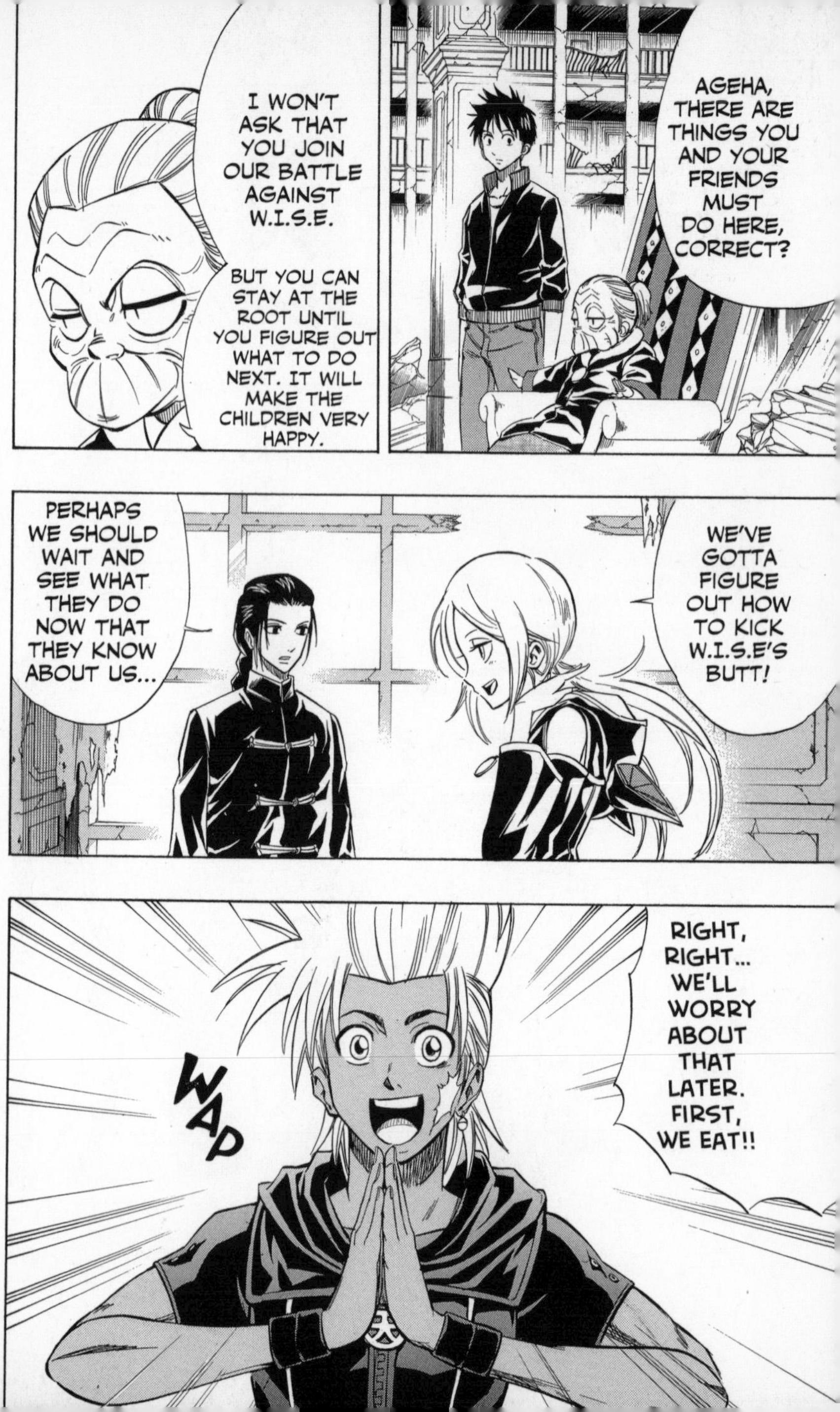
AGEHA, THERE ARE THINGS YOU AND YOUR FRIENDS MUST DO HERE, CORRECT?
I WON'T ASK THAT YOU JOIN OUR BATTLE AGAINST W.I.S.E.
BUT YOU CAN STAY AT THE ROOT UNTIL YOU FIGURE OUT WHAT TO DO NEXT. IT WILL MAKE THE CHILDREN VERY HAPPY.
WE'VE GOTTA FIGURE OUT HOW TO KICK W.I.S.E'S BUTT!
PERHAPS WE SHOULD WAIT AND SEE WHAT THEY DO NOW THAT THEY KNOW ABOUT US...
RIGHT, RIGHT... WE'LL WORRY ABOUT THAT LATER. FIRST, WE EAT!!
WAP

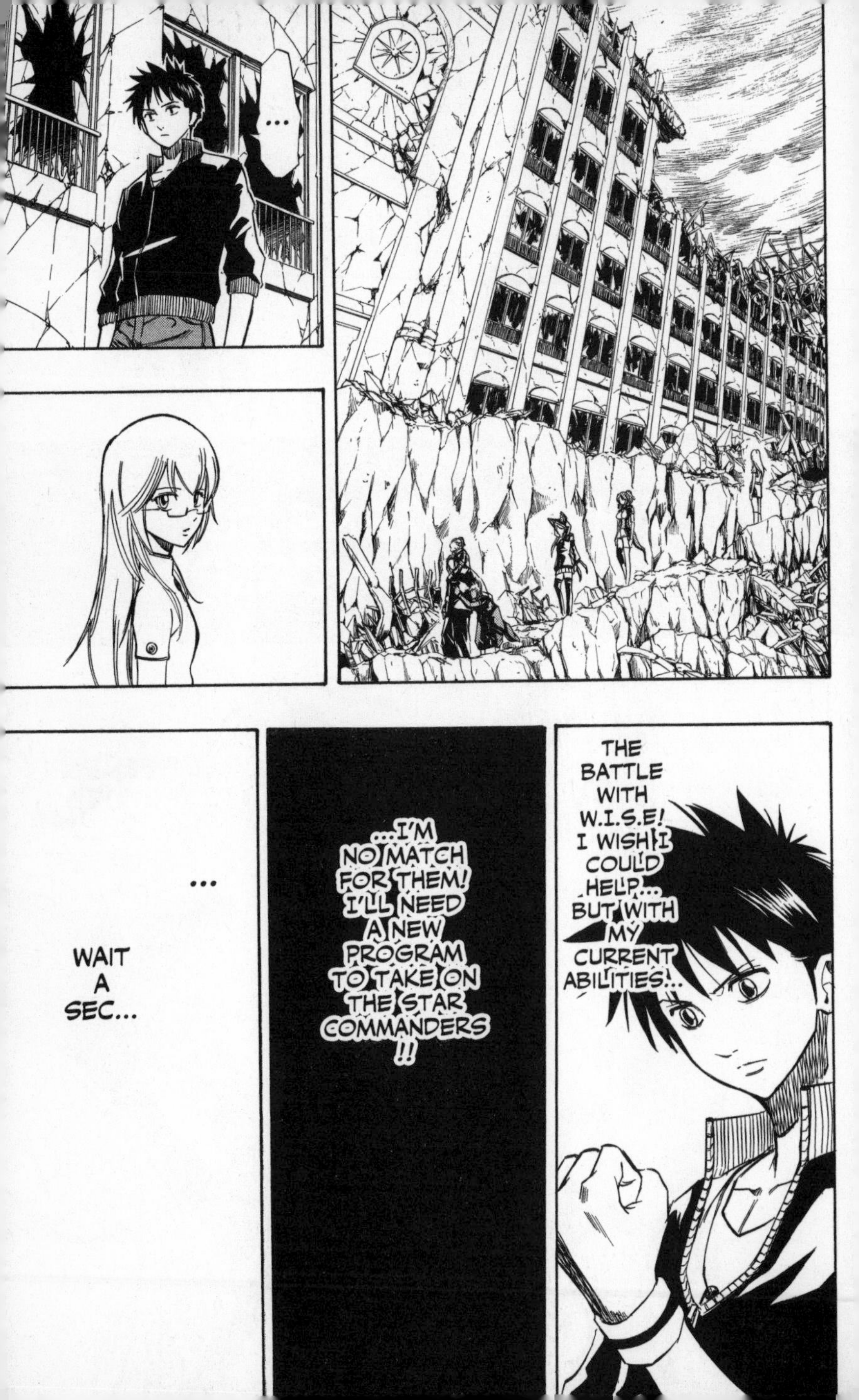
...
THE BATTLE WITH W.I.S.E! I WISH I COULD HELP... BUT WITH MY CURRENT ABILITIES...
...I'M NO MATCH FOR THEM! I'LL NEED A NEW PROGRAM TO TAKE ON THE STAR COMMANDERS!!
...
WAIT A SEC...

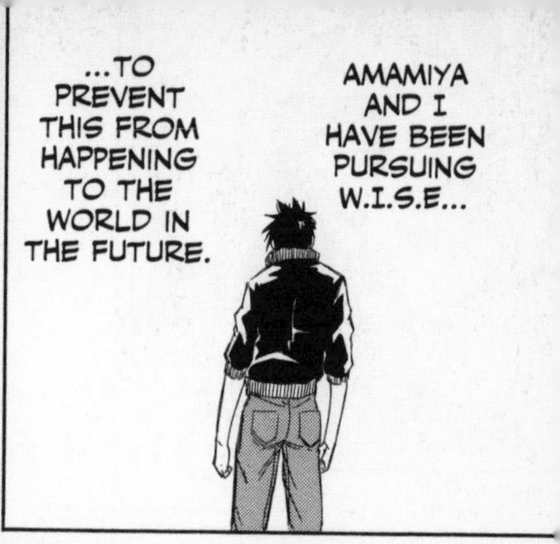
AMAMIYA AND I HAVE BEEN PURSUING W.I.S.E...
...TO PREVENT THIS FROM HAPPENING TO THE WORLD IN THE FUTURE.

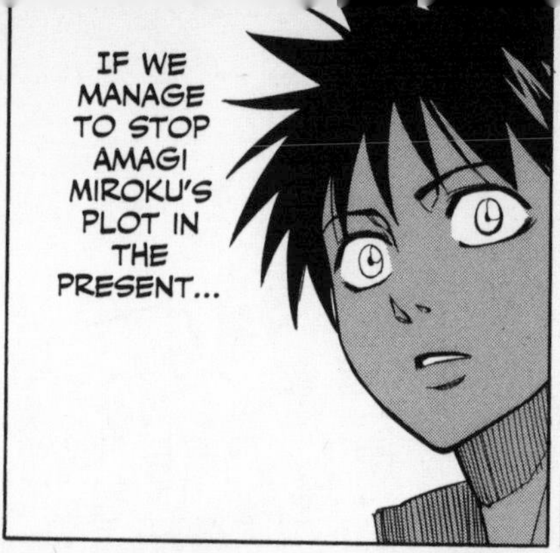
IF WE MANAGE TO STOP AMAGI MIROKU'S PLOT IN THE PRESENT...

WHAT HAPPENS TO THIS FUTURE WORLD?!

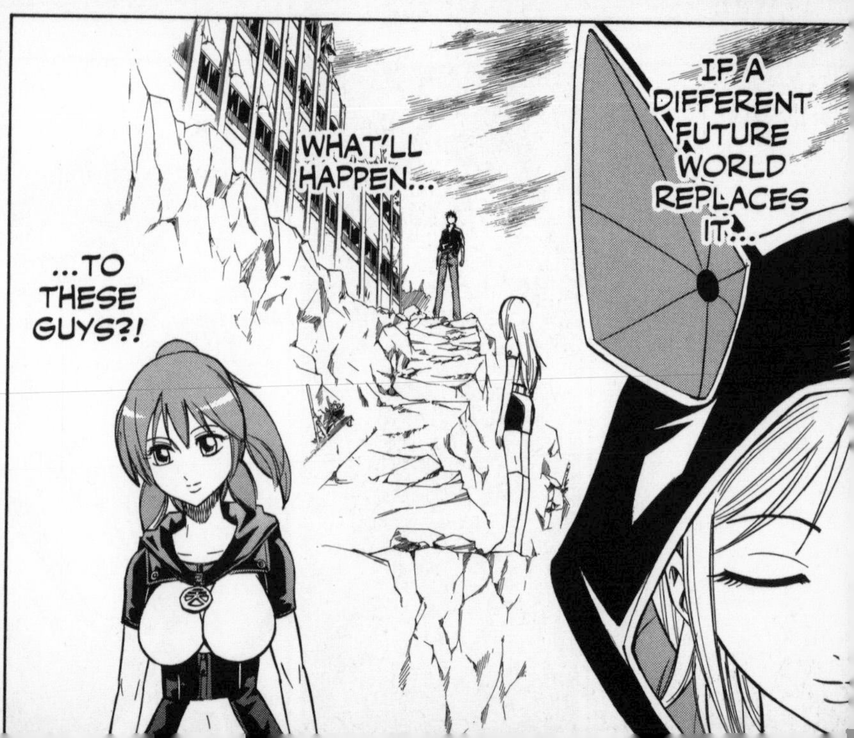
IF A DIFFERENT FUTURE WORLD REPLACES IT...
WHAT'LL HAPPEN...
...TO THESE GUYS?!

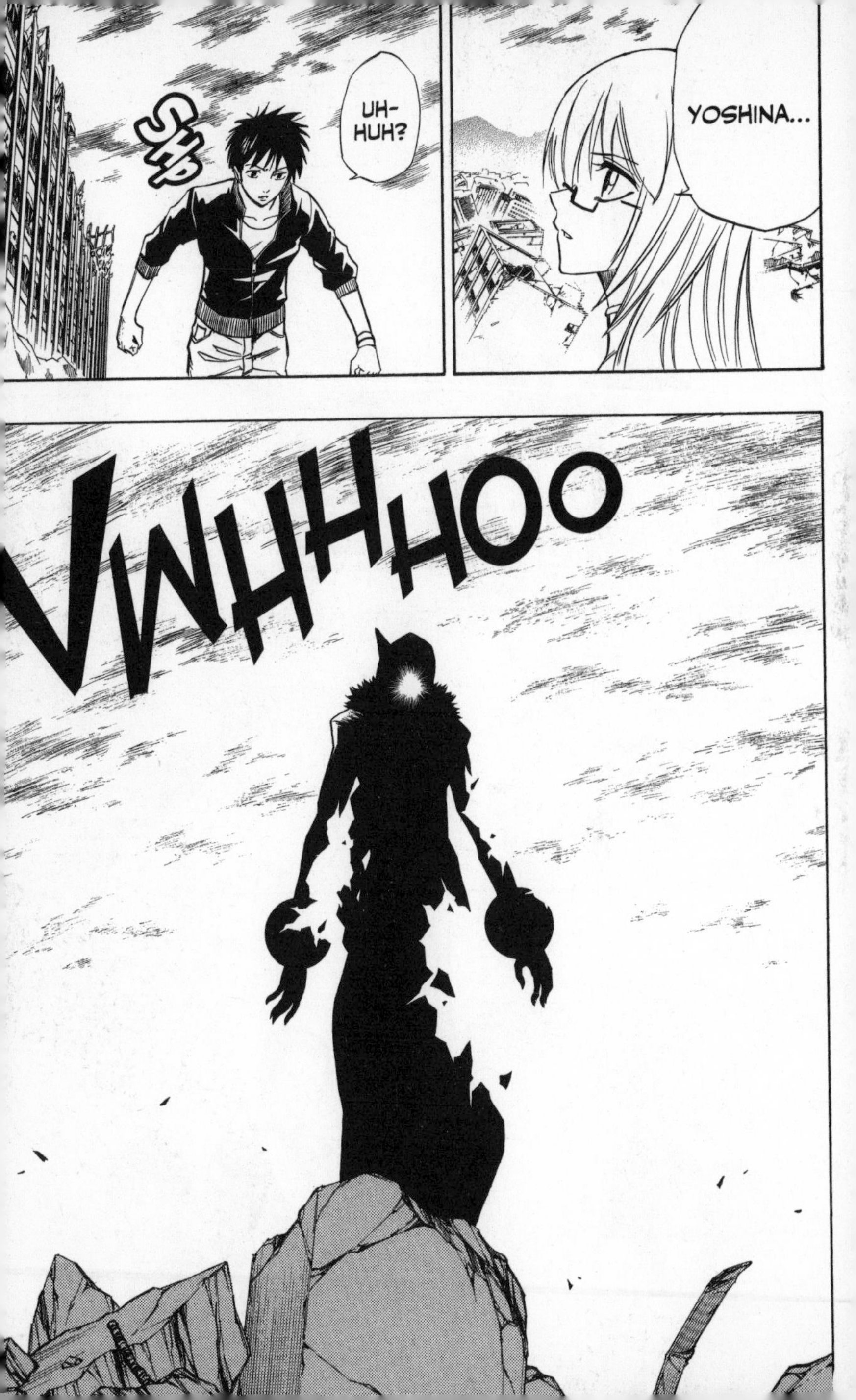
YOSHINA...
SHP
UH-HUH?
VWHHOO

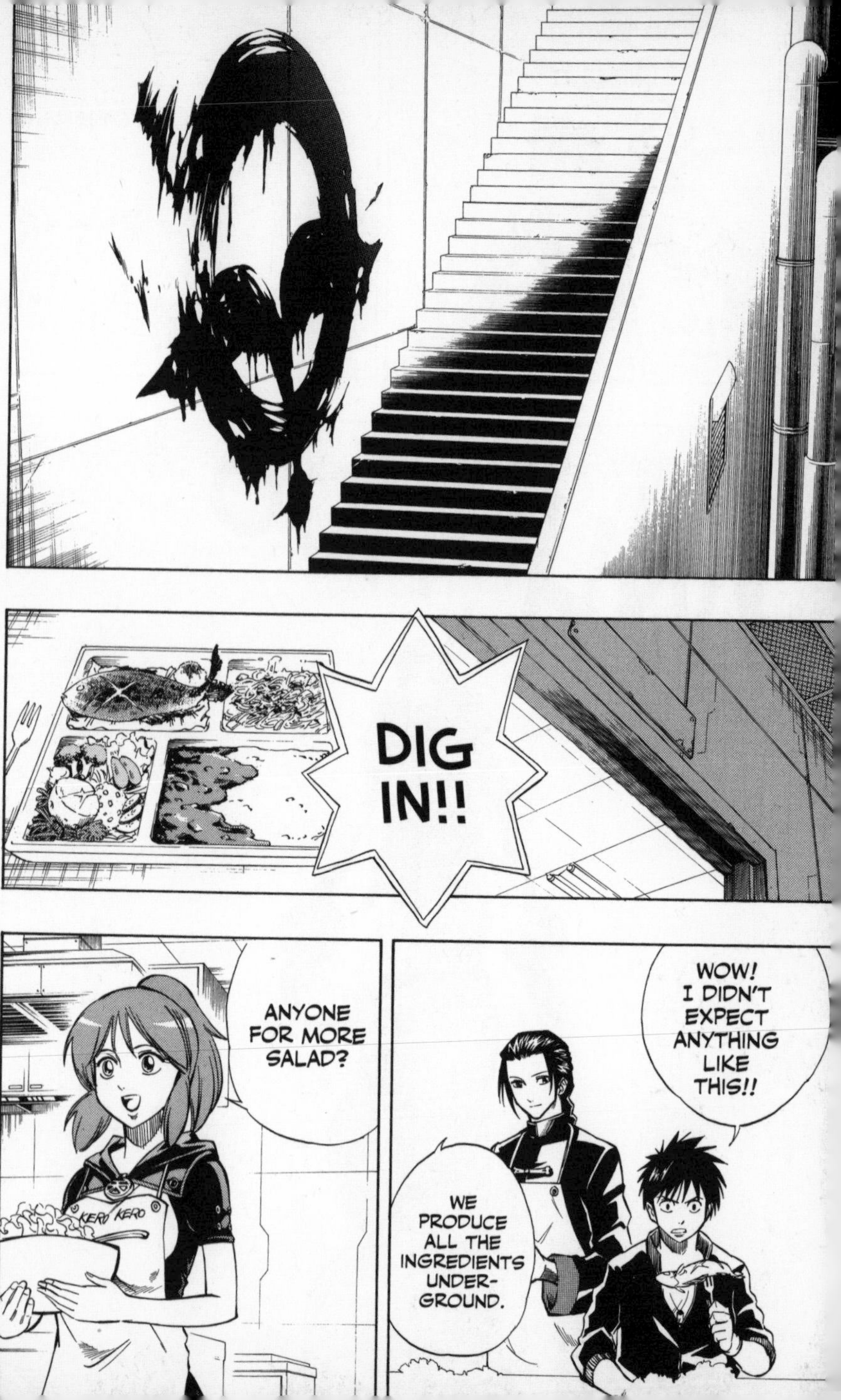
DIG IN!!
WOW! I DIDN'T EXPECT ANYTHING LIKE THIS!!
WE PRODUCE ALL THE INGREDIENTS UNDER-GROUND.
ANYONE FOR MORE SALAD?
KERO KERO

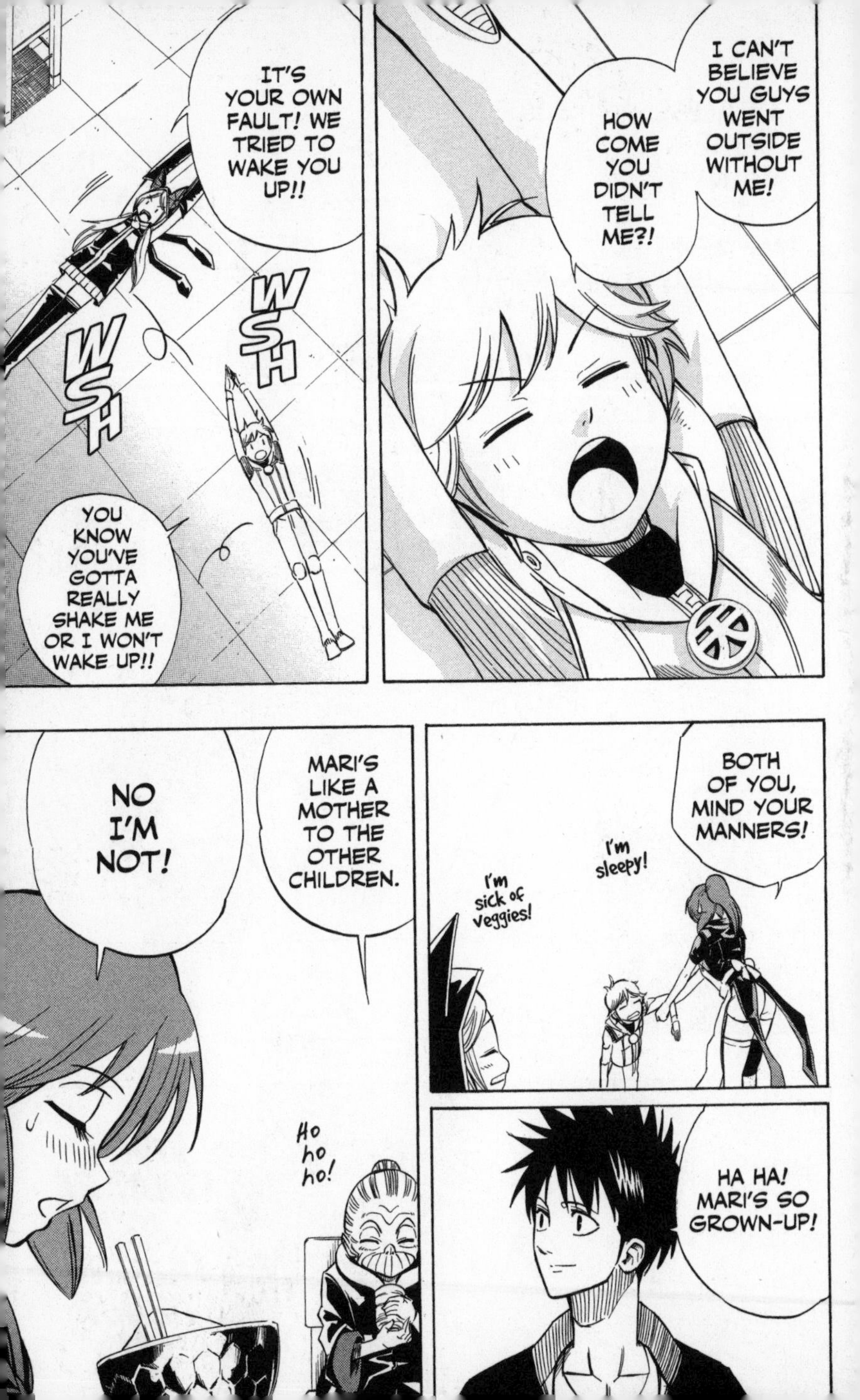
I CAN'T BELIEVE YOU GUYS WENT OUTSIDE WITHOUT ME!
HOW COME YOU DIDN'T TELL ME?!
IT'S YOUR OWN FAULT! WE TRIED TO WAKE YOU UP!!
WSH
WSH
YOU KNOW YOU'VE GOTTA REALLY SHAKE ME OR I WON'T WAKE UP!!
BOTH OF YOU, MIND YOUR MANNERS!
I'm sleepy!
I'm sick of veggies!
HA HA! MARI'S SO GROWN-UP!
MARI'S LIKE A MOTHER TO THE OTHER CHILDREN.
NO I'M NOT!
Ho ho ho!

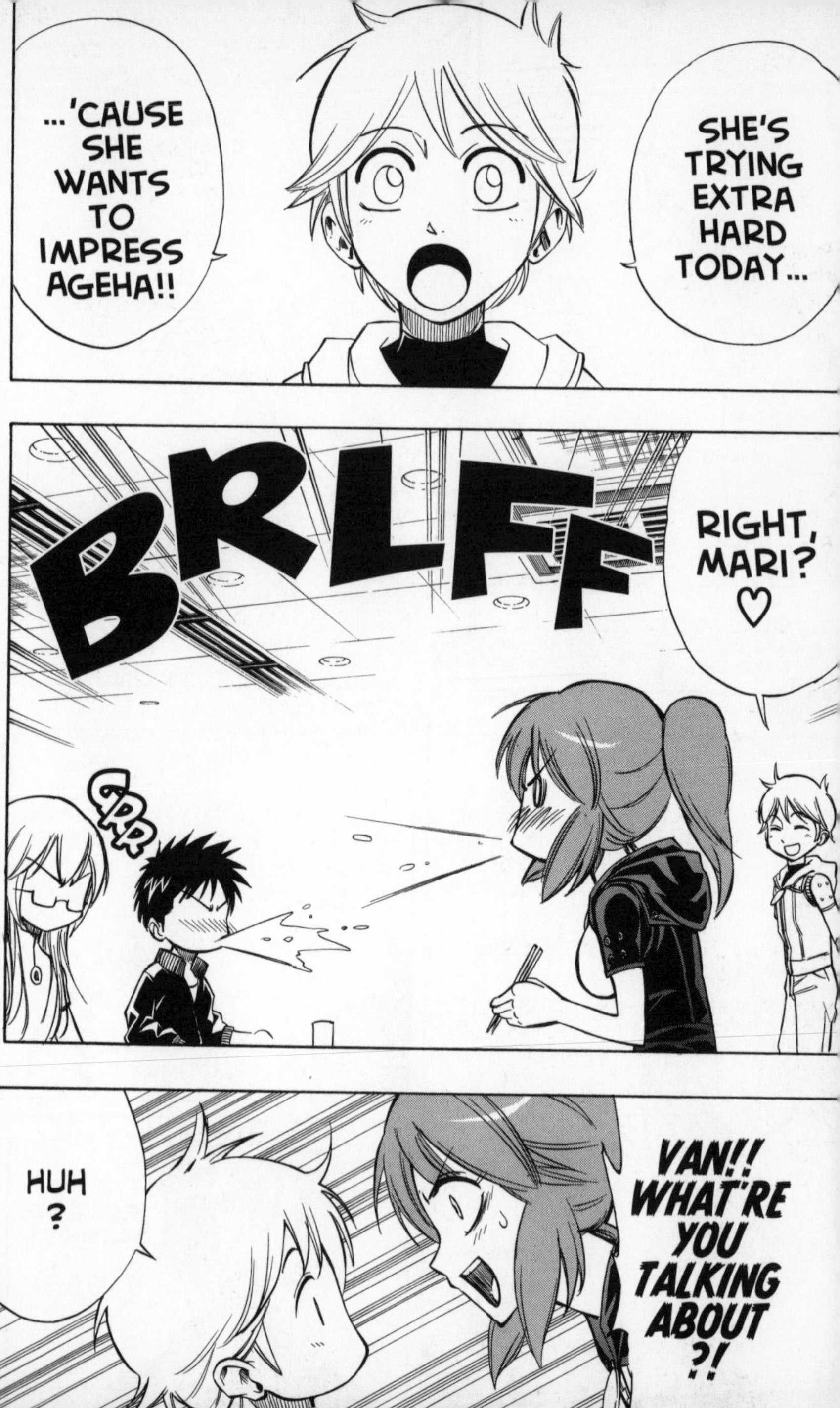
SHE'S TRYING EXTRA HARD TODAY...
...'CAUSE SHE WANTS TO IMPRESS AGEHA!!
RIGHT, MARI? ♡
BRLFF
GRR
VAN!! WHAT'RE YOU TALKING ABOUT?!
HUH?

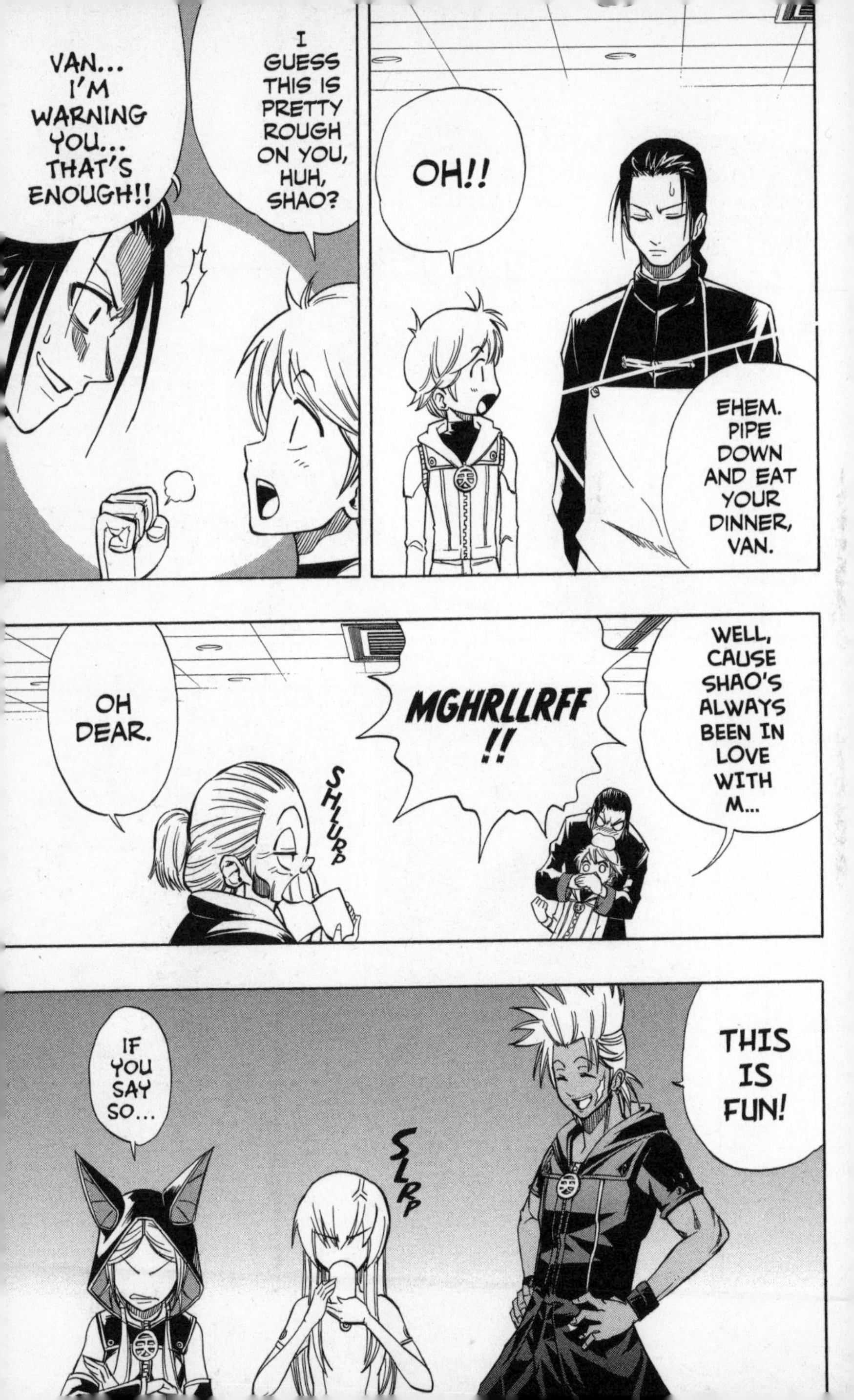
OH!!
EHEM. PIPE DOWN AND EAT YOUR DINNER, VAN.
I GUESS THIS IS PRETTY ROUGH ON YOU, HUH, SHAO?
VAN... I'M WARNING YOU... THAT'S ENOUGH!!
WELL, CAUSE SHAO'S ALWAYS BEEN IN LOVE WITH M...
MGHRLLRFF !!
SHLURP
OH DEAR.
THIS IS FUN!
SLRP
IF YOU SAY SO...

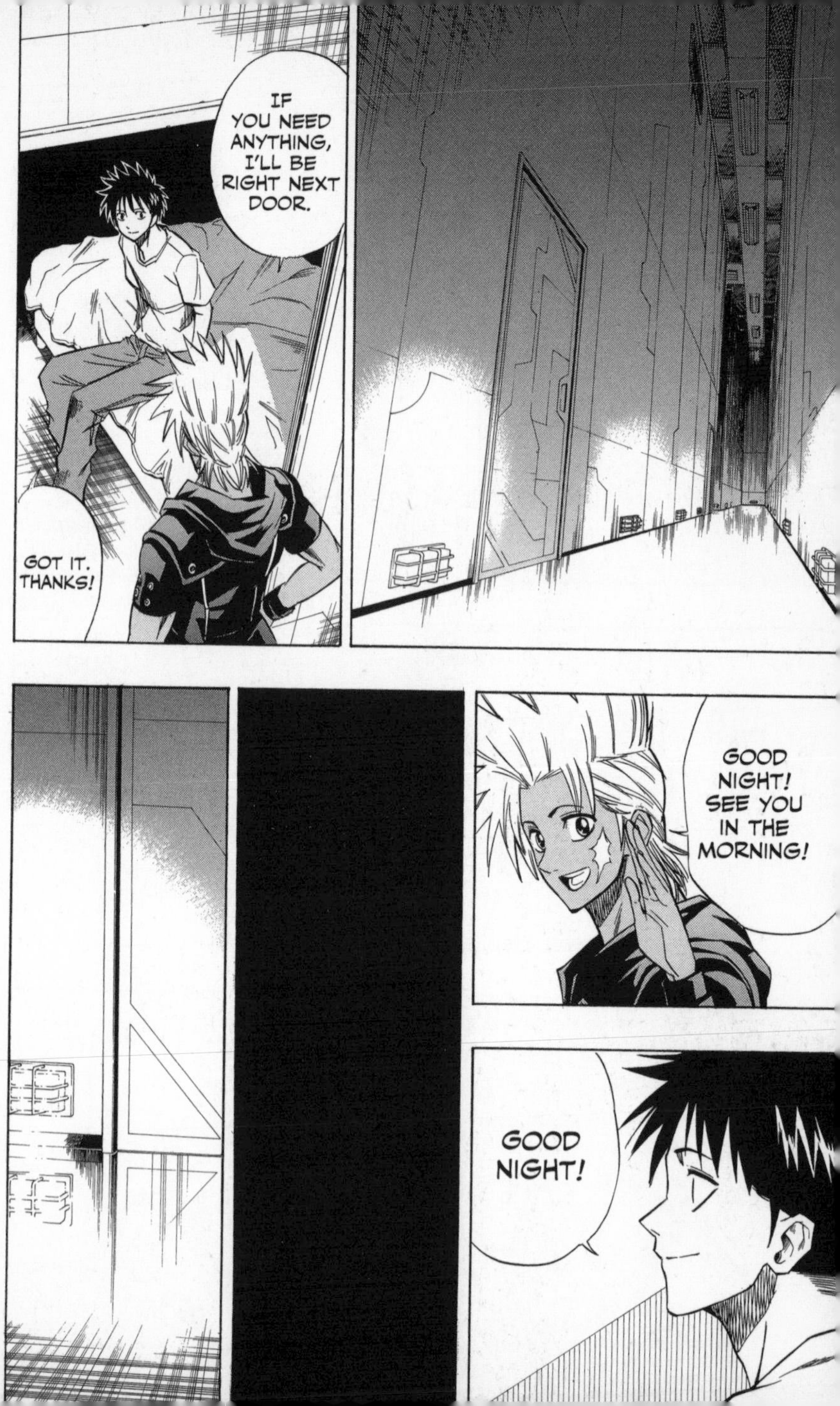
IF YOU NEED ANYTHING, I'LL BE RIGHT NEXT DOOR.
GOT IT. THANKS!
GOOD NIGHT! SEE YOU IN THE MORNING!
GOOD NIGHT!

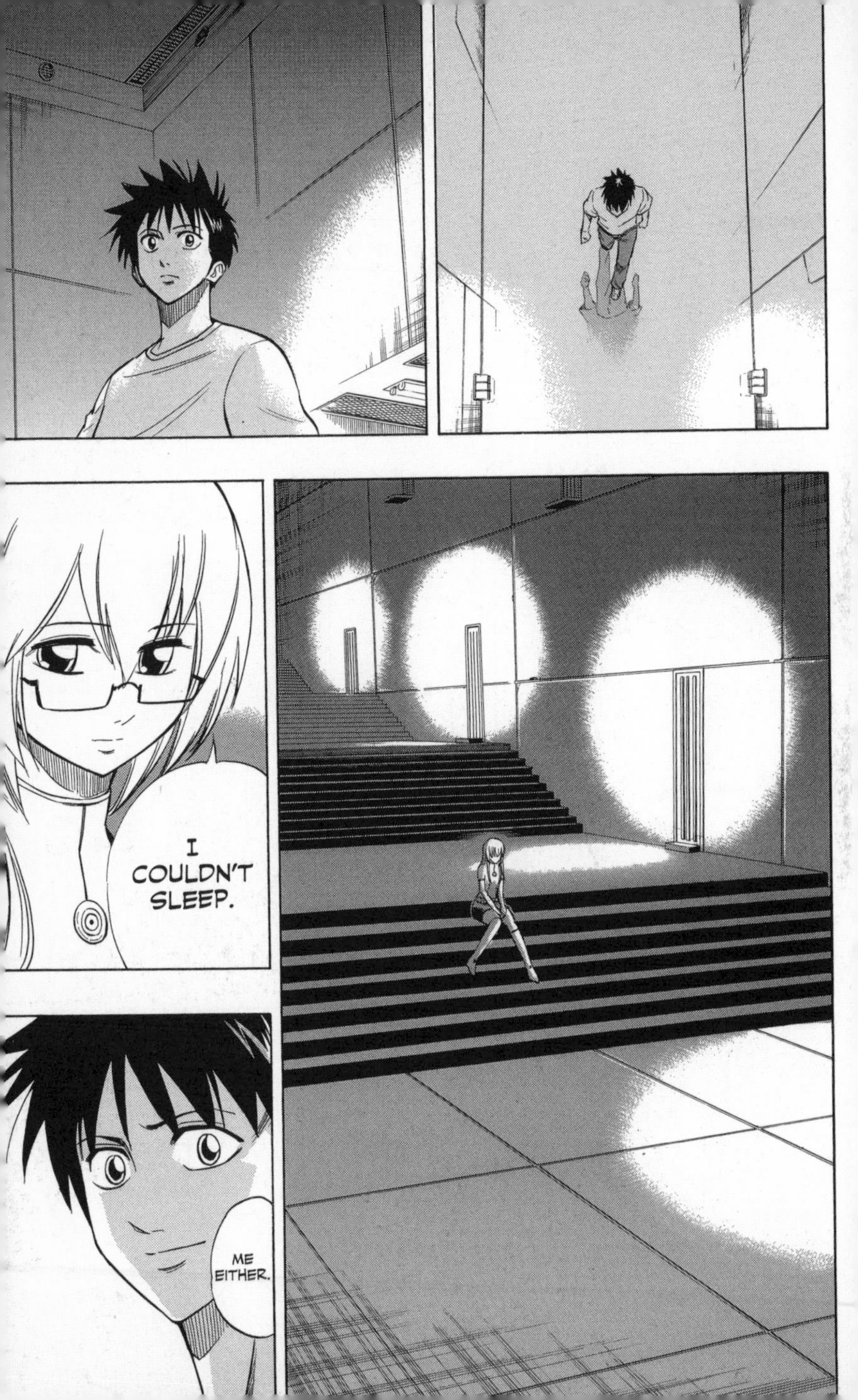
I COULDN'T SLEEP.
ME EITHER.

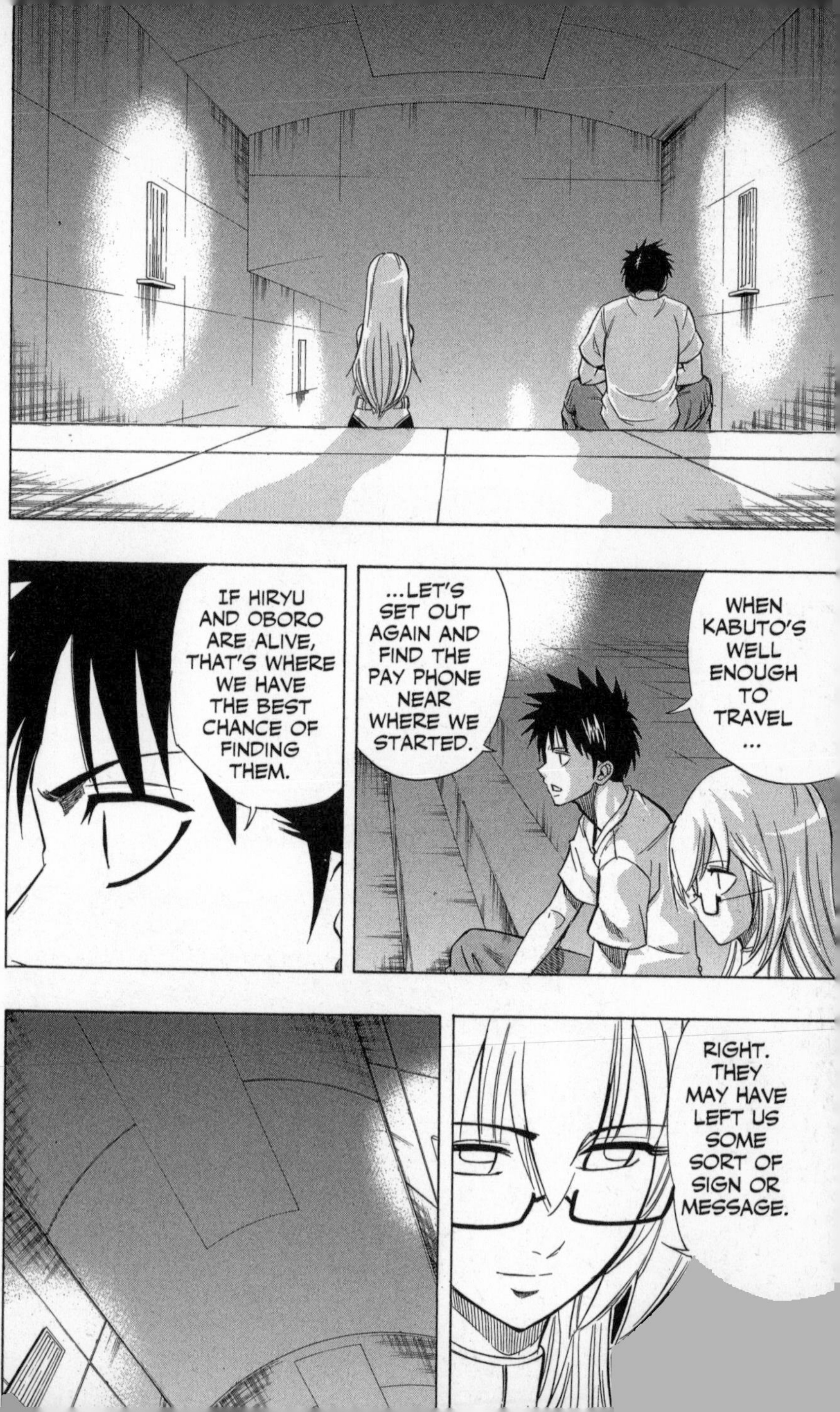
WHEN KABUTO'S WELL ENOUGH TO TRAVEL ...
...LET'S SET OUT AGAIN AND FIND THE PAY PHONE NEAR WHERE WE STARTED.
IF HIRYU AND OBORO ARE ALIVE, THAT'S WHERE WE HAVE THE BEST CHANCE OF FINDING THEM.
RIGHT. THEY MAY HAVE LEFT US SOME SORT OF SIGN OR MESSAGE.

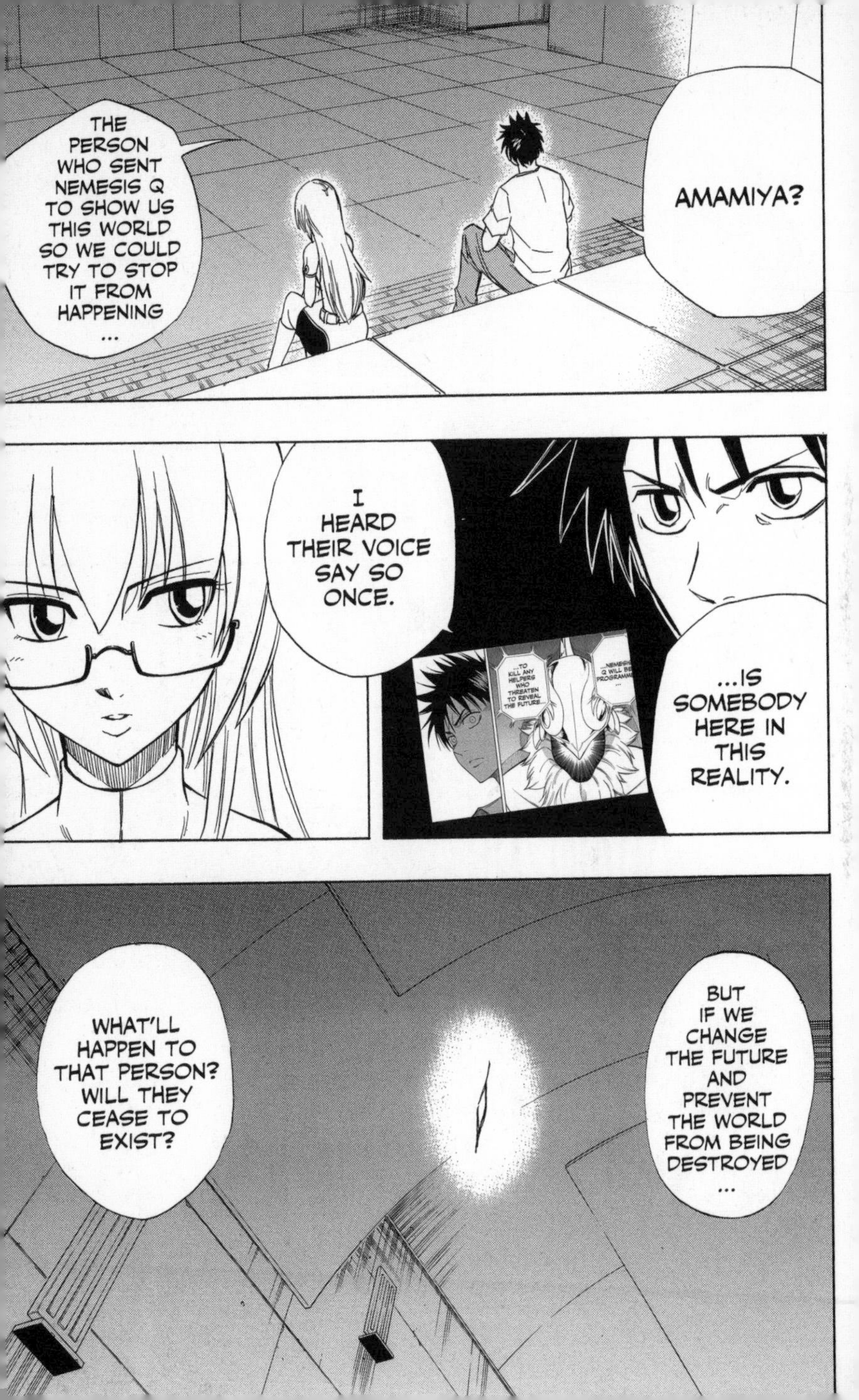
AMAMIYA?
THE PERSON WHO SENT NEMESIS Q TO SHOW US THIS WORLD SO WE COULD TRY TO STOP IT FROM HAPPENING ...
...IS SOMEBODY HERE IN THIS REALITY.
...TO KILL ANY HELPERS WHO THREATEN TO REVEAL THE FUTURE...
I HEARD THEIR VOICE SAY SO ONCE.
BUT IF WE CHANGE THE FUTURE AND PREVENT THE WORLD FROM BEING DESTROYED ...
WHAT'LL HAPPEN TO THAT PERSON? WILL THEY CEASE TO EXIST?

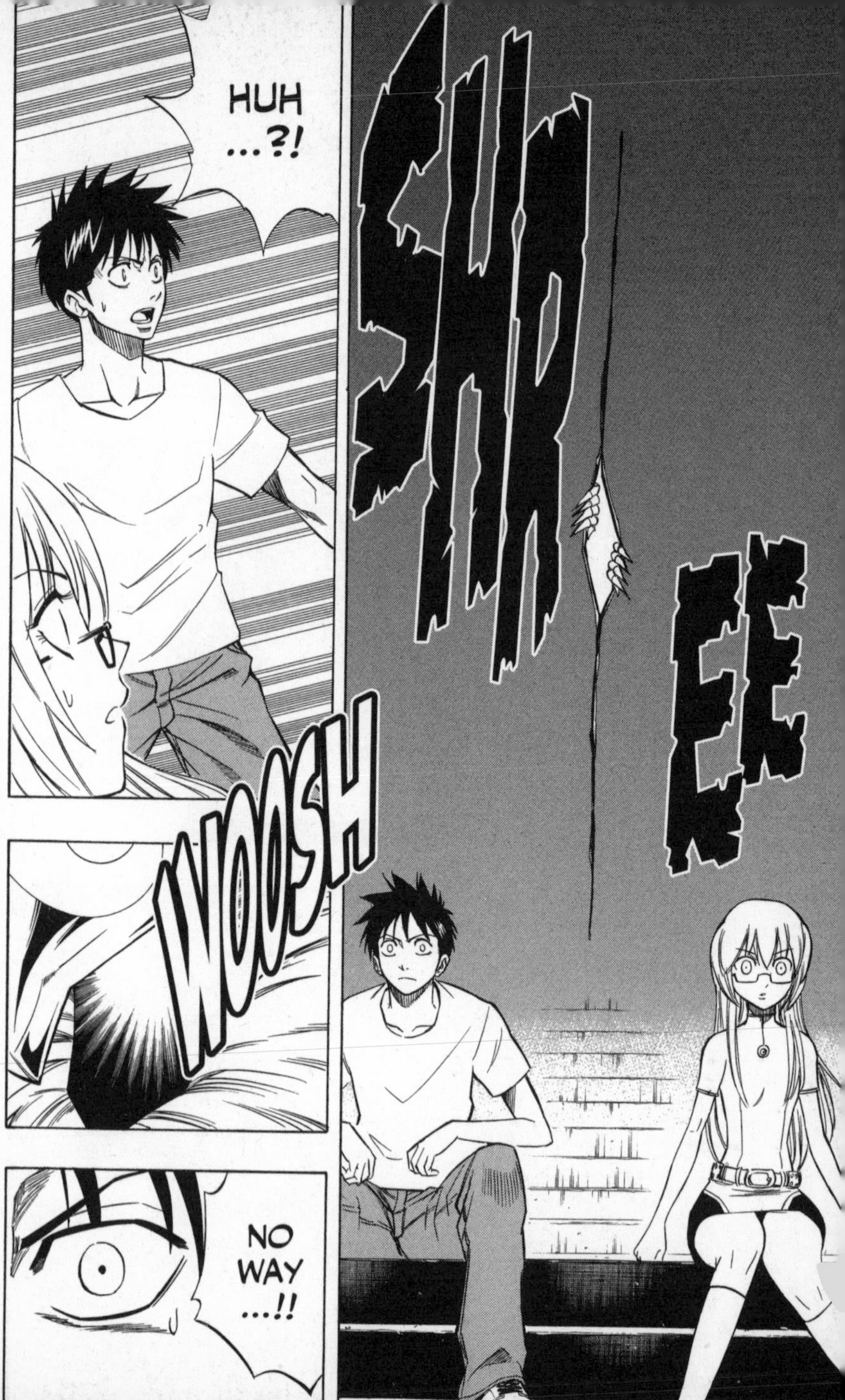
HUH ...?!
WOOSH
NO WAY ...!!

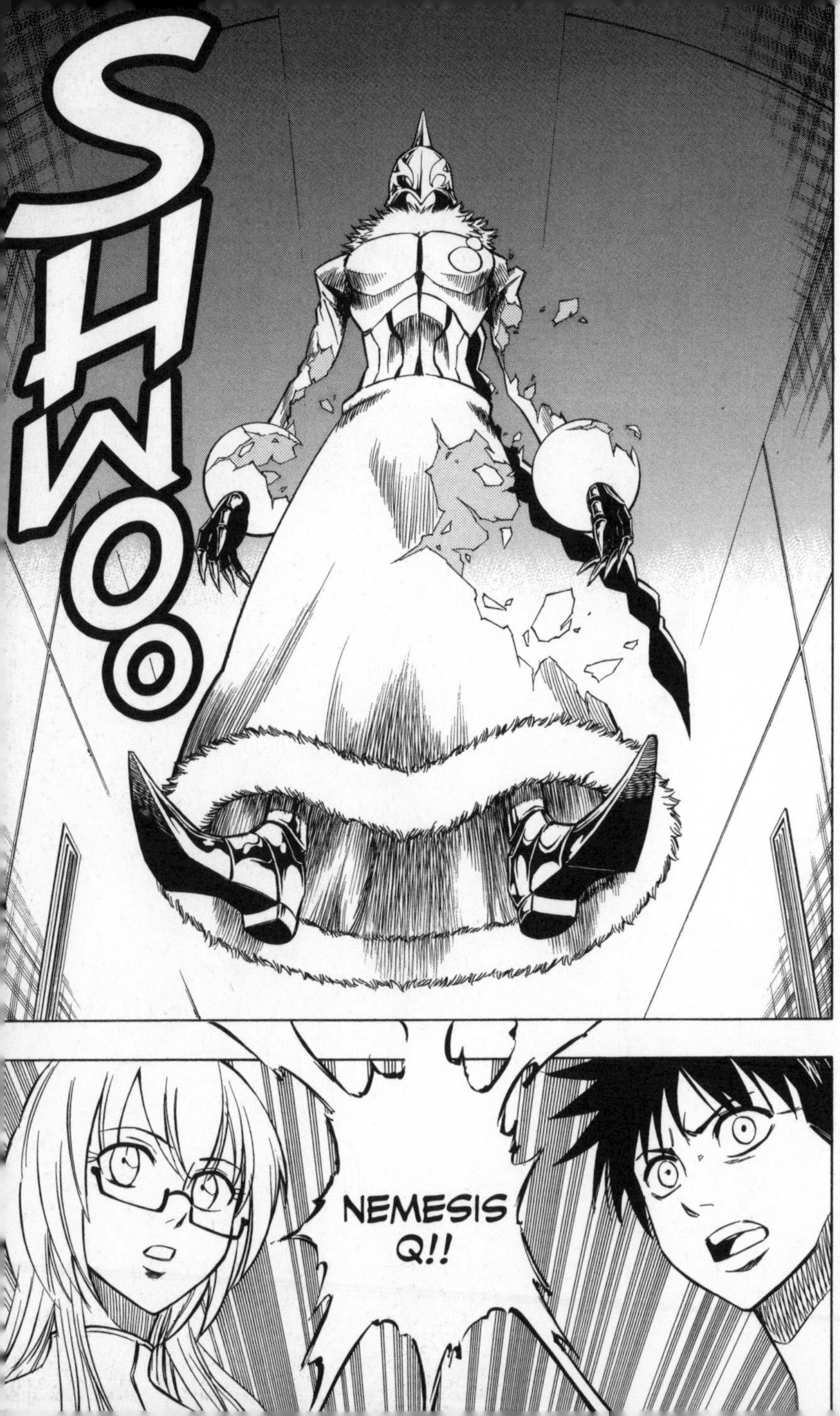
SHWOO
NEMESIS Q!!

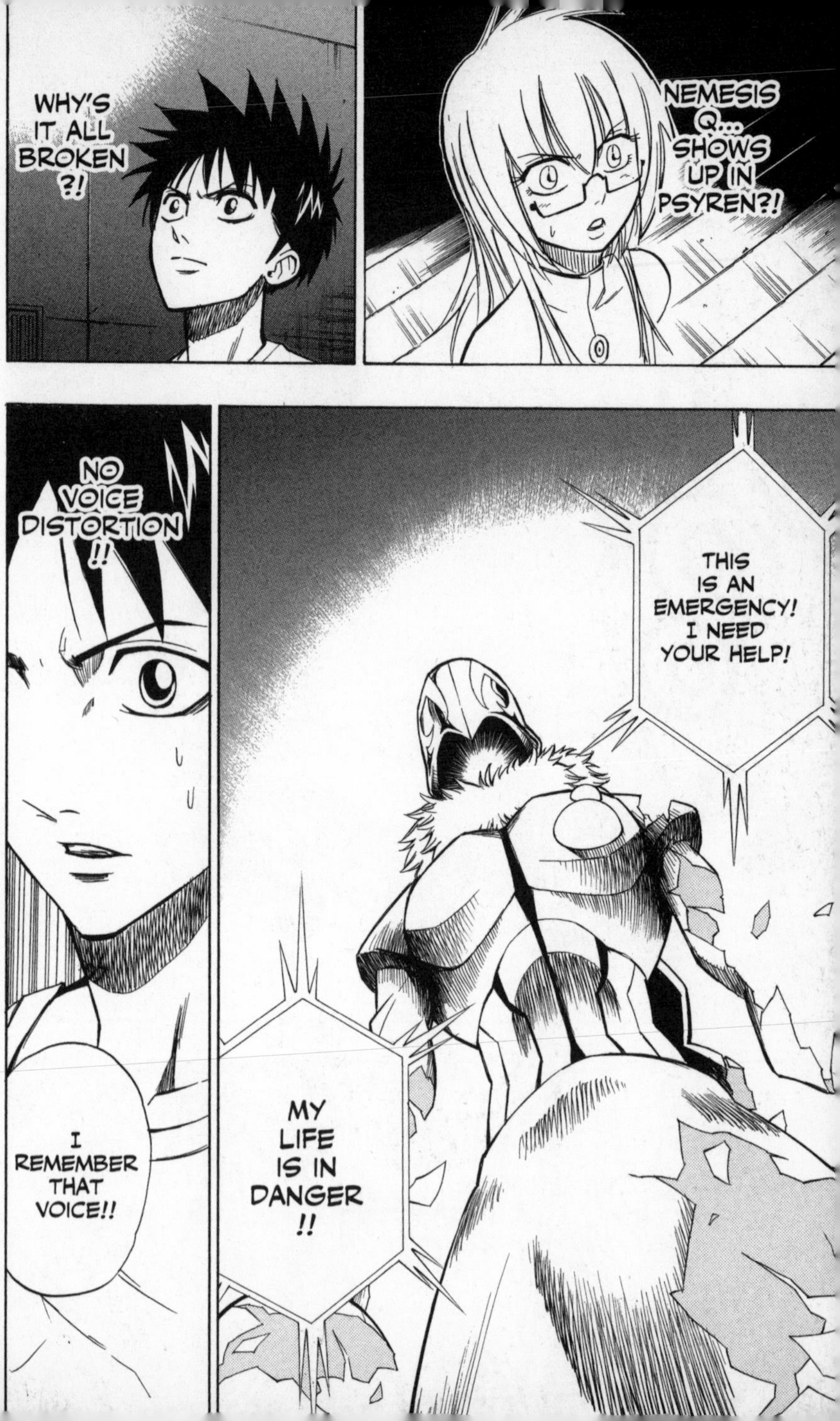
NEMESIS Q... SHOWS UP IN PSYREN?!
WHY'S IT ALL BROKEN?!
THIS IS AN EMERGENCY! I NEED YOUR HELP!
MY LIFE IS IN DANGER!!
NO VOICE DISTORTION!!
I REMEMBER THAT VOICE!!

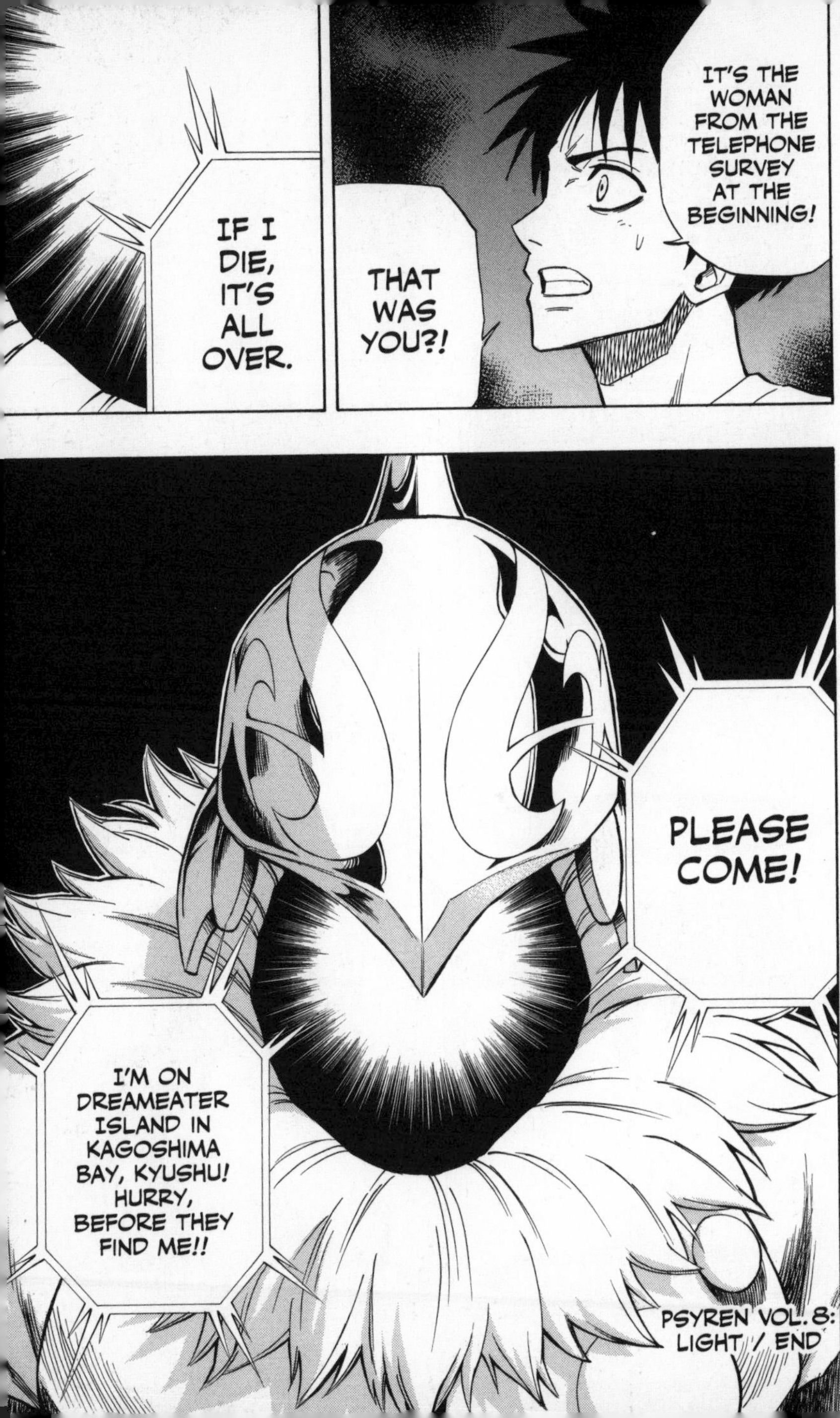
IT'S THE WOMAN FROM THE TELEPHONE SURVEY AT THE BEGINNING!
THAT WAS YOU?!
IF I DIE, IT'S ALL OVER.
PLEASE COME!
I'M ON DREAMEATER ISLAND IN KAGOSHIMA BAY, KYUSHU! HURRY, BEFORE THEY FIND ME!!
PSYREN VOL. 8: LIGHT / END

PSYREN CHARACTER RANKING

PSYREN CHARACTER POPULARITY POLL RESULTS

TOTAL VOTES RECEIVED: 11,055

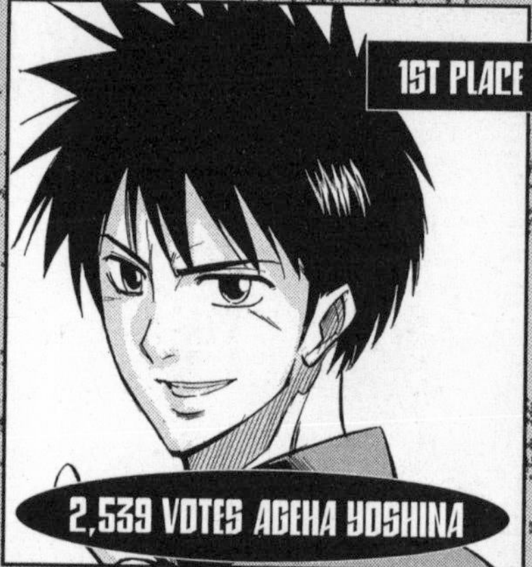
1ST PLACE
2,539 VOTES AGEHA YOSHINA

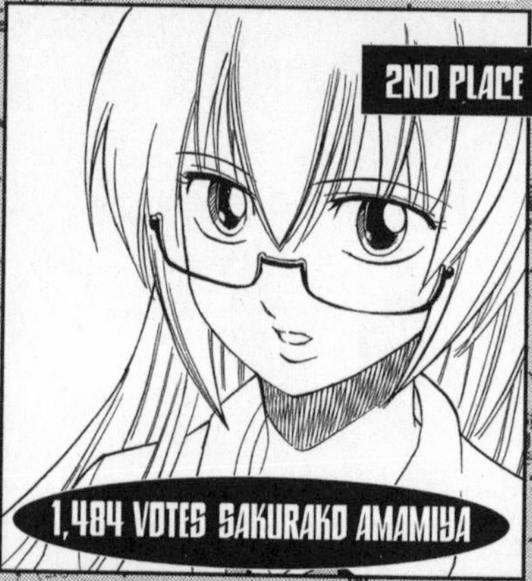
2ND PLACE
1,484 VOTES SAKURAKO AMAMIYA

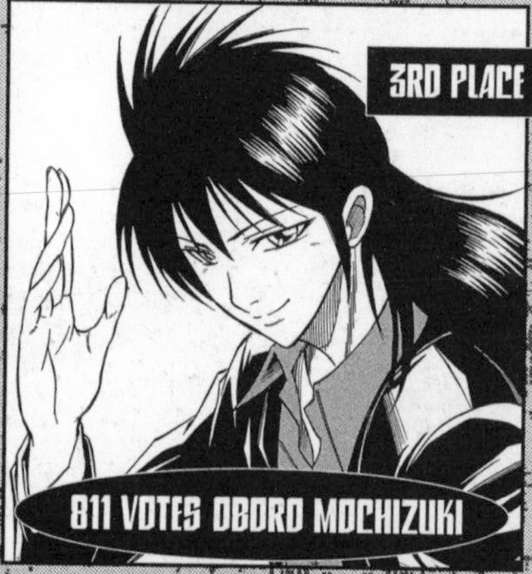
3RD PLACE
811 VOTES OBORO MOCHIZUKI

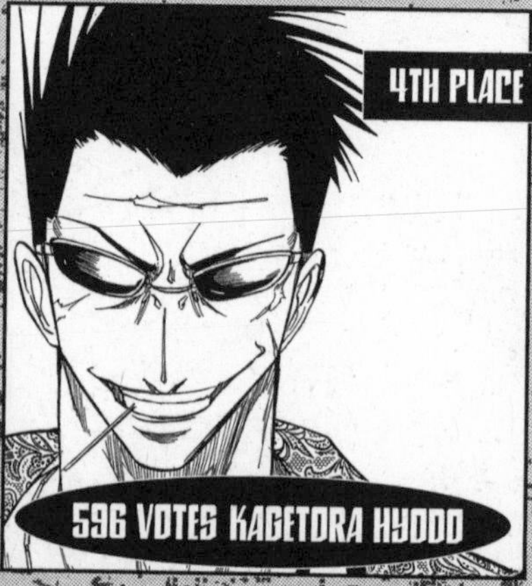
4TH PLACE
596 VOTES KAGETORA HYODO

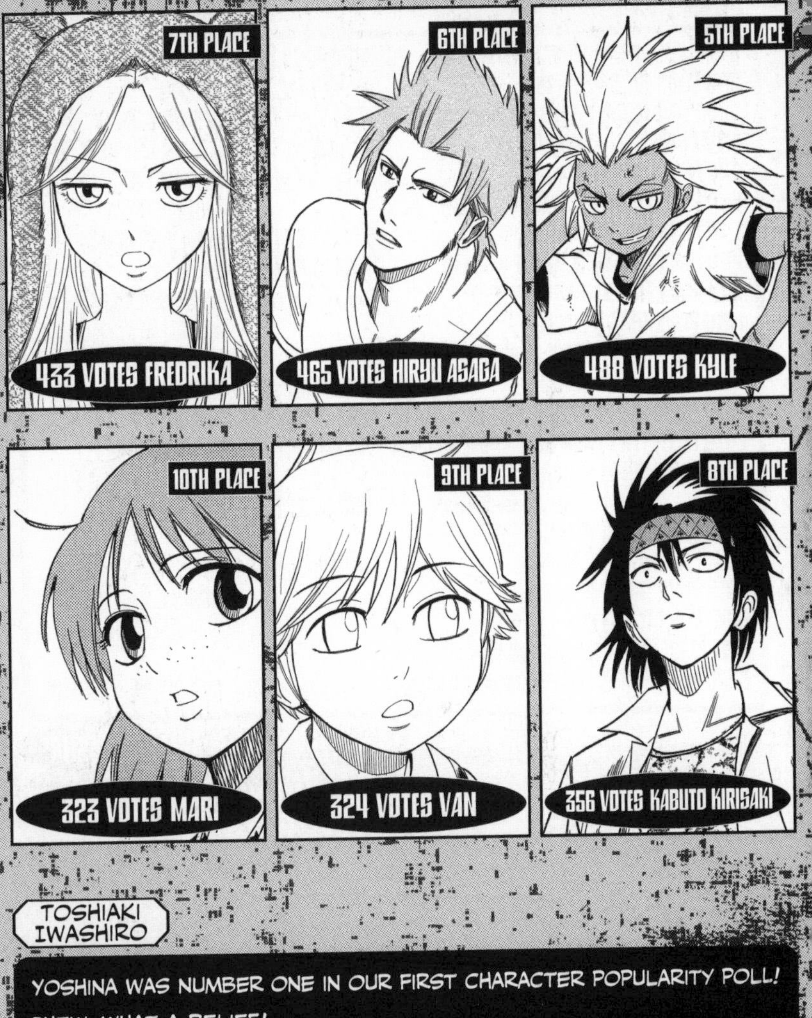
5TH PLACE
488 VOTES KYLE
6TH PLACE
465 VOTES HIRYU ASAGA
7TH PLACE
433 VOTES FREDRIKA
8TH PLACE
356 VOTES KABUTO KIRISAKI
9TH PLACE
324 VOTES VAN
10TH PLACE
323 VOTES MARI

TOSHIAKI IWASHIRO

YOSHINA WAS NUMBER ONE IN OUR FIRST CHARACTER POPULARITY POLL!

PHEW, WHAT A RELIEF!

I THOUGHT AMAMIYA MIGHT BE NUMBER ONE, BUT SHE WOUND UP NUMBER TWO.

I GUESS OBORO'S POPULAR BECAUSE HE'S A CELEBRITY?

SURPRISINGLY ENOUGH, KAGETORA CAME IN FOURTH.

WELL, KAGETORA AND KYLE WERE SEEING A LOT OF ACTION DURING THE PERIOD WHEN WE TOOK THE POLL.

THIS POLL WAS CONDUCTED IN JAPAN.

11TH PLACE [279 VOTES] AMAGI MIROKU	33RD PLACE [38 V] ANDREW THE WOLF-BUNNY
12TH PLACE [256 V] SHAO	34TH PLACE [33 V] GIZZANI
13TH PLACE [250 V] TATSUO MANA	35TH PLACE [26 V] KABUTO'S UNCLE
14TH PLACE [224 V] NEMESIS Q	36TH PLACE [25 V] WOMAN ON PHONE
15TH PLACE [193 V] SHINER	37TH PLACE [20 V] MIYOSHI KUMICHO
16TH PLACE [184 V] HARUHIKO YUMEJI	FAKE COPS
17TH PLACE [181 V] GRANAR	39TH PLACE [17 V] CHIKA SHINONOME
18TH PLACE [163 V] MATSURI YAGUMO	40TH PLACE [16 V] HANDO
19TH PLACE [123 V] KIYOTADA INUI	41ST PLACE [12 V] PSYREN CARD
20TH PLACE [86 V] JUNAS	MI [CAT]
21ST PLACE [84 V] FUBUKI YOSHINA	ANGRY GORY
DOLKEY	44TH PLACE [10 V] AZUMI
23RD PLACE [79 V] NOZOMI SUGITA	45TH PLACE [8 V] HIROKI
24TH PLACE [78 V] RAN SHINONOME	KOJI SEMITANI
25TH PLACE [76 V] KAPLIKO	MIWA
TOSHIAKI IWASHIRO	48TH PLACE [6 V] SAKA
27TH PLACE [70 V] ARFRED	WORM
28TH PLACE [67 V] MADOKA	50TH PLACE [5 V] GAKU INUZUKA
29TH PLACE [60 V] OKUMURA	GOLDORF
30TH PLACE [59 V] IAN	MS. MATSUMOTO
31ST PLACE [45 V] ELMORE TENJUIN	
32ND PLACE [42 V] KUKUCHI SOKUBAKU KAIJU	⟨ET CETERA...SORRY!!⟩

HIRYU CAME IN 6TH, AND AFTER THAT FREDDY, KABUTO, VAN, AND MARI FOLLOW. PERSONALLY, I THINK THAT SEEMS ABOUT RIGHT.

IN 11TH PLACE, AMAGI MIROKU GOT THE HIGHEST MARKS OF THE BAD GUYS, EVEN THOUGH HE HAD ONLY JUST DEBUTED WHEN THE VOTING TOOK PLACE.

BEYOND THAT, THE RESPONSES WERE KIND OF BAFFLING, INCLUDING ME (IWASHIRO), OKUMURA, KIKUCHI AND ANDREW...

IF WE DO THIS AGAIN, I WONDER IF I SHOULD INCLUDE THE ELMORE WOOD KIDS BOTH AS CHILDREN AND AS ADULTS?

NO, I GUESS I SHOULD PROBABLY LIST THEM EACH JUST ONCE. I WONDER IF AGEHA WILL STILL MANAGE TO COME OUT ON TOP NEXT TIME?

THANK YOU FOR VOTING!

PLEASE VOTE AGAIN NEXT TIME!
(IF THERE IS ONE...)

PSYREN

Afterword 8

HELLO, EVERYONE!!
THANK YOU FOR READING VOLUME 8.

THIS VOLUME INCLUDES A LOT OF IMPORTANT
DEVELOPMENTS IN THE STORY.
I REMEMBER IT BEING REALLY HARD, BUT
REALLY REWARDING, TOO.

I DREAMED UP THE PARTS ABOUT ELMORE AND
THE CHILDREN IN THE FUTURE BEFORE THE MANGA
WAS EVEN SERIALIZED, SO IT MEANT A LOT TO ME
TO HAVE ARRIVED AT THIS POINT.

ANYWAY, I'LL CONTINUE TO WORK HARD
ON THE NEXT VOLUME, TOO. ZZZZZZZZ

IWASHIRO TOSHIAKI
OCTOBER 2009

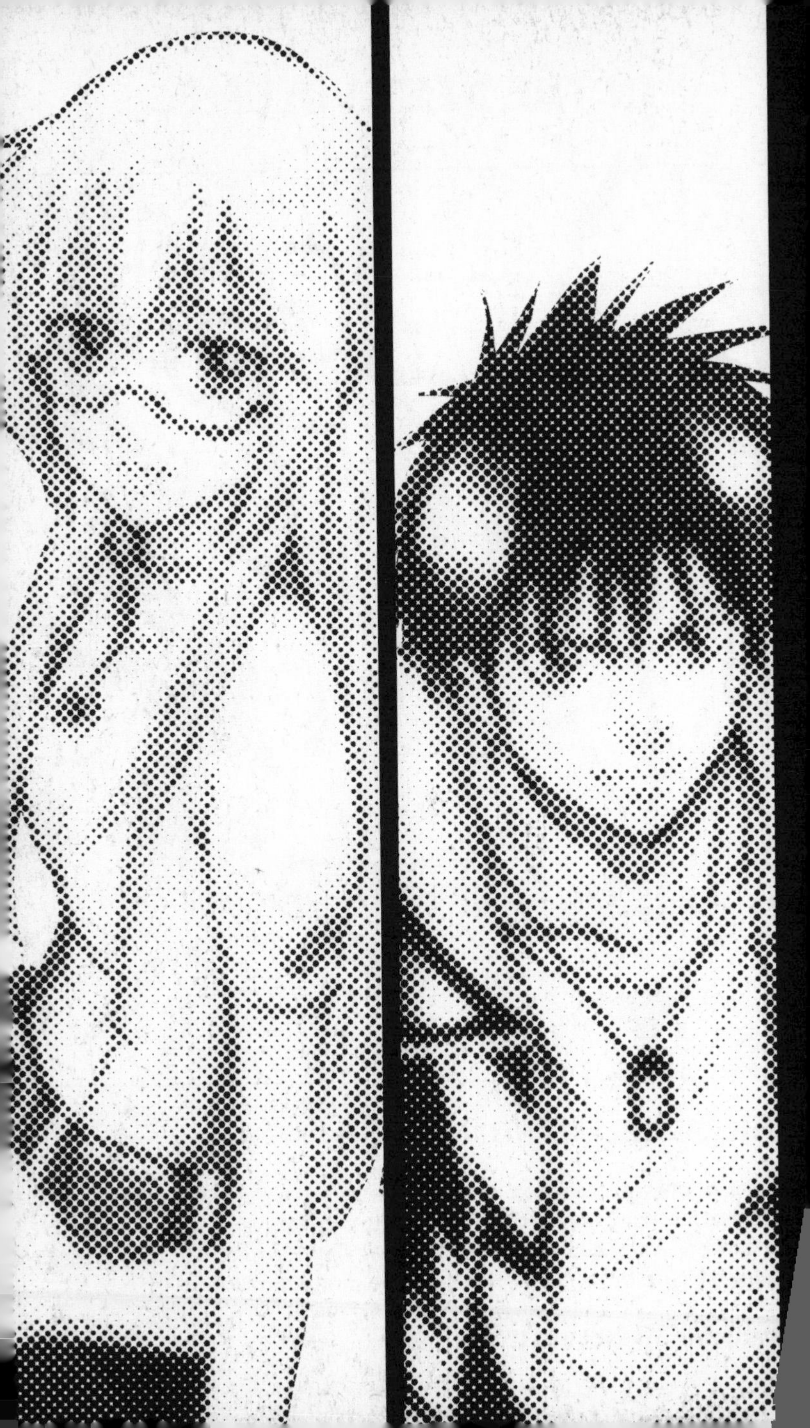

IN THE NEXT VOLUME...

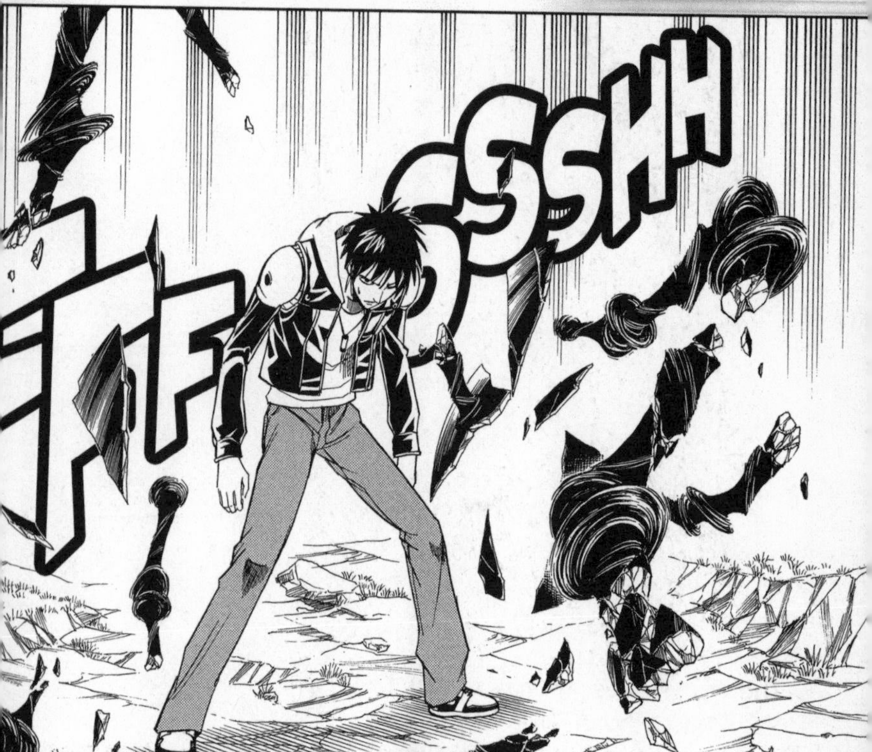
FSSHH

THE LIVING ISLAND

Ageha must assemble a team of fellow Psionists to travel to the mysterious Dreameater Island to help the master of the enigmatic Nemesis Q. They'll have to battle monsters and enemies on the treacherous journey. And their progress is being matched by Usui, a Psionist intent on destroying Nemesis Q!

Available MARCH 2013!

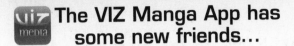

You're Reading in the Wrong Direction!!

Whoops! Guess what? You're starting at the wrong end of the comic!

...It's true! In keeping with the original Japanese format, **Psyren** is meant to be read from right to left, starting in the upper-right corner.

Unlike English, which is read from left to right, Japanese is read from right to left, meaning that action, sound effects and word-balloon order are completely reversed—something which can make readers unfamiliar with Japanese feel pretty backwards themselves. For this reason, manga or Japanese comics published in the U.S. in English have sometimes been published "flopped"—that is, printed in exact reverse order, as though seen from the other side of a mirror.

By flopping pages, U.S. publishers can avoid confusing readers, but the compromise is not without its downside. For one thing, a character in a flopped manga series who once wore in the original Japanese version a T-shirt emblazoned with "M A Y" (as in "the merry month of") now wears one which reads "Y A M"! Additionally, many manga creators in Japan are themselves unhappy with the process, as some feel the mirror-imaging of their art changes their original intentions.

We are proud to bring you Toshiaki Iwashiro's **Psyren** in the original unflopped format. For now, though, turn to the other side of the book and let the fun begin...!

—Editor

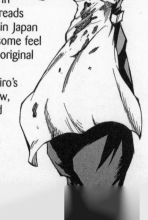